# MALABAR, MYSORE AND A TALE OF TWO SULTANS

## Hyder Ali's Dominions in 1780

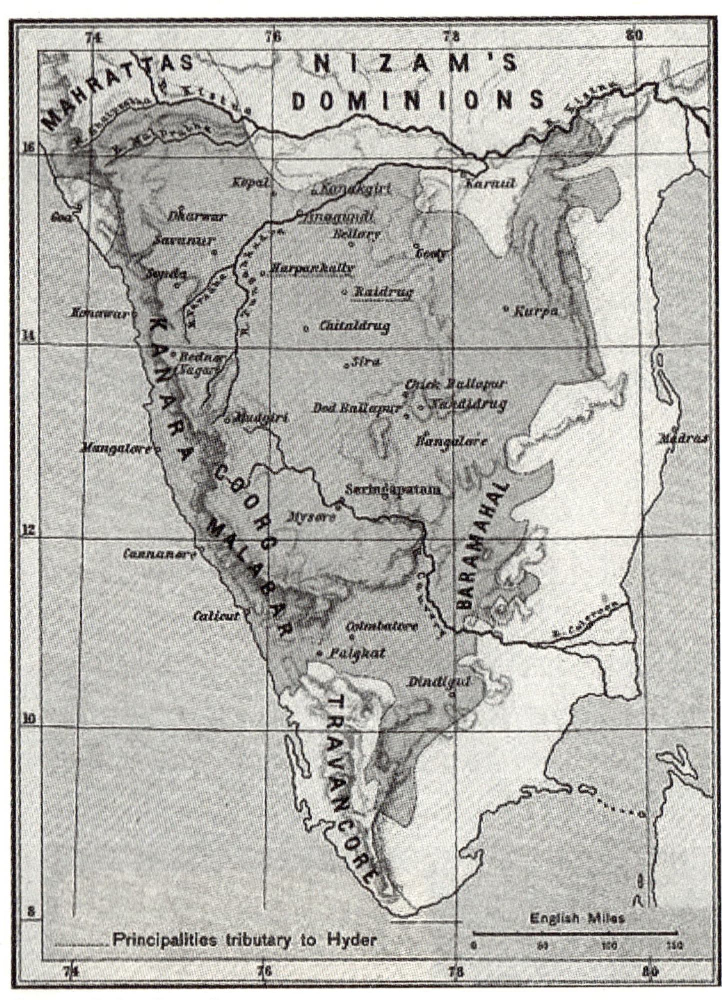


*Source*: Columbia.edu

# MALABAR, MYSORE AND A TALE OF TWO SULTANS

Pushpa Kurup

ink | OCCAM

Cover Photo: Painting in Kowdiar Palace, Thiruvananthapuram, depicting Tipu Sultan's defeat at the Travancore Lines in December 1789. Artist unknown. Photo by Pushpa Kurup.

ISBN: 978-93-92209-96-3

First published in India 2025
This edition published 2025

BluOne Ink Pvt. Ltd
A-76, 2nd Floor, Sector 136, Noida
Uttar Pradesh 201301
www.bluone.ink
publisher@bluone.ink

Printed and bound in India at Nutech Print Services - India

# CONTENTS

# AUTHOR'S NOTE

This book is a layman's humble attempt at comprehending the history of southern India, especially during the colonial era. Poring over history texts can be incredibly tedious and sifting the wheat from the chaff can be a daunting task when there are too many relevant sources. When several accounts appear to coincide, we often assume related facts to be true. Contemporary accounts by writers who were directly acquainted with the protagonists may carry more credibility than later ones. Nevertheless, it is essential to consider the possible motives of the author, as well as the potential for flights of fancy, embellishment, exaggeration and partisan views. Both enemies and friends of the protagonists are likely to present biased perspectives, so their narratives must be considered with a pinch of salt.

Historical sources can misrepresent, distort, peddle lies or mix truth with fiction, making it difficult for serious researchers to ferret out the truths and comprehend the nuances. Sometimes, folk memories and oral transmissions can be just as valid as recorded histories. After all, we live in a country where the Vedas and the great epics, the Ramayana and the Mahabharata, have been transmitted orally for thousands of years. The renowned Sanskrit scholar, Max Muller, in one of his Oxford lectures, cited an instance when he had asked scholars from three different locations (Bombay, Calcutta and Madras), each of whom spoke a different Indian language, to recite the *Rigveda*, and he was astonished to discover that he could detect no difference in their recitations. Here is evidence that oral communications can be flawless too!

While analysing the available data, I have endeavoured to keep all this in mind. The era of the Mysore sultans spans from the 1750s, and there exists a plethora of sources detailing their military activities. Not only the English and the French but also the Portuguese and the Dutch have mentioned them in their despatches, letters and books. Publications relating to Haider Ali and Tipu Sultan are available in various languages. However, the fact that many contemporary accounts were written 200–250 years ago, some by less erudite chroniclers, complicates the task of understanding. Archaic language usages and cultural nuances further add to the challenge. Moreover, conflicting accounts, varying perceptions, exaggeration, bias and other factors abound. Thus, it is no simple feat for a researcher to arrive at definitive conclusions. Some degree of repetition is inevitable, as I cite different versions of the same story by different authors.

As various authors have employed different spellings for the names of people and places, some of which are indecipherable and others outright ridiculous, I have made the difficult decision to alter them to enhance the reader's convenience. This includes proper nouns appearing within quotes, except when they appear in the titles of books authored in the 18th and 19th centuries. We often encounter 'Tipu' spelled as 'Tippoo', 'Sultan' as 'Sultaun', 'Khan' as 'Cawn' and so on. I have generally retained the spellings found in 20th- and 21st-century publications, occasionally providing the best-known spellings within brackets. The East India Company has often been abbreviated to 'EICo.'. Regional variations have been respected; for example, it is 'dalawai' in Mysore and 'dalawa' in Travancore. Thus, we have 'Dalawai Nanjaraj' and 'Velu Thampi Dalawa'. Furthermore, for terms such as 'Zamorin', I have chosen to use the more familiar but incorrect anglicized version instead of the Malayalam word 'Samuthiri', which is the original, correct version but is familiar only to the people of Kerala. 'Samuthiri' or 'Zamorin' is not the name of an individual ruler but rather a generic term that refers to all the kings of an ancient dynasty of Kozhikode (Calicut). Upon ascending the throne, they were all known as 'Mana-Vikrama', and their given names are virtually unknown, contributing significantly to the confusion regarding their identities.

It is believed that in the 16th century, fifteen different Zamorins were pitting their wits against the invading Portuguese, while only four Kunjali Marakkars (yet another generic name!) served as naval admirals during the same period.

The name 'Calicut' is also of foreign origin; the vernacular name is 'Kozhikode', which, unfortunately, contains an unpronounceable syllable. Thus, 'Calicut' it shall remain! On the altar of convenience and simplicity, I am compelled to sacrifice the virtue of accuracy, and I beg to be forgiven for this transgression. I have also used the name 'Coorg' more often than 'Kodagu', 'Cannanore' rather than 'Kannur', 'Tellicherry' rather than 'Thalassery' and so on. While Shakespeare might proclaim, 'What's in a name?', I realize that the sons and daughters of the respective soils may not be pleased with my usage. I plead guilty and seek forgiveness.

Yes, history is invariably judgemental. There are unfathomable unknowns. In the final analysis, we see what we want to see, hear what we want to hear, read what we want to read and believe what we want to believe. I cannot claim to be truly objective. I can only say that I made a sincere effort. My perspective is definitely that of a Malabari, and I am not a trained historian.

Many individuals have assisted me in the task of compiling the oral histories. Their contribution cannot be adequately expressed even in a thousand words. The errors and omissions that discerning readers may discover are entirely my responsibility.

## Disclaimer and Declaration of Intent

Nobody has paid me to write this book. I have not received any advance from my publisher either. No one has inspired, motivated or even patted me on the back. This project was self-inspired, self-driven and self-funded. I am an independent and intensely private citizen. I have no ulterior motives or hidden agenda. I serve no masters – political, religious or corporate.

I have no intention of criticizing, contradicting or belittling anyone, least of all historians and politicians. This book is not intended to hurt anyone - dead, living or yet-to-be-born.

# ACKNOWLEDGEMENTS


**For Help with Research**

- Princess Aswathi Thirunal Gowri Lakshmi Bayi for providing me with a briefing about the erstwhile Travancore state and Tipu Sultan, and for the royals' remembrance of the history of that period. Also, for showing me the painting of Tipu Sultan being carried in a palanquin after being wounded in the attack on the Travancore Lines and for permitting me to photograph it.
- Dr Azad Moopen for sharing valuable information relating to the centuries-old history of his ancestors.
- Sheela Anthony for accompanying me to Kanjoor Church, Our Lady of Snow, Aiycotta and other locations in Thrissur and Ernakulam districts, and for introducing me to erudite stalwarts.
- Jose C. Kokkad for accompanying me to St Francis Xavier Church in Sampaloor.
- Vijayakumari for accompanying me to Emoor Bhagavathy Temple and Palghat Fort.
- Govindasamy for introducing me to Ashraf Ali and arranging for my visit to Vellore Fort and the tombs of the Mysore royals.
- Ashraf Ali for narrating the archaeological history of Vellore and Tipu Sultan's association with the region.
- Bhaskaran Master for sharing his views on Pazhassi Raja and for setting up an impressive memorial to the valiant hero in Pazhassi.

- Arjun S.K. for logistical support and facilitation at various points in Thalassery including Wellesley's Bungalow and the local archives.
- Susmitha Sumesh for organizing my visits to Palakkad and enlisting her brother's support.
- K.P. Sasidharan for being an eternal source of motivation.
- Chengat Radhakrishnan Nambiar for sharing valuable books and insights.

**For Moral Support and Various Other Forms of Assistance**

- My brother, Premchand Kurup
- My sister-in-law, Remani
- My daughter, Sitara Raja
- My son-in-law, Sanjay Kumar M.V.
- My mother, Saroja Kurup
- My aunt (Ammayi), Uma Devi Nambiar
- My cousins, Latha, Anita, Vineeta, Prameela and Prema
- My ever-present battalion of friend-warriors, Sathi, Bindu, Chithra, Girija, Uma, Annie, Sathar and so many others
- My publisher, BluOne Ink, and their highly professional team led by Praveen Tiwari, the publishing director

# TIMELINES: 1721–1947

**Nawab/Sultan I (Haidar Ali: 1761–1782)**

1721 – Birth of Haider Ali (estimated) at Doddaballapur (uncertain).

1729 (date uncertain) – Haider Ali's father, Fateh Muhammed, dies.

Year uncertain – Haider joins the Mysore army along with his elder brother, Shahbaz.

1749 – During the siege of Devanahalli, Haider Ali proves his mettle.

1749–1750 – Haider Ali, with a small contingent of Mysorean troops, goes to Hyderabad to intervene in a succession dispute on behalf of Nasir Jung. Jung is enthroned but soon gets killed. Haider Ali loots a part of his treasure and returns rich. (The French swallow the lion's share.)

1750 – Tipu Sultan is born on 20 November (exact date uncertain).

1751 – Haider assists Nanjaraj in the siege of Trichinopoly (Thiruchirapally). The campaign lasts for years.

1755 – Haider Ali is appointed the *faujdar* of Dindigul.

1757–1758 – The Palghat raja appeals for help against the Samuthiri (Zamorin) of Calicut. Haider Ali sends his brother-in-law Makhdum Sahib, who subdues the Zamorin and exacts a promise of tribute. War reparations are collected from the Palghat raja as well.

1758 – Devaraj, the Dewan (and de facto ruler) of Mysore dies. The Zamorin of Calicut dies. Marthanda Varma, the powerful ruler of Travancore, also dies.

1759 – Haider Ali displaces Nanjaraj and assumes charge as the commander of the Mysore army.

1760 – The queen mother conspires with the Marathas to get rid of Haider Ali. He flees to Bangalore, leaving his family behind. The British defeat the French at the Battle of Wandiwash (Vandavasi).

1761 – Haider usurps the throne of Mysore and virtually imprisons the raja. The nizam of Hyderabad, Salabat Jung, is deposed by his younger brother Nizam Ali Khan. In Poona, Madhav Rao succeeds his father Balaji Baji Rao as the peshwa.

1763 – Haider Ali captures Bidanur. Salabat Jung is murdered.

1766 – Haider Ali invades Malabar from the north. The Zamorin dies by self-immolation.

1767–1769 – The First Anglo–Mysore War, which remains inconclusive.

1769–1771 – War with the Marathas.

1776 – Britain loses her American colonies as America declares independence. India thus becomes invaluable to Britain.

1779 – French mercenary M. Lally leaves the nizam's employ to join Haider Ali. Later, he serves under Tipu Sultan.

1780–1784 – The Second Anglo–Mysore War.

1780 – Haider and Tipu are victorious at Pollilur, near Kanchipuram. Colonel Bailley is taken prisoner and later dies in custody.

1781 – Haider suffers defeat at Porto Novo (Parangipettai).

1782 – Haider is victorious at Kumbakonam (early 1782); he dies in camp in Chittoor on 7 December. Tipu hurries from his camp in Ponnani to take control of the Mysore kingdom.

**Sultan II (Tipu Sultan: 1782–1799)**

1783 – In January, realizing that Tipu will not spare his life, Ayaz Khan surrenders Bidanur and all the surrounding territories to the British. He moves to Bombay and dies in exile in 1799.

1784 – The Treaty of Mangalore (11 March) ends the Second Anglo–Mysore War. The outcome maintains the status quo ante bellum. Malabar and Coorg remain in Tipu's hands (except Tellicherry and Mahe, which are held by the British and the French, respectively).

1785–1786 – Tipu sends an embassy to Turkey, France and England.

1787 – Tipu sends another embassy to France.

1788 – Tipu arrives in Calicut via Thamarassery Pass in January. Nairs join hands with the British to offer resistance. Tipu razes Calicut to the ground.

1789 – Tipu attacks the Travancore Lines in December and suffers reverses.

1790 – Tipu attacks the Travancore Lines in April, leading to the outbreak of the Third Anglo–Mysore War as Lord Cornwallis declares war on Mysore.

1791 – Cornwallis captures Bangalore in March, while the Marathas capture Dharwar in April.

1792 – British troops attack Srirangapatna in February. The Treaty of Seringapatam is negotiated. Tipu cedes Malabar and Coorg to the British on 24 February and hands over his two minor sons (Abdul Khaliq and Muizuddin) to Lord Cornwallis as hostages. A tribute of 3.30 crore rupees is also agreed upon, and Tipu signs the treaty on 18 March.

1796 – Tipu sends a delegation to Turkey and France.

1797 – Tipu sends a second delegation to France. Afghan ruler Zaman Shah invades India's northwest at the behest of Tipu Sultan. Tipu also sends two emissaries to Isle de France (Mauritius), asking for troops to help drive the British out of India.

1798 – The Malartic Proclamation is issued in January by the governor of Isle de France. The proclamation appears in a Calcutta newspaper in June. Tipu conspires with Napoleon and invites him to attack India. 'Dhamaraja' Rama Varma, ruler of Travancore, passes away at the age of seventy-four.

1799 – The Fourth Anglo–Mysore War concludes with the fall of Srirangapatna and the death of Tipu Sultan.

**After Tipu's Death**

October 1799 – Veerapandiya Kattabomman is hanged.

June 1801 – Marudhu Pandiyan's proclamation surfaces at various locations, calling upon the people to resist British occupation.

October 1801 – The Marudhu brothers are hanged together with their sons, grandsons and camp followers, including Oomadurai, the dumb brother of Veerapandiya Kattabomman.

November 1805 – Pazhassi Raja is waylaid and killed by the British in Mananthavady, Wayanad.

1806 – Following the Vellore Sepoy Revolt, Tipu's sons are exiled to Calcutta.

1807 – Around 450 Muslim sepoys are dismissed in Palayamkottai for conspiring to overthrow the British.

1809 – On 11 January, Velu Thampi Dalawa of Travancore issues the Kundara Proclamation, calling upon his compatriots to drive the British out of India. In April, Velu Thampi commits suicide in Mannadi when he finds himself surrounded by British troops. His brother, Padmanabhan Thampi, and other leaders are captured and hanged by the British. The White Mutiny in Madras occurs from June to August.

1818 – The Maratha empire collapses.

1834 – The British annex Coorg.

1839 – The British invade Afghanistan and install Shah Shuja on the throne.

1843 – The British annex Sindh.

1846–1856 – The British annex Punjab, Satara, Sambalpur, Jaitpur, Bagat, Udaipur, Jhansi, Nagpur, Awadh and Thanjavur.

1857 – The War of Independence, also known as Sepoy Mutiny, begins.

1947 – India gains independence from Britain.

# 1

# THE LEGACY OF THE MYSORE SULTANS

It is an oft-repeated fallacy that Tipu Sultan was a martyr for the cause of India's freedom. At the risk of being branded an undercover Sanghini, I humbly propose that if Malabar hadn't come under British protection, I might never have been born or I might have been named Sainaba or Fatima.

Roughly two centuries after Haider Ali's initial incursion into Malabar, I arrived on planet Earth only to find that the agony of those encounters had been seared into the DNA of my kinsmen. Whenever my grandma spoke of British oppression, she also detailed the horrors inflicted by Haider Ali and Tipu Sultan. The father–son duo, during their forty-year rampage across southern India, had mindlessly slaughtered and nearly wiped out the warrior clans of Malabar.

Haider Ali's first attack on Malabar occurred in 1757–1758 when he dispatched his brother-in-law Makhdum Sahib to assist the Palghat raja in a conflict with the Samuthiri (Zamorin) of Kozhikode (Calicut). Emboldened by victory and enticed by the scale of the booty, Haider Ali marched on Kolathunadu, the dominion of the Kolathiri raja, in 1766. In Calicut that same year, his *padayottam* ended in the fiery suicide of the Zamorin. Thereafter, Malabar witnessed a horrific saga of indescribable depredations. It was Tipu's decisive defeat in 1792 at the hands of the British that saved the warrior clans of Malabar from extinction.

In the Malabar–Mysore story, there were two notable instigators who were directly responsible for Haider Ali's attacks on Malabar. The first was Raman Komu Achan of the Tharoor Svaroopam, Palakkad (Palghat), who invited the Mysorean to invade Kerala in 1757. The second instigator was Ali Raja Kunhi Amsa II of the Muslim Arakkal kingdom of Cannanore (Kannur), who extended a subsequent invitation to Haider in 1763 and allied with him, thereby facilitating the second invasion of 1766. In 1751, Marthanda Varma of Travancore had initially sought military aid from Haider Ali to quell internal revolts, but he swiftly retracted his request. At that time, Haider was a mere *naik*. A decade later, he would orchestrate a coup d'état in Mysore.

Haider Ali, initially a common soldier in the Mysore army, gradually rose to become the de facto ruler of the ancient kingdom. In June 1761, he usurped power from Krishnaraja Wodeyar II, the Hindu scion of a centuries-old dynasty, but stopped short of crowning himself king.

The rise of the Mysore sultans more or less coincided with the rise of the British in India. The Mughal Empire was in rapid decline following the death of Aurangzeb in 1707. In 1738–1739, Nadir Shah of Persia sacked Delhi, captured the emperor, Muhammad Shah, and returned to Persia with the Peacock Throne, the Kohinoor, the Darya-i-Nur and the entire contents of the Mughal treasury. In 1746, Dupleix became the French governor of Pondicherry. In 1751, Robert Clive captured the Vellore Fort. By 1755, Haider Ali became *faujdar* in Dindigul (near Madurai, Tamil Nadu). In 1757, at the Battle of Plassey, Robert Clive defeated Siraj-ud-Daulah, the nawab of Bengal, and established British hegemony in the Indian subcontinent. In 1758, Haider Ali's army reached Palghat and subdued the mighty Zamorin of Calicut. In 1760, at the historic Battle of Wandiwash (Vandavasi in North Arcot district, Tamil Nadu), the British defeated the French, thus becoming masters of the south. The Marathas were a major power, and for a while, they held sway in northern India, subduing even the Mughal emperor, but they suffered terrible reverses at the Third Battle of Panipat in 1761 when they fought the Afghans. The same year, Haider Ali wrested control of the Mysore kingdom. In 1763, he defeated the powerful Ikkeri Rajas of Bidanur and annexed their territories extending up to Mangalore. At the decisive Battle of Buxar in 1764–1765, the British defeated the combined armies of the Mughal emperor Shah Alam II and the nawabs of Awadh and Bengal. In 1766, Haider Ali invaded Malabar, triggering a cycle of death and destruction.

The First Anglo–Mysore War, fought between 1767 and 1769, was a struggle for supremacy with no clear outcome. As the years passed, the Mysore kingdom as well as the British East India Company grew in wealth and power.

Haider Ali was primarily a military adventurer, and so was Tipu Sultan. The duo realized that war was a profitable enterprise. Moreover, it was the only business they knew. They attacked their neighbours without the slightest provocation, intermittently invading Malabar, Mangalore and Kodagu (Coorg), besides occasionally making forays into Arcot, Madras and even Travancore. Fate eventually caught up with Haider Ali when he died of cancer in 1782 amid the Second Anglo–Mysore War.

The British besieged Srirangapatna, the capital of the Mysore kingdom, in 1792 and 1799. The first time they stopped short of eliminating Tipu and instead signed a peace treaty. However, by 1798, they were convinced that he needed to be exterminated. Finally, the Marathas, the nizam of Hyderabad and the British ganged up against Tipu. With the fall of Srirangapatna and the death of Tipu Sultan in 1799, a forty-year saga of widespread destruction ended – and a new era of domination by a new enemy began.

The violent intrusions of the Mysore sultans considerably weakened the rulers of Malabar and drove them into the waiting hands of the British. Haider and Tipu had invaded Malabar, Coorg, Mangalore and other regions not to fight the British but to plunder the wealth of the Hindu kingdoms and effect conversions to Islam.

They crippled the economy, sowed the seeds of Hindu–Muslim enmity and facilitated a British takeover.

Malabar paid a heavy price for this exchange of overlords. The British ruled the land with an iron hand from 1792 to 1947, marking the longest period of subjugation in Malabar's history. The story of Coorg is tragically similar. The British turned it into a playground for the elite and held hunting parties long before formally annexing it in 1834.

## Sundry Interventions, Sundry Cruelties

Tipu Sultan did not confine himself to military interventions. His attacks were multi-pronged and often macabre. He ordered the wholesale destruction of pepper vines in Malabar, something unprecedented in the 3,000-year history of the pepper trade. Colonel Mark Wilks, a contemporary of Tipu Sultan, recorded that all the pepper vines of the Malabar Coast were destroyed in 1784 under Tipu's orders.[1] Francis Buchanan, a medical doctor who served in India from 1794 to 1815, travelled through Mysore, Malabar and the Tamil country a year after Tipu's death and wrote an elaborate account of these regions in a book published in 1807. Buchanan makes multiple references to Tipu's destruction of the pepper vines: 'Mr Wye says that in the southern division of Malabar, the cultivation of black pepper, owing to Tipu's having destroyed the vines, is much less than it formerly was.'[2]

There is plausible evidence to suggest that Malabar's pepper trade is over 3,200 years old. When the mummy of the Egyptian Pharaoh Rameses II (died 1213 BCE) was carefully examined, it was found that a peppercorn had been stuffed into each nostril.[3] As the ancient world had no other known source of pepper, it can be surmised that pepper from Malabar was being imported to Egypt in the second millennium BCE. Thus, Tipu Sultan was the only person known to have destroyed the pepper vines of Malabar in the past 3,000 years. He could have had only one aim - to sabotage the flourishing trade. He wanted the people of Malabar to wallow in poverty because they had been fiercely and consistently resisting his sporadic attacks. By destroying their means of livelihood and dismantling the trade networks, he might have hoped to bring the people to their knees. Tipu, however, failed in this sinister attempt. The vines were replanted. They grew and multiplied. The trade was re-established and thrives to this day.

Speaking of the Randathara region, which belonged to the royal family of Chirakkal, Buchanan writes, 'It suffered very severely in the wars with Hyder and Tipu, and within the memory of man it has been twice completely depopulated.'[4] The descriptions are heart-rending. We encounter similar accounts from Coorg as well.

William Logan's much acclaimed *Malabar*, better known as *Malabar Manual* or *Logan's Manual*, provides a long list of temples destroyed by Tipu. It includes Thrichambaram and Taliparamba Temples in Chirakkal taluk, Thiruvangatu Temple in Thalassery and Ponmeri Temple near Vadakara. The versatile Scotsman was the collector of Malabar in the mid-19th century, and his extensive compilation is an invaluable resource for researchers and academicians to this day.

In late 1788, Tipu issued the infamous 'Order of Extermination', exhorting his army chiefs to 'surround and extirpate the whole race of Nairs from Cotiote [Kottayam] to Palacatcherry [Palghat]'.[5] Here he was referring to Kottayam–Malabar in the Kannur district, not the Kottayam district in the present state of Kerala. Tipu, a man who maintained a sizeable harem, was horrified by the liberal sexual mores of the Nairs and the Kodavas (Coorgis), which in his view were similar to that of animals. He threatened the Nairs that if they did not change their habits and customs, he would 'honour' all of them with Islam. It is said that their reply was not to his liking, and it provoked him to issue the extermination order.

Tipu Sultan extended his cruelties to animals as well. Wilks informs us that on his march to subdue Travancore in 1789, Tipu took a detour in Anamalai (spelt 'Animalee' by Wilks) to go elephant hunting. The description of his method of killing a female elephant makes for a gruesome reading.

> The female elephant was chained to the ground by her four feet, and the chiefs of the army being assembled for that purpose, the Sultan made the first cut, the example was followed with reluctance even by the Mahommedans; but this barbarian had the cruelty to insist that even many of the brahmins present should cut in their turn; and it is to this enormity that they continue until this day to ascribe his subsequent repulse from the wall of Travancore.[6]

In December 1789, Tipu attacked the Travancore Lines (a protective barrier built by the Travancore raja in anticipation of invasions from Mysore) and suffered a humiliating defeat at the hands of the Travancore army, losing his dagger, seal and other items in the melee. He was forced to beat a hasty retreat and was wounded in the encounter, while several of his military stalwarts lost their lives. Wilks recounts that the local people attributed Tipu's defeat to the bad karma earned by his wanton cruelty to a cow elephant.

William Kirkpatrick, another contemporary of Tipu Sultan, translated several of the latter's *hukumnamahs* (orders and instructions to his various functionaries) from Persian into English, publishing a select compendium in 1811. In his observations of one of Tipu's letters, Kirkpatrick mentions, 'Colonel Munro (Sir Hector, 1726–1805) assures me that it is an absolute fact that on one occasion he [Tipu] *ordered all the male population of a particular village, which had given him offence, to be castrated*.'[7] (Emphasis added.)

Buchanan writes, 'On the accession of Tipu, the Namboothiris met with much trouble; and many of them were caught and circumcised. Those who could escape fled to Travancore.'[8] The *polygars* of Anamalai and the Coimbatore region did likewise. 'Ten years ago, Tipu endeavoured to seize them, in order, by circumcision, to make them Mussalmans; but they made their escape into the country of the Cochin raja, and continued there until the fall of Seringapatam.'[9]

Princess Aswathi Thirunal Gouri Lakshmi Bayi of the royal house of Travancore writes in her book titled *Sree Padmanabha Swamy Temple*:

> In the course of his invasions of North Malabar areas, Tippu embarked on a series of atrocities like burning down houses, molesting women of other religions, desecrating temples and churches and converting people to Islam by force under penalty of death. Many of the high-born Brahmin, Namboodiri and Kshatriya families who were the main targets of Tippu's hatred as well as Nairs and other Hindus fled to Travancore seeking asylum … the famed idol of Sree Guruvayoorappan from the Sree Krishna temple at Guruvayoor was brought by the priests and other functionaries to Travancore where it was ceremoniously received and worshipped, at first in Ambalappuzha and for a time in the specially erected shrine on the land of the Royal House of Mavelikkara. After the menace of Tippu was removed, the idol was taken back to the original abode in Guruvayoor.[10]

The author informs us that in the year 1772, Rama Varma 'gifted villages north of Periyar River free of taxes per one collective deed of gift to eighteen Namboodiri families hailing from Shukapuram village'.[11] It was during the reign of Haider Ali that the great exodus began. 'More and more families of Namboothiris fled their native land and joined their relatives who had already been settled inside Travancore borders by the king. Descendants of many of these illustrious families still carry with them the emotional scars of those days of terror.'[12]

The Mandyam Iyengars had settled in Melkote (Melukote or Mayilkotta) sometime in the 12th century and were among the earliest followers of Ramanujacharya, the apostle of Vaishnavism. They were pious and learned men, and their lives revolved around two major Hindu temples – the Cheluvanarayana Temple and the Yoganarasimha Temple. They enjoyed the continuous patronage of the Hoysala kings, the Vijayanagara kings and the Wodeyars.

'Deepavali [Diwali]is supposed to symbolize the victory of light over darkness but for the Mandyam Iyengars, it will forever remain a day when darkness descended upon them,' writes Satish Viswanathan in a 2019 article in OpIndia. On this day, over two centuries ago, the 'Tiger of Mysore' slaughtered over 800 Mandyam

Iyengars including women and children in Melkote. The massacre is believed to have occurred between 1783 and 1790. Viswanathan states:

> The dowager queen Lakshmammani's efforts to place a Wodeyar back on the throne were ably assisted by the Mandyam Iyengars. At the forefront was the Pradhan of Mysore, Thirumalai Iyengar, and his brother Narayan Iyengar. Talks were initiated to forge an alliance with the East India Company in order to dethrone Hyder Ali. The plot was uncovered by Hyder Ali and he imprisoned both the brothers and their extended family. Fearing persecution, several members of the community emigrated to the Madras Presidency.

After Haider Ali's death, Rani Lakshmammani made frantic efforts to obtain British assistance to overthrow Tipu. Viswanathan notes, 'Shamaiah Iyengar, a minister in Tipu's court, secretly reached out to Lord George Harris...This correspondence was viewed as treason by Tipu Sultan and his response was to wipe out the entire Mandyam Iyengar community in Melkote.' After the Deepavali-day massacre, the remaining residents fled the area and Melkote became a ghost town. The Mandyam Iyengars began to observe Deepavali as a day of mourning. Sadly, the Melkote massacre has largely escaped the attention of historians.

## Equal Injustice to All

The people of Kerala have inhabited the southwest coast of peninsular India for countless years. Their Chola, Pandya and Pallava neighbours never tried to exterminate them. In the 3rd century BCE, Emperor Ashoka referred to the 'Keralaputtas' as people outside his realm. Judaism, Christianity and Islam came to this coastal paradise in peace and co-existed with Hinduism, Jainism and Buddhism. Despite inevitable skirmishes, business flourished for thousands of years. When the Mysore sultans invaded in the mid-18th century, the British were entrenched in Tellicherry, the French in Mahe and the Dutch were hovering around Cochin. The Portuguese had earlier made an ignominious exit.

Emphasizing that Malabar had never truly been subject to a foreign power, Fra. Bartolomeo, a Carmelite missionary known to the people of Kerala as Paulinus Paathiri, states in a book published in 1796, 'The original Malabar sovereigns still retain peaceful possession of this kingdom, which they have enjoyed for three thousand years. Tipu Sultan once attempted to subdue it; but his troops were beat, and again driven from the country.'[13] Bartolomeo was referring to Tipu's defeat at the Travancore Lines in 1789. He had returned to Europe the same year, but the letters he had received from other missionaries in Varapuzha provided a wealth of information:

> In the years 1788 and 1789 when the cruel Tipu Sultan Bahadur, son of Haider Ali Khan, persecuted the Brahmins and caused them to be either unmercifully beat, or circumcised according to the Mahommedan manner, a great many of them fled to Vikatta [Vaikom], where they received every kind of protection possible from the king of Travancor.[14]

Kodungallur, the Muziris of the ancient world, was attacked by Tipu on many occasions, and the Dutch, realizing that they would not be able to defend the fort, hurriedly sold it to the king of Travancore. However, in 1790, Tipu's French general, M. Lally, seized and dismantled it.[15]

Bartolomeo also writes of the destruction of Calicut:

> This city was razed almost to the ground by Tipu Sultan, who destroyed its flourishing trade; expelled from the country the merchants and factors of the foreign commercial houses; caused all the coco-nut and sandal trees to be cut down; and ordered the pepper plants in the whole surrounding district to be torn up by the roots, and even to be hacked to pieces, because these plants as he said, brought riches to the Europeans.[16]

Bartolomeo observes that Tipu Sultan went to Calicut to teach the people an unforgettable lesson. The Zamorin and his Nairs, from their hideouts in the mountains, were making sporadic guerrilla attacks on the Mysore army. The common folk invariably assisted their displaced sovereign, and this infuriated Tipu.

> He resolved to punish them, and for that purpose took the field in person. He was preceded by 30,000 barbarians, who butchered every person who came in their way; and by his heavy cannon under the command of general Lally, at the head of a regiment of artillery. Then followed Tipu Sultan himself, riding on an elephant; and behind him marched another corps, consisting of 30,000 men also. The manner in which he behaved to the inhabitants of Calicut was horrid. A great part of them, both male and female, were hung. He first tied up the mothers, and then suspended the children from their necks. The cruel tyrant caused several Christians and Heathens to be brought out naked, and made fast to the feet of his elephants, which were then obliged to drag them about, till their limbs fell in pieces from their bodies. At the same time, he ordered all the churches and temples to be burned... Christian and Pagan women were compelled to marry Mahommedan men... Every Christian who appeared in the streets must either submit to be circumcised, or be hanged on the spot. This happened in the year 1789 at which time I resided at Verapole [now Varapuzha, a suburb of Kochi]. I had then an opportunity of conversing with several Christians and Pagans, who had escaped from the fury of this merciless tyrant; and I assisted these fugitives to procure a boat to enable them to cross the river which runs past that city.[17]

The sultan's letters and *hukumnamahs* provide firsthand evidence of his diabolic acts. For instance, he wrote to Rajah Ram Chander on 8 February 1786, 'You write, that you were about to issue to the eighty men of the Naimar [Nair]tribe, who had been incorporated into the Usud Ilhyes [converted Muslims], the regulated rations, and other advances, for their separate expenses...'[18]A few days later, on 13 February, he wrote to Budruz Zuman Khan:

> Your two letters, with the enclosed memorandums of the Naimar captives, have been received. You did right in *causing a hundred*

> *and thirty-five of them to be circumcised*, and in putting eleven of the youngest of these into the Usud Ilhye band, and the remaining ninety-four into the Ahmedy troop, consigning the whole, at the same time, to the charge of the Kilaadar of Nagar. You must give strict orders to the said Kilaadar, to take the utmost care of these people, so that they shall not perish.[19] (Emphasis added.)

The converted Muslims were given innovative group names such as Ahmedy, Usud Ilhye, Chela and so on.

The Hindus of Coorg and the Christians of Canara suffered untold brutalities at the hands of Tipu's army. In a letter to Meer Zynul Abideen on 17 September 1785, Tipu wrote:

> It has lately been represented to us, that the Koorgs have committed some excesses at Zuferabad ... you will proceed, as above directed, to Zuferabad; to the Foujdar of which place, Zynul Abideen, we have addressed another letter, which is enclosed. You are, in conjunction with him, to make a general attack on the Koorgs; when, having put to the sword, or made prisoners of, the whole of them, *both the slain and the prisoners are to be made Musulmans.*[20] (Emphasis added.)

Kirkpatrick, who took great pains with the translation from the Persian original, observes:

> The reader will probably be startled at the order contained in the foregoing letter, for making Mussalmans, not only of the living, but of the dead Koorgs, who might fall into the hands of the Sipahdar; and the extravagance of the proceeding may even lead him to suspect, either the correctness of the manuscript, or the fidelity of the translation. With respect to the former, it will be sufficient to say that there is not the slightest ground for supposing any error of the manuscript in this passage; and as to the latter, I will only observe, that nothing can be expressed with more plainness, or freedom from ambiguity, than the original, which, for the satisfaction of the oriental reader, at least, shall be inserted at the bottom of the page.[21]

Kirkpatrick is certain he has made no mistake in translation – Tipu's order clearly states that the dead must be converted to Islam along with the living. Kirkpatrick avers:

> All his Hukum-namahs, or instructions to the governors of provinces, and others, conclude with a denunciation of the penalties to which they will be liable, in case of disobedience or disregard of the orders contained in them. Sometimes these are generally stated, under the vague, but emphatic, term of 'the worst of punishments', at others, they are specifically named; as crucifixion, in one or two instances, and emasculation, in others.[22]

At the conclusion of the Second Anglo–Mysore War in 1784, Tipu regained possession of all the territories held by his father in Canara and Malabar. Lewin B. Bowring in *Haider Ali and Tipu Sultan and the Struggle with the Musalman Powers of the South,* published in 1899, states, 'He signalized his zeal for the faith of Islam by driving out of the coast region no fewer than 30,000 of its Christian inhabitants, who were forcibly deported into Mysore.'[23] He mentions in a footnote:

> It is stated that Tipu demanded the surrender of the daughters of some of these Christians in order to have them placed in his seraglio, and that, on the refusal of the parents, the latter had their noses, ears, and upper lips cut off, and were then paraded through the streets on asses, with their faces towards the tails of the animals.[24]

Bowring adds:

> Similar cruelties were practised on the people of Coorg, the small hill district where Haidar had barbarously cut off the heads of all who opposed his progress... Tipu marched into the country with his army, and lectured the Coorgs on the iniquity of the custom of polyandry. He warned them that if any further rebellion took place, he would extinguish it by removing the population and Islamizing them. At a later period, he actually carried this barbarous threat

> into execution, devastating the province, and driving the wretched inhabitants like sheep to Seringapatam, where they had to submit to circumcision.[25]

The hard truth is that the common folk on both sides of the Western Ghats were terrorized by the Mysore sultans on the one hand and the British on the other. Bartolomeo writes:

> I was assured also by Father Pavone, who for thirty years had been superintendent of the military establishment at Madura [Madurai], that a great many of the Kshatriyas had fled to the mountains from Madura in order to avoid falling into the hands of Haider Ali Khan, Tipu Sultan, Muhammed Ali and the English.[26]

Bartolomeo does not mince words when he speaks of the English and their ally, Muhammed Ali, the nawab of Arcot. He emphasizes that the English were just as oppressive as the Mysore sultans.

Buchanan informs us:

> During the ten days that General Abercromby waited at Priyapattana [in the Coorg country], the gunpowder of his army was kept in the temple of Jaina. On his retreat it was left behind; but Tipu, instead of applying it to the purposes of war, caused the whole to be blown up, and thus had an opportunity of destroying an idolatrous temple, which was one of his favourite amusements.[27]

This narrative reveals that neither the British nor the Mysoreans had any shortage of gunpowder. The Bombay British army had no business keeping the gunpowder inside a Jain temple or leaving it there when they marched back to their base. Tipu had no business blowing up the shrine. Both parties indulged in several insensitive, irreverent and criminal acts. First, the Jain temple was used by the English for storing gunpowder. What happened to the worshippers who held it sacred? How safe was it to leave behind an explosive substance inside a temple? While Buchanan highlights Tipu's sadism, that of the white conquerors is conveniently glossed over, without any adverse comments. Since Buchanan himself was British, and Abercromby was his compatriot, this comes as no surprise.

A letter dated 16 July 1785 addressed to Tipu's brother-in-law and trusted commander, Burhanudeen Khan, was discovered in the Palghat Fort when the British captured it in 1790. It read:

> Let the ditch be filled, and, with the consent and concurrence of all, let the place be stormed and taken. If, however, the garrison will capitulate, it will be well: and [in this case] with the exception of Kala Pundit, the rest may be allowed their lives and arms; but the Pundit's person must be secured. In the event, however, of the assault of the place, *every living creature in it, whether man or woman, old or young, child, dog, cat or any thing else, must be put to the sword,* with the single exception of Kala Pundit.[28] (Emphasis added.)

James Bristow, who published his memoir in 1792 while Tipu was still alive, reveals:

> He [Tipu] has demolished many of their temples and sanctified places of worship, particularly a much-revered pagoda near the bazaar of Seringapatam, where he found it is asserted, 150,000 coined pagodas, buried under the stone out of which the oval was hewn. He frequently orders calves to be brought before the door of their temples, and sheds the sacred blood under the very nose of the offended deity.[29]

Bristow describes a horrific event that occurred in September 1781, when Sergeant Dempster and fifteen others were selected for the purpose of circumcision and forcibly carried off by the prison guards. 'They resisted a long while, and bore very cruel treatment before they submitted to this operation, nor did they submit at last, until they were stupefied with *majum* [a strong opiate], which they had been forced to swallow.'[30] He continues, 'In January 1782 the same persons re-entered our prison, accompanied by Sergeant Dempster, and made a second selection of fourteen, in which number I had the misfortune to be included.'[31] He goes on to describe how they swallowed the narcotic potion, how they were shaved and circumcised, and how those who offered resistance were held down by stout and strong guards.[32] 'After the operation our right ears were perforated, and small silver rings with round knobs fixed in them, this being a mark of slavery among the Mahommedans.'[33] Thereafter, he says their fetters were removed, and they were incorporated into the Chela battalions comprised almost exclusively of prisoners of war. This happened during the last phase of Haider Ali's reign.

Bristow's memoir is filled with horror stories that eerily resonate with truth. Describing the tragic tale of the English prisoners who had the misfortune to fall into Tipu Sultan's hands after he had recaptured Bidanur in 1783, Bristow writes:

> Four European women, with their husbands, belonging to the Bedanore garrison, were brought to Seringapatam, where they were torn from the men, whom the villains sent to Chittledroog [Chitradurga], and afterwards allotted the women to four of the black slaves. Two became the property of the natives of Mysore, and the other two became the property of a couple of abominable Abyssinians, with whom they were compelled to live. I saw the women myself, they were good looking females.[34]

The posthumously published memoir of the English sailor James Scurry, who was captured at sea by the French admiral Suffrein and handed over to Haider Ali in 1781, gives a touching account of his decade-long captivity in Srirangapatna, his forced conversion, circumcision and daring escape to freedom.

A letter written by Tipu Sultan on 22 November 1786 to Urshud Baig Khan, faujdar of Calicut, tells a chilling tale of forced migration.

> Enclosed is a letter which we have received from Gopa, the Aumil of Koorumnad [Kurumbranad], relating to the depredations of the robbers and highwaymen [who infest that district]. Peruse the same, and settle the business. Such of the authors of these flagitious

> proceedings as have been already killed, are killed. But why should the remainder of them, on being made prisoners, be put to death? Their proper punishment is this. *Let the dogs, both black and white, be regularly dispatched to Seringapatam.*'[35] (Emphasis added.)

Kirkpatrick, who translated the letter from the original, acknowledges his inability to figure out who the 'white dogs' are, and therefore, he includes the actual Persian phrase as a footnote. He also shares a wild guess, 'Is it possible that, by the white dogs, he could intend the native Christians of Malabar? This supposition is, it must be owned, opposed by a strong fact, which is, that the Christians in question are as black as any other people in India.'[36] My own guess is that Tipu could just as well have intended the Mappilas, who though fair-skinned, were just as unhappy with the Mysorean domination as the dark-skinned Hindus.

James W. Hoover in *Men without Hats: Dialogue, Discipline and Discontent in the Madras Army, 1806–1807*, states:

> During the Second Anglo–Mysore War, Haidar Ali had besieged British-held Vellore, but to his dismay local Muslims had aided the Company garrison with men and supplies. Haidar Ali's forces had retaliated against the people of Vellore by brutally torturing all civilians who fell into their hands – cutting off ears and noses.[37]

K.K. Nair, in his book *By Sweat and Sword: Trade, Diplomacy and War in Kerala through the Ages,* writes, 'Going by Tipu's correspondence with his staff, the flight of the Moplahs [Mappilas] gave him as much pleasure as that of the other inhabitants.'[38] Describing the impact of Tipu's actions on Malabar, Nair avers, 'The Nairs lost their power, the Moplahs their money, the merchants their trade and the agriculturists their occupations.'[39]

It seems likely that the father–son duo simply played the Muslim card whenever it suited them. Haider Ali and Tipu Sultan had no special affection or consideration for the Muslim dynasties in their neighbourhood or even a modicum of respect for the Mughal emperor. The nawab of Arcot was the sworn enemy of both father and son. The nizam could well have been a friend, but they turned him into an enemy. Ali Raja and the Arakkal Beevi of the Muslim dynasty of Cannanore were simply exploited to serve their narrow ends. While Ali Raja Kunhiamsa (1745–1777) consciously allied with Haider Ali and even invited him to invade Malabar, there are ample indications that the Arakkal Beevi Junumabe Sultana II (1777–1819) made concerted efforts to evade face-to-face encounters with Tipu Sultan, although her minor daughter had been betrothed to one of Tipu's minor sons in an opportunistic political alliance in 1789.

## Damning Testimonies by Friendly Contemporaries

Mir Hussein Ali Kirmani was a Persian immigrant and contemporary of the Mysore sultans. He served six years at the Mysore court between 1781 and 1786 and was thus personally acquainted with both Haider and Tipu. After Tipu's death, Kirmani wrote an elaborate history of the two sultans from his residence in the Vellore Fort, where Tipu's family was confined.

Describing the capture of the Nargunda Fort by the Mysore forces and the imprisonment of the chief and his family, Kirmani writes, 'Some however say that the daughter of the Poligar who was one of the most beautiful women of her time, after she was honoured by reception into the Mussalman faith and the performance of the marriage ceremony was received into the Harem of the Sultan.'[40] The 'honour' described here was the forcible conversion of a hapless prisoner. Doesn't Islam teach that 'consent' is required for the performance of a marriage ceremony? Did the true believer, Tipu Sultan, ask for the woman's consent?

After Tipu captured Adoni in 1785, he sent troops to Kanchan Garh to capture the widow of the polygar who had died recently. Tunguma, who had been ruling Kanchan Garh after her husband's death, learnt of the sultan's sinister intentions and fled in the dead of night, leaving her minor son behind. Kirmani's account reveals, 'Her son, however, whose name was Mudkum Kuru, and about ten or twelve years of age, was taken prisoner in the small fort of

Surkah, his residence; and was honoured by being circumcised and made a Muslim, and he thenceforward received the name of Ali Mardan Khan.'[41] After some time, Ali Mardan Khan was married to the daughter of Khan Jehan Khan, also an 'adopted son' of the late Haider Ali. If Tipu is to be absolved of the crime of forcible conversion, his own accounts and those of Kirmani must be dismissed as blatant lies.

Another contemporary of the Mysore sultans was Maistre de la Tour (aka MMDLT), a French trooper who served in the army of Haider Ali. He rose to become the head of the artillery, commanding 10,000 troops. He authored *The History of Hyder Shah, alias Hyder Ali Khan Bahadur, and of His Son, Tippoo Sultaun,* which was published in 1784, two years after Haider Ali's death. De la Tour traces Haider Ali's French connection to the year 1750 when the latter first encountered the professionalism of the French troops. The French were then hobnobbing in Hyderabad during the succession dispute which saw the incumbent Nasir Jung assassinated by the nawab of Cudappah. This was five years before Haider Ali became the *faujdar* of Dindigul and eleven years before he seized power in Mysore. Realizing the immense value of French military tactics, Haider Ali began hiring French officers to train his private army, soon gaining a reputation as a formidable fighter.

De la Tour describes Haider Ali's hurried march to Ponnani to quell the rebellion of the Nairs in mid-1766: 'Their path was everywhere marked by ruin and destruction, for their orders were to burn and pillage, and they exerted themselves so much in this horrible work that they left behind them nothing but heaps of ruins.'[42] The Frenchman's account leaves no room for doubt. Haider Ali was a ruthless invader with a destructive purpose.

The Nairs had no bayonets or cavalry but only swords and sabres. In this kind of battle, courage alone would not suffice. Their methods and tools were primitive, whereas Haider's army comprised European-style fighters. The result was a major rout. 'The poor inhabitants who fled to the woods and mountains in the most inclement season, had the anguish to behold their houses in flames, their fruit-trees cut down, their cattle destroyed, and their temples burned.'[43] Soon dysentery broke out in Haider's camp, and he was compelled to return to Coimbatore. 'Before he quitted the country, Haider, by a solemn edict, declared the Nairs deprived of all their privileges.'[44] Thereafter, he issued a second edict announcing that those who 'took the turban', that is, embraced Islam, would have their privileges and assets restored. Despite this concession, only a small minority adopted the faith.

## Like Father, Like Son

Haider Ali, though uneducated, was a brilliant military strategist, a brave fighter and a clever statesman. He knew when to fight, when to flee, when to beg for mercy, when to surrender and when to make peace. He accumulated immense wealth but eventually succumbed to a fatal illness at the age of sixty-one. His Islamic faith did not deter him from consuming alcohol. He ordered forced migrations and forcible conversions and performed acts of remarkable cruelty.

According to De la Tour, Haider Ali went hunting twice a week. The author paints a vivid picture of the tiger hunt when Haider is accompanied by his Abyssinians, his nobles and several footmen armed with spears. They encircle the beast and move closer to contract the circle gradually. The hunt invariably culminates in a perfect win for Haider Ali and death for the tiger. 'When he prepares to spring on someone to force a passage, he is attacked by Hyder himself, to whom the honour of giving the first stroke is yielded, and in which he seldom fails.'[45]

Haider Ali had a standing army of entertainers, all of whom were women. 'No Bayadere of the prince's company is more than seventeen years old. At this age they are dismissed; and either travel over the province, or attach themselves to the Pagodas. [Footnote: Every pagoda maintains a number of Bayaderes, whose charms produce one of the most certain revenues of the Brahmins.]'[46] Here the Frenchman refers to the *devadasi* cult and the role played by Brahmin priests in fostering this hoary tradition in Hindu temples.

MMDLT elaborates:

> If the friends are retained to sleep, they choose each a companion for the night among the performers, for which the directress is likewise paid one hundred rupees each; and the master of the house must present his friend with some trinket, or piece of stuff, to be given to the damsel when she is sent away in the morning.[47]

Such were the pastimes of the budding Mysorean general and his cronies.

The Portuguese military adventurer, Eloy Joze Correa Peixoto, wrote *Memoirs of Hyder Ally from the Year 1758 to 1770*. Having served for over a decade in Haider Ali's army before and after the latter's usurpation of the Mysore kingdom, he penned his memoirs soon after leaving the service in 1770. A summary of the anecdotes recounted by Peixoto appears in the *Annual Report of the Mysore Archaeological Department for the Year 1937*, published by the Government Press, Bangalore in 1938. Peixoto reveals that while preparations were in full swing for the wedding of Haider's son Tipu, it was rumoured that Haider too would marry. 'He had already three wives and upward of 4000 concubines who had been distributed in all the countries but principally housed in Bednur, Bangalore and Seringapatam. The concubines were of all castes; there were even European mistresses among them.'[48]

Describing Haider's love of sport, Peixoto states,

> Sports were held for several days by order of Haider – sports like tigers fighting with elephants, fireworks and so on. In one of the sports, two tigers were brought, of which one was a cub, which when let loose, injured several people. The men fell upon it with swords and killed it, at which Haider laughed.[49]

The 'Mysore Report', citing Peixoto's narrative, recounts:

> On another occasion he ordered a royal tiger to be let loose in his garden to fight with two hogs reared up by himself though he was

> a Moor [Muslim]. These two hogs, as soon as they saw the tiger, joined together to fight it. The tiger climbed up a tree to attack them but was forced to descend. It leaped into a dry ditch and the Nawab ordered a Rocket Boy to throw rockets at it. The tiger jumped on the man but before it could fall on him Haider shot it dead.[50]

Here we find evidence that Haider Ali had rockets and rocket-boys in 1769–1770. Tipu, in all likelihood, inherited his obsession with tigers and rockets from his father.

Peixoto reveals that as soon as Haider Ali had left Malabar in early 1766 and retired to Coimbatore, the Nairs rose in revolt and imprisoned his governor Madanna in a pagoda. In August, Haider returned to wreak vengeance. Several authors have described the mad fury and vicious retaliation on the part of Haider Ali, but Peixoto writes with the intimate knowledge of an insider:

> The entire Nair country was plundered, their houses were burnt, and a universal massacre of the Nair caste was ordered. The Nairs were hunted down and butchered. Haider gave Rupees 5 to anyone who brought him the head of Nair that was able to fight; if it was of an old man, he gave four, and if of a boy he gave three rupees. A price of three rupees was also paid for every Nair woman captured alive. Many women were thus captured and transported to distant places as presents to governors and chiefs.[51]

Haider Ali's innate cruelty is attested by Peixoto with several examples:

> Hyder used to chastise his concubines if for any reason he suspected them of infidelity. A certain concubine casually lifted her eyes at a servant on the 5th of the month [August]. He killed her with his own hand and ordered the skin of the servant to be taken off.[52]

Peixoto adds that the nawab's son, Tipu, is cruel beyond description and that no chief desires to accompany him on account of his capriciousness. He also predicts that 'his fortune will last no longer than his father lives'.[53]

Kate Brittlebank, author and historian, is a modern-day admirer of the Mysore sultans, especially Tipu. In *Tiger: The Life of Tipu Sultan*, she tells us, 'The Cholas seized temple images from the Calukyas; and Vijayanagara's Krishnadevaraya, to celebrate his defeat of the Gajapati king, removed an image of Balakrishna from Udayagiri to the capital. We can see this process in operation with Tipu's demolition of the Varahaswami temple at Srirangapatna.'[54] While confirming that Tipu destroyed the temple, Brittlebank sees no difference between the seizure and transfer of sacred Hindu idols from one temple to another and the obliteration of a Hindu temple by a Muslim conqueror. Describing Tipu's destructive acts as part of an ongoing 'process', she rationalizes, 'It was the Wodeyar's direct association with Vishnu's boar incarnation that led to Tipu's demolition of the Varaha temple.'[55] This is a rather strange proposition, for if religious and political causes warranted the destruction of the temple, one wonders why Haider Ali in his twenty-one-year reign left it untouched. Brittlebank further reveals that the Venkataramana Temple in Nagar (Bidanur) has a bell that was cast in Amsterdam in 1713. Apparently, Tipu removed it from a church in Malabar.[56] How it ended up in a Hindu temple so far away is anybody's guess. Perhaps Tipu intended to melt it down to make guns or ammunition and he carted it away, but before he could do anything with it, he lost the territory to the British. The local Hindus might have simply 'saved' the bell by housing it in a temple.

'Neither the English, nor the Dutch, nor even the ruthless Portuguese, showed themselves more alien to or disruptive of the entire region's political and social fabric than the two dictators from Mysore,' writes Denys M. Forrest in *Tiger of Mysore: Life and Death of Tipu Sultan*, published in 1970.[57] Succinctly summarizing the impact of the Mysore sultans, he states, 'They came and conquered and killed and converted –and then disappeared forever.'[58]

## Modern Perceptions

Even after 225 years since his death, Tipu Sultan remains a divisive force. The Bombay Kerala Samajam took legal action when actor–director Sanjay Khan adapted Bhagwan S. Gidwani's novel *The Sword of Tipu Sultan* into a television series. They argued that it was historically inaccurate. The dispute reached the Bombay High Court and later the Supreme Court, but the series was ultimately broadcast by Doordarshan in 1990.

In 2015, the Karnataka government decided to celebrate Tipu Sultan's birthday, sparking a major controversy and provoking the people of Coorg to raise the banner of revolt. Chief Minister Siddaramaiah could have chosen to honour Abbakka Rani of Ullal, who fought the Portuguese until her last breath, or Kittur Rani Chennamma or Sangoli Rayanna, among other home-grown martyrs. However, vote bank politics prevailed over common sense.

The celebrated Kannada actor Girish Karnad had to tender a public apology in November 2016 after his remark lauding Tipu Sultan attracted public condemnation. Karnad had expressed the view that the Bangalore airport ought to be named after Tipu Sultan, akin to the Kolkata airport being named after Subhash Chandra Bose.

In 2018, the Tipu Jayanthi celebrations triggered much controversy, as Union Minister Anant Kumar Hegde described Tipu Sultan as 'a brutal killer, wretched fanatic and mass rapist', and Chief Minister H.D. Kumaraswamy diplomatically skipped the event. In May 2019, Tipu's death anniversary was remembered only by the Pakistani prime minister, Imran Khan, and the distinguished Parliamentarian from Thiruvananthapuram, the erudite Shashi Tharoor. The irony is that if Tipu had realized his dream of exterminating the Nairs, Tharoor, if he had the good fortune to be born, would have been known as Abubacker or Moosakka today! When the Bharatiya Janata Party came to power in Karnataka later that year, they curtly announced that there would be no more Tipu Jayanthis. Om Shanti!

With the passage of centuries, Tipu Sultan's hagiographies have overshadowed the achievements of his father. The supreme irony is that Haider Ali was the winner and Tipu Sultan the loser of the Mysore kingdom. Today, Tipu lovers and Tipu haters are mostly arrayed along communal lines, while the great mass of commonfolk is clueless about the merits and demerits of the father–son duo.

Only the questions remain: Were the Mysore sultans courageous warriors or merciless monsters? Were they patriots and freedom fighters or looters and freebooters? Were they religious bigots? History has the answers, but we need to turn the pages.

# 2

# ORAL HISTORIES AND WHISPERING WALLS

When I record and recount oral testimonies, I know I could be completely off the mark. Or I may be partially right and partially wrong. If I am lucky, I may stumble upon some hidden truths. If I am unlucky, I may find myself barking up the wrong tree. I, therefore, call upon you, my readers, to suspend your judgement, put on your thinking caps and take every word with a liberal dose of scepticism.

The testimonies I have collected are from genuine individuals with ample decency, integrity and honesty, untainted by political or religious biases. They have no incentive to conspire in distorting history. They have simply narrated their stories, family histories and the tales passed down from their parents and grandparents. I have merely documented their narratives, endeavouring to capture the details, spirit, emotions and nuances to the best of my ability.

**Madhavi Amma (1909–1999), Kalliasseri, Kannur District**

Kunnathu Puthiyaveetil Madhavi Amma of Kalliasseri village in the Kannur district was the first witness who introduced the Mysore sultans to me. Born in Malabar 110 years after the death of Tipu Sultan, she had no firsthand experience of the era of Mysorean dominance. However, she had ample experience of the brutality of the British police, as they were regular visitors to her ancestral home during India's struggle for freedom. Her cousin, the fiery communist leader, K.P.R. Gopalan, often had the police on his trail. The men in uniform would make routine visits to the *tharavad,* followed by the breaking of pots and pans, rattling of chairs and tables and intimidation of the occupants. Being a direct beneficiary of these unholy visitations, Madhavi Amma had no love lost for the British. (Years later, two of her sons would go to London for higher studies and bring home white-skinned wives, but that is another story.)

Madhavi Amma was my maternal grandmother. She imparted a great deal of knowledge to me before I even started school. This included the Malayalam alphabet, basic social skills, lessons in nobility as well as stories (histories and 'herstories'), both traditional and her own personal experiences.

Grandma told me that the British were real monsters, but she considered Haider Ali and Tipu Sultan to be the biggest villains ever. According to her, Mahatma Gandhi and Jawaharlal Nehru had led the struggle for India's freedom. She mentioned that Gandhi had intervened with the British to save K.P.R. Gopalan from the gallows. (Later, when I was old enough to understand, K.P.R. himself recounted this story to me.) Thus, before I began formal schooling, there were only four historical figures I knew of: Gandhi, Nehru, Haider and Tipu. The first two were seen as messiahs who had saved Indians from eternal bondage. The latter two were viewed as merciless rulers who had brutally slaughtered our forefathers.

## Princess Aswathi Thirunal Gouri Lakshmi Bayi, Royal House of Travancore

Aswathi Thirunal Gouri Lakshmi Bayi resides in the Kowdiar Palace in Thiruvananthapuram. An erudite scholar, author and polyglot, she adeptly navigates Sanskrit, Malayalam and English with remarkable finesse. History, culture and religion are her favoured subjects. She was recently honoured with a Padma Shri award.

The Princess asserts that Tipu Sultan was not particularly interested in converting Dalits and other lower castes. What he enjoyed most was converting the upper caste Namboothiris and Nairs. Tipu wrote a threatening letter to Rama Varma, the ruler of Travancore, warning him that unless he promptly expelled the Malabar Nairs and Namboothiris who had taken refuge in his kingdom, he should expect a Mysorean attack on his kingdom.

The raja's reply was unequivocal: 'We do not have a tradition of abandoning those who are under our protection.'[1]

Such a response required extraordinary courage, considering the Mysorean army's overwhelming superiority in both numbers and firepower, and the sultan's reputation for atrocious cruelty and religious outrages. Thenceforth, Karthika Thirunal Rama Varma came to be known as Dharmaraja – the royal upholder of dharma – for this act of extreme nobility. It is said that the pope wrote a letter to the raja, appreciating the nobility of his stance. (The letter is not traceable in the state archives, and an attempt is being made to get a copy from the Vatican.)

Tipu did indeed attack, breaching the Travancore Lines. However, Lord Padmanabha was on the side of Travancore. Tipu broke his leg and had to make a hasty escape, losing his turban, flag, dagger and shield to the Travancore army in the process. Later, with the nawab of Arcot acting as a mediator, the dagger and shield were returned. The cap and flag remained in the possession of the Travancore royals. (This narrative is related by Mir Hussein Ali Khan Kirmani, a contemporary of the Mysore sultans, although the details differ. Kirmani insists that the cap belonged to a common soldier – a fact that lends credibility to the tale of the captured cap.)

In the book *Sree Padmanabha Swamy Temple*, the Princess writes:

> Tippu had advanced twice in the direction of Travancore but had to pay a high price for his ambitions. During his second advance, Tippu had openly declared his decision to tether his own flag at the gold flag-mast inside the Sree Padmanabha Swamy Temple, since Sree Karthika Thirunal [Rama Varma] had outright rejected Tippu's conditions of peace which involved Travancore acknowledging the overlordship of Mysore and denying refuge to those who fled to the State to escape persecution by the Sultan.[2]

Upon learning of Tipu's desire to have his horse tethered at the temple, Rama Varma remarked that the horse should be brought to him along with its master. The Princess asserts:

> The desire of either ruler about the horse did not materialize but Tippu's flag, sword, shield and cap, were brought by the jubilant Travancore Forces as trophies to the King. While the sword and shield were returned following the request of the Nawab of the Carnatic who was good friend and ally of Sree Karthika Thirunal, Tippu's dark green serrated flag, however, was taken out in triumph by the flag-bearers at the head of the *Arat* processions of Sree Padmanabha Swamy, as a symbol of the victory of Travancore by Divine grace.[3]

To date, during the annual '*Arattu*' procession, when the eldest male scion of the erstwhile royal family travels from the Kowdiar Palace to the Padmanabha Swamy Temple, replicas of Tipu's green serrated flag and red cap are carried along with immense pride atop an elephant.

The Princess also showed me an old painting depicting the defence of the Travancore Lines by the Travancore army when Tipu Sultan attacked. The painting depicts Tipu lying wounded in his palanquin, being carted away to safety. Legend has it that he sustained a leg injury and, unable to walk, was carried across the river by faithful soldiers. In her characteristically blunt manner, the Princess remarked, '*We* did not defeat Tipu. The Periyar River defeated him.'

The painting had once adorned the walls of her bathroom, but when she grew weary of seeing Tipu's face every day, she ordered its removal. However, when we searched for the painting, it was nowhere to be found. Finally, one of the palace staff members was tasked with locating it, which he did with utmost diligence. The painting, now lacking a frame and covered in a thin layer of dust, was rejuvenated by Aswathi Thirunal, who arranged for it to be reframed. It will undoubtedly take pride of place beside a painting depicting the Colachel War of 1741, when the inimitable Marthanda Varma decisively defeated the Dutch. Two historic victories. Two glorious feathers in the Travancore cap. Two exquisite paintings.

## Narayanan Peruvannan, Theyyam Performer and Padma Shri Awardee, Taliparamba, Kannur District

Narayanan Peruvannan, a spectacular *theyyam* performer from Taliparamba in the Kannur district, shared with me his surprise discovery during a visit to the house of a Muslim friend in Nilambur, Malappuram district, several years ago. To his astonishment, he found that the ancestral house possessed all the features of a traditional Namboothiri *illam*, complete with exquisite carvings and even a Lakshmi-*vilakku*. Narayanan inquired about the family's cultural heritage from the owner, and he learned that they were originally of Namboothiri descent. However, their ancestors had hastily converted to Islam during Tipu Sultan's *padayottam* to protect their clan from a massacre. Although two centuries had passed and many generations had practised Islam, the Lakshmi-*vilakku* had not been discarded, sold or gifted. It remained within the family as a gentle reminder of their long-lost heritage.

Conversion was often a one-way street. Once an individual lost caste, there was no route to regain it. This was the fate of many Hindus in Malabar and Coorg during the 18th century. If someone consumed beef even once, if they were formally or informally converted to another religion, if their men were circumcised or if their women were raped, they would be cast outside the Hindu fold. There was simply no way for them to reintegrate into Hindu society. There was no *ghar-vapasi*, purification ritual or acceptance by the parent community. It is highly probable that many who converted to Islam during the reign of the Mysore sultans remained Muslim not because they wholeheartedly embraced the new religion but due to the absence of any option to rejoin the Hindu community. Subsequent generations were born into the Muslim faith, and the painful past was gradually forgotten. While some families preserved their oral histories, others chose to erase them from memory.

## Dr Azad Moopen, Business Tycoon, Dubai, UAE

Dr Azad Moopen is the founder of Aster DM Healthcare, a global conglomerate of hospitals with 380 facilities in 8 countries. Born in Kalpakanchery in Tirur taluk of Malappuram district, Moopen studied medicine at Calicut Medical College before relocating to the UAE and achieving great success as a healthcare entrepreneur. He was awarded the Padma Shri in 2011.

Moopen recounts that his family is descended from two Hindu brothers, Krishna Menon and Govinda Menon, who converted to Islam in the mid-18th century. He was kind enough to share the 250-year history of the Mandayapurath Menon Moopen family of Malabar. Krishna Menon, the founder of the Moopen clan, was a protégé of Raja Rama Varma, the last ruler of Vettathunad (Kingdom of Light). The rajas of Vettathunad, who ruled the Tirur and Ponnani taluks (currently in the Malappuram district), had pledged allegiance to the Zamorins of Calicut.

Diwan Bahadoor C. Gopalan Nair, who also recounts the family history of the Moopens in his 1917 book *Malayalathile Mappilamar*, traces their origins to the Mandayapurath Menon family in the Mulliarkurussi village of Valluvanad. Two sisters of this family were married to two Namboothiri brothers from Achipra in Ponnani taluk. Govinda Menon, the son of the elder sister, and Krishna Menon, the son of the younger sister, grew up in Achipra. When the young Krishna Menon gained renown for his intelligence and resourcefulness, the raja of Vettathunad summoned him to his palace in Tanur. Impressed by his capabilities, the raja took him under his wing, and in time made him a minister. Later, Krishna Menon was appointed as the prime minister, and thereafter, the entire family shifted to the fertile village of Kalpakanchery, where the raja granted them large tracts of land. Here, the Moopens' ancestral *tharavad*, Mandayapurath Thekethil House, was constructed in the late 18th century and still stands today.

Krishna Menon frequently interacted with Muslim traders from Arabia and was drawn to the customs and practices of Islam. One day, he made the decision to embrace the Arabian religion. With much hesitation and apprehension, he sought permission from the Vettathunad raja. The ruler was taken aback, but nevertheless, he was magnanimous enough to grant permission for the religious conversion. Thus, Krishna Menon and Govinda Menon, along with their family members, were converted to Islam, with the Imam of the Ponnani Mosque, Makthoum Thangal, officiating at the ceremony. Thereafter, Krishna Menon and Govinda Menon were given the Muslim names Mohidin and Mohammad, respectively. After the conversion, Mohidin continued to guide the fortunes of Vettathunad, and the raja conferred upon the two brothers the title of Moopen (meaning 'leader' or 'elder'), decreeing that henceforth all members of the *tharavad* and their descendants would be known by this title.

When Tipu Sultan of Mysore overran Malabar, Raja Rama Varma of Vettathunad fled to Travancore, where he was granted asylum. (He would later die in exile.) Mohidin Moopen stayed behind and continued to oversee the lands of Vettathunad. Tipu Sultan was pleased with Mohidin and entrusted him with the task of collecting revenues from Eranad, Valluvanad, Vettathunad and Palakkad taluks.

*Logan's Manual* states that taxes were collected by 'Mohidin Muppan and Haidros Kutti' from 1773 onwards. (Haidros Kutti was another converted Muslim.) After Haider Ali's invasion of Malabar in 1766, this privilege had been granted to the Coimbatore raja. However, the Zamorin was able to collect taxes between 1768 and 1773, probably due to the Mysore usurper's inability to maintain control over the conquered territories. 'In 1773 Chunder Row [Rao] and Sreenivas Row came with troops and wrested the country from the Zamorin. By their orders, the Nads were rented to Mohidin Muppan and Haidros Kutti, who collected 100 per cent of the *pattam*.'[4] It is, therefore, evident that the Menon brothers were entrusted with this responsibility during the reign of Haider Ali (as Tipu came to power only in December 1782). Logan's narrative reveals that tax collection was an arduous process, largely due to the exorbitant rates fixed by the Mysore sultans.

The Moopen family account states that in the late 1770s (while Haider Ali was the de facto ruler of the Mysore kingdom), Mohidin Moopen defaulted on the payment of taxes to Mysore as he was unable to meet the collection targets. A furious Tipu Sultan sent his soldiers to Kalpakanchery to bring Mohidin to Srirangapatna. Mohidin was terrified and sought refuge with the maharaja of Travancore. Tipu demanded of the maharaja that he surrender the Vettathunad raja along with Mohidin. The maharaja politely declined. Thereafter, Haider Ali passed away, and Tipu Sultan became the ruler of Mysore. While Haider Ali was alive, Tipu was often tasked with managing the Malabar territories, while Ayaz Khan was posted in Bidanur, and Haider himself focused on the Carnatic. However, after Tipu's accession to the throne, life became more difficult for people in the conquered territories. Thus, for the Moopens, returning to Kalpakanchery was not an option.

The Travancore maharaja granted the Moopen family a vast area of land in Eloor (present-day Udyogamandal in Ernakulam district), where they lived in exile. Mohidin Moopen and Mohammad Moopen died and are buried in Eloor. Some members of the Moopen family returned to Kalpakanchery after the death of Tipu Sultan in 1799, while others relocated to nearby locations such as Chembra and Ponmundam. Dr Azad Moopen belongs to that branch of the family that returned to the native village. He is a sixth-generation Moopen, while the youngest members of the *tharavad* now constitute the tenth generation.

Azad Moopen's father, Mandayapurath Ahmedunni Moopen, popularly known as M.A. Moopen, was an agriculturist, trader, businessman and community leader of Kalpakanchery. In the mid-20th century, he constructed a local school and hospital and introduced many innovations such as the post office, electricity and telephones. In 1942, he built Ameer Manzil, which served as an unofficial court-cum-residence where locals would come to settle disputes and resolve conflicts. M.A. Moopen also acted as a bank, where people entrusted their gold and cash for safekeeping. His wife, Ayshu Kalliyath, a gracious and noble lady, was beloved by the populace for her generosity, compassion and philanthropic activities.

Eventually, Azad Moopen's seven siblings all moved out of Kalpakanchery. Ameer Manzil is still owned by the Moopen family. They have founded the Moopen Institute of Local Empowerment (MILE) to empower community-level workers, the M.A. Moopen Memorial Special Needs School for children and a mosque in Kalpakanchery to perpetuate the family legacy. Today, MIMS (Malabar Institute of Medical Sciences) and Aster Medicity are household names in the state of Kerala. The chain of hospitals established by Dr Azad Moopen provides world-class healthcare facilities in several countries.

## Muhammed Ashraf Ali, Archaeological Explorer, Vellore, Tamil Nadu

On a visit to Vellore to explore the historic Vellore Fort, where Tipu's descendants were housed after the fall of Srirangapatna, I met Muhammed Ashraf Ali, an archaeological explorer who had literally left no stone unturned in the vicinity of Vellore. A retired employee of BSNL (Bharat Sanchar Nigam Ltd), Ashraf Ali has a lifelong passion for the exploration of ancient sites and artefacts. A keen sportsman and self-taught historian, he made innumerable discoveries and pointed out several interesting facts to me.

I was aware that after the Vellore Revolt of 1806, Tipu's family had been exiled to Calcutta (Kolkata). However, Ashraf Ali told me that only the male members had been exiled, and many of the females had lived and died in Vellore, with their graves located outside the fort. Later, I visited the tombs of the Mysoreans. The graves included that of Bakshi Begum, the principal wife of Haider Ali, Fathima Begum, daughter of Tipu, Mir Raza, a son-in-law of Tipu, and many nobles and commoners.

In August 1806, Lieutenant Colonel Charles Marriott had prepared a list of princes exiled to Calcutta. It included Tipu's brother Karim Sahib, his nephew Hyder Hussein Khan and ten other princes, who may have been his sons. The names of Fateh Hyder, Abdul Khaliq, Sultan Mohi-ud-Deen and Sultan Moiz-ud-Deen are on the list. Abdul Khaliq, the second son of Tipu, died on arrival in Calcutta. The names of Tipu's daughters (except two) are not on the list, lending credence to Ashraf Ali's contention that they continued to live in the fort until their deaths several years later. With the male heirs out of the way, the British would have convinced themselves that there would never be another mutiny.

Ashraf Ali had another interesting piece of information. He told me that Haider Ali had proclaimed his son Tipu as the nawab of Arcot after winning a battle in the area and had repeated the coronation function inside the Vellore Fort. Thus, Tipu was twice proclaimed as the nawab of Arcot, but the Mysoreans failed to hold the fort for long. Apparently, Tipu Sultan hung around the fort for a while and used to hold court in a particular location called Sultan's Pavilion. Today, it looks more like an open-air assembly hall with whitewashed pillars, a flat roof and little else. A row of prison cells overlooks the pavilion. They are fairly decent and airy and are currently being used to house police cadets during their training period.

Many areas inside the fort are presently under the control of the Tamil Nadu Police. As the security officer of VIT (Vellore Institute of Technology) University accompanied me to the fort, I was allowed into the police quarters and other areas that are routinely forbidden to visitors. I learnt that LTTE (Liberation Tigers of Tamil Eelam) captives had escaped from the prison by digging a tunnel under one of the cells. (The LTTE was a Tamil militant group led by Velupillai Prabhakaran in the Sri Lankan civil war during the last decades of the 20th century. Prabhakaran was killed in action in May 2009, and the movement was brutally wiped out by the Sri Lankan army.)

A mystifying tomb inside the fort is of Dewan Purnaiya's daughter, who had converted to Islam. Her name is not mentioned on the tombstone, which simply says 'Dewan Puraniya's daughter'. I was unable to ascertain when and how the lady came to Vellore and when her conversion took place. The most logical assumption is that she came along with the slain sultan's retinue in 1799. In that case, she may have been converted earlier and wedded to a Muslim. It would have been impossible for an unmarried Brahmin girl to accompany Tipu's family into exile. As Purnaiya continued as a Dewan under the Wodeyars, there would have been no pressing need for him to send his unmarried daughter with a Muslim group to a distant location. Thus, it seems likely that the Brahmin girl who lies buried outside the Vellore Fort had become a Muslim before the death of Tipu Sultan. One can only speculate on Purnaiya's role in the conversion. Was it forced, fear-driven or voluntary? Was it a consequence of the Dewan's ambition? Did the sultan himself play a role in the conversion? Was the girl wedded to a member of the Sultan's family? Some authors have mentioned that it was the calming influence of his mother that prevented Tipu from converting Purnaiya himself. The tomb merely indicates the fact that Purnaiya's daughter 'embraced Islam', died in 1832 and lies buried there.

## Achuthankutty Menon, Emoor Bhagavathy Temple Functionary, Palakkad (Palghat)

The Kallekulangara Emoor Bhagavathy Hemambika Temple, popularly known as Kaipathi Kshethram (the Temple of the Hand), lies 8 km from Palghat on the road to the Malampuzha Dam. The 'murthy' or consecrated idol consists of a pair of hands. According to legend, Goddess Durga emerged from the waters of a pond to bless an ailing priest who had fervently appealed to her, as he was unable to walk through the forest to the shrine atop Muthiramkunnu where he used to perform the daily rituals. Taking pity on him, the goddess appeared in the pond adjacent to his humble abode. The dazzled Namboothiri dived into the pond and grabbed hold of her two hands, which promptly turned into stone and were henceforth worshipped in lieu of a full-bodied idol. The name 'Kallekulangara' originates from this legend. ('Kallu' means 'stone' and 'kulangara' means 'bank of a pond'.)

Hemambika is the patron deity of the Palakkatusseri royal house. (Balambika, Hemambika, Lokambika and Mookambika are believed to be the four Durga temples consecrated by Parashurama, the sixth avatar of Lord Vishnu.) My friend Vijayakumari accompanied me from Ottapalam to Palakkad to visit the Hemambika Temple. One of the temple functionaries, Achuthankutty Menon, acquainted us with the history of the temple. Vijayakumari ventured to ask Menon whether it was true that the temple jewels were given away to Haider Ali. He answered that when the jewels were taken in a procession to the temple from the abode of the raja, the Mysorean soldiers snatched them away. He was merely being circumspect. It does appear that the devi's ornaments eventually reached Mysore in the form of gold ingots. Whether the raja gave them away fearing the new interloper or whether Haider Ali looted the temple is a moot point.

Menon was kind enough to give me a 2017 booklet written by Chandrika Hariharan Iyer titled *Hemambika: The Elixir of Life*. The author states, 'As read from *History of Kerala* by K.V. Krishna Ayyar, the Shekari rajas original place and tharavad were once located close to the present Victoria College grounds but moved to Akathethara-Kallekulangara after Hyder came to Palakkad.'[5] Iyer also notes:

> Brother-in-law of Hyder Ali, Muqadam Ali's forces withdrew after collecting their compensation by way of gold melted out of the ornaments worn by the Emoor Bhagavathy, the tutelary deity of the Palakkad achans, as *rakshabhogam* equivalent of 12,000 old Viraraya fanams ... The Raja of Palakkad became a tributary to Mysore and agreed to pay a sum of 5000 fanams to Mysore annually as protection money.[6]

She quotes an article by the late P.C.N. Raja wherein he stated that Tipu Sultan caused damage to the Hemambika Temple.[7] It is said that when Tipu arrived, the royal family took to the hills, and the deity was hidden in the pond. Later during the British occupation, the family returned, and the deity was retrieved and reinstalled in the sanctum sanctorum.[8] Thus, it is evident that each of the sultans harmed the temple in their own unique ways.

Chandrika Iyer's account of the loss of the temple jewels offers a more plausible and detailed explanation. There exists a centuries-old tradition known as 'Ponnakambadi Ezhunnallathu', during which the *thiruvabharanam* (sacred ornaments) of the goddess are ceremoniously taken in a procession from the royal house to the temple and back. 'Nowadays in the place of the thiruvabharanam, a gold *thirumangalyam* is brought in silk cloth kept in a *chembu* vessel tied in a stick,' notes Iyer.[9] This alteration highlights how the intervention of the sultans led to significant changes in long-cherished customs or *acharams*.

We met the 96-year-old scion of the erstwhile Palghat royal family. Despite being wheelchair-bound and hard of hearing, Shekari Varma Valiya Thamburan K.K. Chathu Acchan exuded dignity and calmness. While monarchy has transitioned into democracy, some old customs persist, such as the 'Ariyittu-Vazhcha' ceremony that continues unabated to this day. 'Do they have any connections with the Travancore royals?' I asked. 'None,' they replied. I wondered whether this had any relation to the centuries-old boycott of the Palghat raja by other Kerala royals. Buchanan notes that the Nairs of Palghat faced a complete social boycott: 'As this family invited Hyder into the country, they are considered by all the people of Malabar as having lost cast[e], and none of the Rajas of Kshatriya descent will admit them into their company.'[10]

Regardless of whether the Namboothiris actually boycotted the Palghat raja, it seems certain that a mass migration did occur in the past. Some individuals testified that when the raja married a woman from a lower caste (*vedan* community), the Namboothiris boycotted him and left Palghat. However, this reasoning appears unsound, as it was common for kings to have many wives from diverse backgrounds. Moreover, succession to the kingship followed the 'marumakkathayam' tradition, making the caste of the king's sons irrelevant. Only his nephews needed to be of pure blood because one of them would eventually inherit the throne. Therefore, the story of the *vedathi* was recounted by the Shekaripuram Namboothiris, a priest from Alathur and a few others, but it appears dubious nevertheless. The exodus of the Namboothiris may have been triggered by some other event.

The priests of the Hemambika Temple are Namboothiris, a tradition that has persisted for several generations. Did the Palghat raja eventually succeed in winning back the Namboothiris who boycotted him in the mid-18th century? Neither the Namboothiris nor the Iyers I met had an answer to that question.

The Iyers claim they migrated from Thanjavur centuries ago, with some mentioning a time span of 400 years. Krishnaprasad of Alathur suggested it could have been a chain migration rather than a mass exodus. What prompted their departure from their fertile homeland, Thanjavur, and drew them to faraway Palghat? Was it due to famine or Maratha attacks, or were they tempted by incentives offered by the Palghat raja? There is no doubt that the Namboothiris left Palghat en masse. Today, only a few clans remain, and most of them seem to trace their roots to other districts. While the Iyers constitute the predominant Brahmin community in this district, many have pursued other professions and migrated to more developed regions, with temple service no longer being their preferred occupation. Meanwhile, the Namboothiris have returned to resume their temple duties.

## Speaking Stones, Screaming Walls

Every stone bears a story, and every wall echoes with wails and whispers. Each structure stands as a silent witness to the relentless march of history. Some were ravaged, while others were spared, as the Mysore sultans swept through Malabar, Thrissur, Alwaye and other parts of central Kerala.

Some say that Tipu came here and destroyed everything, while others claim he never arrived, attributing the preservation to divine intervention. Some believe their prayers to a saint led to miraculous outcomes. Some credit a divine flood that rendered the Periyar river impassable. These ideas, with minor variations, were elucidated by different people at different locations in central Kerala during my visits in early 2022. Today, Hindus and Christians of various denominations continue to pass on these beliefs orally. They heard it from their parents and grandparents and convey the same to their children and grandchildren.

It is a fact that Tipu's army camped in the region for an extended period. The common people were gripped with fear as they lacked the power to resist the might of the Mysoreans. They prayed fervently, and by divine intervention, they survived to share their tale. While we may suspect the veracity of the myriad accounts, and even discount the miracles, the ultimate truth remains unassailable. The mighty Tipu Sultan failed in his effort to conquer Travancore and Cochin. The British East India Company declared war on Tipu, forcing him to abandon Travancore and rush to defend his other territories, including his capital. At Tirurangadi in 1790, Tipu's army suffered a crushing defeat, with the British and the Nairs joining forces against him. In 1792, Tipu found himself besieged in Srirangapatna and was forced to agree to a humiliating peace treaty, ceding Malabar to the British formally.

### Thazhekkad St Sebastian Church, Thrissur District

The area around this church is home to one of the oldest St Thomas Christian communities in Kerala. Legend holds that Thomas the Apostle of Jesus arrived in Kerala in 52 CE, attracted many followers, converted many locals, built many churches and was finally martyred in Mylapore in present-day Chennai. The Thazhekkad Sasanam, an ancient stone edict, dated between the 8th and 10th centuries, describes the grant of special privileges to the Christian community. The church itself dates back to 800 CE.

The church bears a plaque stating that in 1789, during the *padayottam* of Tipu Sultan, the shrine was set ablaze, and the idols were either thrown away or destroyed. The terrified local residents scattered in all directions. Later, they returned and searched for the lost idols. Finally, after many fervent prayers to the saint, one of the idols was retrieved from an old well. It was installed near the altar, and the church was rebuilt. The well sits adjacent to the outer wall of the church, and its water is believed to possess magical, healing properties. While sultans may come and go, beliefs endure eternally.

**Basilica of Our Lady of Snow (Manjumatha), Pallipuram, Ernakulam District**

During a visit to the Pallipuram Fort, I came across a splendid church situated on the banks of the Chalakudy River, a tributary of the mighty Periyar. I discovered an ancient Portuguese-style church (perhaps rebuilt by the Dutch), a new modern church standing alongside it, and an old watch-tower-like structure crowned with a blue dome. The church was originally built by the Portuguese in 1507 and refurbished over the centuries. Upon the arrival of the Portuguese, the region already boasted a sizeable Christian population, likely due to its proximity to the supposed landing site of St Thomas in 52 CE. Subsequently, the Dutch seized control of the area in the 17th century before it was ultimately sold to the raja of Travancore in the late 18th century.

The legend of Our Lady of Snow is truly astonishing. When Tipu Sultan's forces encamped on the opposite bank of the river, they spotted the outline of a church in the distance and prepared to unleash cannon fire. Given Tipu's reputation for destroying numerous Christian churches and Hindu temples, the people of Pallipuram were terrified. They gathered inside the church and fervently prayed to Our Lady to save the community from certain annihilation. And lo and behold! A dense fog enveloped the church and its surroundings, making them invisible to the invaders. Unable to locate their target, the gunners ceased their assault, leaving the church and the people unscathed. Through a miraculous intervention, the venerated saint had outsmarted the advancing forces of the marauding sultan of Mysore. Following this magical event, Our Lady came to be known as Manjumatha (Our Lady of Snow).

This church has a namesake in Rome, Italy. The Basilica di Santa Maria Maggiore is one of the Seven Pilgrim Churches of Rome. Built in the 5th century, it is also known as Our Lady of the Snows, commemorating a miraculous event from the 4th century when Mother Mary purportedly signalled her presence by causing snowfall on a summer night (5 August) atop the Esquiline Hill. Today, the church is a major attraction for devout Catholics and tourists alike. (I had the privilege of paying obeisance at this shrine when I accompanied a Christian group to Rome in 2014.) It is noteworthy that the annual feast of Our Lady is celebrated in Pallipuram on 5 August! Myths and beliefs tend to migrate.

### Varapuzha Basilica, Ernakulam District

The Basilica of Our Lady of Mount Carmel and St Joseph, located in the northern suburbs of Kochi (Cochin), is known to the locals as Varapuzha Basilica or Varapuzha Palli. Built in 1673, it is dedicated to two saints, Our Lady of Mt Carmel and St Joseph. Like many other churches, the annual feast is celebrated here between 31 July and 15 August.

The old Varapuzha Basilica has a fascinating history. Paulinus Paathiri or Fra. Bartolomeo described it in his 18th-century publication as a 'Church of Latin and Chaldean rites'. Situated on an island, it was spared the depredations of Tipu Sultan, whose army ravaged many other churches located nearby. During that turbulent time, Varapuzha received many refugees, whom Fr Paulinus helped in crossing the river to safety. The Carmelite missionaries cared for these displaced individuals until the Muslim conqueror eventually withdrew from the region. Before the outbreak of the Third Anglo–Mysore War in 1790, Paulinus Paathiri returned to Europe. However, he received letters from his fellow missionaries in Varapuzha, informing him that the Mysorean army had invaded the island and seized control of their church.

Describing an incident from 15 April 1790, when Tipu's army breached the Travancore Lines and entered Verapole (Varapuzha), the Bishop of Varapuzha wrote to Paulinus Paathiri:

> The troops advanced to Verapole and set some houses on fire, but did not enter the island. We were visited only by a few marauders, who converted our church, our seminary, and our convent into real dens of thieves. They plundered and destroyed whatever they could lay their hands on; for it had been almost impossible for us to remove anything out of the way. By the peculiar providence of God, however, and of St Joseph, neither our church nor our convent fell prey to the rapacity of the soldiery or to the flames.[11]

The church fathers were immensely relieved that the Mysoreans did not set fire to the church upon their departure. However, the seminary had to be closed following the attack, and it was not until 1832 that services could resume.

**Sampaloor, Thrissur District**

Sampaloor (originally named Saint-Paul-Oor) is often referred to as the Goa of Kerala, as it was a significant hub where many famous missionaries arrived to propagate the gospel. Among them were St Francis Xavier, St John Britto (Swamy Arulananda), Arnos Paathiri and Fr Joseph Constantine Buski (Veeramamunivar).

Meticulously preserved records indicate that St Francis Xavier made visits to Sampaloor in 1542, 1544 and 1548. Throughout the Portuguese era, numerous Jesuit priests resided in Sampaloor. The area, therefore, is home to a church dedicated to St Francis Xavier as well as the St Paul's Seminary, the St Paul's Monastery and the St Paul's Press.

Arnos Paathiri, who was ordained at the St Paul's Seminary, made significant contributions to Malayalam literature. It was in Sampaloor that Jesuit priests established Kerala's first printing press in 1663. However, when Tipu Sultan arrived in 1789–1790, the church was completely destroyed. It would take considerable time before the clergy could rebuild it in 1862, with active support from the vicar apostolate of Varapuzha. The Historical Museum and the Anglo-Indian Cultural Museum house numerous artefacts that highlight the tumultuous history of the region.

One evening, I arrived at the Church of St Francis Xavier to find the place deserted. The church doors stood wide open, and I took the opportunity to pay my respects. However, to my utter disappointment, the adjacent museum was closed. My friend Jose Kokkad went in search of the chief priest, who was overseeing some construction work nearby. The priest was kind enough to return and open the museum for us. Despite having several others waiting to see him, he graciously took the time to explain the history of the church and highlight the uniqueness of the preserved artefacts.

I learnt that the church had indeed been destroyed by Tipu Sultan and was rebuilt six decades later. We are repeatedly reminded by various visuals – both inside the museum and on the church premises – that Francis Xavier arrived by sea. The well he used to baptize the locals is still preserved in the basement of the modern edifice. Statues and paintings on the walls depict his conversion of Brahmins and other castes, his healing of the sick and his performance of miracles. The stones of the original church, recently unearthed by researchers and construction workers, have been preserved by erecting a small structure alongside the modern church, labelled Xavier's Castle. Inside the museum is an evocative black-and-white painting portraying a battle between the invading Mysorean forces and the defending locals. The invaders, bearded horse riders armed with muskets, face off against *mundu*-clad locals wielding swords, shields and spears. In the background, dark clouds of smoke fill the sky, indicating destruction and arson. The field is littered with bodies, and blood drips from wounds. As the saying goes, 'A picture is worth a thousand words.' In this manner, the pain is kept alive by Christians and Hindus in numerous areas mauled by the Mysoreans during their twenty-five-year rampage across Malabar.

## Kanjoor St Mary's Forane Church, Ernakulam District

Kanjoor is situated near Kalady, the birthplace of Adi Shankaracharya. Here, the St Mary's Forane Church, established in 1001 CE, stands testimony to a long history of conflict. The church has weathered many a storm. A book published in 2014 by Dr Jomom Thachil titled *Kanjoor Christava Pazhama* gives an intriguing account of the church's history.

An exquisite 'elephant lamp' or *aana-vilakku*, gifted to the church by the Cochin ruler Sakthan Thampuran (1790–1826), is only taken out during festival processions. According to legend, the raja was incensed when a servant failed to pay obeisance to him, leading him to order the breaking down of the church door. Simultaneously, an elephant attacked his own mansion, humbling the raja. As a peace offering, he donated an elephant lamp to the church. It is modelled after the traditional Lakshmi-*vilakku* with a large elephant in place of Goddess Lakshmi.

A Jesuit father at the nearby Sameeksha Retreat informed me that Christians and Nairs had joined forces to resist the Mysorean troops when Tipu Sultan arrived on the scene. He also mentioned the great flood that had washed away Tipu's army. He suggested to our common friend Sheela Anthony that we visit the church and take a look. We followed his advice. On one of the walls, there is a modern mural said to be a replica of an old mural painting, depicting several scenes from the church's history. Tipu Sultan is depicted seated on an elephant, his head held high and haughty accompanied by foot soldiers, drummers, cannons and horsemen. The image portrays horses, elephants and soldiers being swept away in the floods. It also shows Sakthan Thampuram standing at the church door with a servant insolently seated, refusing to rise and bow to the reigning monarch. Beneath this scene, the painter depicts an elephant striking at the king's mansion. In another scene, a sleeping king appears to be dreaming of a solution to the impasse, with the elephant lamp prominently featured in his dream.

## The Miracle Flood Theory

At various locations in Thrissur and Ernakulam districts, there is a widely held belief that a miraculous flood in the Periyar River washed away the soldiers and horses of Tipu Sultan's army when they attempted to breach the Travancore Lines and attack the army of Travancore. Tipu had to cross the river to enter the territory of the southern kingdom, which was an ally of the British. He did so with a few thousand soldiers, leaving the bulk of his forces on the opposite bank of the river. Once Tipu and his advance guard had crossed over and the fighting began, the river swelled in size and drowned all those who tried to flee to the safety of the opposite bank. The Nair soldiers slaughtered all those who had crossed into their domain. Tipu himself narrowly escaped. This event is recounted by the Persian chronicler Kirmani, a contemporary of the sultan. The version of the Travancore kingdom is presented by Princess Aswathi Thirunal, who opines that the flood in the Periyar turned the tide in favour of the Travancoreans.

Was the flood real or was it a myth? It is well known that the 27-km-long Vypin Island was formed as a result of a massive flood in the Periyar River in the year 1341. Vypin lies in the Arabian Sea at the estuary of the Periyar. The flood is said to have washed away the ancient port of Muziris (now Kodungallur). Muziris was known from Roman times as a flourishing port, yet it was washed away in an instant. Thus, flooding in the Periyar is no miracle. Kirmani mentions that the river was in spate, and, therefore, Tipu was advised to avoid crossing. Disregarding this advice, the sultan crossed the river with 4,000 soldiers. He was routed – and the rest is history. Whether God sent a flood to defeat the sultan is a matter of faith and conjecture.

## Hindu Legends

Far north in the Kasargod and the Kannur districts, the *padayottam* of the Mysore sultans gave rise to a variety of legends. As mentioned earlier, the historical accounts of the desecration of various temples are intertwined with fanciful stories of divine intervention to halt the carnage.

The Rajarajeswara Temple in Taliparamba was one of the most prominent temples of the erstwhile Kolathunadu kingdom. The region, then known as Perinchelloor, fell under the sway of the Cholas in the 11th century, and it is likely that the temple was named after Rajaraja Chola. Numerous legends envelop this ancient site. According to one, Lord Parashurama himself guided King Sathasoman of the Mooshika dynasty in constructing the temple. It is also believed that Lord Shiva, the main deity, visits Annapoorneswari Devi of Cherukunnu daily. S. Jayashanker in his book *Temples of Kannoor District* records, 'The gigantic gopuram at the entrance was destroyed by Tippu's army.'[12]

The story goes that during the siege, the chief priest sought refuge inside the *srikovil*, fervently praying for hours on end. According to Jayashanker:

> The Lord heard his prayers. Tippu's forces had to retreat as the Commander of the army was bitten by a *kari-nagam* [black serpent] and a serpent appeared in front of every soldier. Thus, the temple was saved from total destruction. However, some Nampoothiri families had to flee for safety and they settled in the erstwhile Travancore state ... The temple had large properties which were lost during the attack of Tippu's forces and also due to the implementation of land reforms.[13]

The Sree Katamberi Chuzhali Bhagavathy Temple near Morazha boasts of ancient origins, with legends suggesting that the sage Agastya once worshipped Goddess Bhadrakali here. 'During Tippu's attacks an attempt was made to ransack the temple but the sudden appearance of swarm of bees and wasps by the grace of the Goddess protected the temple,' says Jayashanker.[14]

A beetle attack supposedly thwarted the advance of Tipu Sultan's marauding forces at the ancient Subramanyaswamy Temple in Meethala–Punnaat near Iritty. Swarms of beetles also emerged from the temple, deterring the invaders.[15]

In the Anthoor locality of Taliparamba, there are two very ancient Shiva temples known as Mel-Thali (upper Thali) and Keezh-Thali (lower Thali). Jayashanker notes, 'The forces of Tipu Sultan plundered and caused heavy damages to the Mel-thali temple and the neighbouring Thrkkapaaleswaram Devi temple.'[16] However, the Keezh-Thali Temple was spared as a *karnavar* of the Meppaat *tharavad* stood in front of the temple in the guise of a Muslim imam and convinced the marauders that the temple was soon to be converted into a mosque. Thereafter, though a staunch believer, the gentleman never entered the temple, considering himself unworthy of the goddess, as he had impersonated a Muslim imam.'[17]

# 3

# THE WILD RAMPAGE OF HAIDER 'NAIK'

The Wodeyar dynasty of Mysore traces its origins back to 1399. They served as long-time feudatories of the powerful Vijayanagar kingdom, which met its demise in 1565 at the hands of an alliance formed by four Bahmani sultanates of the Deccan. Following this, the Wodeyars gained independence. However, by the time Haider Ali arrived on the scene, the raja was a mere figurehead, completely at the mercy of his ministers, the brothers Devaraj and Nanjaraj.

As a young man, Haider enlisted in the army, rose through the ranks and quickly gained the raja's trust. Mastering both the art of war and the rare skill of palace intrigues, he soon displaced the wily brothers and became the de facto ruler of Mysore. He strengthened his army, arranged for French training for his troops, invaded neighbouring states and enriched himself through plunder. Once firmly in control, he set about expanding his domain, quickly subduing the neighbouring principalities led by various *nayakas* and polygars. (Polygar, the anglicized version of *palayakkar*, literally means 'leader of the military camp'.)

## Obscure Origin

Not much is known about Haider Ali's ancestry. He was the son of Fath (or Fateh) Muhammed and grandson of Muhammed Ali. Muhammed Ali's father, Sheikh Wali Muhammed, is believed to have immigrated from northern India to Gulbarga in Karnataka.

Muhammed Ali married the daughter of a humble worker in a dargah. Later, he moved to Bijapur and lived for a while with the seven brothers of his wife, all of whom perished in the battle against Aurangzeb in 1686. Thereafter, the family relocated to Kolar. When Muhammed Ali passed away around 1697, his fourth son, Fath Muhammed, entered the service of the nawab of Arcot. Later, he served the ruler of Mysore, but subsequently moved to serve the ruler of Sira (in Tumkur district, Karnataka). He was entrusted with the fort of Doddaballapur, where his son Haider was born in 1721. Fath Muhammad also had another son, Shahbaz, who was three years older than Haider. Forrest notes, 'Fath Muhammad had married in his Arcot days the daughter of a holy man from Tanjore and had a son called Shahbaz.'[1]

Bowring has documented a family tree where Haider Ali's great-grandfather is listed as Muhammed Bhalol. His grandfather is Ali Muhammed, also known as Ali Ghulam Dost Muhammed, who married the daughter of Sayyad Parsa Munshi. His father, Fath Muhammed, also known as Fateh Ali or Shuja Sahib, wed Majida Begum, the daughter of Meer Akbar Ali Khan. Fath Muhammad passed away in 1729. Haider Ali is reported to have married Fakhrunissa, the daughter of Moinuddin, as well as an unnamed daughter of Makhdum Sahib.

Upon the death of the ruler of Sira, a succession dispute erupted, leading to an attack by the nawab of Arcot. Fath Muhammed perished in the ensuing battle. His widow, Majida Begum, and his minor sons endured immense suffering as Fath Muhammed had left behind debts. The boys were imprisoned and badly mistreated by the creditors. Finally, a relative intervened on their behalf, and Devaraj, the dalawai of Mysore, wrote to the subedar of Sira demanding their release. It is said that the Wodeyar took pity on the widow and paid 10,000 varahas for the release of her underage sons.[2] Thus, Majida Begum and her sons arrived in Srirangapatna, where they found refuge under the protection of Haider Saheb, a nephew of Fath Muhammed.

Shahbaz and Haider Ali received training in the use of firearms and horse-riding, growing up well-versed in the art of war.

As the boys matured, they departed to serve elsewhere, but their mentor brought them back and introduced them to Nanjaraj, the commander of the Mysore army, 'who gave them the command of 300 foot and 50 horses'.[3] When Haider Saheb passed away, Shahbaz took over his detachment.

Wilks, providing a slightly different account, states:

> Mohammed Bhelole, a religious person, who came from the Punjab to the south, accompanied by two sons, Mohammed Ali, and Mohammed Wali, and settled at the town of Alund in the district of Calburga [now Kalaburagi, erstwhile Gulbarga]…. He married his son Muhammed Ali to the daughter of one of the servants of the celebrated mausoleum at Calburga, and Muhammed Wali into another family in the same neighbourhood.[4]

Later, the sons ventured to Sira in search of employment. 'Fath Muhammed, the son of Muhammed Ali and the father of Haider, was born at Sera.'[5] Subsequently, 'the two brothers came to Kolar, where Muhammed Ali died, and Muhammed Wali, seizing on all the domestic property, turned Fath Muhammed and his mother out of doors'.[6] An unnamed naik took pity on the widow and her son, offering them refuge. When Fath was old enough, the unknown benefactor enlisted him as a peon under his command. Fath Muhammed eventually rose to the rank of naik.[7]

Wilks states, '[Fath's] first wife was Seydanee Saheba, the daughter of Burra Saheb, a religious person at Kolar, who bore him three sons, Wali Sahib, Ali Sahib, and Bhelole Sahib.'[8] The lady died young, and later Fath married the elder daughter of a destitute widow whose husband had been robbed and murdered while the family was travelling from Konkan to Kolar. Fath found a new patron, Sadatullah Khan, the nawab of Arcot, likely by 1721. Upon the death of his second wife, he wed her younger sister, who bore him two sons, Shahbaz and Haider, both born in Boodicota.[9] In 1728, Fath Muhammed and his son Wali from his first marriage perished in battle. His widow and minor sons found themselves in dire circumstances. A creditor appeared and demanded money.[10] Wilks recounts:

> The usual methods were resorted to and succeeded; but not before the torture, in its most cruel and ignominious forms, had been applied to both the boys and probably to their mother. This inhuman conduct was not forgotten; and … Haider, in his prosperous fortune, sought his revenge after the lapse of thirty-two years, with all the virulence belonging to the memory of a recent injury.[11]

While there is disagreement regarding Haider Ali's family history, there is no doubt that he ascended from very humble beginnings. His rise was gradual, with his exploits becoming well-documented only in the 1760s, when he was forty years old.

## From Naik to Nawab

Wilks testifies:

> At the eight-month-long siege of Devanahalli in 1749, Haider Ali showed exemplary courage and impressed Nanjaraj with his fighting skills … first appearing as a volunteer horseman in his brother's corps, and afterwards occasionally entrusted with the command of parties of infantry in the trenches. He was observed on every service of danger to lead the way, and to conduct himself with a coolness and self-possession seldom found in a young soldier.[12]

He was conferred the title of 'Khan' and granted a distinct command. Haider Ali Khan would steadily rise in prominence and swiftly leave his mark on the tumultuous political landscape of south India. Titles such as 'nawab' and 'khan bahadur' would follow later.

When Nanjaraj dispatched a contingent to Hyderabad to intervene in a succession dispute following the nizam's demise, Haider Ali seized a golden opportunity. The main contenders were the nizam's son, Nasir Jung, and grandson, Muzaffar Jung. Mysore stood alongside Nasir Jung, who had seized power upon his father's passing. The French were also present, aiming to capitalize on the turmoil.

Nasir Jung managed to overpower and imprison Muzaffar Jung. However, on 16 December 1750, he was treacherously assassinated by the nawab of Cuddapah. In the ensuing chaos, the French seized a significant portion of Nasir Jung's wealth, while Haider Ali absconded with the remainder. Wilks states:

> Haider had already prepared the means of availing himself of such opportunities, by keeping in his pay a body of three hundred select Beder Peons, who may well be characterized as brave and faithful thieves ... During the confusion of this day they mixed with the crowd near the treasure of Nasir Jung, which, as usual, the treasurer had begun to load at the first alarm; and these expert marauders, exclusively of minor thefts, separated from the crowd two camels laden with gold coins, and before the confusion had ceased, were clear of all the outposts, and well advanced on their route towards Devanahalli [Haider's fixed home and station], whither, during this service, about three hundred horses and five hundred muskets occasionally picked up upon the field, or stolen in the quiet of night, had also been conveyed.[13]

With his newfound wealth, Haider bolstered his army and enlisted French mercenaries to train his soldiers. It proved to be a wise investment.

Haider Ali encountered other opportunities as well. A power struggle unfolded between Muhammad Ali and Chanda Sahib for the nawabship of the Carnatic. The French supported Chanda Sahib, while the British aligned with Muhammad Ali. The latter appealed to Mysore for aid and pledged to cede Trichinopoly (Trichy for short, now Thiruchirapally or Thiruchi) and its surrounding territories to Mysore if they were to secure victory with their assistance. The Wodeyar and Devaraj were not in favour of this risky venture, but Nanjaraj could not resist the temptation.

In February 1752, Nanjaraj led an army to Trichinopoly to confront Chanda Sahib and the French, with Haider Ali by his side. Chanda Sahib was lured away to Tanjore (Thanjavur) and assassinated in May. However, the victorious Muhammad Ali only conceded the temple island of Srirangam to Mysore. Subsequently, the Mysoreans switched sides and tried to capture Trichinopoly with French support. The attempt proved unsuccessful, prolonging the conflict for years. In 1755, Nanjaraj was recalled to Mysore, and Haider Ali was appointed as the *faujdar* of Dindigul.

While Nanjaraj was away in the Carnatic, the nizam, accompanied by his French commandant De Bussy, descended on Srirangapatna and demanded the outstanding tribute. Devaraj hurriedly raised funds by plundering temples and parting with the crown jewels, but the 18 lakh rupees he could muster amounted to only a third of the owed tribute. Shortly thereafter, the Marathas also arrived. Bowring states, 'In March 1757, the Peshwa Balaji Baji Rao suddenly appeared before the capital, exacting the payment of a heavy contribution, of which five lakh rupees were paid in cash, while certain districts were surrendered in pledge for an additional sum of twenty-seven lakhs.'[14] Haider was summoned back to the capital, where he discovered the troops on the brink of mutiny due to unpaid wages. He quickly restored order, and the overdue payments were released, enhancing his reputation and popularity. Nanjaraj and the Wodeyar now found themselves indebted to him.

During his long stay in Dindigul, Haider Ali focussed on subduing the minor chieftains in the neighbouring areas and enhancing the strength of his army. Undoubtedly, he also managed to improve his financial situation during this time.

It appears that Haider Ali's brother Shahbaz died in 1756. According to Wilks, Devaraj relinquished his post in February 1757,[15] but apparently, he retained considerable influence for some time thereafter. By this time, Haider had modernized his army by extensively employing European mercenaries, weaponry and military manoeuvres and had a few hundred Europeans under his command. While Cossigny and Lally were French, Budene hailed from Germany. There were Dutch and Portuguese officers as well. Haider Ali poached them from other kingdoms by offering higher pay and perks. As early as 1758, Peixoto, the captain of the Portuguese troops in Goa, had joined the Mysore army.[16] His memoirs provide valuable insights into Haider Ali's early campaigns before he assumed control of the Mysore kingdom.

In 1758, the Marathas invaded Mysore. Haider Ali, hastily appointed as commander of the Mysore army, led a march to repel the invasion. He quickly negotiated peace, bringing a sense of relief to Mysore. However, the Marathas would repeatedly invade Mysore in the following years to extract tribute.

In March 1758, the Mysore soldiers revolted once more, besieging Nanjaraj's residence and blocking the supply of food, water and provisions. Once again, Haider Ali intervened and successfully quelled the rebellion.

Charles Stewart, author of the 1809 publication *A descriptive catalogue of the oriental library of the late Tippoo Sultan of Mysore: to which are prefixed memoirs of Hyder Aly and his son Tippoo Sultan*, provides a detailed account of Haider Ali's actions to depose Nanjaraj. Upon receiving intelligence from his spies that Nanjaraj was plotting against him, Haider Ali arrived at the dalawai's residence with a group of armed men and captured him. Stewart explains:

> A detachment was then sent to reduce the palace, but the Raja submitted voluntarily, and sending for Haider Ali, received him most graciously, and declared before the whole court, that the conduct of Josachuri Nanjaraj having for some time past given him great offence, it had been his serious intention to depose him from the office of Dalawai, and confer that honour on his general, Haider Ali, but that measure being now happily effected without his interference, he had much pleasure in placing the reins of government in so able hands. Haider seeing the Raja sufficiently intimidated, was profuse in his protestations of fidelity and attachment, and alleged the minister's design upon his life as the sole cause of the commotion which had taken place.[17]

Stewart reveals that the following day, Haider Ali approached the raja, requesting a patent or commission granting him and his successors the hereditary office of dalawai. Fearing the consequences of refusal, the raja agreed, with the condition that Haider and his successors demonstrate loyalty and obedience.[18] In this way, Haider Ali initially seized power in Mysore in 1759, but his grip on the kingdom was precarious.[19]

The same year, the peshwa dispatched an army to Mysore to recover the arrears of tribute. They seized Bangalore and Chennapatna, but Haider Ali dispatched Lutf Ali Beg to surprise them and recapture the two towns. Peace negotiations ensued, and the Marathas agreed to relinquish the pledged districts upon payment of thirty-two lakh. Half of this amount was paid upfront, and the army withdrew. Haider had averted the annihilation of the Mysore kingdom once again. In gratitude, the raja bestowed upon him the title of 'Fath Haider Bahadur'. Prior to this, he had been known as Haider Naik. Wilks observes that when Haider Ali assumed command of the army in 1759, 'many of the senior-most military servants of the state resigned, rather than serve under the Naik'.[20]

For a while, Haider Ali maintained a respectful demeanour toward the raja, despite the latter being merely a figurehead. Haider's grip on the kingdom was tenuous; nevertheless, in May 1760, he demonstrated boldness by dispatching the bulk of his troops, numbering 5,000, under the command of Makhdum Sahib to aid Comte de Lally, the French governor of Pondicherry. Exuding supreme confidence in his military prowess, he stayed in Dariya Bagh, barely 3 miles from Srirangapatna Fort, with a modest armed guard of 300 soldiers.[21] In the meantime, the British and the French were engaged in a life-and-death struggle amid the Seven Years' War (1756–1763), a worldwide conflict between the two European powers for global supremacy. In India, the Battle of Wandiwash in 1760 ended in a decisive victory for the British over the French. Eyre Coote led the British army, while the French were led by Comte de Lally.

Haider Ali paid a heavy price for his overconfidence. In a final attempt to oust Haider Ali, the dowager rani conspired with Khande (Kanhere) Rao to enlist the assistance of the Marathas.

Subsequently, a Maratha contingent arrived in Srirangapatna, forcing Haider to flee to Bangalore on 12 August 1760, leaving behind his wife and ten-year-old son Tipu.[22] Fortunately for Haider Ali, the Marathas suffered a resounding defeat at the hands of the Afghans the following year. This provided him with the much-needed opportunity to regain control in Mysore. Initially, he faced defeat in Nanjangud in a battle against Khande Rao. 'Haider then adopted the singular course of throwing himself as a supplicant at the feet of Nanjraj.'[23]

Nanjaraj, moved by compassion, reinstated Haidar Ali's command and appointed him as dalawai or commander-in-chief. However, the challenge of facing Khande Rao still loomed large. At the outset, Haider Ali seemed destined for defeat. Yet, employing a cunning stratagem, 'He fabricated letters in the name of Nanjaraj to the officers of the latter's troops, desiring them to surrender Khande Rao in accordance with a pre-arranged agreement. These letters were designedly carried to Khande Rao, who, fearing a conspiracy, abandoned his army, and fled to Seringapatam.'[24] Months later, having seized control of several forts previously held by Khande Rao, Haider Ali besieged Srirangapatna and demanded the surrender of Khande Rao. Bowring observes, 'The ladies of the palace interceded for the unfortunate Brahman, whereupon Haider replied that he would cherish him like a *tota* (parrot), a promise which he kept by keeping him in an iron cage and feeding him on rice and milk till the end of his life.'[25]

After assuming control of the Mysore kingdom in 1761, Haider shifted his family to Bangalore. That same year, Salabat Jung, the nizam of Hyderabad, was deposed by his brother Nizam Ai Khan, while another brother, Basalat Jung, governed Adoni, a district bordering Mysore. Following an unsuccessful bid to retake Sira from the Marathas, Basalat Jung accepted 3 lakh rupees from Haider Ali and declared him the nawab of Sira, bestowing upon him the title of 'Haider Ali Khan Bahadur'. Ironically, Basalat Jung lacked the authority to confer titles as he was not the nizam of Hyderabad.

Nonetheless, this did not dissuade Haider Ali from adopting the newfound title.[26]

## Haider Conquers Bidanur

Haider Ali swiftly expelled the Marathas from Sira and subdued the palayakkars of Chickaballapur, Raidurg, Harpanhalli and Chitradurga. Then, in 1763, he seized an opportunity to attack Bidanur.

Bidanur had long been ruled by the Nayaks of Ikkeri, who had gained independence following the collapse of the Vijayanagar kingdom. They had accumulated significant wealth through trade with the Portuguese. K.M. Panikkar mentions in his book *A History of Kerala, 1498–1801*:

> In 1737 Somasekhara Nayak, the thirteenth ruler of the dynasty, attempted an invasion of Chirakkal, but had to withdraw after an unsuccessful campaign, but the frontier quarrels continued with the Rajas of Nileshwaram, a branch of the Chirakkal family, and so late as 1750, Ikkeri forces attacked Nileshwaram, but were driven back by the Regent of Chirakkal.[27]

The principality boasted a long and glorious history. Although the Ikkeri Nayaks often clashed with their Malabari neighbours, trade rather than conflict was the hallmark of their kingdom. C. Hayavadhana Rao, historian and author of *History of Mysore (1399 to 1799)* avers that Sivappa Nayaka I (1645–1660) had provided asylum to approximately 30,000 Christians who sought sanctuary in his territory to escape the horrors of the Inquisition in Goa and Salsette.[28] Channammaji, the widow of Somasekhara I, had also offered protection to Rajaram, the son of Shivaji, while he was in hiding from the Mughals. At the time of Haider's assault, Bidnaur boasted around 60,000 inhabitants, with at least half of them being Christians.[29]

Panikkar asserts, 'On the death of Basavappa Nayak in 1755, the regency of the state of Bednore passed to a rani, who in order to maintain her own power, murdered her adopted son.'[30] This event supposedly happened in 1757. However, in 1763, during Haider Ali's siege of Chitradurga (referred to as 'Chiteldrug' by Panikkar and the British), a young man approached him, claiming to be the slain prince and seeking assistance to reclaim the throne. Recognizing this as a golden opportunity, Haider Ali reached a tacit understanding with the 'Pretender' as well as the palayakkar of Chitradurga. According to this arrangement, the Pretender was to be reinstated on the throne, and Haider was to receive 40 lakh rupees for campaign expenses, 'besides the port of Mangalore, together with a tract of country to form a communication from thence to the kingdom of Mysore'.[31]

Haider then advanced towards Bidanur accompanied by the Pretender and the palayakkar of Chitradurga. Rao reports:

> At Ayanur, a petty place occupied by a hundred men, Haider first encountered opposition. The garrison here, fearless of consequences, fired at the troops. They were promptly surrounded and taken, their ears and noses being cut off, and, in this state, they were dismissed to spread terror before them.[32]

When Haider reached Anandapur, Queen Virammaji proposed a payment of twelve lakh pagodas in exchange for his withdrawal. Disregarding her offer, Haidar pressed on towards Bidanur. When he reached the formidable fortifications of Bidanur, she raised the offer to eighteen lakhs.[33] But Haider, aware of the kingdom's immense wealth, had no inclination to negotiate. Rao says:

> He sent word demanding the Rani's immediate surrender, guaranteeing honourable treatment to her as a pensioner at the fort in Seringapatam. Virammaji proudly rejected the proposal and preferred to defend her capital city with the aid of Abdul Hakim Khan of Savanur.... When intelligence of what Virammaji had done and was determined to carry through reached Haidar, his rage knew no bounds. He became, it is said, violently incensed.[34]

Virammaji displayed great valour in defending her capital. Rao observes that her soldiers bravely withstood the siege, holding their ground despite significant losses. Abdul Hakim's Pathan troops put up a brave resistance as well. 'Haidar, seeing that the siege, "defended by a woman", had been protracted beyond his calculation, and that the monsoon would soon be on him and his army, ordered the assault to be given.'[35]

When the rani realized her situation was dire, she made a decisive move: she set fire to her luxurious palace, burning most of her jewellery. Accompanied by only two or three attendants, she fled on foot via a water drain to the fortress of Kabbaladurga, approximately 15 miles away.[36] Her trusted confidante, Nimbaiya, and her adopted son, the nominal raja, Somasekhara Nayaka III, were part of her entourage.

It is said that Haider himself personally assisted in extinguishing the flames. Upon learning of Virammaji's escape, he followed her and laid siege to Kabbaladurga. After a valiant resistance, the garrison eventually surrendered, and the rani was captured. 'Thus fell Bednur, after a protracted siege of one month, on January 19, 1763.'[37] In this manner, Haider Ali supplanted another 200-year-old dynasty. The founder of the dynasty, Sadashiva Nayaka, and his descendants had ruled Bidanur for 203 years, from 1560 to 1763.

Haidar returned and installed the Pretender, Channabasappa Nayaka, on the throne. He received Virammaji graciously and feigned reconciliation between her and the Pretender.[38] However, she was soon stripped of her jewellery and imprisoned on Maddagiri (Madhugiri) Hill along with her adopted son, Somasekhara. They remained there until their liberation by the Marathas in 1767.[39]

Initially, Haider contemplated making Bidanur his capital. According to Bowring:

> He formed designs for building there a palace and arsenal, with a local mint, besides constructing a dockyard on the coast. But a severe attack of malaria, and a conspiracy in which many hundred persons were implicated, seem to have deterred him from this

> project. Three hundred of the conspirators were hanged, and all signs of revolt suppressed.[40]

For the first time, Haider Ali issued coins bearing his own name, known as the Haidari-varaha or Bahaduri-varaha. He fortified the ports of Honavar, Basrur, Barakur and Mangalore, where he initiated the construction of ships and other vessels.[41]

After the fall of Bidanur, Mirza Hussain Beg, Haidar's brother-in-law, proceeded to attack Basavarajadurg, a fortified hill located about 10 miles offshore in the Arabian Sea. Rao says:

> Here was secreted immense treasure belonging to the Rani. Hussain Beg took hold of a few boats from the fishermen and sailed with his followers towards the island hill and there intimating that Bednur had fallen, asked the garrison to surrender. The garrison, having heard that the worst had happened, surrendered after a siege of three days.[42]

Hussain Beg then occupied the fort, seized the treasure and upon his return to Bidanur, presented it to Haidar.[43] Rao also mentions Haider's younger son Karim Sahib's purported involvement in this campaign alongside Hussain Beg. However, it appears unlikely as Karim would have been under ten years old at the time. Even his older brother, Tipu, was only thirteen years old in 1763.

According to Maistre de la Tour:

> When Hyder took possession of the place [Bidanur] he found an immense treasure in gold, coined and in ingots, in trinkets and precious stones, that was indeed stupendous, if credit may be given to the accounts of the French, who accompanied him in that expedition.[44]

Haider then disbursed half a year's pay to his troops across his dominions. He renamed Bidanur as Haider-Nagar and Mangalore as Corial Bunder or Port Royal and declared himself king of Canara and Coorg. Considering Coorg had long been a vassal state

sustained severe losses and was forced to retreat the next day to Anavatti. Madhav Rao pursued him to his new encampment.[53]

Haider found himself surrounded on all sides. To add to his woes, his artillery failed to fire. Rao states:

> Haidar, utterly undismayed, at length dismounted from his horse, and taking a match in his hand, placed it on the touch-hole of one of his guns. It was, however, of no use, as the fuse did not take fire... [The Marathas] charged in a body, and mixed with the Mysore troops, shoulder to shoulder, and breaking through their ranks, threw them into confusion and slaughtered them mercilessly. Venkata Rao, Haidar's Dewan, was killed in the melee, while Zaman Khan, his bosom friend, was wounded. Some of his troops, under pretence of bringing aid or ammunition, actually ran off to avoid destruction...Haidar just managed to escape from the general slaughter, followed by but fifty of his cavalry, mainly through the fleetness of their horses, the remainder being destroyed to a man.[54]

'About the middle of July, the Peshwa, having posted Gopal Rao Patwardhan at Savanur, advanced with the main army against Haider.'[55] Rao further adds, 'Haidar withdrew to Hangal and eventually disappeared in the forests, suffering heavily in a skirmish he had with Gopal Rao. The Peshwa, proceeding further, invested Mudhol... Towards the close of September, Madhav Rao invested Dharwar, which capitulated early in November, after offering a stout resistance.'[56]

Madhav Rao was unaware of his uncle Raghunatha Rao's secret alliance with Haidar Ali, and thus, 'what had been won by him on the battlefield was to be lost almost immediately by the treachery of his uncle'.[57]As the Marathas began to cut down the gigantic trees behind Haidar's camp, Haidar panicked and beat a hasty retreat. The Marathas set out in pursuit. 'Madhav Rao tried to move a column between Haidar and Bidanur.'[58] This compelled Haidar to engage in a decisive confrontation. However, his forces were unable to withstand the Maratha onslaught. 'The action terminated in a disorderly rout in which he lost in killed alone, it is said, 3,000 horse and double that number of infantry.'[59] Haidar managed to reach Bidanur with only 2,500 horse and 10,000 infantry. He sought peace, but the negotiations swiftly collapsed. 'As Madhav Rao advanced, garrison after garrison surrendered on the first call. Thus fell to him Harpanahalli without resistance; next fell Ikkeri without a fight; and Kumsi was reduced after a resistance of but two days, while Anandapur ... held out for a while and finally surrendered.'[60]

Haider Ali's defeat at Anavatti occurred in December 1764.[61] Rao explains, 'Haidar had been beaten back successively from Rattihalli to Anavatti, and from Anavatti to Bidanur. The trench warfare at Anavatti began early in January 1765 and went on for nearly a full year, until the treaty of Bednur was signed.'[62]

By the end of January 1765, Haider arranged to secretly dispatch his family, 'by a route through the woods, to Seringapatam, while successive detachments with treasure followed them to the same place'.[63] After capturing Anandapur in February 1765, Madhav Rao prepared to besiege Bidanur. At this point, his treacherous uncle Raghunath Rao (Raghuba) advised Madhav Rao that the time had come to seek peace. The unsuspecting peshwa 'agreed to the suggestion and left the conduct and conclusion of the treaty to his uncle'.[64] Raghuba craftily negotiated favourable terms for Haidar, resulting in the 'Peace of Bednore', which was literally dictated to Haidar under the walls of Bidanur. According to the treaty, Haidar agreed,

> (1) to restore to Gopal Rao of Miraj, Bankapur, Harihar, Basavapatna and other places (2) to relinquish all claims on Nawab Abdul Hakim of Savanur and his country (3) to cede back to Murari Rao Ghorpade of Gooty all his places; and (4) to pay twenty-eight lakhs towards the expenses of the war, besides five lakhs as a gift [nazar] and a further two lakhs for other expenses, the total thus to be paid in cash amounting to Rs. 35 lakhs. Madhav Rao, on his part, was to retire on receipt of the money.[65]

Rao adds, 'Haidar paid the full indemnity before Madhav Rao crossed the Tungabhadra.'[66] He further states, 'Haidar's occupation of Sira appears to have been tacitly admitted in the negotiations that preceded the treaty of Bednur.'[67] Tragically, the treaty overlooked Rani Virammaji, leaving her imprisoned until 1767 when the Marathas finally liberated her from Haider Ali's custody.

Following his defeat at Rattihalli, Haider abandoned the idea of establishing Bidanur as his new capital.[68] Rao suggests that although Tipu, in a later period, tried to rebuild the town and renew its trading potential, 'his regulations for the protection of the internal trade dealt a severe blow to its prosperity'.[69] Furthermore, the Kazi he appointed worsened matters by demolishing the Christian church and Hindu temples, destroying several inscribed slabs and constructing a mosque from the ruins.[70]

In January 1767, Peshwa Madhav Rao marched towards Sira with support from the nawab of Savanur, Murari Rao of Gooty, and the palayakkar of Chitradurga.[71] Sira surrendered, followed by Gurramkonda, while Madhugiri resisted for a month. Haider had imprisoned Rani Virammaji of Bidanur and her adopted son here. The peshwa soon released them and proceeded towards Channarayadurga.[72] Haider Ali 'to effectually arrest the progress of the Mahrattas, issued the most peremptory orders to his officers, civil and military, to break down the embankments of tanks; to poison the wells with milk-hedge; to burn all forage; to drive off the villagers and cattle to the woods'.[73] The war concluded with the peshwa returning the occupied territories to Haider Ali upon payment of 35 lakh rupees. On his return march, he took the rani and her son with him. Unfortunately, the rani passed away during the journey to Poona.

Rao states:

> Madhav Rao's next Mysore campaign came off in the cold weather of 1769. But in the middle of this campaign, he fell ill and left its completion to one of his generals. The campaign ended by the treaty of Seringapatam between Haidar and Triambak Rao in June 1772. Haidar was compelled to surrender Kolar, Bangalore,

> Hoskote,Chikkaballapur, Dodballapur and Sira, besides the fortresses of Maddagiri and Gurramkonda.[74]

With his kingdom significantly reduced, Haider found himself in a precarious position. Madhav Rao had the opportunity to reinstate Rani Virammaji's adopted son or a scion of that family to the throne of Bidanur. However, Madhav Rao passed away on 18 November 1772, and soon after, the adopted son of Virammaji also died. By 1773, Mysore had reclaimed all the territories ceded to Madhav Rao two years earlier.[75]

## Conflicts Galore

In 1779, Haider Ali attacked Chitradurga. He bribed the Muslim soldiers within Madikeri Nayak's force, leaving Nayak with no choice but to surrender when he realized he had been betrayed. Haider imprisoned Nayak in Srirangapatna, looted and ravaged Chitradurga, and 'carried off to his capital 20,000 of the inhabitants'.[76] The young boys among them were swiftly incorporated into the Chela battalions.

Around this time, Haider sent his brother-in-law to subdue the nawab of Cuddapah (Kadapa), but the attempt proved unsuccessful. Subsequently, Haider himself marched to Cuddapah, where he emerged victorious in a battle against the Afghan defenders, forcing them to surrender. However, approximately eighty troopers refused to lay down arms, and strangely Haider chose not to press the issue. This decision proved to be a colossal blunder. In the dead of night, the troopers overpowered their guards in a daring attempt to murder Haider Ali. Bowring relates the sequence of events:

> [The troopers] penetrated to the tent of Haider, who, disturbed by the noise, made up the semblance of a person asleep with a pillow, cut a hole through his tent, and succeeded in escaping. On the alarm being given, most of the assassins were slain. Such of them as survived had their hands and feet chopped off, while a few were killed by being dragged round the camp, attached to the feet of elephants.[77]

The nawab of Cuddapah swiftly surrendered and was sent to Srirangapatna with his family, 'but his beautiful sister was compelled to marry the destroyer of her house, who placed her at the head of his harem with the title of Bakshi Begam'.[78] Bowring avers that Haider 'was a man of the loosest morals, and never spared any one of the sex who had the misfortune to attract his attention'.[79] Bakshi Begum is buried outside the Vellore Fort.

Haidar Ali subsequently targeted the Savanur Nawab, Abdul Hakim. He seized control of Dharwar Fort with the assistance of its governor, Rustum Khan, and advanced towards Savanur. Hakim's Pathan army suffered a decisive defeat. The conflict concluded with a double matrimonial alliance: Haider offered his daughter to the eldest son of the nawab, while Haider's son Karim married the nawab's daughter. Bowring notes, 'The marriage ceremonies were conducted, in 1779, with pomp and magnificence at Seringapatam.'[80]

An interesting development occurred amidst the marriage ceremonies. Bowring discloses, 'During the progress of these festivities an ambassador named Ganesh Rao arrived at Haidar's capital with proposals from the Poona Darbar that he should join the Marathas and the nizam in expelling the English from Southern India.'[81] Later historians would claim it was Tipu Sultan who initially recognized the English threat and sought to unite the Indian principalities against them.

Bowring also informs us that Haider Ali did make overtures to the English, but 'all his endeavours to effect a friendly alliance with the English had been thwarted by the evil influence of the Arcot Nawab'.[82] In fact, when the Marathas proposed reconciling their differences with Haider Ali in 1771, on the condition that he assist them in subduing the eastern provinces, Haider revealed their plans to the British in an attempt to win the latter's favour. He threatened that if the Madras government rejected his offer of an alliance, he would not hesitate to align with the French. 'In 1773, he renewed his endeavours to procure a treaty.'[83] However, once again, Muhammad Ali of Arcot played a double game and prevented this alliance from materializing.

Following the conclusion of the First Anglo-Mysore War in 1769, Haider became entangled in several conflicts, mostly with the Marathas. A decade later, in 1780, war broke out once again with the British. In December 1782, Haider Ali died of cancer in his military camp in Chittoor. His death was kept secret, and a messenger was sent to inform his eldest son, Tipu Sultan, who was preparing to attack British forces at Ponnani in Malabar. In a puzzling turn of events, Haider Ali's younger son, Karim, was quickly appointed as the dewan, while Tipu rushed from Ponnani to take over the reins of Mysore.

## Mysore and Hyderabad

The nizamat of Hyderabad was established in the post-Aurangzeb era by Asaf Jah I, who is commonly known as Nizam-ul-Mulk. Originally named Mir Kamaruddin, he soon became known simply as nizam. Starting as the governor of the Deccan under the Mughals, he later served as the Wazir of the declining Mughal Empire from 1722 to 1724. Returning to the Deccan in 1724, he started ruling independently, although he did not formally declare independence. His rule was characterized by efficiency, a people-friendly approach and tolerance towards Hindus. He conferred titles and gifted *jagirs* without seeking approval from Delhi, engaged in warfare, negotiated peace treaties and effectively kept the powerful Marathas in check. Subsequently, all his descendants were commonly referred to as nizams.

Narendra Luther, in *Legendotes of Hyderabad*, explains:

> The title of 'Asaf Jah' was not conferred upon the second, third and fourth Nisams who ruled during 1748–1762 and spent all their time in internecine warfare. When the fifth Nizam, Mir Nizam Ali Khan, ascended the *masnad* in 1762, he was given the title and so became Asaf Jah II.[84]

In the early 19th century, the Ram Bagh Temple was built by Raja Bhavani Prasad Bhatnagar, who invited the nizam, Sikandar Jah, to preside over the installation ceremony of the sacred idols of Rama, Sita and Lakshmana. The ceremony was duly performed in the year 1812. Luther observes, 'It is both surprising and inspiring that a Hindu temple should have been inaugurated by a Muslim. This did not "contaminate" the faith of either.'[85] Lalitha Iyer, in a 2017 article in the *Deccan Chronicle*, provides a conflicting date for the installation, stating it occurred in 1802, but she also mentions the presence of the nizam at the event.[86] The nizamat came to an end in 1948 when Hyderabad was integrated with the Union of India.

Although Hyderabad, Arcot and Mysore were all governed by Muslim rulers, they often found themselves at loggerheads. It is possible that the nizam (Asaf Jah II, who ruled from 1762 to 1803) felt threatened by the aggressive tactics and brutality of the Mysore sultans. To counter this perceived threat, he may have sought the friendship of the British as a strategic alliance against the larger menace posed by Mysore. During the First Anglo-Mysore War, Haider Ali and the nizam initially joined hands as allies. However, at some point during the conflict, the nizam abandoned Haider and reconciled with the British.

The nizam, being immensely wealthy, understood that Haider was primarily motivated by the prospect of plunder. In the Fourth Anglo-Mysore War, the nizam sent his forces to augment the British army in Srirangapatna with the aim of defeating Tipu Sultan.

## Mysore and Travancore

After Marthanda Varma rose to power in Travancore in 1729, he rapidly expanded his domain in all directions. He achieved a significant victory by defeating the Dutch in Colachel in 1741. Additionally, he subjugated and punished the Ettuveetil Pillaimaar, the powerful Nair chieftains belonging to the eight noble clans, who had previously exerted significant control over Travancore. Despite successfully centralizing power to a great extent, Varma still faced challenges to his authority due to a series of rebellions in the territories he had newly conquered.

To quell the intermittent insurrections within his expanded domain, Marthanda Varma sought military assistance from Haider Ali in 1751. It is uncertain where Haider was positioned at this time. In December 1750, Haider had achieved considerable success in Hyderabad. From 1752 to 1755, he participated in the Trichinopoly campaign under Nanjaraj. According to several accounts, Haider assumed the position of *faujdar* of Dindigul only in 1755. It seems likely that prior to 1755, Haider was engaged in military operations in the southern part of modern Tamil Nadu, bordering the kingdom of Travancore, thereby capturing Marthanda Varma's attention. Panikkar cites Marthanda Varma's appeal to Haider Ali and portrays him in a somewhat negative light.

Haider took no significant action beyond preparing to send a force to Travancore. Before the troops were dispatched, Marthanda Varma informed Haider Ali that his assistance was no longer required. Haider then demanded compensation, citing the expenses incurred in making military preparations. Marthanda Varma, however, refused to pay.

Marthanda Varma's success in averting a crisis unwittingly unleashed a Frankenstein's monster. Haider Ali's gaze would greedily shift towards Kerala, ultimately bringing untold tragedy to this verdant paradise in the years to come. K.K. Nair suggests:

> The appeal drew the attention of Haider Ali to the anarchy, internal weakness and rivalries within Kerala. He took full advantage of the prevailing confusion and on his part demanded compensation and considered the excuses of the Travancore maharajah specious. Haider Ali's assistance once sought was not easy to shake off.[87]

Haider Ali harboured a deep-seated grudge against Travancore, which persisted until the end of his life. Following Marthanda Varma's death in 1758, Haider Ali wasted no time in taking action. He sent his army to Palghat in the same year at the invitation of the Palghat raja. Subsequently, in 1766, he invaded and subjugated the kingdoms of the Kolathiri and the Zamorin. Additionally, he forced Cochin to pay tribute in exchange for non-aggression. However, the outbreak of the First Anglo-Mysore War in the following year, and Haider Ali's subsequent conflicts with the English and the Marathas, prevented him from directly attacking Travancore. After his death, his long-standing grouse against Travancore was carried forward by his son, Tipu Sultan.

## Early Testimonies

Jean-Marie Lafont, a senior fellow at the Centre for Social Sciences and Humanities (CSH) at the French Embassy in New Delhi, translated the 'memoires' of Lieutenant Colonel Russel concerning Mysore. His translation is included in the 2001 publication *State and Diplomacy under Tipu Sultan*, edited by Irfan Habib.

Lafont observes:

> Russel gives a detailed account of Hyder's unfolding coup d'etat in 1761, with the help of Hugel and 300 Hussars who joined him in Bangalore after the fall of Pondicherry. We find details of the help Hugel gave to Hyder in the capture of Srirangapatnam. Having secured his hold on the country, Hyder embarked on a policy of conquest, seeking to seize Kolar, Hoskote, Matagueri [Madhugiri], and Sira. He received the title of Nawab from Basalat Jang in 1762, following which he changed his name from Hyder Naik to Hyder Ali Khan.[88]

Russel also mentions that Hugel's French troops showcased their valour at the battle of Savanur.[89] 'Hyder would have besieged Goa, had not Hugel decided to leave him at that time: a decision which obliged the Nawab to change his plans.'[90] This suggests that Haider Ali's dependence on French troops was significant during the initial years of his reign.

We learn that in 1772, 'Hugel and his officers had arrived in Srirangapatnam a few days before the battle of Melkota', and they joined Haider just before the fateful day when 'Mr Fortin was killed, all the other officers wounded, and Mr Hugel died from his wounds in the first days of May 1772'.[91] Thereupon, Russel hastened from Pondicherry and assumed command of the French troops. This account strongly suggests that Haider Ali and the French in Pondicherry were staunch allies.

Habib cites Russell's narrative:

> During the six years I commanded [the Hussars], I did not leave Haider for one single day. I followed him in all his expeditions, being twice a day with him or his son in the trenches during the sieges. I was always in the most perilous places in the battles or in the storming parties, and I was often consulted for erecting the batteries, conducting the siege works and dealing with the military service.[92]

This description of Haider's modus operandi and the French commandant's role in his military campaigns holds significant weight. Russel portrays Haider Ali as an outstanding general, consistently leading from the front, overseeing the construction of fortifications, setting up artillery positions, devising strategies and paying attention to every detail.[93] 'As soon as the first entrenchment is ready, he builds a "cannoniere" for his son, who does not leave the trenches until the surrender of the place.'[94] Russel also observes Haider Ali's dedication to training his son in the art of warfare. Additionally, he explains how Haider Ali invariably ensured that his army was stocked up on provisions, stating, 'He always has at Patan [Srirangapatna], his capital, enough provisions to feed for 10 years 10,000 cavalry and 20,000 sepoys. The storehouses at Haidernagar and Bangalore have more or less the same capacity.'[95]

Peixoto also provides interesting details regarding the events in Srirangapatna. On 2 August 1770, the 12-year-old Wodeyar king died suddenly. Peixoto notes that the king was not sick but was discovered dead in the morning.[96] Despite his young age, he had already started to exhibit a royal presence and had begun asserting himself. 'In the night after supper, he drank a cup of milk which Hyder had sent him.'[97] The surgeon involved in the incident was apprehended, imprisoned and fined a huge sum. The *Haider-nama*, a 1784 publication, dates this event to 1771. Wilks says he was strangled by a *jetti*. The annals of the Mysore royal family agree with Peixoto's account regarding the date of the incident. Peixoto observes, 'In this manner, the Nawab shews his sorrow by the surgeon's prison, and by the condemnation, utility to his treasury, where all the Nawab's interest do center.'[98] He also adds, 'During the burial even the silver vessels belonging to the royal family had to be brought from Hyder's palace.'[99]

Peixoto describes Nanjaraj's reaction to the death of the child raja. Nanjaraj was acutely aware of Haider Ali's tyranny, and he felt the nawab was 'endeavouring to extinguish the generations of the kings of that kingdom. He also bewailed the new king [Chamaraja Wodeyar] for he believed Haider would soon dispose of him also.'[100]

In summary, Haider Ali may be described as a self-made ruler who established a vast empire through his strategic military skills. He demonstrated brilliance in warfare and was known for his ruthless tactics. Betraying his king and mentor, he seized control of Mysore and expanded his dominion by conquering Bidanur, Malabar, and several territories from the Marathas and the nizam. With French support, he challenged the British East India Company and amassed wealth through looting. Haider Ali hired soldiers from diverse backgrounds, modernized his army and imported weapons from France. He also ensured his sons received military training.

Haider, though illiterate, possessed sharp wit and cunningness. He enjoyed hunting tigers and maintained a large harem. His cruelty and debauchery are attested by several historians, including military officers like Russel, De la Tour and Peixoto, who worked closely with him in the early years of his reign.

One cannot help but wonder how the history of southern India might have unfolded in the 18th century had cancer not halted Haider Ali's ambitions.

# 4

# MALABAR INVASIONS AND STRANGE ADOPTIONS

The first Muslim invasion of Kerala occurred in 1757–1758 when Haider Ali sent his brother-in-law, Makhdum Sahib, to assist the Palghat raja, Raman Komu Achan, against the Zamorin of Calicut. This event was a defining moment in Kerala's history, as it was the first instance of a Muslim army setting foot on the soil of Cheranadu, as the region was historically known.

The 'petty' kings of Malabar had a history of internal conflicts. In 1756–1757, the forces of the Zamorin attacked Palghat, compelling the Palghat raja to seek help from external sources. Mysore, a formidable kingdom, had its military leader Haider Ali stationed at Dindigul. Haider had established a significant arsenal in Dindigul, and his troops had received training from French officers. He was raring to go.

## The First Mysorean Invasion, 1758

The Zamorin had driven a deep wedge into the territory of the Palghat raja and called it Naduvattom. Concerned that the Zamorin aimed to annex the entire region, the Palghat raja 'despatched in 1757 a deputation to Haider Ali, then foujdar of Dindigul, under the nominal sovereignty of the puppet Chick Kishen Raja [Chika Krishnaraja] of Mysore'.[1] Haider's private army, led by Makhdum Ali, arrived to assist the Palghat Nairs, prompting the Zamorin to hastily buy peace by agreeing to pay a tribute of 12 lakh rupees.

The Malabar campaign appears to have been Haider Ali's independent project. There is no evidence of the involvement of Nanjaraj and Devaraj, who wielded significant power in Mysore at that time. In fact, a quarrel had erupted between the brothers in 1758, leading Haider to hurriedly travel to Srirangapatna, probably to support his godfather, Nanjaraj, while Makhdum Ali led a formidable force to Palghat.

The Zamorin promptly initiated negotiations with Devaraj, resulting in an understanding that the war indemnity would be paid to Devaraj instead of Haider Ali. Soon, Devaraj sent the Rajput corps of Hari Singh, the most zealous of his supporters to collect it.[2] Wilks' narrative states, 'They had now sent secret agents to Devaraj, offering to pay the money to him, provided he would rid them of the Mussalman troops of Haider, and send Hindus to receive it.'[3] He adds, 'Hari Sing was not only the rival, but the personal enemy of Haider; whom he considered as an upstart, indebted for his success in life more to fawning and flattery than to military merit; and would never condescend to address him, or speak of him, by any other designation than the Naik'.[4]

Hari Singh's attempt to collect the money was thwarted when he received news of the sudden death of Devaraj at Srirangapatna on 17 June 1758. Following this, he hurried to Avinashi in Coimbatore, where he was treacherously murdered by soldiers led by Makhdum Sahib, perhaps acting under orders from Haider Ali. Consequently, the war indemnity promised by the Zamorin remained unpaid. Logan notes, 'The claim to this war subsidy was never relinquished, and to recover it was one of Haider Ali's avowed objects in invading Malabar.'[5] However, it remains unclear why Haider selected the domain of the Kolathiri raja for his subsequent invasion, rather than invading the Zamorin's territory through Palghat or the Tamarassery route.

Even though the tribute promised by the Zamorin remained unpaid, the Palghat campaign of 1758 had proved highly lucrative for Haider Ali, as he acquired not only the treasures of Goddess Hemambika but also those of the royal household of Palghat. Eight years later, he would once again launch an offensive in Malabar.

The Nairs of Palghat invited the wrath of Nairs across all of Kerala for inviting Haider Ali to invade Malabar. Similarly, the Namboothiris of Palghat boycotted the Palghat raja for the same reason, leading to a mass exodus of the priestly class from the region. In response, the raja settled Brahmins, known as Pattars or Pardesi Brahmins, from Tamil Nadu in 64 villages. Logan observes, 'The great *Pattar* settlements in Malabar lie in the Palghat taluk, a taluk which, if it ever was occupied by the Namboothiris, has for a very long time past been deserted by them.'[6] The departure of the Namboothiris from Palghat may have been triggered by the desecration of the Hemambika Temple by the Mysore army or perhaps by the fear of circumcision. Logan made these observations more than a century after the events occurred.

An ASI (Archaeological Survey of India) inscription at the entrance to the Palghat Fort states that it was built during the medieval period by an unknown builder and later strengthened and refurbished by Haider Ali in 1766. However, many local residents mistakenly attribute the construction of the massive rhomboidal structure with seven bastions to Haider Ali, and some even credit Tipu Sultan with its construction! Between 1766 and 1790, the fort changed hands several times. The British finally acquired it in 1790.

## The Second Mysorean Invasion, 1766

A few years after the initial invasion of Palghat by the Mysore army, Ali Raja of Kannur (Ali Raja Kunhi Amsa II of Arakkal, who reigned from 1745 to 1777), an arch-rival of the Kolathiri raja, invited Haider Ali to launch another attack on Malabar. Haider Ali welcomed the idea, but he proceeded cautiously, taking his time to meticulously plan his course of action.

*Logan's Manual* reveals that the British were already aware of Haider Ali's motives long before the second attack took place.

'The [Tellicherry] factors received intelligence that even so early as January 1763 he [Ali Raja] was endeavouring to persuade Haider Ali to the conquest of Malabar, but for a time it did not suit the potentate's schemes to comply with the request.'[7] It was only in 1766 that the dreaded invasion began.

In his memoir, the Portuguese Eloy Joze Peixoto provides interesting details of Haider's annexation of Bidanur on 10 January 1763, and the subsequent events leading up to the Malabar invasion of 1766.[8] Following the conquest of Bidanur, Haider embarked on a campaign to subdue Mangalore and its surrounding provinces. Upon his triumphant return, he ordered Peixoto to proceed to Mangalore, where Lutf Ali Beg had been appointed as governor. Beg then took Peixoto to 'Kumbla where the fort was besieged by Uda-Parssu, a prince of the woods near Nileshwar with an army of about 1,000 Nairs, who fought valiantly but appeared disorganized'.[9] At the approach of the Mysoreans, the Nairs retired into a pagoda and fought terribly, though the walls were scaled on all sides.[10] More than 400 Mysoreans were killed by them. 'However, the place was taken before daybreak and all the Nairs were put to the sword.'[11] Although this battle is not mentioned by other authors, it appears unlikely that Peixoto fabricated this account. It stands to reason that if the Nairs of Nileshwaram had met such a terrible fate at the hands of the Mysore army in 1763, it would explain their lack of spirited defence in 1766 when Haider Ali began his famed *padayottam*.

In May 1763, the day after the battle at Nileshwaram, Peixoto marched with the Mysorean army, under the command of Barki Venkata Rao, to Mangalore 'from whence the pagoda "Irur", the capital of Uda Parssu was attacked'.[12] 'Uda Parssu and his family stayed in their Pagoda with an army of about 6000 Nairs, whereas Barki Venkata Rao had in all about 3000 men.'[13] Peixoto and Captain Ioxe Bento were bringing up the rear, struggling with a three-pounder gun. Peixoto explains:

> The Nairs, though they were on either side, did not make bold to attack … Uda Parssu received succour in the meanwhile from

> Nileshwar. But they were surrounded and forced to surrender. Uda Parssu retreated into the tower of his pagoda. Since it was Haider's order that he should be taken alive, Barki Venkata Rao had to use many tactics and hold out many promises for him to surrender.[14]

What followed makes for interesting reading. The chieftain was escorted to Bidanur along with his family and children, where Haider initially treated them with courtesy. However, at a later date, Narain Rao, one of Haider's high officials, questioned him about the whereabouts of the treasure for which his kingdom was renowned. Dissatisfied with the chieftain's reply, Haider ordered him to be hanged on 7 October 1763.[15]

The British were in a state of panic as soon as they learned of Haider Ali's intentions regarding Malabar. Their Tellicherry factory faced imminent peril, and it was imperative to find a way to contain Haider. Logan reports, 'A treaty dated 27th May 1763 was accordingly arranged at Bednur in the shape of a "Phurmaund" from the "Nawab Haider Ali Khan Bahadur" permitting the Honourable Company to export rice from Mangalore for Tellicherry, and binding both parties not to assist their enemies.'[16] Logan further adds, 'The factors were fully alive to the fact that Haider Ali's invasion of Malabar was only a question of time.'[17]

In January 1764, the British sent a reconnaissance mission under Ensign Parker to trace the route from Cotiote (Kottayam–Malabar) to Srirangapatna, and onward to Vellore, in case they needed to mobilize their troops along that route. By October of the same year, Haider Ali sent a letter to the British, hinting at his intention to invade Malabar once he had settled his conflicts with the Marathas. Although the British may have lodged feeble protests, another letter arrived on 6 November, with Mysorean emissary Anant Rao requesting the British to refrain from opposing their army in the event of an invasion. The letter revealed Haider's determination to subjugate the Kolathiri, the Zamorin and the Cochin raja, and exact tribute from them. 'Anant Rao invited the Honourable Company to assist Hyder Ali in carrying out his designs or at least to remain neuter.'[18]

In response, the British presented economic proposals aligned with their own interests. On 12 February 1766, reports reached the British in Tellicherry that Haider Ali had reached Nileshwaram with a 12,000 strong army. (Dutch sources suggest the number was 40,000).

The term *padayottam*, with its ominous connotations, likely originated at this time. The Kolathiri raja fled to Tellicherry, enabling Ali Raja to quickly seize Chirakkal. Aided by Mysorean soldiers, the enterprising Ali Raja proceeded to conquer the Maldives, where he blinded the king and transported him to Mangalore, presenting him before Haider Ali. However, Haider was unimpressed by this vulgar exhibition of brutality.

Peixoto supplies invaluable details of Haider's dreaded incursion into Malabar:

> Towards the end of January 1766, the march began from Mangalore, the army proceeding by land and a fleet of 80 vessels by sea ... The army marched by way of Mangiseram, Combelom, Decalla, and Tekal to Maday, the fort of which place was captured easily after passing a pretty large river in spite of this passage being defended by the Nairs.[19]

Here, Peixoto was referring to Manjeswaram, Kumbla, Bekal and Madayi. (Decalla is difficult to identify.) Peixoto's spellings are rather quaint. In fact, he does not spell any proper nouns correctly. Or perhaps the blame has to be laid at the door of the translator.

'The whole country was disturbed by robbing, setting the houses on fire and killing the Nairs without discretion.'[20] Peixoto states that the Kolathiri, the Zamorin and the Cotiote raja sought peace, but Haider, disregarding their entreaties, proceeded to attack and capture Valapattanam. Subsequently, Chirakkal, the capital of the Kolathiris, was abandoned and fell under Haider's control. 'The Moplahs were enlisted in his army and the Nawab of Cannanore [Ali Raja] was made the governor of the place.'[21]

'The country of the four Nambiars was then attacked and abandoned. The king of Zamorin was captured at an annual feast to which Haider sent 500 of his men dressed as Brahmans.'[22] He was lodged in a pagoda, and tribute was demanded.

Other accounts, primarily from British sources, state that Haidar Ali's campaign in Malabar met with little resistance. 'The first engagement took place at Baliapatanam [Valapattanam], where 500 Nairs offered obstinate resistance; but they were dispersed by artillery fire.'[23]

The Mysorean forces faced strong resistance only at Kadathanad, where many Hindus, including women and children, were massacred. Upon Haider's arrival in Kurumbranad, the Zamorin sought a meeting with him on 11 April 1766, to negotiate terms of surrender. By this time, a contingent of the Mysore army had already reached Calicut, and the defenders of the fort had fled. However, the heir apparent continued to resist in the southern part of the kingdom. Haider Ali detained the Zamorin and his ministers, demanding immediate payment of 12 lakh rupees promised to him in 1758, as well as additional sums as war reparations. There were unconfirmed reports that he made an exorbitant demand of 1 crore rupees. Subsequently, the family members and Brahmin supporters of the Zamorin escaped to Travancore. Shortly after, the Zamorin set fire to himself and the palace in a horrific incident reminiscent of the Rajput practice of *jauhar*. Wilks avers, 'I have been assured by more than one eye-witness that several of the Raja's personal attendants who were accidentally excluded when he closed the door, afterwards threw themselves into the flames and perished with their master.'[24]

Peixoto describes the subsequent developments:

> The Nairs were attacking Haider's men every moment as they were waiting only for his retreat. Haider was obliged to leave the kingdom in charge of a governor and quit the place. After being in possession of it for about two years he received from the king of Zamorin Rs. 12,00,000 and delivered the kingdom on the 8th of March 1768.[25]

At that time, the First Anglo-Mysore War was in progress. Peixoto's narrative indicates that Haider Ali faced challenges and obstacles during this period.

## Death and Deportation

The Dutch suspected that Haider Ali's next target would be Cochin and Travancore. Consequently, agents of the Dutch Company approached Haider Ali at Calicut, requesting that their colony in Cochin be spared. Haider stipulated that the Cochin and Travancore kings provide cash and elephants in exchange for the safety of their kingdoms. He demanded 4 lakh rupees and eight elephants from Cochin and 15 lakh rupees and twenty elephants from Travancore. The Cochin raja opted for peace by agreeing to pay tribute.

Rama Raja of Travancore politely refused, citing that he was a tributary of the nawab of Arcot and therefore under the protection of the British East India Company. However, he offered to contribute a substantial sum provided that the Kolathiri raja and the Zamorin's heirs were reinstated to their former territories. Surprisingly, the Cochin raja expressed similar sentiments, despite his ongoing conflict with the Zamorin. Despite their frequent skirmishes, these rulers were interconnected through marriage and adoptions, and regarded each other as brothers. The idea of dispossessing a sovereign of his kingdom was anathema to the people of Kerala.

When the monsoon arrived, Haider Ali retired to Coimbatore, where he seized the palace and deposed the local ruler. Three months later, the Nairs in the conquered territories of Malabar revolted. A Muslim force led by Raza Sahib was sent to quell the rebellion but found themselves surrounded by the Nairs, unable to advance or retreat. Haider Ali quickly came to the rescue, and despite heavy losses due to the monsoon rains and flooded rivers, the Mysorean army pressed on determinedly. 'A French officer in Haidar's service gallantly led a storming party, which carried the enemy's position and completely routed them.'[26]

'Haidar at first beheaded or hanged all who were taken prisoners, and then resorted to the expedient of deporting the wretched inhabitants wholesale to the plains of Mysore, where thousands of them perished from hunger and misery.'[27] Of the 15,000 individuals who were deported, only 200 managed to survive.

Haider Ali proceeded to capture Guruvayur and demanded 10,000 fanams to spare the temple. The ransom was paid. Additionally, the ruler of Palghat, Kelu Achan, was deposed, and Ittikomu Achan was appointed by Haider in exchange for a hefty tribute. Every action or threat carried financial implications, and with each invasion or threat, Haider Ali's wealth increased.

The Dutch governor Moens wrote in his *Memorandum* in 1781 that Haider returned to his capital in January 1767 upon receiving the intelligence of potential attacks by the Marathas and the nizam. Subsequently, the British besieged Mangalore and destroyed his navy in 1768, prompting Haider to dispatch emissaries to Oman and Persia seeking assistance.

In May 1768, Haider Ali managed to recapture Mangalore from the British. However, facing pressure on other fronts, he had to redirect his forces to the Carnatic region. Recognizing the challenges of controlling the Nairs of Kerala, he commenced negotiations for the restoration of their territories. The conditions he imposed included the payment of war reparations by the Nairs and the retention of the Palghat Fort by the Mysoreans. With the rulers of Malabar agreeing to these conditions, the Mysore armies withdrew in December 1768, after an uneasy occupation lasting roughly three years. The French commandant at Mahe and the Dutch at Cochin acted as mediators between the local Rajas and Madanna, the civil governor appointed by Haider Ali. For the next five years, Haider did not return to Kerala, as he was preoccupied with conflicts elsewhere. In December 1773, the Mysoreans returned to Malabar. With the Maratha threat subsiding following the death of Peshwa Madhav Rao in 1772, Haider Ali could now focus on Kerala. Led by Srinivasa Rao and Saiyyad Sahib, Haider's army descended through the Tamarassery Pass and once again overpowered the Malabar chiefs. On 12 January 1774, the Zamorin signed an agreement with the French commandant at Mahe, Governor Duprat, accepting French overlordship in exchange for protection. The French flag was raised at Calicut, but as the Mysore army advanced, the French evacuated the fort since they lacked the resources to defend it.

According to Moens' *Memorandum*, 'When the Zamorin fled, he wanted to take shelter in our territory, but I diverted him from it. So, he retired with his family by sea to the south on a native vessel to the kingdom of Travancore, where with the connivance of that ruler he still resides.'[28] Thereafter, Calicut and other areas of Malabar came under direct Mysorean administration.

Towards the end of 1774, the Tellicherry factors reported to Madras that Haider Ali was preparing to march south and occupy Cochin and Travancore. In August 1776, when an army led by Sardar Khan entered Cochin territory, the raja quickly brought peace by agreeing to pay the arrears of tribute. Thereafter, 'Haider Ali renewed his request to the Dutch Governor, Moens, to allow free passage to his army towards Travancore through the Dutch possessions of Chetwai and Cranganore (Kodungallur). Since Moens evaded giving a satisfactory reply, Sardar Khan captured the fort by a surprise attack'.[29] While several areas fell into his hands, the Travancore Lines proved to be an effective barrier to further expansion. Sardar Khan marched on Thrissur and seized it on 18 September 1776. The Cochin raja hurriedly sent emissaries to Srirangapatna, and Haider agreed to withdraw his army upon the payment of a specific fee, in addition to the annual tribute. A tense peace prevailed for two years, but in 1778, rebellion erupted once more.

In August 1778, Haider Ali learned of the outbreak of war between the English and the French in Europe. He quickly negotiated a six-year truce with the Marathas and prepared for hostilities against the British. Meanwhile, the British captured Pondicherry and devised plans to capture Mahe, the sole French settlement in Malabar. Mahe served as the port through which the French imported firearms and supplied them to the Mysore army. Haider Ali recognized that if Mahe fell, his weapon supply would be disrupted. On 19 March 1779, Haider wrote to the British at Madras, asserting, 'Now you have set on foot an expedition against Mahe. There are many factories in my country belonging to the Dutch, English, French, Portuguese and Danes, who trade in my country on the footing of subjects.'[30] This statement is noteworthy as it implies Haider Ali's assertion of authority over British, French and other factories in his territory, including the British factory at Tellicherry and the French colony of Mahe. However, in reality, neither of these places was under his control.

In March 1779, the British captured Mahe with the support of the Nairs, dealing a significant blow to Haider Ali. Thereafter, the Nairs in the occupied territories rebelled once more, but Haider quickly overpowered them with the assistance of the Arakkal Beevi, Junumabe Sultana II (1777–1819). Meanwhile, the Tellicherry factors were advised by their superiors to take a defensive stance and avoid any overt hostility towards Haider Ali. This inaction on the part of the British facilitated Haider Ali's suppression of the Nair princes.

An army led by Sardar Khan reached Malabar in February 1780. After dealing with some of the recalcitrant rajas, they commenced the siege of Tellicherry in July. On 20 July 1780, Hyder Ali descended upon the Carnatic with a massive army, marking the beginning of the Second Anglo-Mysore War. The siege of Tellicherry lasted for eighteen months. Author and researcher C. K. Kareem notes:

> The Factors at Tellicherry showed unabated vigour and inexhaustible heroism in defending the fort. By the end of the year 1781, reinforcements arrived from Bombay under Colonel Humberstone with the instructions to act in conformity with Major Abington of Tellicherry factory. On February 8th, 1782 Sardar Khan who invested Tellicherry was defeated by Major Abington and was taken prisoner with 1200 men. The author of the *Haider Nama* writes that Sardar Khan who was very much ashamed of this defeat ended his life by committing suicide.[31]

The British captured Calicut. Concurrently, along the coast, the Nairs rose in revolt against Mysore, destroying Haider Ali's garrisons and blockhouses. Haider Ali then sent Makhdum Sahib to Malabar. In a battle against the British and others on 8 April

1782, Makhdum was killed, and his army was routed. Left with no choice, Haider Ali dispatched Tipu Sultan and the French general, M. Lally, to Malabar. Colonel Humberstone marched from Calicut to Palghat, but for some reason, he retreated to Ponnani. Either he had learned of Tipu's march to Palghat and decided that discretion was the better part of valour, or he had received instructions from Bombay. When Tipu's army arrived, the Ponnani River was flooded. Despite this, Humberstone's men managed to cross the swollen waters under the cover of night and reach Ponnani town, where reinforcements under Major McLeod had arrived from Bombay.

The Mysore army camped within two miles of Ponnani. After a week of waiting, Tipu launched an attack, but the outcome was inconclusive. The stalemate persisted. Then, on 12 December, the Mysore army suddenly disappeared. Haider Ali had died at Chittoor, and Tipu was rushing to Srirangapatna to secure his own succession.

The British under Fullarton marched from Ponnani and captured the Palghat Fort after a brief siege. The fort held strategic significance as it was the most accessible point to enter Kerala through the Palghat Pass. Fullarton subsequently advanced to Coimbatore, leaving the Zamorin to maintain control over Palghat. However, the Zamorin abandoned the fort, allowing Tipu's forces to reclaim it. The war persisted beyond the death of Haider Ali, concluding only in 1784 when the British and Tipu signed a peace treaty.

## Social Change in Malabar

Quoting a British officer named Brown, Buchanan states that Malabar, before the arrival of Haider Ali, was a most prosperous country, 'For ages, the inhabitants had been accumulating the precious metals that had been given them for the produce of their gardens.'[32] Malabar was indeed rich, and while there were minor skirmishes among the rajas, there was no significant drain on wealth. Buchanan states:

> Haider's only object, in the countries that he conquered, was to acquire money; and, provided he got plenty of that, he was very indifferent to the means which his officers took to obtain it. Immediately after the conquest of Malabar, vast sums were extorted from its inhabitants by the military officers, and by the Canarese Brahmans placed over the revenues. Of these extortions Haider received a share; and no want of a system of revenue was felt until these systems began to fail.[33]

Thus, Haider dismantled the ancient revenue system that had favoured agriculture and failed to implement an alternative system. Economic collapse was inevitable under these circumstances. 'The country, however, was daily declining in produce and population; in so much that, at the accession of Tipu...they were reduced to one-half of what they had been at the time of Haider's conquest.'[34] While Haider Ali's reign greatly damaged the social fabric of Malabar, the rule of his son brought about total devastation and completely destroyed religious tolerance and unity.

In the 18th century, the Nair nobility suffered greatly under the firm rule of Marthanda Varma of Travancore, the machinations of Paliath Komu Achan of Cochin, and the onslaught of the Mysore sultans. However, the Namboothiris retained their spiritual dominance, although many had to flee to Travancore to escape conversion to Islam. Travancore transformed into a military state with a standing army of mercenaries from neighbouring regions, governed by a Tamil bureaucracy after Marthanda Varma defeated the Pillais of the eight noble clans collectively described as Ettuveetil Pillaimaar. Panikkar suggests, 'Before the time of Marthanda Varma, rebellion was the recognized form of protest and Kerala law did not allow either confiscation of property or even capital punishment in the case of nobles.'[35]

Not all social changes can be attributed to the Mysore sultans. Opium virtually disappeared from Kerala's shores by 1730, as the Dutch found it more profitable to sell the deadly product in Java and the East Indies. As the drug became scarce, the habit also disappeared, and people began to rely on good old toddy and arrack, which remain popular to this day.

In 1725, the French naval officer Bertrand-François Mahé de La Bourdonnais established a French colony at Mayyazhi, which soon came to be known as Mahe. Years later, this port proved useful for Haider Ali to import French canons, firearms and ammunition. La Bourdonnais' life ended in tragedy, but his name lives on in India and Mauritius. The island of Mauritius has a town named Mahebourg, while in India, the town of Mahe forms part of the union territory of Puducherry (erstwhile Pondicherry) and still bears the Frenchman's name.

It was firepower that gave the Europeans their military advantage. The methods of warfare changed considerably with the introduction of firearms, cannons, cavalry and other modern weaponry. The Nair militia relied on traditional weapons such as swords and daggers. When the Mysore sultans invaded Malabar, the local rulers were at a significant disadvantage as they lacked standing armies and cavalry, and only had limited access to modern military equipment. It was only the fearless courage of the Nair nobility that prevented the complete extinction of the people of Kerala. However, by the dawn of the 19th century, the Nairs had lost considerable influence, and they never regained the supremacy they once held in the political landscape of Kerala.

Haider's invasion and occupation of Malabar triggered a series of excesses. Besides terrorizing the populace, the invaders committed numerous acts of depravity. A prime example is their treatment of the famous Thiruvarkkattu Bhagavathy Temple, better known as Madayi Kavu, in the Kannur district:

> During the incursion of Hyder Ali into Malabar, circa 1780, Madayi Kavu was desecrated with the entrails of slaughtered cattle, following which a local Nair warrior named Vengayil Chathukutty beheaded the miscreant responsible for the act, delivering the severed head to the temple authorities. Thereby the Nair family of Vengayil received the title of Nayanar.[36]

During this phase, Kerala witnessed far-reaching social, political and economic changes. Pepper production declined, and agriculture suffered as lands were laid waste and farmers sought refuge in the forests and mountains. Harsh taxation, extortion and looting impoverished the common folk, while prisoners were either killed or deported. Temples were desecrated, and the rigid caste hierarchy was upended. The Namboothiris fled, and the Nairs were declared persona non grata. People from all castes were either persuaded or compelled to convert to Islam, and there was significant transfer of landed properties.

The involvement of some Muslim groups in aiding and abetting the atrocities committed by the invading armies quickly disrupted the religious harmony that had prevailed along the Malabar Coast for centuries. Nonetheless, there were several factions of Mappilas who actively resisted the Mysorean invasions.

## Unintended Consequences

On the northern bank of the Ponnani River in Malappuram district lies the ancient Thirunavaya Navamukunda Temple, where the glorious Mamankam festival was held once every twelve years, perhaps starting from the 8th century. It was an occasion marked by pomp, pageantry, revelry and commerce during the Middle Ages. The Zamorin captured Thirunavaya in 1486, gaining the right to host the Mamankam. Since then, a long-standing tradition of blood feuds commenced, with suicide squads known as *chavers* from Valluvanad attempting to assassinate the Zamorin and reclaim their lost territory. Representatives from all kingdoms in Cheranadu (Kerala) attended, drawing tourists and pilgrims from distant lands, including Arabia, Greece and China.

The last occurrence of the Mamankam was in 1755, and with Haider Ali's arrival in 1766, the festival abruptly ceased. The temple was destroyed by Tipu Sultan during one of his customary rampages but was later rebuilt. Today, devout Hindus congregate at Thirunavaya to perform the last rites for their ancestors. The vendettas and bloodshed of yesteryears are now a relic of the past.

## Mysore and Lakshadweep

Buchanan mentions, 'Lacaday [Lakshadweep] is in the territory formerly belonging to the Tamuri [Samuthiri] Raja.'[37] Whether the Zamorin ever had control of the islands is uncertain. The Arakkal Beevi of Cannanore was known to have control of the islands. Panikkar informs us, 'The Rajas of Cannanore conquered the Maldives in the 12th century, and the Kolathiri who was the sovereign of the Laccadives leased out the islands to Ali Raja on an annual payment.'[38]

When Haider Ali conquered Malabar, he spared the Arakkal kingdom and did not show much interest in Lakshadweep, perhaps due to the absence of a navy at that time. Later, he established a small fleet of ten ships, but the British quickly thwarted his naval ambitions.

Lakshadweep, a small group of coral atolls in the Arabian Sea, is first mentioned in the 1st century CE when a Greek sailor wrote about these numerous islands lying off the Malabar Coast. Arab traders were regular visitors here from time immemorial. It appears that Islam came to Lakshadweep in the 7th century, and very soon all the islanders were converted. At the turn of the 12th century, the islands were captured by the Kulasekhara Perumals and later came under the Kolathiri dynasty of Cannanore. When the Arakkal kingdom of Cannanore, a Muslim matrilineal dynasty, came into existence, the islands were probably passed on to them. (Legend has it that the Arakkal Beevis trace their origin to a woman from the Kolathiri family who was wedded to a Muslim commoner.)

Centuries later, Vasco da Gama arrived in Lakshadweep and built a fort. In 1545, the islanders revolted against the Portuguese. Later, in the 1780s, Tipu Sultan took over the Amindivi Islands in the northern group, probably after his son was betrothed to the daughter of the Arakkal Beevi. With Tipu's death, the British gained control of Amindivi. It was not until 1908 that the Arakkal Beevi finally ceded the remaining islands of Lakshadweep to the British.

Buchanan refers to the 'Lacadives' as worthless islands belonging to the 'Biby of Cananore or Canura'. He mentions that her ships sailed to Arabia, Bengal and Sumatra. 'The people here have no communication with the Maldives, although the Sultan and inhabitants of these islands are Moplays.'[39]

## Velluva Kammaran Nambiar Becomes Hyat Sahib

Though a battle-hardened military man, Haider Ali had a soft spot for a few individuals. One of them was Ayaz Khan, a captive from Chirakkal. Another was Velu Nachiyar, the fugitive queen of Sivaganga, whom he chose to shelter for eight long years.

Kammaran Nambiar from the Velluva Puthiyaveedu at Chirakkal was one of the numerous individuals who were captured and deported following Haider Ali's 1766 invasion of Malabar. Legend has it that he was either the son or nephew of the raja of Chirakkal. Haider Ali purportedly took him under his wing as his own son. According to Mohibbul Hasan, 'Ayaz was a Nair from Chirakkal who had been taken prisoner by Haidar during his Malabar campaign of 1766. He became a Muslim, and because of his abilities and handsome personality, he gained the confidence of Haidar, who enlisted him in his Asad-i-Ilahi troops. In 1779 he was appointed Governor of Chitaldrug, and early in 1782 he was put in charge of the more important province of Bednur [Bidanur].'[40]

There are discrepancies in the given name and family name mentioned by various British and Indian chroniclers, but all agree that the Nambiar boy ended up in Mysore, where he was converted, circumcised and named Muhammed Ayaz Khan. (Logan gives his name as Kumaran, but this seems to be incorrect.) Another version states that Kammaran was trapped by the Ikkeri Nayaks when he went to Bekal for peace talks as a representative of the Kolathiri raja. When the Mysoreans overran Bekal, they liberated him and sent him to Haider Ali, who was greatly impressed by his dignified demeanour, exemplary courage and martial skills.

Ayaz became a prime favourite of Haider Ali and was raised at the palace. His gradual ascent to the position of governor of Bidanur was documented by Mark Wilks and William Logan, with curious observations noted by the English prisoner James Scurry. Wilks, states:

> Sheick Ayaz had, while a youth, and a common chela of the palace, rendered himself unacceptable to Tippoo by the independence of his character, and had, in consequence, been treated by that prince with gross and repeated indignity. In mature age, Hyder's extravagant praises of his valour and intellect, and the habit of publicly contrasting the qualities of his slave with those of the heir apparent, perpetually embittered all the feelings of former enmity, and rendered the death of Hyder a crisis which Ayaz must necessarily have contemplated with alarm.[41]

Wilks notes that Tipu 'sent secret orders to the officer next in authority to put him to death and assume the government'.[42] Upon learning of Tipu's plan to have him executed, Ayaz Khan swiftly surrendered the Bidanur Fort and the neighbouring areas to the British and sought refuge in Bombay.[43] The British confiscated his treasury, which contained 12 million pound sterling and erroneously dubbed him as 'Hyat' Sahib. Tipu unjustly accused the 'ungrateful Malabari slave' of absconding with the booty. Would the British have allowed Ayaz or anyone else to escape with the treasure?

Bowring states:

> Bednur fortress was at this time governed by Sheikh Ayaz or Haiyat Sahib, a Nair of Malabar, who had been forcibly converted to Islam, and for whom Haidar had an extraordinary affection on account of his fidelity and trustworthiness. Tipu, however, resenting this partiality, had a personal dislike to him, and had sent orders to supersede him in his post. But before his successor, Lutf Ali Beg, could reach his destination, Ayaz, distrusting his sovereign's intentions towards him, and despairing of holding his own against the English, surrendered the fort and town of Haidernagar to Matthews.[44]

K.K. Nair writes:

> In the interval between Haider's death and Tipu's arrival in the camp, Haider's provincial governor of the districts of Chitteldoorg, Bednore, Gorial Bunder [Mangalore], etc., known as Hyatt Sahib or Sheikh Ayaz received intelligence of General

> Matthews approach. He communicated the same to Mysore as also his intention to withdraw his troops from Bullum and march without delay to oppose General Matthews. What made Bednore extraordinarily important was the aspect that its metropolis Haidernagar held the enormous wealth of Haider's conquests. It was also the prime depository of his arms, ammunition and military stores.[45]

Nair adds, 'What made the assault of Bednore imperative to the English was the aspect that their position in the Southern Presidency had become critical with an empty treasury following the severe famine of Madras in 1782.'[46]

Some writers have suggested that perhaps Haider Ali had nominated Ayaz Khan as his successor. Why did Haider Ali appoint Ayaz as the governor of Bidanur instead of his two biological sons? Was it because there was more treasure in Bidanur Fort and Haider needed a staunch loyalist to protect it? We do know that when Bidanur eventually fell into British hands after the death of Haider Ali, the East India Company gained £12 million. The treasures looted by the soldiers were not quantified. Did the unfortunate Ayaz Khan depart for Bombay empty-handed? We simply do not know. All we know is that Tipu was frustrated at the loss of Bidanur and immediately launched an attack to recapture it. He managed to regain the fort, but not the treasure.

Kirmani writes with a flourish:

> The Sultan's spies brought intelligence that Ayaz Khan, the adopted son of the late Nawab, and who had been appointed by him to the government of the districts of Nagar, Gorial Bunder [Mangalore], the cup of his unworthiness being at this time filled to the brim, had followed the path of treachery and ingratitude, and with the greatest perfidy had delivered up the whole of the forts of that country [Malabar] to the English of the port of Bombay; and that unfortunate man, with a great quantity of gold, jewels, baggage and followers had embarked on board ship, and had taken his ill-starred route to Bombay.[47]

Ayaz Khan's decision not to march to Srirangapatna following Haider Ali's death raises several questions. Was he merely awaiting orders from Tipu Sultan? Or was he aware of the British advance towards Bidanur and thus determined to defend the fort? British narratives suggest they did not expect Ayaz Khan's capitulation. For Tipu, this came as a rude shock. Perhaps he awaited news of Ayaz Khan's murder. Or was he preoccupied with establishing control over Srirangapatna?

Ayaz would have been around 32 years old when his foster father died. After surrendering to the British, he spent 16 years in exile in Bombay. A decade after going into exile, Ayaz Khan staked a claim for his properties in Chirakkal, but the British refused. Instead, they awarded him a meagre pension. Unfortunately, Ayaz died soon thereafter, in 1799, leaving his wives and children destitute. What eventually became of his descendants remains unknown. In the same year, Tipu Sultan was defeated and killed, and his descendants eventually fell into poverty despite receiving generous pensions from the British for over a century.

## Velu Nachiyar Finds a Muslim Brother

Velu Nachiyar was the first queen of Hindustan to decisively defeat the British in battle. Yet, remarkably few people have even heard of her.

Velu Nachiyar, the daughter of the raja of Ramanad, was a skilled warrior, proficient in several languages, including English, French and Urdu. In 1746, at the age of sixteen, she was married to Muthu Vaduganatha Thevar of Sivaganga. In 1750, her husband became the king.

In the late 1750s, Haider Ali was encamped at Dindigul with a substantial army, and by 1761, he had emerged as the de facto ruler of Mysore. In 1757, Robert Clive's victory at Plassey had established British supremacy in India. The First Anglo-Mysore War between the British and Haider Ali occurred from 1767 to 1769, a time when both powers were in their early stages of territorial expansion.

In 1772, the British, assisted by the son of the nawab of Arcot, launched an invasion of Sivaganga. Velu Nachiyar's husband was killed, and Sivaganga was occupied by the Arcot royals. The widowed queen and her daughter sought refuge in Virupakshi Palayam, where the palayakkar Gopala Nayak provided them sanctuary.

The British conducted an extensive search to locate the queen. They resorted to torture and ultimately killed a young girl named Udaiyal, who steadfastly refused to divulge Velu Nachiyar's whereabouts. Later, Velu Nachiyar would raise a women's battalion named 'Udaiyal Padai' in honour of the brave Udaiyal, appointing a Dalit woman named Kuyili as its commander. Kuyili, too, was destined to leave her mark on history.

Thandavarayan Pillai, the chief minister of Sivaganga, and the Marudu brothers followed their queen into exile. Together, they formed a delegation and approached Haider Ali with a request for 5,000 soldiers. Impressed by the queen's fluent Urdu, Haider awarded her 400 gold coins and offered her protection. He promised to provide military aid when the time was right.

It is unlikely that brotherly love motivated Haider to assist the queen of Sivaganga as it was not in tune with his known character traits. Whenever Haider Ali sent troops to assist any ruler, he invariably exacted a price. As explained earlier, he had demanded a steep price from the Palghat raja for aiding him against the Zamorin of Calicut; he had also sought monetary compensation from Marthanda Varma of Travancore for merely 'preparing' to send him military aid. However, he made an exception for Velu Nachiyar, who remained under his protection for eight years before embarking on the campaign to reclaim Sivaganga. Even though Haider offered protection to the queen and her retinue over an extended period, he did not actively engage in fighting on her behalf. Velu Nachiyar formulated and executed her own plans for reclaiming her kingdom. The exiled queen spent eight years preparing for war. During this time, Thandavarayan Pillai passed away, and the Marudu brothers assumed leadership roles as her chieftains.

In 1780, as Haider Ali descended on the Carnatic, igniting the Second Anglo-Mysore War, Velu Nachiyar decided it was time to strike. On the day of Vijayadasami (or Dussehra) festival, her women's battalion infiltrated the Sivaganga Fort disguised as ordinary worshippers carrying baskets of flowers. Kuyili doused herself with oil and ghee from the festival lamps, setting herself ablaze. She then detonated the British ammunition depot, thus becoming the first woman suicide bomber in recorded history. Seizing the opportunity, the women warriors grabbed their hidden weapons and quickly seized control of the fort.[48]

Sivaganga was reclaimed through what was essentially a women-only military operation on Vijayadasami, the day commemorating Goddess Durga's defeat of the buffalo-demon Mahishasura. Preceded by Navaratri, nine nights of festivities dedicated to worshipping the goddess in her various forms, Vijayadasami symbolizes the ultimate victory of righteousness. Thus, Velu Nachiyar and her all-woman Udaiyal Padai chose this auspicious day to take on the mighty British.[49] Velu's story cannot be told without honouring two great women warriors – Udaiyal and Kuyili. The narrative of India's freedom struggle remains incomplete as long as such names are omitted from our history books, while only the most violent males are glorified.

Following Haider Ali's death in 1782 during the ongoing war with the British, Velu Nachiyar secured peace and preserved her kingdom by paying tribute to the nawab of Arcot. She reigned as queen from 1780 to 1790, while her daughter Vellachi ruled from 1790 to 1793. Together, they maintained control over Sivaganga for 13 long years amid a tumultuous political milieu.[50]

# 5

# LIVING BY THE SWORD

Haider Ali's troops-for-hire business model had been highly successful from the outset. War proved to be a profitable enterprise. Victorious outcomes often resulted in indiscriminate looting, leading to overnight riches. Unlike farming, industry and trade, which offered gradual returns, war promised swift and substantial rewards. In a way, this was exactly what the Europeans did in India.

Once Haider Ali had gained the trust of the Mysore raja and the dalawai Nanjaraj, he parked himself at Dindigul and frequently launched raids into the surrounding territories, fighting and looting. A string of quick victories made him rich. By dispatching Makhdum Ali to Palghat in 1758, he gained considerable wealth. In 1759, he sent 5,000 men to Pondicherry at the request of M. Lally. With his resources multiplying, he strengthened his army and fought more battles. He seized control of the Mysore kingdom in 1761, following a failed attempt in 1759. Thereafter, he continually strengthened his position.

However, the father–son duo made a significant tactical error – they allied with the French and opposed the British. During the latter half of the 18th century, these two European powers vied for dominance in India. There was a fleeting moment when it seemed the French might prevail, especially during Dupleix's tenure as the governor of Pondicherry. However, unfortunately for the sultans, the tide quickly turned in favour of the British.

Haider's hostility towards the English originated from his desire to secure the coveted fiefdom of Arcot, which he hoped to confer upon his son, Tipu Sultan. However, the British supported Mohammed Ali Khan Wallajah for the position. Haider fought several battles in pursuit of this goal but in vain. While he briefly seized the Vellore Fort and proclaimed his son as the nawab of the Carnatic, he could not maintain control for long. Despite the collapse of his Arcot dream, the bitterness remained. His hatred of the Arcot royals and the British persisted, a sentiment shared by Tipu Sultan.

## Profile of Haider Ali

At the time of Tipu's birth, Haider Ali had not yet acquired any titles; he was simply known as Haider Naik. Tipu is said to have been born in Devanahalli, the location where the Bangalore airport now stands. His mother, Fakhrunissa, had been residing in Devanahalli since its capture by the Mysoreans in 1749.

Bowring paints a compelling portrait of the upstart of Mysore:

> Haidar was a born soldier, an excellent rider, and skilful alike with his sword and his gun. Trained by early habits to active exertion, he could undergo great fatigue without suffering from it, and when at the head of his troops, he was reckless of personal danger, thus stimulating the courage of his followers. Cool and sagacious in war-time, he excelled in cavalry tactics, and seemed to possess by intuition the knowledge how to launch his horsemen with the greatest effect on the enemy.[1]

Haider heavily depended on the ability and expertise of the French officers in his service.

Bowring shares some graphic depictions of the prisoners held captive by Haider, 'Sad tales might indeed be told of many of his English captives, who were half-starved, and sometimes forcibly circumcised.'[2] However, his sympathies appear to be reserved for the English prisoners, while the fate of the Indian captives was overlooked. Nonetheless, Bowring's estimation of Haider Ali's character is convincing:

> He had no compunction in devastating whole tracts of his own country in order to prevent an enemy from subsisting his troops on local supplies, nor did he evince any compassion for the conquered, or show liberality to the distressed. His every action was regulated by a cold calculating temperament.[3]

Haider was of 'medium height with rather coarse features, which were embrowned by the sun; his nose small but aquiline, his eyes also small, and the lower lip thick'.[4] He was clean-shaven and 'his turban was of brilliant scarlet, flat at the top, and of immense length'.[5] Bowring further reveals:

> He is said to have been very accessible to all and to have conversed with great readiness. In close intercourse with his boon-companions he did not hesitate to make use of the foulest abuse. In matters of business his shrewdness and capacity were remarkable, and he had the faculty of giving his attention to several subjects at the same time, so that he could hear a letter read, dictate orders, and witness a theatrical exhibition all at once, without being distracted by any one of these occupations. Although he was unable to read or write, the answer to every document of importance was read over to him by a second person after it had been written by one of his scribes, thus ensuring absolute accuracy, after which he scrawled his signature. All State business was transacted under his own eyes with regularity and despatch, his retentive memory enabling him to supervise closely everything that was done by his subordinates. The evenings were enlivened by comedies, and the performances of trained groups of dancing girls, and not unfrequently ended in a debauch with some chosen friends. He had an extensive harem, and did not scruple to seize and place in it any girl who possessed superior attractions.[6]

Occasionally, Haider had Brahmin advisers. 'To assist him in organizing the system of plundering, which he carried on for many years, he took into his service a Maratha Brahmin named Khande Rao.'[7]

Wilks observes that Haider Ali, though illiterate, possessed an extraordinary memory and demonstrated exceptional proficiency in handling figures and accounts.[8] Together with the cunning Brahmin Khande Rao, he devised an innovative system of plunder, allowing the looters to keep half of the spoils while Haider Ali claimed the other half. This get-rich-quick scheme proved highly successful for all involved parties, ensuring mutual benefit for Haider and his Bedar peons, Pindaris and others.[9] Wilks further explains how Haider accumulated wealth through various unscrupulous means, including the falsification of accounts:

> Nanjaraj on the receipt of Hyder's dispatches with a long list of killed and wounded, sent a special commissioner with rich presents for Hyder and the officers who were represented to have distinguished themselves, and Zuckhum puttee [compensation] for the wounded... The allowance on this occasion was fourteen rupees a month, until the cure should be completed. Hyder marshalled his wounded men, to be inspected by the commissioner: sixty-seven was the true number; but about seven hundred had their legs or arms bound up with yellow bandages, and acted their parts with entire success. The money was paid to Hyder according to the muster and to the probable time of cure reported by the attending surgeons, at the rate of fourteen rupees per man per month. To the really wounded he gave seven.[10]

Thus, it is evident that Haider was not only cold and calculating but also cunning and deceitful.

Wilks remarks:

> During these operations Kunde Row was perpetually sounding the exploits of his master to Nanjaraj; exaggerating the disturbed state of the country, and the necessity of augmenting the forces; which was accordingly authorized from time to time, and assignments on the revenues of other districts were added for that purpose to his other resources. Special commissioners were always deputed to muster the new levies; and on one occasion, Jehan Khan saw exhibited the manoeuvre which he calls a circular muster, by which ten thousand men were counted and passed as eighteen thousand... while claiming merit for public economy in being able to defray

> the expense of the augmented forces from the allotted funds, he was, in fact, accumulating an immense treasure.[11]

Haider Ali also had a penchant for pomp and pageantry. Bowring provides an elaborate description of his extravagant military parades, 'Lastly, at the end of the procession came Haidar himself, mounted on a white elephant which was captured in the Bidanur country.'[12]

De la Tour recounts a peculiar tale involving a French military man named Constantin, who came to India along with some French troops in 1754. He married a Portuguese woman and had a beautiful daughter. Serving as a sergeant under M. Hugel, who commanded the French troops in Mysore, Constantin was rumoured to have entered into an agreement with Haider Ali to 'sell' his daughter to the 'nabob'. Recognizing the dishonour this transaction would bring upon Europeans, Hugel confronted Constantin, who vehemently denied the allegation. A young Frenchman volunteered to marry the girl, and Constantin accepted the proposal. However, that very night, he sold his daughter to Haider Ali for a princely sum of 50,000 rupees. He then absconded to Bangalore with considerable riches that local people had handed over to him for safe-keeping. He eventually relocated to Goa and Bombay, before departing for Europe. De la Tour adds, 'Hyder's French surgeon affirms, that the girl has since told him that she esteemed herself fortunate in being sold to the Nabob; as her father and mother might have made a more shameful traffic with her if she had stayed with them.'[13]

The 1937 Mysore Report, citing Peixoto's memoir, presents a startling revelation: 'Hyder had even thought of giving him [Raja Sahib] in marriage his only living daughter who had been preserved by Modin Saib in spite of his custom of killing his daughters as soon as they were born.'[14] This shocking revelation is not corroborated elsewhere, but it does provide food for thought. Haider Ali, despite having numerous partners, is known to have had only two sons, Tipu and Karim, and a daughter who was married to the son of the Pathan nawab of Savanur.

Haider was known to resort to harsh methods of extortion, which he applied to friends and foes alike. 'Those who were suspected of having money were chastised until they gave up the whole for no other reason than that it was the Nawab's pleasure ... The Nawab used cruelty, killing, robbing and other oppressions without remedy.'[15] Regarding his political strategy concerning the de jure ruler of the Mysore kingdom, Peixoto notes that while Haider pretended to act as regent for the raja, he posted Muslim (Moorish) governors in all the provinces and stationed Muslim commanders in every fort.[16]

Chetti narrates a tale of Haidar Ali's innovative approach to choosing a (nominal) successor for the throne of Mysore. In 1775, following the death of the puppet ruler, Haider Ali took it upon himself to nominate a successor. 'He collected all the children of the royal family and threw a heap of toys among them. One of the princes, Chama Raja Wadiyar, took up a dagger. He was considered the fittest for the throne, and made king accordingly.'[17] Beatson says that Haider gathered a group of small children from the royal family and distributed some fruits among them, observing their subsequent behaviour. While some children ate the fruit and others stored it away, one four-year-old boy gave the fruit to his father. Upon witnessing this gesture, Haider declared that the boy was best suited to be king and proceeded with the coronation. Undoubtedly, Haider retained the de facto control of the kingdom, and the coronation was merely a facade.[18]

According to C. Hayavadhana Rao:

> Haider indeed stands out as an exceedingly capable organizer. He virtually built up a new army; developed a new technique of warfare; and provided for the proper guarding of the passes that could lead the enemy against him. Even more than all this, he developed a policy that subordinated everything to the single idea of expanding Mysore.[19]

Rao adds:

> Two other factors helped Haidar in his active policy of aggression. One was that he was, both by predilection and by upbringing, one

> on whom religion sat lightly. He befriended generally the Hindus and respected their scruples, their beliefs, and their religious observances. The characterisation that he was 'half-a-Hindu' was not inapt in its application to him. This friendliness towards the Hindus in a Hindu state ruled by a Hindu sovereign made him, if not exactly a persona grata with the people generally, at least one who was regarded with a feeling akin to goodwill. This initial goodwill proved a great asset to him. It enabled him to gather strength during the beginnings of his career as Regent.[20]

Describing Haider Ali as a master strategist, Rao observes:

> Inland, towards the South, he already held the strong fort of Dindigul, and he befriended Mahfuz Khan, brother of Muhammad Ali, who had been appointed to the charge of the Madura and Tinnevelly [Tirunelveli] countries. At the same time, he kept [in] close touch with Muhammad Yusuf Khan, the rebel Commandant of Madura, in order to use him, if possible, in his own interest.[21]

Rao further states:

> The necessity of European discipline and European instructors, the preparation of his own military supplies, such as muskets, guns, cannon balls and powder, the supply of his own horses to his cavalry, possibly the advantages of attacks by night, were all matters in which Haidar Ali followed, if he did not actually imitate, Yusuf Khan.[22]

Muhammed Yusuf Khan was born Maruthanayagam Pillai, but he converted to Islam and gained a reputation for his brilliant military manoeuvres. He served the EICo but later fell out with the British as well as Muhammad Ali, the Arcot nawab. 'In a letter to the Madras Council, dated 12th February 1763, Muhammad Ali, writing of the machinations of Yusuf, states that he had *"entered into a union with Haidar Naik"*.'[23] Eventually, Yusuf was captured by the French, and subsequently handed over to the British and Muhammad Ali, who hanged him on 15 October

1764. Thus, Haidar forfeited an opportunity to gain control over Madurai and Tirunelveli, and to recapture Trichy.[24] Rao reveals that Yusuf's collaboration with Mysore, Travancore and Thanjavur 'was abundantly proved from the papers found in Madura by the captors'.[25]

While Haidar missed the opportunity to acquire new provinces for Mysore, he gained new recruits for his army and forged a friendship with Ali Zaman Khan. Khan, known for his jovial nature, soon became an inseparable part of Haider's entourage. 'Being a very stout man, the Khan was not able to mount a horse, and therefore, when he went out, Haidar, evidently to secure his pleasant company, gave the loan of his own elephant.'[26] Ali Zaman Khan served as one of Haidar's representatives during the peace negotiations with the English in 1769 at the gates of Madras. He participated in the battle of Rattihalli and was wounded.[27] Subsequently, he was captured alongside many other officers of Haidar at Chinkurli but was later released by Triambak Rao.[28]

Hayavadhana Rao states:

> In regard to buying of horses, he (Haider) followed ... the time-honoured system that had descended to him. As to preparation of supplies, there was a well-regulated system in vogue in Mysore, which he improved ... Haidar never yielded the command over his whole army into the hands of the European officers he employed. Nor did he ... allow them to deal with troops that were not distinctively their own ... Thus, while his army in 1767, for instance, was about 200,000 strong including 26,000 cavalry, the number of Europeans was only 750, with 250 cannoners ... He never allowed the European officers and their portion of the army to domineer over the Indian sections or to dictate to him.[29]

## Portrait of Tipu Sultan

According to Mohibbul Hasan and several other historians, Tipu's date of birth was 20 November 1750. While this date is widely accepted today, other chroniclers have proposed alternative dates. Kirkpatrick refers to a circular issued by him '[to] the Dewan and

Bakshy of each of the Seven Kucherries of the Seat of the Sultanat [or Seringapatam]' on 17 December 1785 'directing the birthday of the Sultan, or the approaching 14th day of Tulooey [20th December] to be celebrated, in the manner appointed in the Hukm-nameh'.[30] He further informs us:

> In a loose paper in my possession, containing directions for the regulation of military salutes on various occasions, there is a note, or memorandum, purporting, that the Sultan was born on the 14th of Tulooey of the year of the Higera 1165, on the anniversary of which day it is ordered, that a salute of thirty-one guns shall be fired at ten o'clock in the morning, and all the people of the city observe the same as a festival.[31]

Tipu Sultan's given name was Fath Ali. According to a popular story, when Fakhrunissa was expecting a child, she accompanied her husband to the tomb of Tipu Mastan Aulia at Kolar and prayed for the birth of a son. The infant was later named Tipu after the saint. How 'Mastan' became 'Sultan' is anybody's guess. Interestingly, Tipu continued to add 'Sultan' to the names of his sons. During Haider Ali's lifetime, British and French accounts invariably referred to Tipu as Tipu Sahib. Similarly, Haider Ali's wife's brother was called Makhdum Sahib, and Tipu's younger brother was known as Karim Sahib. However, immediately after Haider Ali's death, the British began to address his successor as 'Tipu Sultan'. This seems to suggest that Tipu assumed the title of 'Sultan' at this stage. In 1787, after concluding his war with the Marathas, Tipu adopted the title of Padshah (Badshah). Among his demands to the peshwa was the curious suggestion that he should henceforth be addressed as 'Tipu Sultan Khan Bahadur'. The peshwa might have silently acquiesced, as this concession did not entail any financial costs.

Sometime in 1789, Nizam Ali Khan Asaf Jah Bahadur proposed an offensive and defensive alliance between Hyderabad and Mysore and sent an emissary to Tipu at Coimbatore to discuss the matter.[32] Wilks observes:

> To this proposition, the Sultan distinctly replied, that he was ready to return the pledge, and establish an offensive and defensive treaty, on the condition of an intermarriage in the families, but not without this preliminary alliance; but on this subject, the envoy had no orders, and could give no reply.[33]

Wilks suggests that a supremely confident Tipu Sultan sent two emissaries to Hyderabad to formally present the proposal. 'The Sultan, foreseeing no impediment, sent an embassy in return, consisting of Kuttub-u-Deen and Ali Reza, who accompanied the envoy in his return to Hyderabad. Nizam Ali, however, distinguished between political union, and the degradation which he attached to the proposed alliance.'[34] Wilks testifies that when Ali Reza requested to partake in the Sheker-Bhat, the dish of rice and sugar sent as the first preliminary ceremonial of marriage, Nizam Ali did not reply, and the meeting was abruptly terminated.[35] The same year witnessed the betrothal of Tipu's minor son Abdul Khaliq to the minor daughter of the Arakkal Beevi of Cannanore. Did Tipu use his own brand of bulldozer politics to initiate this alliance? One can only speculate.

On 1 June 1790, the British resident at Poona signed a treaty with the peshwa (and the nizam) on behalf of the governor-general. While the substance constituted an offensive and defensive alliance in the war against Tipu, it is interesting to note how the respective personalities are addressed. The Company is referred to as 'the Honourable United English East India Company', the peshwa as 'Peshwa Savai Mahadeo Narain Pundit Pradhan' and the nizam as 'Nawab Nizam Ali Khan Asaf Jah Bahadur', while Tipu is mentioned as 'Futh Ali Khan known by the Denomination of Tipu Sultan'.[36] Tipu is neither addressed as 'nawab' nor 'bahadur'. This suggests that 'Tipu Sultan' is not his given name but an assumed one. When the Third Anglo–Mysore War ended and a treaty was signed on 17 March 1792, it was noted that the signatories were (apart from the EICo., the Peshwa's agents and the nizam's nominees) 'Ghulam Ali Khan Bahadur and Ali Reza Khan on behalf of Tipu Sultan'.[37] Again, no prefixes or suffixes are attached to Tipu's name. However, the very first article of the said treaty refers to 'the late Nawab Haider Ali Khan'. Haider Ali is titled as nawab, but his son is not. One wonders why.

It is true that Tipu was not as well-educated as many writers and eulogists claim. While he was the literate son of an illiterate father, his 'dream book' contained numerous spelling errors. Having been on the battlefield from the age of fifteen or earlier, he could not have received much formal education. However, he spoke many languages, including Farsi, had a keen curiosity and displayed an eagerness to learn. He had diverse interests, with dream analysis and rocket science among them. Undoubtedly, he was drawn by the destructive potential of rockets, though he also used them for ceremonial purposes.

When Haider Ali invaded Malabar in 1766, a teenaged Tipu was ordered to accompany him to gain battle experience. In June 1767, when the nizam marched against Bangalore alongside the British, Haider Ali dispatched Tipu, along with two senior nobles, to negotiate with the nizam on his behalf. Impressed with Tipu's negotiation skills and the costly gifts sent by his father, the nizam bestowed upon him the title of Fath Ali Khan Bahadur. (Clearly, he was not yet addressed as 'Sultan'.) Shortly thereafter, Tipu was sent to Madras at the head of an army, accompanied by his military mentor, Ghazi Khan, as well as Makhdum Sahib and other nobles. Tipu distinguished himself, plundering San Thome and unleashing terror in Madras.

In the meantime, Haider Ali suffered defeat at the hands of the British at Thiruvannamalai, approximately 200 km southwest of Madras. He promptly recalled Tipu, who then marched to Vaniyambadi in the Salem district of present-day Tamil Nadu. With the onset of monsoon, the Mysore army remained in the region, laying siege to Ambur without success. In December, Tipu was dispatched to the west coast where the British posed a significant threat to Haider Ali's newly conquered territories. Upon reaching Bidanur, Tipu learned that the British had captured Mangalore. Engaging in minor battles with them for two months in early 1768, Tipu alternated between attacking and retreating until he finally succeeded in seizing the main bazaar. Although the Mangalore Fort resisted, panic spread among the British upon hearing news of Haider Ali's impending arrival. They hastily withdrew, leaving Tipu to revel in his triumph. When Haider Ali arrived, he quickly evicted the British from the rest of his Malabar territories. Thereafter, both father and son continued to fight until the conclusion of the war (First Anglo–Mysore War) in March 1769. Tipu Sultan was still in his teens, but his 'tiger' avatar was gradually emerging.

By the time Haider Ali passed away in 1782, Tipu had risen to immense power. He took over the reins of the Mysore kingdom, subdued his adversaries and continued the Second Anglo–Mysore War that was ongoing at the time. Peace was concluded only in 1784.

Tipu referred to his government as 'Sarkar-i-Khudadad' (God-given Government) and his kingdom as 'Ahmedy Sircar'. He maintained a highly centralized system of administration and issued detailed written instructions to his officers. Interestingly, after the French Revolution, Tipu began calling himself Citizen Tipu.

Bowring states:

> From his youth upwards he was deficient in stability and straightforwardness, so much so as to excite the wrath of his father. Haidar, besides publicly flogging Tipu at Chinkurli, exacted from him an agreement, in which the youth declared that if he committed theft or fraud or be proved guilty of prevarication, misrepresentation, or deceit, or if he should be detected in taking presents without orders or carrying on secret intrigues, he consented to be strangled or to undergo some other condign punishment. It is evident from the contents of this curious paper, which was discovered at Seringapatam after the siege in 1799, that Haidar was well aware of the unstable and fickle temperament of his son. It was also asserted by many who knew Tipu in later life that his understanding was at times clouded over in a way that betrayed symptoms of mental aberration.[38]

Bowring describes Tipu's 'singularly eccentric character', noting that he was 'so modest that no one ever saw any part of his person, save his feet, ankles, and wrists; while in the bath he always covered himself from head to foot'.[39]

The French officer Lieutenant Colonel Russel, writing in 1781, provides interesting insights into the character of Tipu Sahib. He notes that Tipu is 'not as tall and strong as his father. He has a distinguished appearance, is very smart and quick in physical exercises. He is the best horseman of the whole army'.[40] According to Russel, at 32 years old, Tipu displayed an 'eagerness to learn', an 'interest in politics and war' and a 'love for glory'.[41] Russel further remarks, 'He has the same passions as his father, but not the vices. He is particular about following exactly the commands of his religion. He has moral principles, is careful not to depart from them, and is critical of his father's behavior.'[42] Russel also mentions that at the time he departed Mysore in mid-1778, Tipu had only one daughter.

He further adds:

> When I was him, which happened at least twice a day when we were besieging a place, while waiting for his father in the trenches, he questioned me on our manners and customs, our military forces, our way of conducting military operations. He asked me what he should do when he would be master [of Mysore]. He told me his reign would be advantageous for France, for my troop [of Hussars] and for me. He enquired whether the French had any territorial ambitions in India. I reassured him, telling him that all we wanted was to maintain our position and protect our trade. He was then making plans to fight the English [whom he hates].[43]

Russel's remarks indeed provide food for thought. He makes another interesting observation: 'Tipu Sahib fears his father more than he loves him. He is ambitious like him, and impatient to reign.'[44] Additionally, Russel notes that Tipu's impatience could not have escaped the notice of his father, who took care not to grant him any independent authority. Haider ensured that Tipu was provided only with the minimum resources required to sustain his activities. Haider 'gives him money with such parsimony that that he is obliged to borrow from the *sowcars* or *sahukars*, or money-lenders for his necessary expenses'.[45]

Russel notes that Tipu 'spends sparingly, loves order, and is very strict in military discipline'.[46] He concludes with the remark that it is impossible to say whether Tipu's ascension to power would lead to good or bad outcomes.[47]

## Alien Connections and Modus Operandi

Haider Ali's association with the French was no secret. He was hand in glove with the French at least from the 1750s. As mentioned earlier, he obtained his military supplies through the French port of Mahe.

Hayavadhana Rao discusses Haider's early attempts to cultivate favour with the British in the 1760s. In February 1764, Haidar wrote a letter to the governor of Madras expressing his desire 'that everything that will conduce to the increase of our friendship may be done by us both'.[48] During his conflicts with the Marathas, he corresponded with the British at Tellicherry, requesting them to supply arms and ammunition. 'During 1766–1767, the friendly relations between Haidar and the Hon. Company continued, except that he came into conflict with the Factors at Tellicherry on their refusal to help him with powder and shot during his invasion of Malabar [1766].'[49]

In 1768, the British decimated Haider's minor fleet of ten ships, prompting him to send emissaries to Oman and Persia seeking assistance from his Muslim brethren. In 1775, Haider Ali imported a contingent of 1,000 horses and horsemen from Shiraz in Persia.[50] This occurred during the interval between the First and Second Anglo–Mysore Wars. Obviously, these troops were employed in conflicts with other non-European neighbours. Haider Ali was not averse to doing business with the British either. In 1777, he provided them with sandalwood and pepper from Malabar and acquired 6,000 muskets and 4,000 grenades in exchange. Three years later, he declared war on the British.

On 4 September 1781, amid the Second Anglo–Mysore War, Haider Ali signed a treaty with the Dutch at Nagapattinam in which the two powers pledged mutual assistance against the British. The Dutch governor and Haider Ali jointly defended Nagapattinam when the English, led by General Hector Munro and Admiral Edward Hughes, bombarded the town from both land and sea. However, the 8,000-strong garrison was forced to surrender on 11 November.

Tipu Sultan later sought troops from the Ottoman sultan and offered the port of Mangalore in exchange for the port of Basra. However, this offer was politely deflected.

Irfan Habib, in his introduction to the 2001 publication titled *State and Diplomacy under Tipu Sultan: Documents and Essays*, says:

> Tipu wished, through his ambassadors, to propose to Turkey that a Turkish expeditionary force be sent to India. The explanation to be given to the Ottoman ruler of the need for this intervention was that the English had seized large territories of Hindustan and were oppressing Muslims. Again, the identification of the English as the principal enemy is manifest, although Tipu was at this time at peace with them and at war with the Marathas.[51]

Habib elaborates, 'The Turkish court, however, had no interest in Tipu Sultan's main proposal of a fight against the English and saw no particular profit in developing the kind of commercial ties Tipu wanted, especially the lease of Basra.'[52]

Tipu Sultan sent a one-man embassy to Constantinople in 1784 following the conclusion of the Second Anglo–Mysore War.[53] The selected emissary was Uthman Khan. The information provided by Uthman may have prompted the sultan to send a second embassy the following year, consisting of four men and four elephants. Upon the ambassadors' arrival at Constantinople, Uthman returned to Mysore. Subsequently, upon his arrival at Srirangapatna, Tipu sent another three-member delegation (including Uthman Khan) from Pondicherry directly to France at the beginning of 1787.[54]

Tipu's letter dated 19 November 1786 addressed to Monsieur Monneron in Pondicherry, states:

> You write that five thousand soldiers' muskets will arrive immediately, either at Calicut or Mangalore; and that you will bring five thousand more along with yourself, when you return [to Pondicherry] from the Mauritius. It is understood. We have written to the Talukdars of Calicut and Mangalore, directing them to receive the muskets you may send, whenever they arrive, provided you shall have fixed a proper [or just] price upon the same.[55]

The Mysore sultans were not the sole powers to employ French mercenaries. The nizam of Hyderabad and the Maratha confederacy also utilized the services of various French adventurers. One such figure was Monsieur Michel Joachim Marie Raymond, who rose to prominence in Hyderabad during the 1780s. Raymond had been present at Pondicherry in 1778 when the town fell to the British. Subsequently, he relocated to Mysore and served in the army, coming under General De Bussy after the death of Haider Ali. In 1785, Raymond entered the service of the nizam, Asaf Jah II, where he quickly won the trust of the nizam and the admiration of the locals. Referred to as Musa Ram by Hindus and Musa Rahim by Muslims, Raymond fought against Tipu's army in the Third Anglo–Mysore War (1790–1792). He was later defeated by the Marathas at the Battle of Kharda in 1795. Raymond died under mysterious circumstances in March 1798 and was laid to rest in Hyderabad. His tomb remained a site of pilgrimage until around 1940, and Musa Ram Bag is named in his honour.

Haider and Tipu recognized the crucial role played by European mercenaries, especially the French, in their military campaigns. The valour and professionalism of French troops often contributed to Mysorean victories. However, when Haider Ali sought to attach Goa after capturing Karwar, the French troops refused to fight the Portuguese, leading Haider Ali to realize that while the French could be utilized, they could not be trusted. Similarly, when Tipu Sultan tried to recapture Bidanur from the British in 1783, news arrived from Europe of a peace treaty between Britain and France. This prompted the French soldiers in Tipu's camp to lay down their arms and refuse to fight. Like his father, Tipu learned through experience that the loyalty of European soldiers was not unconditional. Nevertheless, his dependence on the French left him with limited options. In a letter to Cossigny on 28 December 1786, Tipu stated, 'You write, that a strict friendship subsists between the Hollanders and the Rajah of the French; and that it is expedient that we, also, should establish a good understanding and correspondence with that people. It is comprehended. Whosoever is united with the French, is, in fact, united with us.'[56]

Tirthankar Roy highlights in *The East India Company: The World's Most Powerful Corporation*:

> The three heroes of the French political mission in India La Bourdonnais, Dupleix and de Lally, faced severe criticism at home for adventures that had cost the treasury and the French company an enormous sum of money. La Bourdonnais lost his property, was imprisoned, and died in poverty in 1753. Dupleix, who had staked his personal fortune on the Indian mission, went bankrupt and died unknown and poor in 1763. De Lally was executed in 1766.[57]

Haider Ali may have chosen the wrong allies, but his military acumen and well-trained battalions allowed him to devise clever strategies and secure victories in some of his battles against the British.

Haider refurbished and strengthened the Palghat Fort in 1766. According to James Scurry's narrative, Tipu built a mosque at Srirangapatna in 1787–1788. Additionally, the fort of Srirangapatna was strengthened under the sultans' rule. Tipu Sultan also enhanced the Bekal Fort in the Kasargod district of northern Kerala, believed to have been originally built in 1650 by the Keladi Nayaks. Tradition suggests that Tipu Sultan added a water tank, magazine and watchtower to the fort. However, beyond these endeavours, little construction occurred during their forty-year reign in Mysore, Malabar and Coorg. Their legacy is primarily one of wanton destruction.

Tipu issued several written orders to his Mir Asafs or revenue collectors between 1795 and 1798. A collection of about fifty such orders, found in the Persian Manuscript section of the Salar Jang Museum in Hyderabad, was translated by I.G. Khan, a reader in history at the Aligarh Muslim University.[58] Order No. 34 says:

> It is ordered that *pucca* brick *masjids* are built in all the forts. They shall be utilized to provide education to the children of the soldiers and the officers. Exhort them to come for prayers. And they must be taught the books *Zad al Mujahidin* and *Murid al Mujahidin* which can be taken from the royal chancery [*nawishtkhana*].[59]

Order No. 39 states, 'It has been decided that in your territories 50 workshops of iron will be established. Of these ten will produce steel and forty, iron.'[60]

The preservation of wildlife was not among the sultan's objectives. His Order No.18 states his desires in this respect: 'Let the *muqaddams* and *aumils* be warned that they must not let the population of tigers and bears in their areas survive at all. They must be killed and the skins sent to the sultan.'[61] The 'Tiger of Mysore' did not want a single tiger to be spared. He imprisoned them, imitated them, and openly admired them, but he felt they had no right to exist. No wonder the tiger population of India has dwindled to the point of near extinction, and huge efforts are required today to bring this exotic animal back from the brink.

Abdul Khaliq was one of the child hostages taken by Lord Cornwallis in 1792 when he was still a minor. Upon their return from Madras, Tipu found him and his brother Muiz-ud-Din to be rather unmanageable, prompting him to decide to send them to France for education.[62] However, this plan did not materialize due to Tipu's involvement in multiple conflicts and the ongoing political upheavals in France.

When Tipu sent his delegation to France, he prepared a draft treaty to be signed by the king. His briefs to his ambassadors to Turkey and France (1785–1786) have been translated by Iqbal Husain, a retired professor of history at the Aligarh Muslim University.

Tipu's draft treaty with France comprised five clauses.[63] While the first clause stipulated that France and Mysore would join hands to fight the British in India, the second stated that 'Ten thousand Europeans ['hat-wearers'] with war-tried high commanders should be despatched [from France])'.[64] The third clause stated that Tipu would command the combined forces. The fourth clause addressed the division of the spoils. Chennapattan (Madras), Pondicherry and other ports on the Coromandel Coast would fall to the lot of the French, while Trichy, Thanjavur and other places in the hinterland would be held by the sultan. The fifth clause revealed the towering height of the sultan's ambition. After conquering Chennapattan, the combined French–Mysorean army would proceed to capture Bombay and Calcutta. Once again, the French would obtain the ports, and the sultan would acquire the provinces in the interior.[65] One is inclined to conclude that either the sultan was truly building castles in the air, or he was attempting to seduce the French by dangling some tempting carrots before their eyes.

Tipu had even more peculiar demands to make of his embassy. He instructed the delegates, 'Twelve eunuchs of nine or ten years, of the Abyssinian race or any other, should be purchased and brought back.'[66] He also ordered, 'Five or six fair-faced [slave] girls from among Turks, Arabs, or Mughals, should also be brought, after paying whatever amount has to be expended [in making their purchase].'[67]

A *hukumnama* issued on 17 November 1785 instructed the ambassadors on what representations to make before the king of France. They were advised to tell the king that Haider Ali had once written a letter to Souillac, the governor of Mauritius, stating:

> For six or seven years the British had occupied Pondicherry and expelled the French. For meeting the old obligations of the bonds of unity that exist with the King of France, we had waged war with the English for one year. We captured and killed many of them. If your army also arrives, we will capture Pondicherry and hand it over to you, and inflict on your enemies a severe punishment.[68]

The ambassadors were instructed to explain that 'upon receipt of this letter, Monsieur Souillac sent Monsieur [de] Suffrein, the admiral, with ten war-ships, and Monsieur Duchemin with 2000 Europeans. On learning of their arrival, our master [Haider] captured the fort of Cuddalore, Mahmud Bandar and other places'.[69] While informing the French monarch that lakhs of Mysoreans had 'tasted the cup of martyrdom in the war', they were to appeal to him that some ships be sent immediately 'so that the fort of Chennapattan could be captured soon and handed over to the French'.[70] Tipu also stated, '*Our master wrote many times to Monsieur Souillac* that the entire country of the Carnatic has come under the control of this Government, and just one fort, that of Chennapattan, remains' (emphasis added).[71] If this statement is true, then Haider Ali had also sought help not merely from the French in India but also from France and Mauritius.

## The 'Tiger' of Mysore

Buchanan describes Tipu's persecution of Hindus, alleging he seized their wealth, women and children. The atrocities are described in detail: 'The ancient government of this country was at last completely destroyed, and anarchy was introduced... During this period of total anarchy the number of Moplays was greatly increased, multitudes of Hindus were circumcised by force, and many of the lower orders were converted.'[72]

Buchanan implies that Haider Ali was more lenient in his treatment of Hindus. However, his assessment is not entirely accurate. Haider Ali also conducted conversions, as attested by the case of the English sailor James Scurry, who became 'Shum Sher Cawn', and the documented history of Velluva Kammaran Nambiar, who became Ayaz Khan. It was just that Tipu's brutality eventually eclipsed the sins of his father.

The Second Anglo–Mysore War concluded in 1784 with both sides agreeing to restore the status quo ante bellum. Thus, Malabar and Coorg once again came under the control of Tipu Sultan. In the following years, he conducted frequent raids into Malabar, leaving destruction in his wake. In 1784, he ordered the destruction of the pepper vines. In 1788, he virtually destroyed Calicut and terrorized the common folk, including the Mappilas. That same year, he issued his infamous 'Order of Extermination', calling for the genocide of Nairs.

In December 1789, Tipu Sultan attempted to breach the Travancore Lines in a failed attempt to invade Travancore. Despite laying siege to the fortifications, he only succeeded to effect a breach, allowing his forces to move into the territory of the Nairs. However, in the ensuing pitched battle, Tipu injured his leg and was forced to beat a hasty retreat during which he lost his sword, seal, red cap and green banner. Following this, he camped on the outskirts of the fortifications for three and a half months.

When Tipu breached the Travancore Lines again in April 1790, the British came to the defence of their southern ally, sparking the Third Anglo–Mysore War. The Mysore army initially enjoyed some success near Cochin. However, in December 1790, Tipu suffered a decisive defeat at the Battle of Tirurangadi (near Calicut), and the Mysore–Ali Raja alliance was routed at Cannanore.

In March 1791, Cornwallis captured Bangalore. Srirangapatna was attacked in February 1792. After three weeks of resistance, Tipu sued for peace. He ceded half of his territories, including Malabar, to the British and handed over two of his minor sons as hostages. The Treaty of Seringapatam marked a tragic defeat for the 'Tiger' of Mysore. It is significant that he did not go down fighting but instead chose to accept the humiliating terms.

Tipu Sultan had lost nearly all that his father had gained, yet he persisted in seeking foreign allies to aid him in his struggles against the British. He sought help from France, Mauritius, Afghanistan and Turkey.

The British soon resolved to eliminate Tipu. The Fourth Anglo–Mysore War began in 1799 with the Marathas and the nizam of Hyderabad aligned on the British side. The siege of Srirangapatna on 4 May 1799 concluded within a couple of hours. Tipu's body was discovered inside the fort amid a heap of corpses.

Brittlebank analyses Tipu's intentions as follows:

> It is pure romanticism to think that Tipu would have preferred to go down fighting rather than surrender – if that had been the case, he would have done so at the end of the Third Anglo Mysore War; instead, he chose to sign a treaty with his foe.[73]

She is spot on. The truth is that even in 1799, Tipu did try to negotiate. He was not inclined to go down fighting. However, Richard Wellesley, the belligerent governor-general, refused to negotiate. Wellesley did not want peace; he wanted Tipu's head.

## Maratha Neighbours and a Rare Gem

During the reign of the Mysore sultans, the Marathas were the most powerful indigenous force. They had surpassed the Mughals in strength and extended their influence into the far north and the deep south. In the northwest, they conquered Peshawar after defeating the Afghans in May 1758. The Mughal emperor found himself virtually under the protection of the Marathas. (A century later, a Maratha woman named Manikarnika would gain eternal fame as Lakshmibai, rani of Jhansi, through her valiant defence of her husband's kingdom and her eventual martyrdom.)

The 17th century witnessed the meteoric rise of the Marathas. In the far south, Shivaji Bhonsle captured the Vellore Fort in 1676, just a few years before his death. Shivaji's half-brother Venkoji (or Ekoji) became the first Bhonsle ruler of Thanjavur. The Marathas ruled Thanjavur until 1855 when the British finally annexed it under Dalhousie's infamous Doctrine of Lapse.

The Maratha empire formally commenced with the crowning of Chhatrapati Shivaji in 1674, flourished for a century and a half, and ended with the defeat of Peshwa Baji Rao II in 1818. However, its origin can be traced back to 1645 when a teenaged Shivaji, along with a small group of young Mavalas, swore a solemn oath to pursue the goal of Swarajya. At that time, Shivaji's father, Shahaji, was working for the Adilshahi sultan of Bijapur. The Mughal emperor Shahjahan ruled in Delhi, while his son Aurangzeb held many of the forts in the region of present-day Maharashtra. In 1646, Shivaji led a guerrilla force to capture the Prachandagad Fort, which he later renamed Torna. In 1658, Aurangzeb ascended the Mughal throne, imprisoning his father and murdering three of his brothers, including Dara Shikoh, the heir apparent.

The Marathas had been in power for nearly a century when Haider Ali rose to prominence in the early 1760s. They would retain power for barely two decades after the death of Tipu Sultan. It was in November 1659 that Shivaji killed Afzal Khan at Pratapgad and routed the army of the Bijapur sultan. Since then, the Marathas gradually extended their domains. However, in 1665, they were defeated by the Mughals at Purandar Fort and had to sue for peace, surrendering twenty-three forts and paying tribute. In 1666, Aurangzeb invited Shivaji to Agra and arrested him on arrival, but Shivaji managed to make a daring escape, concealed in a basket of sweets. When Shivaji died in 1680, the Marathas were a force to be reckoned with.

The Marathas suffered some setbacks during the rule of Sambhaji, the son of Shivaji. Aurangzeb shifted his base to the Deccan soon after the death of Shivaji and remained at Aurangabad for twenty-seven years until his death in 1707 at the ripe old age of eighty-eight. In 1689, Sambhaji was captured by Aurangzeb's forces and tortured to death. His wife Yesubai and his son Shahuji were imprisoned. Sambhaji's half-brother, Rajaram, was anointed as the new ruler, but he was constrained to escape farther south to the Tamil country, while his wife Tarabai ably ruled the kingdom. Soon after his return in 1700, Rajaram contracted a fever and died. Seven years later, when Aurangzeb died, Shahuji was released from prison and returned to take over the throne of the Marathas. Balaji Vishwanath Bhat, a Chitpavan Brahmin, became the peshwa. Tarabai shifted her base to Kolhapur along with her son. The age of the peshwas had begun.

Balaji Viswanath soon re-established Maratha power in the Deccan, despite the internecine conflicts and intrigues within the Maratha camp. After his death in 1720, his twenty-year-old son, Baji Rao I, became peshwa. He reigned for about twenty years and fought forty-one battles. In 1728, he defeated the nizam at Palkhed near Aurangabad.

In 1737, Baji Rao I conquered Delhi. In 1739, the Marathas under Chimaji Appa, brother of the peshwa, defeated the Portuguese at Vasai (Battle of Bassein). This region, which included present-day Mumbai, had been held by the Portuguese since 1534 when they acquired it from Bahadur Shah, the ruler of Gujarat. Thus, the Maratha victory at Vasai was hailed as a historic event. When Baji Rao I died, he was succeeded by his son Balaji Baji Rao or Nana Saheb I. Between 1741 and 1748, the Marathas undertook six expeditions into the prosperous Bengal region, each time returning with substantial loot. They annexed Orissa and extracted tribute from the nawab of Bengal. When the Afghan chieftain Ahmed Shah Abdali captured Attock, Multan and Peshawar in 1756, the Marathas under Raghunath Rao and Shamsher Bahadur (son of Baji Rao I and Mastani, the daughter of Raja Chhatrasal of Bundelkhand by a Persian concubine) launched a surprise attack causing him to abandon all the forts and retreat.

In 1761, the Marathas suffered a significant setback due to their defeat at the hands of the Afghans at Panipat. As a result, they lost control of Delhi, and it took them another decade to regain it. Mahadji Shinde (Shindia or Scindia) accomplished this feat with the assistance of the French military adventurer, Benoit de Boigne. In 1772, they sacked Rohilkhand to punish the Afghan Rohillas, who had supported the Afghans at Panipat a decade earlier. In 1775, the Marathas emerged victorious in the First Anglo-Maratha War. In 1783, Mahadji Shinde conquered the Gwalior Fort.

Sadashivrao 'Bhau' was the son of Chimaji Appa, the gallant brother of the peshwa. He lost his mother in infancy and his father when he was only ten years old. He grew up at Satara in the company of his cousins Shamsher Bahadur and Raghunath Rao under the tutelage of his aunt Kashibai (the first wife of Baji Rao I) and his grandmother Radhabai. Sadashiv Rao won his first battle in 1747 at the age of seventeen against the nizam's forces at Udgiri with the help of Raghunath Rao and Shamsher Bahadur. In 1760, he recaptured Delhi, which was then held by Najib-ud-Daulah of the Rohilla clan. Najib escaped to Kandahar and sought the aid of Ahmed Shah Abdali.

In 1761, as Haider Ali seized power in Mysore, the Afghans invaded Hindustan and clashed with the Marathas at Panipat. Leading the Maratha army was Sadashivrao Bhau. Among the warriors were the peshwa's eighteen-year-old son, Vishwasrao, along with Jankoji Shinde, Malharrao Holkar, Yeshwantrao Pawar, Sardar Nimbalkar, Shamsher Bahadur and several other stalwarts. The Jat chieftain, Surajmal, joined the Marathas, while the nawab of Awadh, Shuja-ud-Daulah, chose to support the Afghans. The battle was fast and fierce, resulting in heavy losses on both sides. Najib-ud-Daulah was killed, and the young Vishwasrao was felled by a stray bullet. Shamsher Bahadur and Jankoji Shinde were badly wounded. In the face of adversity, Sadashivrao Bhau ordered Malharrao Holkar to retreat to Pune with the women and camp followers. He and his brave warriors fought valiantly and attained martyrdom. Their bodies were never found. Shamsher Bahadur, the brave son of Mastani, succumbed to his wounds, while Jankoji Shinde was captured and tortured to death by the nawab of Awadh. The peshwa soon died of grief.

Abdali hurried back to his country upon receiving intelligence that his brother had captured Kandahar in his absence. Later, he wrote to the peshwa expressing his deep anguish at the latter's loss and stating that he would never come to Hindustan again. Years later, his grandson, Zaman Shah, would make an unsuccessful foray into Hindustan at the behest of Tipu Sultan.

Despite the setback at Panipat, the Marathas quickly regained their lost glory. Haider Ali had by now firmed up his hold on Mysore, the British were rapidly expanding their sphere of influence and the nizam was attempting to reclaim his lost territories.

Peshwa Nana Sahib was succeeded by his sixteen-year-old son Madhav Rao.

Peshwa Madhav Rao soon defeated Haider Ali's forces and captured Dharwar. The Marathas pursued the usurper of Mysore, who fled before them. Haider Ali was defeated at Rattihalli. Thereafter, they pursued him to his newly conquered kingdom of Bidanur. Haider Ali bought peace by relinquishing a large portion of his treasure. Between 1764 and 1777, the Marathas sought revenge on all their enemies, launching attacks on Bundelkhand, Rohilkhand and other territories in the north while also expanding their power southwards. In the region of the Tungabhadra, they met the forces of Haider Ali once again. Gopal Rao led the Maratha forces, and Haider Ali was forced to retreat. However, news arrived that the young peshwa was seriously ill. The battle was hurriedly concluded, with Haider Ali agreeing to pay tribute, and the Maratha army returning to Pune. Peshwa Madhav Rao died in 1772 at the age of twenty-seven, and his widow Ramabai committed sati. (Earlier, in 1680, three wives of Chhatrapati Shivaji had burned themselves on his funeral pyre.) Madhav Rao's brother, Narayanrao, was made peshwa, but he was assassinated the following year, and his infant son, Sawai Madhav Rao, was named peshwa. Nana Phadnavis was chosen as the regent.

Fortune favoured the Marathas in 1782, when they won the First Anglo-Maratha War, with Nana Phadnavis and Mahadji Shinde leading the charge.

As explained earlier, Haider Ali had several conflicts with the Marathas in his struggle for supremacy in southern India. While he did manage to capture some of their domains, most of the time he preferred to buy them off rather than engage in direct conflict. When he did fight, he was mostly unsuccessful. In 1767, he was defeated by Madhav Rao I at Sira and Madhugiri. Madhav Rao also released Rani Virammaji from prison, whom Haider Ai had imprisoned in 1763. At the time of his death, Haider was paying tribute to the Marathas, and the latter soon demanded the arrears from Tipu Sultan. Between 1785 and 1787, the Marathas and the Mysoreans waged war. The Marathas under Tukoji Rao Holkar defeated Tipu Sultan at Gajendragad.

In 1788, when the Rohilla chieftain, Ghulam Kadir, took over Delhi and blinded Emperor Shah Alam II, Mahadji Shinde was quick to exact revenge. The Marathas attacked and captured Delhi, reinstating the blind emperor, but the Rohilla chief managed to escape. However, the Marathas tracked him down and imprisoned him. Shah Alam II then wrote to Mahadji asking for the eyes of Ghulam Kadir, whom he had once treated as his own son. Mahadji gladly obliged and included the traitor's nose and ears for good measure. Thereafter, Ghulam Kadir's hands and feet were hacked off, and he was finally hanged from a tree in March 1789.

In June 1790, the Marathas achieved a decisive victory over the kingdoms of Jaipur and Jodhpur at the Battle of Patan. Marwar was also captured a few months later. In 1791, under the leadership of the seventeen-year-old Peshwa Sawai Madhav Rao and other generals, the Marathas defeated the Mysore army and captured Tipu's general, Mushramulk Khan. Later, Tipu himself was defeated by the Marathas.

In 1791, the Marathas also raided the Sringeri Mutt, said to have been consecrated by Adi Shankaracharya himself, and looted its possessions, prompting the head priest to appeal to Tipu Sultan for help. Tipu ordered the governor of Bidanur to provide funds to the swami for the restoration of the mutt. About thirty letters written in Kannada and exchanged between the sultan and the Sringeri Shankaracharya have been found. The letters reveal that Tipu had made several grants to the temple over the years. Here we have an example of a Hindu army looting the temple of Goddess Sharada and a Muslim ruler paying to restore it. This incident is often cited by scholars who wish to establish that Tipu Sultan was truly secular and non-partisan. However, this portrayal is far from the truth, as one cannot ignore Tipu's diabolic interventions in other temples.

In 1795, the nizam's forces suffered a crushing defeat at the hands of the Marathas in the Battle of Kharda. The same year, the peshwa died under mysterious circumstances. Nevertheless, despite severe odds, Nana Phadnavis and Mahadji Shinde continued to keep the

Marathas united. After the fall of Tipu Sultan in 1799, the British turned their attention to eliminating the Marathas.

The Second Anglo-Maratha War in 1803 weakened the Maratha confederacy as it resulted in significant territorial losses to the British. The Third Anglo-Maratha War commenced in November 1817. The peshwa was defeated at Pune and fled to Koregaon, where he faced another defeat. Subsequently, he moved from place to place to evade capture, finally surrendering on 3 June 1818. He was offered a generous pension and exiled to Bithur, near Kanpur. His territories were annexed by the East India Company and incorporated into the Bombay Presidency. While Kolhapur and Satara remained under Maratha rulers, Gwalior, Indore and Nagpur became British protectorates.

During the final conflict with the Marathas, the British managed to loot the 89-carat Nassak Diamond (also known as the Eye of the Idol) that belonged to the Trimbakeswar Shiva Temple in the Nasik district. Mined in the 15th century in the Kollur Mines of Golconda state, the gem was set in the idol, probably by the year 1500. (The Kohinoor and the Darya-i-Nur were products of the same diamond mines.) Col J. Briggs is said to have 'acquired' the Nassak Diamond from Peshwa Baji Rao II and faithfully handed it over to his superiors. The gem was taken to London by Warren Hastings. It was promptly sold to British jewellers and soon ended up as an adornment in the sword of one of the nobles. In 1927, it made its way to America. Thereafter, it changed hands many times and now resides in a private museum in Lebanon. It is said to be owned by a Lebanese financier, and its current weight is approximately 43 carats. The Trimbakeswar Temple Trust had demanded the return of the stolen diamond. Lebanon is presently embroiled in a war with Israel, and the fate of the Nassak Diamond hangs in the balance.

A *New York Times* report on 23 March 1927 states, 'It was purchased [by the Parisian jeweller George Mauboussin] from the Duke of Westminster and is one of the jewels brought back to England from India by Warren Hastings, thc manner of whose conquests led to his famous impeachment trial.'[74] When this report was published, India was still a British colony. Predictably, the Americans described it as looted material. Two years later, the jeweller's establishment was looted by burglars, but strangely the Nassak Diamond was overlooked.[75] In April 1970, when the gem was up for auction once again, the *New York Times* reported:

> The story that enhances the brilliance and size is that, centuries ago, it was set in an eye of a Hindu statue that stood in a cave temple at Nassak, India, near Bombay. Covetous local nabobs are said to have stolen the diamond in the 18th century, but they, in turn, lost it to the British army in 1818.[76]

Interestingly, the extraction of the jewel from the idol is attributed to 'covetous local nabobs'. For the British, it was war booty; in other words, it was considered legitimate plunder.

## Afghan Brothers and Other Gems

The Afghan strongman Ahmad Shah Durrani (also known as Abdali) rose to power after the assassination of Nadir Shah of Persia and founded the modern state of Afghanistan in 1747. He invaded India eight times in the next two decades. In 1756–1757, during his fourth invasion, he was accompanied by his son Timur Shah Durrani. Together, they captured Lahore, Mathura and Delhi, and arranged strategic matrimonial alliances for themselves with the family of the Mughal emperor. Timur Shah married the daughter of Alamgir II. On his return, Ahmed Shah captured Amritsar and sacked the Golden Temple. Punjab, Sindh and Kashmir fell into Afghan hands. The fifth Afghan invasion in 1759 was fended off by the combined armies of the Sikhs and the Marathas.

In January 1761, when the Afghans and the Marathas clashed at the Third Battle of Panipat, heavy casualties were incurred on both sides. Ahmed Shah achieved a Pyrrhic victory and subsequently left India forever. The Sikhs quickly rose to prominence, and by 1764, they had driven the Afghans out of Punjab and Peshawar. Ahmad Shah passed away, and Timur Shah ascended the throne. Following Timur Shah's death in 1793, his son Zaman Shah succeeded him.

In *Return of a King*, William Dalrymple states, 'In 1797, Shah Zaman, like his father and grandfather before him, decided to revive his fortunes and fill his treasuries by ordering a full-scale invasion of Hindustan – the time-honoured Afghan solution to cash crises.'[77] Nothing came of the invasion, however. The British had received intelligence regarding Zaman's plans, and they resorted to stratagem, instigating a Persian invasion on his western front, and compelling him to march in a haste to Herat. When Zaman Shah retreated from Punjab in 1799, he gave control of Lahore and the surrounding regions to a nineteen-year-old Sikh, Ranjit Singh.[78] This man would grow in power and stature over the next forty years and come to be hailed as the 'Lion of Punjab'.

Zaman Shah lost power in 1800 and was captured and blinded by his enemies. Shortly before his blinding, he hid the Koh-i-Nur Diamond in a crack in the wall of his prison cell. A decade later, he revealed the secret to his younger brother, Shah Shuja, who dispatched a mission to find the missing heirloom.[79] Zaman Shah had inherited the gem from his grandfather, Ahmed Shah Abdali, who had acquired it sometime after Nadir Shah's assassination in 1747.

A decade after its disappearance, the invaluable gem was found being used as a paperweight. Years later, as Shah Shuja wandered in exile and ended up in a prison in Kashmir, his wife, Wafa Begum, promised Maharaja Ranjit Singh the Koh-i-Nur Diamond in exchange for freeing her husband from his enemies. In 1813, Shah Shuja was liberated by a Sikh expedition to Kashmir, brought to Lahore and placed under house arrest. Ranjit Singh now demanded the Koh-i-Nur Diamond. It is said that he placed Shuja in a cage and tortured his eldest son in his presence to obtain the gem.[80] Later, he seized the remaining treasures, including the Timur Ruby and the Darya-i-Nur. Shah Shuja remained in incarceration. However, in 1816, he managed to escape to Ludhiana, which was then a British outpost. Shuja attempted now and then to recapture his lost kingdom, which he had briefly ruled between 1803 and 1809. But he was singularly unlucky and destined to remain powerless until 1839 when the British installed him on the throne of Afghanistan.

He was assassinated in 1842. Two years later, Zaman Shah died in exile in Ludhiana at the ripe old age of seventy-seven.

Following the death of Ranjit Singh in 1839, the British compelled his minor son, Duleep Singh, by a clause inserted in the Treaty of Lahore, to pass on the Koh-i-Nur Diamond to Queen Victoria. In 1850, after a difficult voyage to Britain, the gem was formally presented to the queen by the deputy chairman of the East India Company. Today the Koh-i-Nur resides in London, and the Darya-i-Nur in Teheran. The Timur Ruby, actually a red spinel, is part of the British Crown jewels.

# 6

# FIGHTING THE ENGLISH

In the latter half of the 18th century, the British and the Mysore sultans engaged in four major conflicts. Tipu Sultan was involved in all of them. Haider Ali passed away during the Second Anglo–Mysore War, and Tipu continued the war until its resolution in 1784. The conclusion of the third war in 1792 resulted in Tipu losing half his territory, including the pepper-rich Malabar region. The fourth war ultimately led to his downfall.

Historians typically concentrate on the wars and overlook the periods of peace in between. There was an eleven-year hiatus (1769–1780) between the end of the first war and the outbreak of the second. What actions did Haider Ali undertake during this period of calm? Did he contribute to the well-being of his subjects? Did he commission any monuments, plant any saplings, dig any wells, improve the administration or bolster the economy? Regrettably, he did nothing of the sort.

During the interregnum between the two wars, Haider Ali engaged in conflicts with the Marathas and suppressed revolts and rebellions in the conquered areas such as Malabar and Coorg. This period witnessed four major battles, multiple skirmishes and frequent confrontations between Mysore and the Marathas. Exchange of money and territories occurred, temporarily quelling the thirst for blood.

Following the conclusion of the Second Anglo–Mysore War in 1784, Tipu Sultan remained active. He fought the Marathas and other adversaries, ravaged Calicut and breached the Travancore Lines.

Between 1790 and1792, he fought the Third Anglo–Mysore War. After his defeat in 1792, Tipu grew increasingly paranoid and tried to involve various foreigners in his domestic conflicts. Eventually, the British decided to eliminate him and, in 1799, they marched on Srirangapatna, together with the nizam and the Marathas. Tipu died an ignominious death, killed by an unknown soldier. Despite having numerous children and a vast retinue of courtiers, it was the invading British who discovered and identified his body.

## The First Anglo–Mysore War (1767–1769)

In 1761, Haider Ali seized Mysore, followed by Bidanur in 1763 and Malabar in 1766. Meanwhile, the British controlled Madras and Bengal, besides Bombay, which had been gifted to them a century prior by the Portuguese, along with Tangiers in Morocco, as part of the dowry of Catherine of Braganza when she was married to Charles II of Britain.

In the 1760s, Mir Nizam Ali Khan took control as the nizam of Hyderabad. The coastal belt of Andhra and Odisha, referred to as the Northern Circars, was under French control until 1758 when it reverted to the nizam. Initially, the British proposed paying rent for the territory, but the nizam rejected the offer. Subsequently, Robert Clive appealed to the Mughal Emperor Shah Alam II, who, despite lacking authority over the region, issued a decree in August 1765 granting the East India Company full rights to the Northern Circars. When the British began occupying the region in March 1766, the nizam raised objections. However, faced with a series of threatening letters and considering his precarious financial position, he signed a treaty with the British in November, relinquishing four out of the five districts to the company. In return, the British agreed to provide troops to the nizam whenever he requisitioned them.

Prior to these events, the nizam and peshwa Madhav Rao had been collaborating to address the perceived threat posed by Haider Ali to their dominions. Haider Ali harboured resentment towards the British due to their establishment of a garrison in Vellore Fort and rejection of his offers of friendship. The Nawab of the Carnatic (Arcot) maintained an alliance with the British. Haider Ali joined hands with some of the adversaries of the Nawab, including his own brother. The stage was set for a mighty confrontation.

In January 1767, the Marathas launched an invasion of Mysore from the north. When they reached the banks of the Tungabhadra River, Haider Ali sought peace, offering to pay 35 lakh rupees if they would withdraw to the banks of the Krishna River. By March, the Marathas withdrew after receiving half of the agreed amount upfront, and the district of Kolar was pledged to ensure payment of the remaining balance. The outstanding amount was settled soon afterward.

On 11 June 1767, Haider sent Tipu, accompanied by Mahfuz Khan and Mir Ali Raza, to the nizam 'with five elephants, ten beautiful horses, and cash and jewels as presents for him'.[1] A few days later, Tipu received his initial nominal command and was sent to Madras, escorted by Makhdum Sahib and other trusted individuals. They initially set out to plunder San Thome but were soon informed of Haidar's defeat at Thiruvannamalai in the South Arcot district of Tamil Nadu. Tipu quickly joined his father's army near Vaniyambadi.[2] Subsequently, months of intermittent fighting and waiting ensued.

Haider Ali and the nizam began negotiating a clandestine alliance, with Haider agreeing to give 18 lakh rupees to the nizam. In return, the nizam agreed to recognize Tipu as the Nawab of the Carnatic once the region was captured by Haider's troops. Sometime in 1767, they launched a joint attack on the British but were defeated near the fort of Changama by Col Joseph Smith. The next battle occurred at Tiruvannamalai, where the combined forces of Col Wood and Col Smith routed the forces of Haider Ali and the nizam in September 1767.[3] However, after the rains ceased, Haider recaptured Tirupatur and Vaniyambadi and besieged Ambur Fort. Captain Calvert defended the fort until reinforcements arrived from Vellore. Subsequently, the English attacked Vaniyambadi, forcing Haider to retreat. When a large convoy with supplies for the

English arrived, Haider attacked it at Singarapetta, resulting in the loss of several of his officers. According to Bowring, Haider's horse was shot from under him, and he narrowly escaped with his life.[4]

Soon after, the nizam and Haider Ali's alliance deteriorated, leading the nizam to forge a new treaty with the British in 1768. Although Haider tried to negotiate peace with the British, his efforts were rebuffed. Subsequently, British forces marched along India's west coast to seize control of Malabar. The Mysorean navy deserted en masse, allowing the British to quickly capture Mangalore. This prompted Haider Ali to abandon his campaign in the Carnatic and rush to Malabar. In December 1767, the teenage Tipu Sultan led an advance force to Mangalore at Haider's behest to reinforce Lutf Ali Beg. Forrest opines that Tipu and Beg realized their limited capacity to act independently, and 'they, therefore, sat down in front of Mangalore to await the arrival of Haidar Ali with his siege train'.[5] Hasan writes:

> On the 7th [March 1768] there was a skirmish, but Tipu avoided giving battle and retreated. He attacked the English on the 15th and the 16th, but was repulsed. On May 2, however, he succeeded in capturing the bazaar of Mangalore but failed in his attempt to capture the fort.[6]

In April 1768, Haider reached Bidanur and hurriedly recruited 20,000 peasants through his local governors. Forrest notes, 'Armed with dummy muskets of ebony, and with a black, white, or yellow flag flying over every 1,000 men they marched upon Mangalore.'[7] The British, deceived by this display, hastily boarded their ships and decamped, leaving behind their sick, wounded, stores and ammunition. Haider Ali took revenge on those left behind. Shortly after, small groups of men arrived at Tellicherry 'with their noses and ears missing, to the utter horror of the English factors'.[8] Thus, the Mysore army recaptured Mangalore and brutally punished the Nairs who had aided the British.

During this period, the British forces at Madras regained control of some territories recently captured by Haider Ali and advanced towards Dindigul, a long-standing stronghold of the Mysoreans. Concurrently, the Marathas made preparations to attack Bangalore, prompting Haider Ali to return to defend it. Facing the imminent Maratha threat, Haider resorted to desperate measures to counter their advance. Bowring mentions:

> Haidar resorted to the device of breaking down the embankments of the reservoirs, poisoning the wells, and driving away the miserable peasantry, so as to make the country a waste. But the Peshwa overcame all these obstacles and reached Sira, then held by Mir Ali Reza Khan, Haidar's brother-in-law, who treacherously surrendered the fort and deserted Haidar's cause, receiving in reward the district of Gurramkonda.[9]

Bowring reveals that fearing an attack on Bangalore, Haider 'sent off his family and treasure to the rock fortress of Savanadrug'.[10] Meanwhile, the nizam clandestinely reached out to the British and returned to Hyderabad to protect his capital.

In November 1768, the Mysorean army entered the Coimbatore district, seized Karur and proceeded to march on Erode. Subsequently, Erode surrendered, followed by Vaniyambadi and Kaveripuram. In January 1769, 'marking the direction of his course by a wide expansion of flaming villages, Haider descended by the banks of the Coleroon into the Tanjore country, accepting a contribution of rupees four lakhs from the Raja for sparing his country'.[11]

Haider Ali dispatched entire garrisons to languish in prison at Srirangapatna. Soon thereafter, he recaptured all the forts lost to the British during the conflict. He then advanced towards Madras, prompting the terrified British to seek peace. Although the initial peace talks failed and hostilities resumed, when Haider Ali reached St Thomas Mount, the British had no option but to negotiate peace. Haider demanded an offensive and defensive alliance, recognizing the need for British assistance to fend off the incessant attacks of the Marathas. Finally, on 29 March 1769, a treaty was signed, with both parties agreeing to support each other in case of an attack by a third party. The outcome was a return to the status quo ante bellum, with the exception that Haider Ali retained control of Karur.

## No 'No-War' Interregnum

The concept of 'peace' seemed absent from the destiny of the Mysore sultans. Their chosen path did not allow for it. When they were not fighting the British, they were battling the Marathas, the nizam of Hyderabad, the Nairs of Malabar, the Kodavas of Coorg and various other adversaries.

According to Stephen Chetti, the Marathas invaded Mysore on several occasions during the reign of the sultans. In 1757, Balaji Rao attacked Srirangapatna and squarely defeated Dalawai Nanjaraj, who was compelled to surrender a large portion of territory.[12] Gopal Rao Hari of Mirritch (Miraj) invaded Mysore in 1760. Buni Visaji Pandit invaded in 1761, while Madhav Rao made incursions in 1765, 1767 and 1770. Triambak Rao arrived in 1771, followed by Raghunath Rao in 1774, and Hari Pant Phurkia in 1776 and 1786. Parasuram Bhau ravaged Mysore territory in 1791 and 1792.[13]

In November 1769, eight months after the conclusion of the First Anglo–Mysore War, the Marathas attacked Mysore. Mohibbul Hasan states:

> Haidar wanted to avoid pitched battles; his policy was to harass the enemy and thus compel them to withdraw from his kingdom. Accordingly, Tipu was despatched to destroy forage, poison wells and tanks, and to persuade the people to retire from their villages into the neighbouring forts.[14]

'To kill the mouse, burn the house' may not be the most effective strategy. While destroying crops and water bodies might hinder the advance of an army, it also disrupts the livelihood of the populace. Without crops, who will till the soil, and where will the people get food?

As Haider prepared to confront the Marathas, he sought the help of the British in accordance with the March 1769 treaty. However, the British did not offer any assistance. Faced with the overwhelming

Maratha assault, Haider retreated to his capital, laying waste to the countryside as he went. As his position grew increasingly precarious, he sent a messenger to negotiate peace terms. Madhav Rao, in response, demanded 1 crore rupees and proceeded to occupy all the northern and eastern districts of the Mysore kingdom. After a three-month siege, he captured the Nijagal Fort, located 30 miles northeast of Bangalore, and 'ordered the noses and ears of all the survivors of the garrison to be cut off'.[15]

In 1770, Haider Ali faced several serious conflicts with the Marathas. In one battle, the Mysore army suffered a defeat, and Haider himself sustained wounds. De la Tour discloses that although he was not present at the scene of action, he received accounts of the events from a trusted confidante. According to these reports, 'Hyder Ali himself is wounded, and many of his friends slain, and among others, Ali Jami Khan, Nabob of Vendevachi [Vandavasi]. Almost all the troops threw down their arms.'[16] Haider Ali was lucky to escape with his life. De la Tour mentions, 'Hyder, after running the greatest risks, arrived at his camp with the entire loss of his army, artillery, baggage, ammunition, and colours.'[17] He further adds:

> Many French officers lately arrived were present at this battle simply as volunteers; they were almost all wounded and one was killed. M Hughel, who had formerly served Hyder as commander of the French cavalry from Pondicherry, was wounded, and afterwards died at Tranquebar in consequence of his wounds.[18]

De la Tour recounts a curious anecdote linked to this event. Mirza Ali Khan, the prodigal brother-in-law of Haider Ali, who had once betrayed him by surrendering Sira to the Marathas, later made amends by bringing a large force to assist Haider against the Marathas. However, the battle was lost, Haider was wounded, and Mirza was captured by the Marathas. Surprisingly, Mirza was released by Madhav Rao on condition that he swore an oath never to wage war against the Marathas again. Mirza readily took the oath and upon returning home, relinquished all his possessions to

Haider Ali and became a fakir. However, whenever Haider engaged in battles against anyone other than the Marathas, Mirza would take up arms and join his army.[19]

Tipu was stationed on the outskirts of Bidanur, anticipating a potential incursion from Poona. However, in February 1770, Haider Ali summoned him back as his own forces struggled to withstand the Maratha onslaught. On 5 March 1771, when the Mysore army retreated from Melkote to Srirangapatna, it was a virtual rout. Haider Ali led the retreating forces, while Tipu, positioned somewhere towards the rear of the army, could not be traced. A few days later, he reappeared at Srirangapatna disguised as a wandering fakir. Haider was reportedly furious at his son's perceived cowardice, but Tipu Sultan survived to fight another day. Wilks reports:

> Haider was dead drunk, Tipu was at the back with the baggage train, and the retreat was completely chaotic. When Tipu finally turned up in the morning, disguised as a fakir, Haider showered him with verbal abuse and even picked up a cane and beat him up.[20]

Luckily for Haider Ali, the Marathas did not press their advantage. Instead, they focussed on plundering Melkote, giving Haider time to reinforce his defences. Although Triambak Rao besieged Srirangapatna unsuccessfully, the Marathas remained in the area for a year, compelling Haider Ali to pay them off, as was customary. A sum of 30 lakh rupees was agreed upon, with 50 per cent of the amount paid in June 1772 upon the conclusion of peace, while some of the richest districts were offered as collateral. Once again, Tipu was dispatched to Bidanur, where he succeeded in capturing a large convoy arriving from Poona. This was perhaps the only gain made by the Mysore army during the two-year war with the Marathas.

Hasan observes, 'In July 1772, Haidar agreed to a humiliating peace with the Marathas.'[21] However, upon the death of Peshwa Madhav Rao in November, Haider promptly sent his son to recapture the territories occupied by the Marathas. 'Tipu first besieged Sira and captured it after a three-month siege. He then attacked Maddagiri (Madhugiri) which fell in four days.'[22]

By the beginning of 1774, Tipu had managed to recover the districts lost to the Marathas. Seeing the power struggle between Raghunath Rao (Raghuba) and Nana Phadnavis for the position of peshwa, Haider agreed to recognize the former, provided that the tribute payable to him was reduced to 6 lakh rupees.[23]

Bowring states, 'Shortly afterwards a serious insurrection broke out in Coorg, owing to the oppressive exactions of the Brahman officials whom Haidar had appointed to collect the revenue.'[24] However, Haider Ali quickly suppressed the rebellion and executed all the leaders involved. Subsequently, he sent an expedition to Bellary to support the *palayakkar* in his attempt to break free from allegiance to Basalat Jung. In response, Jung sent forces under M. Lally to attack Bellary. Haider, however, caught the attacking party off guard and seized the fort. Lally narrowly escaped. Haider then besieged Gooty, where Morari Rao surrendered after the water supply ran out. He was subsequently sent to the dreaded Kabbaladurga, where he met his end.

Bowring recounts how the Mysoreans ingeniously captured Dharwar through a well-thought-out strategy:

> A fictitious letter was sent to the commandant telling him that aid was coming to him from the Marathas. Haidar then dressed up some of his troops in the guise of Marathas and directed another detachment to attack them and fire at them with blank cartridges. The garrison, believing that the first-named body constituted the expected relief, admitted them into the fort, when they seized the commandant, disarmed the defenders of the place and took possession of it for Haidar.[25]

The *palayakkar* of Chitradurga, Madikeri Nayak, and his brave band of Bedars had become marked men ever since they helped Madhav Rao in his assault on the Nijagal Fort. Seeking revenge, Haider Ali laid siege to the fort. 'The siege was protracted for three months, the defenders constantly sallying out, and carrying back the heads of Haidar's soldiers as a propitiatory sacrifice to the goddess Kali.'[26] However, upon learning of the approaching Maratha army, Haider collected a ransom and lifted the siege. Thereafter, he confronted the Marathas at Raravi and emerged victorious. The Maratha army retreated, allowing Haider Ali to seize virtually all the territories between the Krishna and the Tungabhadra.[27]

Madhav Rao's uncle Raghuba, who had served as regent during his minority, greatly enhanced the power and prestige of the Marathas by defeating the Mughal emperor and wresting control of Delhi. However, after Madhav Rao ascended to the position of peshwa, Raghuba felt resentful of his inferior status. In November 1772, despite advice to the contrary from the nobles, Madhav Rao insisted on marching towards Delhi. However, he failed to achieve any substantial gains. Upon his return march to Poona, he was discovered assassinated in his tent in early 1773.[28]

Raghuba once again assumed the role of regent as Madhav Rao left behind only a minor son. However, public sentiment turned against him amid suspicions of his involvement in the assassination, prompting him to flee to Bombay. The British welcomed and induced him to sign a treaty relinquishing the fifth part of the revenue from all lands conferred upon the Marathas by Emperor Aurangzeb several decades earlier. Nevertheless, when the Maratha army surrounded Bombay, the governor capitulated and annulled the treaty in 1774.

Meanwhile, the British in Calcutta dispatched an army led by General Goddard, which advanced to the banks of the Indus. Goddard rejected the terms agreed upon by the Bombay governor, leading to the outbreak of war. While the Marathas were preoccupied, Haider managed to recapture many of the regions they had previously seized from him.[29] Wilks refers to 'Hyder's re-conquest of Malabar in 1773', indicating that he had lost control in the intervening period.[30]

In 1775, Haider wished to invade Travancore and sought permission from the Dutch for his troops to pass through their possessions in the Cochin region. Wilks notes:

> The refusal of this request, and the delay of a reply to his letter to the Supreme Government of Batavia, enraged him; and Sirdar Khan, with about ten thousand men, ravaged the country with fire and sword, and laid siege to the Dutch fort of Chetwa.[31]

When the Dutch navy captain Johan Splinter Stavorinus, who later authored *Voyages to the East Indies*, visited Cochin in 1776, he found the Dutch Company at war with Haider. According to Wilks, the Dutch received reinforcements from Ceylon in November 1776 and unsuccessfully attempted to relieve Chetwa, which eventually fell despite their best efforts. Thereafter, they confined themselves to Cranganore (Kodungallur) and Aiyakota. Wilks mentions, 'The kings, of Cochin and Travancore threw up strong and fortified lines on the opposite side of the river, in order to defend their lands from an irruption on that side.'[32] He also observes that the construction of the Travancore Lines took place in 1775.[33]

In January 1777, the long-awaited letter from Batavia (now Jakarta, Indonesia) arrived, together with gifts for Haider Ali. The Dutch at Cochin sent an envoy to deliver the gifts to Haider, who graciously accepted the gesture. He promptly declared that the ongoing conflict was the result of a misunderstanding. Wilks says, 'Stavorinus ascribes this unexpected facility, first, to his war with the Mahrattas, second, a revolt of the Nairs as well as Mappilas, and third, the improved state of the Travancore wall.'[34]

## The Second Anglo–Mysore War (1780–1784)

In July 1780, Haider Ali descended on the Carnatic with an army of 80,000 men. Hasan suggests the figure may have been as high as 90,000.[35] While various historians provide other figures, it is undisputed that Haider commanded a massive army. His soldiers burnt villages along their route and besieged forts in the North Arcot district. Responding to the threat, the British sent Col Hector Munro to Kanchipuram, while Col Bailley led a southern march from Guntur. Haider, abandoning the siege of Arcot, redirected his forces towards Kanchipuram and deployed Tipu to tackle Bailley's contingent in the north. Thus, the Second Anglo–Mysore War commenced.

France had declared war on Britain in 1778, and the British had responded by capturing Pondicherry in the same year. The following year, they had seized Mahe, the French port on the Malabar Coast, crucial for importing weapons and supplies for both the French armies and Haider Ali. Haider Ali's soldiers had assisted in the defence of Mahe. Now, facing a dilemma, he threatened to invade Arcot in retaliation, but the English stood firm and refused to be intimidated.

Muhammad Ali had alerted the British to Haider's intended invasion, but they had not made adequate preparations. It was not until Haider started ravaging villages near St Thomas Mount that the British hurriedly prepared for defence.

Basalat Jung had ceded the district of Guntur to the British, prompting them to send a detachment to march towards Adoni via Kadapa, a region then under Haider's control. Haider Ali acted swiftly and 'despatched troops, which ravaged the whole country up to Adoni, and stopped any further advance'.[36]

Britain lost its American colonies in 1776, shifting the focus of its strategic interests to India. So, Crown troops were sent from Britain to bolster the strength of the company's forces.

The British gained some initial success when Lieutenant Flint managed to capture and hold the fort of Wandiwash for the following six months. Bowring avers that Haider abandoned the siege of Arcot 'on August 29th [1780] on learning of the approach of a sizeable force under Hector Munro'.[37] In early September, Col Bailley's force from Guntur met an ignominious end near Pollilur as they were ambushed by Tipu while marching to join Munro. Bailley and 250 of his men were captured. Hasan notes that it was only after Haider Ali joined the attack that Bailley finally surrendered. Bowring states, 'Had it not been for the humane interposition of Lally and a French officer named Pimorin, it is probable that not a man would have escaped. Even as it was, 700 Europeans were killed.'[38] Among the prisoners was David Baird, who endured more than three years of imprisonment.[39] Nineteen years later, Baird would exact his revenge.

Bowring further states:

> Haidar is said to have sat in state after the battle to distribute rewards for the production of prisoners, and to enjoy the sights of the heads of the slain. Of those who were captured none were released; some of them died and others were put to death ... This disaster was the most fatal that had ever overtaken the British arms in India, and was commemorated at Seringapatam by an elaborate painting on the walls of the Dariya Daulat garden, where it is still to be seen.[40]

One hundred years later, Bowring, then chief commissioner of Mysore, saw the painting and rued the tragic fate of his countrymen.

In 1780, after the Pollilur fiasco, Col Munro retreated to Madras, disposing of his cannons in the water tank at Kanchipuram. Rather than targeting Madras, Haider Ali besieged Arcot and successfully captured it on 3 November. This gave the British ample time to reinforce their army at Madras and fortify their defences. British forces led by Sir Eyre Coote faced initial setbacks at Chidambaram but achieved three consecutive victories at Porto Novo, Pollilur and Sholingur. They also compelled Tipu to lift the siege of Wandiwash. However, a determined Tipu redirected his efforts towards besieging Vellore instead.

Sir Eyre Coote, a distinguished veteran of the British army, was advised by the governor-general to proceed to Madras in November 1780. Despite being over sixty at this time, Coote won a string of battles, including relieving Chingleput, occupying Karanguli and reaching Wandiwash to provide assistance to Flint, who had held out until then. Haider's forces abandoned the siege, and Coote experienced the satisfaction of liberating a fort that he had similarly relieved twenty-one years earlier. He then moved southward, reaching Mutipaliam near Porto Novo in July 1781. On 1 July 1781, Haider suffered a humiliating defeat at Porto Novo at the hands of

Eyre Coote.[41] Bowring avers that Haider was nearly captured on this occasion and lost 10,000 men in killed and wounded.[42] Coote proceeded to capture the village of Pollilur and then moved to relieve Vellore, which was on the verge of surrender. Haidar's army was driven back, resulting in an estimated loss of 5,000 men.[43]

Bowring notes:

> In order to procure supplies for the starving garrison of Vellore, Coote made an expedition into the territories of the petty chiefs of the Chittur district north of Vellore. But as Haidar had recently ravaged the country, owing to its defection from his cause, the relief derived from this source only amounted to provisions for six weeks, which Coote succeeded in throwing into the besieged fortress. Shortly afterwards he returned with his army to Madras.[44]

One cannot help but marvel at the ingenuity and fighting spirit of this elderly English gentleman.

In mid-September, Haidar proceeded to besiege Arcot. After six weeks, two breaches were created. On 31 October, Tipu and Maha Mirza Khan were ordered to launch a simultaneous assault. Tipu initially failed, but Maha Mirza Khan managed to enter the breach. Hasan notes, 'Tipu, thereupon, rallied his men and made a fresh attack. This time he succeeded and easily occupied the town.'[45]

As war erupted between Britain and the Netherlands in Europe in 1781, the British in India sought to conquer Dutch territories. In November 1781, they captured Nagapattinam, where 2,000 of Haider Ali's soldiers were fighting on the Dutch side. 'Colonel Braithwaite, then commanding a field force at Tanjore...not only drove Haidar's troops out of the town of Nagur but took by storm Negapatam itself.'[46] In December, Tipu managed to seize Chittoor from the British. At Annagudi near Tanjore on 18 February 1782, Tipu defeated Col Braithwaite and took the entire detachment as prisoners. Tipu now had 400 Europeans in his army, and Bowring asserts that the outcome of the encounter was decided by 'the gallantry of M. Lally, who led his French soldiers gallantly on, and made a desperate charge with the bayonet against the English square. The Mysore cavalry rushed in upon the broken square and destroyed the little English force.'[47] Tipu remained in the area until November, when he was ordered to march to Malabar.[48]

Hasan states:

> On February 8, 1782, Sardar Khan, who had invested Tellicherry, was defeated by Major Abington. He lost all his military equipment and was taken prisoner with about 1200 men. But he felt so ashamed of his defeat that he committed suicide soon after. The English followed up their victory by capturing the French fort of Mahe the next day, and Calicut on the 13th.[49]

Hearing of these losses, Haidar dispatched Makhdum Ali to Malabar. Meanwhile, Colonel Humberstone had been sent by the Bombay government to aid Major Abington at Tellicherry. On 7 April, Makhdum Ali was defeated and killed at Trikalur, near Calicut.[50] This was a major blow for Haider Ali.

The Treaty of Salbai was concluded on 17 May 1782 but was formally ratified by the peshwa only after Haider's death. 'It had the effect of severing the coalition between the Marathas and Haidar, who thus stood alone against the English.'[51]

Meanwhile, French troops landed at Porto Novo, and occupied Cuddalore and Permakoil, but their numbers did not exceed 1,200 Europeans, and M. de Bussy was unwilling to risk a general action until he could arrive with further reinforcements.[52] Coote advanced towards Wandiwash, while the Mysore forces moved towards Pondicherry. 'Coote determined to proceed to Arni, which from its central position was the chief depot which Haidar still held below the Ghats for storing his supplies and ammunition.'[53] Hearing of his approach, Haidar sent Tipu to strengthen Arni, and he followed soon thereafter. On 2 June 1782, Coote's army was attacked by Tipu and M. Lally as he was about to encamp near the fort.[54]

Bowring mentions, 'This was the last engagement in which Coote and Haidar encountered one another, and both of them died within a year.'[55] In this encounter, the English suffered heavy losses.

In August, the Bombay government dispatched a force under Colonel Humberstone to invade Malabar. He seized Calicut and advanced towards Palghat, capturing many minor forts along the way.

The northeast monsoon arrived, necessitating the cessation of hostilities. The English returned to Madras, the French retired to Cuddalore and Haidar encamped with his troops sixteen miles north of Arcot.

Tipu reached Palghat on 16 November. Discovering that Humberstone had already departed, he immediately set out in pursuit, reaching the Ponnani River on the evening of the 19th. The river was swollen, leading Tipu to presume that the Englishmen were trapped, but this assumption proved costly. They forded the river under cover of darkness and reached the town of Ponnani.[56] Soon after, Col Macleod arrived from Calicut with reinforcements, and Tipu and Lally blockaded the town. The British prepared for an inevitable assault, but were surprised when on 12 December, the Mysore army abruptly disappeared. Tipu had received news of his father's demise and was rushing to his capital to assume control of the kingdom.

According to Bowring, '[Haider] had for a long time suffered from cancer in his back, and the disease was aggravated by the fatigue incurred in his numerous campaigns...and he died in his camp at Narsingh Rayanapet, near Chittur, on Dec. 7, 1782.'[57]

Tipu arrived on the evening of 28 December and held discussions with key functionaries. The next morning, he conferred with his brother Karim Sahib and army chiefs. 'Then at 9 o'clock in the night, he sat on the throne of his father with all pomp and ceremony and assumed the title of Nawab Tipu Sultan Bahadur. His army saluted him with 121 guns and the French with 21.'[58]

Hasan states, 'He succeeded to a treasury at Seringapatam containing three crores of rupees, besides large quantities of jewels and valuables.'[59] There was also a large treasury at Bidanur, but it fell into the hands of the British after the capitulation of Ayaz Khan. Tipu also inherited a massive, well-trained army that was one of the best fighting forces in India.

Meanwhile, an English force under Brigadier General Richard Matthews had been dispatched from Bombay to reinforce the troops in Malabar. Upon receiving intelligence of Haider Ali's demise, the Bombay authorities issued peremptory orders to Matthews to seize Bidanur. 'Matthews landed at Kundapur, and in three days reached the foot of the Hosangadi Pass. The ascent from this to Haidargarh at the top of the ghat, a distance of about eight miles, is tremendously steep, rough, and stony.'[60]

Matthews was soon joined by Col Macleod from Ponnani. Tipu had to rush from the capital to Bidanur as the English had commenced their siege of the area.[61] Ayaz Khan 'sent an English prisoner named David Campbell, with a proposal to surrender not only the town and fort of Bednur but the whole province, provided he was allowed to retain its governorship as before'.[62] Matthews agreed, and Ayaz surrendered Bidanur on 28 January1783. With the fall of the capital, many other places in the vicinity also surrendered.

Soon after the English had taken control of Bidanur, Tipu managed to recapture it. Mathews and seventeen other Englishmen were taken prisoner and marched off to Srirangapatna, where they all suffered horrible deaths.

According to Bowring:

> [Tipu] had the mortification, however, to find the treasury empty. So irritated was he at this unexpected result that, although Matthews had capitulated on condition that his troops should be permitted to withdraw unmolested to the coast, the conqueror placed him, with many other officers and men, in irons, and sent the party to Seringapatam.[63]

Bristow reports that this triggered a wave of rejoicing in Srirangapatna but deepened the depression of the English prisoners. He reveals:

> Sugar and sweetmeats were carried about the town in baskets, and distributed to the inhabitants under the discharge of cannon. I do not recollect the spirits of the prisoners to be so much depressed at any one time during the whole of my captivity as on this

> mournful occasion.... To add acuteness to our distress, we were desired, or rather compelled to partake of the sweetmeats prepared for the rejoicings, and our positive refusal was construed into a stubbornness, which deserved correction.[64]

This culminated in a severe flogging. Bristow also reveals that Tipu unearthed a conspiracy to overthrow him and reinstall the Wodeyar on the throne. The Europeans were aware of the plot, and one of them divulged the information. All the suspects were sentenced to capital punishment, which included methods such as being dragged to death by elephants.

Bristow mentions,

> The inhuman murder of General Matthews, who was certainly poisoned in a very barbarous manner, being starved until he had consented to eat the food which he had discovered contained poison... He swallowed a plentiful portion of the victuals prepared for him, and a few hours after expired in violent convulsions.[65]

Bristow asserts his confidence in this fact, as he had conversed with the general's two European servants who were witnesses to the tragic event.[66]

In 1783, when news reached India that France and Britain had made peace, the French withdrew their support for Mysore.

Mangalore had fallen to the British in March 1783, but Tipu later recaptured the town, with the garrison surrendering after enduring a devastating bout of scurvy and starvation.

In the meantime, Fullarton moved to Palghat, which quickly surrendered. He then proceeded to capture Coimbatore.[67] Bowring presents the view:

> As his force consisted of 13,000 men, and as he himself was an officer of great ability and energy, it is probable that his junction with the British troops on the west coast would have led to a complete defeat of Tipu. But...the vigorous efforts of the English military commanders were paralyzed by the timidity and hesitation of the civil authorities at Madras.[68]

The Treaty of Mangalore was signed on 11 March 1784, as the Crown insisted that company officials should make peace with Mysore. The British commissioner travelled all the way from Madras to Mangalore seeking peace. Tipu was now in a position to dictate terms.

The outcome was status quo ante bellum. All parties withdrew to the territories they had held before the outbreak of hostilities. Therefore, the net gain for all parties involved in the conflict was zero. However, the net loss encompassed the thousands of soldiers who lost their lives, civilians who were killed, women who were enslaved, crops that were destroyed, buildings that were set on fire and lands and lives that were laid waste.

Tipu did not release all the prisoners as stipulated by the treaty. Bowring states:

> Indeed, the great majority of those who had suffered imprisonment had either perished from the hardships they endured or had met with a violent death at the hands of Tipu's executioners. Many of the English officers, besides General Matthews, had been ruthlessly murdered, by poison or other foul means, while natives of the country had been frequently sent to die at Kabaldrug.[69]

## The Third Anglo–Mysore War (1790–1792)

In the six-year gap between the second and third wars with the British, Tipu Sultan remained active. He engaged in battles against the Marathas and the nizam, beginning in 1785.

Tipu had been furious when the Travancore raja purchased the Dutch forts of Aiykota and Cranganore in the Cochin area and fortified his border with Cochin by constructing what later became known as the Travancore Lines (*Nedumkotta* in Malayalam).

Wilks notes that in 1775, Haider had requested the Dutch at Cochin to allow free passage of his troops through their territories to Travancore:

> The refusal of this request and the delay of a reply to his letter to the Supreme Government of Batavia [Dutch East Indies], enraged

> him; and Sirdar Khan with about ten thousand men, ravaged the country with fire and sword, and laid siege to the Dutch fort at Chetwa.[70]

It was at this precise juncture that the raja of Travancore purchased a strip of land from the Dutch on the island of Vypeen. 'The Dutch had shown a disposition to part with Ayacotta and Cranganore; and it was feared that they might even sell them to Tippoo, rather than incur the risk and expense of defending them.'[71] Wilks adds, 'The Sultan himself recognized the right of sale, by offering to the Dutch double the sum contracted to be paid by the Raja.'[72]

Lord Cornwallis assumed the role of governor-general of India in 1786. In 1788, the company gained control of Guntur, the southernmost district of the northern Circars, as stipulated by an earlier treaty with the nizam. In exchange, the nizam received two battalions of British troops. This strategic move facilitated easier access for British troops to the Mysore kingdom in the event of a conflict.

Travancore had been an ally of the British since Haider Ali invaded Malabar. The British had warned Tipu that any attack on Travancore would be considered a declaration of war against them. On 23 September 1789, Cornwallis wrote to the governor of Fort St George, 'But if you should receive certain information that Tippoo has invaded any part of the dominions of the Nabob of Arcot, or of the Rajah of Travancore, you are to consider him from that moment as at war with the Company.'[73]

In 1788, Tipu descended on Malabar and ravaged Calicut, disregarding that the majority of the town's population were Mappilas. The following year, he attacked other places in Malabar, causing a mass exodus of Hindus to Travancore. When Tipu demanded that the Travancore raja evict the Nair and Namboothiri refugees from his dominions, the raja politely refused. Tipu became incensed and began massing troops at Coimbatore in preparation for an assault on Travancore. Lieutenant Roderick Mackenzie, in his 1792 publication, cites the Travancore raja's communication to Sir Archibald Campbell on 8 June 1788:

> Should Tippoo take offence with me, who am the Company's firm friend and dependant, for writing such an answer, and raise hostilities against me on that account, I must look up to the Company for protection and assistance, as my only resource. From all circumstances of the conduct of Tippoo, and what has passed between him and the Rajah of Cochin, I am led to suspect, he will raise some troubles, I take the Almighty to witness, that, as long as I breathe, I shall never depart from my friendship to the Company, and I hope your Excellency will take care of me.[74]

Two weeks later, on 24 June 1788, Campbell wrote to Cornwallis, enclosing the transcript of Tipu's letter to the Travancore raja. He expressed his view that Tipu 'intended to usurp the territories of every independent Rajah in his neighbourhood, and if possible, to extirpate all the Europeans from the Peninsula'.[75]

In 1789, Tipu strengthened his alliance with the Arakkal Beevi of Cannanore and even betrothed his second son, Abdul Khaliq, to her daughter. It is highly unlikely that the actual nikah took place, as Abdul Khaliq was known to be a minor in 1792 when he was offered as a hostage to Lord Cornwallis at the close of the Third Anglo–Mysore War. He was said to be seven years younger than Fateh Haider, Tipu's eldest son by a concubine, who was born in 1771 or 1772. Thus, at the time of the betrothal, Abdul Khaliq would have been less than ten years old. Some authors suggest it was Fateh Haider who was betrothed to the Beevi's daughter.

Tipu wrote to Holland, the governor of Madras, on 11 November 1789, outlining three demands. First, he requested that the raja of Travancore surrender the princes and chieftains of Malabar who had sought refuge in his territory. Second, Tipu insisted that the raja vacate the fort of Cranganore, recently purchased from the Dutch, as Tipu argued it rightfully belonged to the Cochin raja, who was his tributary. Third, Holland was urged to prevail upon the raja to demolish the part of the Travancore Lines that ran through Cochin territory.

On 24 December 1789, Tipu reached Nedumkotta with a massive army. On that very day, the Travancore raja wrote to the governor, 'With respect to the Rajahs of Chirkul from the time that Hyder Ally-Cawn, carrying terror and destruction into their countries, subdued them; filled with fear and dread, they took protection with me here, as I stand in the relationship with them as a brother.'[76]

The Travancore forces under Kesava Pillai executed a strategic retreat across the Periyar, carefully regrouping to prevent the Mysorean army's attempt to cross the river. Nevertheless, on the night of 28 December, Tipu made an attempt to cross. His army suffered a humiliating defeat, losing their flag to the Nairs. Tipu himself sustained a leg injury and was forced to hastily withdraw, leaving behind his sword, cap and seal, much to the utter delight of the Travancore forces.

Wilks's description of the events is vivid:

> The panic [in Tipu's army] became general, and the confusion irretrievable. The Sultan, himself, was borne away in the crowd; the rear, now become the front, rushed into the intended road across the ditch ... the foremost leaped or were forced into the ditch; and such was the pressure of the succeeding mass, that there was no alternative but to follow. The undermost, of course, were trampled to death; and in a short time, the bodies, by which the ditch was nearly filled, enabled the remainder to pass over. The Sultan was precipitated with the rest, and was only saved by the exertions of some steady and active chelas, who raised him on their shoulders, and enabled him to ascend the counterscarp, after having twice fallen back in the attempt to clamber up; and the lameness, which occasionally continued until his death, was occasioned by the severe contusions he received on this occasion. His palankeen remained in the ditch, the bearers having been trodden to death, his seals, rings, and personal ornaments, fell as trophies into the hands of the enemy; and the fortune of a day, which was turned by 20 men [of Travancore], cost the Sultan's army upwards of two thousand.[77]

Bowring's account states that Tipu 'escaped with the greatest difficulty, through the exertions of some faithful servants, but lamed in the efforts he had made to save himself. In the hurly-burly he lost his sword and shield, which were taken away in triumph to Trivandrum (Thiruvananthapuram), the capital of Travancore'.[78] Bowring adds, 'The Sultan's panegyrist, Mir Hussen Ali Khan, ascribes this disaster to the Travancore troops having broken down a mound which had been erected to prevent the inroads of the sea, its destruction causing the tide to rush in.'[79]

Roderick Mackenzie explains, 'The Sultan at the head of ten thousand men, on the morning of the 29th December obtained Sharapootamally, a steep and rugged hill.'[80] It seems there was initially some laxity on the part of the Nairs, who were caught off guard by the attack at this juncture. However, they quickly regrouped, and approximately 800 men blocked the path of the aggressors. Mackenzie adds, 'A Chela battalion that led the enemy, exhausted by fatigue and want of water, could not be prevailed upon to charge this resolute phalanx. Another battalion, and another, was then ordered to advance; but the Nairs, by this time reinforced from Remiseram, stood firm as a rock. The Sultan pressed onward to the front with his best troops.'[81] A letter written by the Travancore resident George Powney to Cornwallis on 30 December mentions that the Travancore raja lost 200 men, while the sultan's forces suffered a loss of 1,000 men.

George Powney once more corresponded with Cornwallis on 4 January 1790: 'The conflict lasted four hours, when the enemy were repulsed with great slaughter. Tippoo himself was present, and had a horse shot under him.'[82]

The Mysoreans had filled the ditches with cotton, which inexplicably caught fire, adding to the casualties. Mackenzie states that no fewer than 1,500 individuals were killed. 'Amongst the dead, there were three men of high rank. The first is reported to have been an illegitimate son of the Sultan, and second in command.'[83]

Powney's letter to the governor on 10 January reveals:

> That he is wounded is corroborated by some Hircarrahs, who came from his Camp the night before last; they say, that Tippoo had been obliged to leap from the ramparts of the lines. As he had filled the ditch with bales of cotton at the place where his troops entered, and these had been set fire to. That in his fall he had been very much bruised and torn by a bamboo hedge which grows in the ditch. This account I think probable; others mention that he is wounded in the shoulder by a musket ball. The Hicarrahs likewise add that there was a general mourning in his camp on account of the death of his brother-in-law, Meer-o-Dein Cawn.[84]

In another letter to the governor three days later, Powney mentioned:

> Every account which has been brought in says, that he was wounded, in the attack, to which cause it is reasonable to ascribe his present inaction; that he was there himself is without doubt, as his Palanquin was left in the ditch, in which was a silver box, containing several valuable diamond rings and other jewels; his large seal, with his titles ... and likewise his sword.[85]

As expected, there are conflicting narratives regarding the specifics of Tipu's mode of transportation – some claim he rode a horse while others suggest he sat in a palanquin. However, all accounts agree on certain points – Tipu's defeat, the significant loss of life, his narrow escape and his injury. The only dissenting voice is that of the erudite Mohibbul Hasan.

Hasan puts forth the hypothesis that Tipu Sultan was not at the forefront of this disastrous assault on the Travancore Lines. By stating that the Travancore raja 'did not give up his policy of inciting rebellions in Malabar and extending protection to the rebels of his [Tipu's] kingdom', the author attempts to justify Tipu's unprovoked attack.[86] However, he acknowledges that the Mysoreans were routed and suffered heavy casualties. He expresses the following view:

> No reliable evidence exists to prove that Tipu was personally present during the attack by his troops upon the lines. He himself denied it; he even maintained that the engagement had taken place without his knowledge and that as soon as he heard of it he at once recalled his troops and sent back the Travancore prisoners of war to the Raja. It appears that the rumour of Tipu's narrow escape and his being wounded was spread by some *harcarahs* who claimed to have returned from Tipu's camp.[87]

Hasan concludes that the accounts provided by the spies are unreliable. Instead, he favours the version presented by Tipu Sultan in a letter to the British on 1 January 1790. However, the question arises how Tipu's personal effects fell into the hands of the Travancoreans if he had not participated in the attack. This fact is attested even by Kirmani, who was essentially a court chronicler of the Mysore sultans, not to mention several other contemporary authors.

Chetti recounts an interesting anecdote that circulated in Tipu's capital nearly one hundred years after his death:

> It is also said that one of the captive Christians, while serving as a personal attendant of Tipu Sultan accompanied him in one of his incursions into the Travancore territories. The Sultan was being carried in a palanquin when suddenly the enemy was seen to surround him. The Native Christian attendant then quickly persuaded his master to exchange his garments for those humbler ones of his own, and as the Sultan got down and effected his escape along with his other followers, the Christian servant took his seat in the palanquin. When the enemy approached, they mistook the Christian for the Sultan, and killed him on the spot.[88]

Tipu inflicted unimaginable cruelty upon the Christians of Mangalore. Surprisingly, despite being one of his victims, one individual willingly sacrificed his life to save the sultan from the wrath of the Travancore Nairs. This incident is not mentioned by any contemporary historians, but the rumour was circulating in Mysore several decades later.

Kirmani provides a detailed account of Tipu Sultan's defeat at the Travancore Lines. He attributes the victory to the kingdom of Kochi, though it was the Travancore army that defended the Lines. (He may be excused for his inability to distinguish between the two groups of 'infidels'.) Kirmani relates how Tipu, disregarding the advice of his commanders, opted to cross the river at night and breach the Travancore Lines, a feat he accomplished with around 2,000 horsemen. He says:

> All of a sudden the treacherous enemy finding this the critical moment for them to obtain the victory, cut down the mound which they had raised above in order to stop out the sea, and the tide rushing in with great violence filled up the rivers to the brim, and the road of succour and assistance to the advanced division of the Sultan's troops was cut off.[89]

In simple terms, it was a masterstroke by the Travancoreans, while the Mysoreans, led by their reckless sultan, had unwittingly fallen into a trap.

Kirmani further adds, 'The enemy attacked the Sultan's troops on all sides with arrows and musketry and caused [incalculable] distress and confusion among them.'[90] He recounts that 'three or four hundred brave horsemen...were all killed and wounded in front of the Sultan'.[91] Thereafter, Tipu's life was saved by one of his loyalists, Kamaruddin Khan, who 'took him out of his palki ... and caused him to be carried through the water to the opposite side of the river' to the safety of his army camp.[92] Kirmani adds, 'But of those present in that battle not one man ever returned safely to the presence. The Sultan's Palki with its bed, the great seal of the exchequer and a dagger were taken by the infidels.'[93] The revelation that Tipu was in a palanquin is intriguing. Was he wounded or was he simply lazy? The painting in the Kowdiar Palace in Thiruvananthapuram depicts Tipu Sultan lying on his back in a palanquin.

Kirmani does not mention that the flag also fell into the hands of the enemy. Judging by his description of the events, one can reasonably conclude that the account provided by the Travancore royals is trustworthy. Tipu did indeed lose his flag, cap, dagger and seal. In warfare, the loss of the flag symbolizes a significant defeat, underscoring the profound meaning behind the exhortation to soldiers to 'keep the flag flying'.

Kirmani was aware of the Nairs' claim to have seized the sultan's cap. He provided an elaborate description of how a footman in front of the palanquin was killed, and his cap fell into the palanquin and so on. This appears to be a desperate attempt to establish that it was not Tipu's cap. It seems highly unlikely that amidst a desperate battle, either Tipu or anyone else could have closely followed the trajectory of a footman's cap. In any case, Kirmani reveals that only Tipu Sultan and Kamaruddin Khan returned. 'The rest of the Khans, such as Turbeut Ali Khan, Muhammad Omra, Urzbegi, and Sayyed Khan, the Daroga of the treasury, were never after heard of.'[94]

This narrative clearly illustrates that Tipu had a narrow escape, while all his senior lieutenants were killed. Tipu embarked on the attack on the Travancore Lines not on horseback but while riding in his palanquin. His escape did not involve riding, running or swimming; instead, he was carried across the swirling waters by his attendants. Kirmani reveals that Tipu 'caused his drums to beat for victory [as if he had gained one]'.[95] Thus, the cunning nature of the sultan becomes evident. What is noteworthy is that this is not the prejudiced narrative of the British or the Nairs, who were sworn enemies of the Mysore sultans. It is the truthful account of a fellow Muslim.

James Bristow's memoir supplies an intriguing insight into the war: 'The intelligence of Tipu's repulse at the Travancore lines put a total stop to the immense preparations which for a time had engrossed the whole attention of the capital.'[96] The author adds that 'the loss of his great seal, turban, and palanquin, captured in the before-mentioned repulse, together with several valuable jewels, and the narrow escape of his own person' disheartened his supporters in the capital, while simultaneously unleashing a variety of rumours and speculations.[97] According to Bristow, 'He would certainly have fallen into his enemy's hands if a mean disguise had not protected him; the very bearers of his palanquin were cut down some moments after he had deserted it.'[98] This is similar to Chetti's version. Bristow elaborates:

> Tipu having thought proper to substitute another inscription on his new signet, this circumstance gave fresh alarms at Seringapatam, and many took it for granted the tyrant had either been killed or dethroned ... but the general anxiety dissipated when a new state palanquin was dispatched with great pomp.[99]

This constitutes clear evidence that Tipu did lose his signet ring and his palanquin during his assault on the Travancore Lines. Given that Bristow was a prisoner at Srirangapatna during this period and published his book in 1792, shortly after the peace treaty was signed, his testimony warrants serious consideration. Bristow further reports that 'on [Tipu's]return from this expedition, he brought a number of different sorts of guns, and a large quantity of sheet copper, of which he had stripped the domes of the Roman Catholic churches on the Malabar coast'.[100]

Following his setback in December, Tipu did not retreat but instead remained in the vicinity for months, biding his time for the right opportunity to launch another attack. Wilks explains:

> In a mixed paroxysm of rage and humiliation, he swore that he would remain fixed on that encampment until he should carry this contemptible wall. He accordingly ordered the recall of Burhan-u-Deen from Coorg, and of nearly the whole of his detachments for the conversion of the infidels from Malabar. Battering guns were to be brought from Seringapatam and Bangalore.[101]

Sandeep Balakrishna states that on 19 January 1790, Tipu wrote a letter to Budruz Zaman Khan, stating, 'I have achieved a great victory recently in Malabar and over four lakh Hindus are converted to Islam. I am now determined to march against the cursed Raman Nair.'[102] Here, Tipu was referring to Raja Karthika Thirunal Rama Varma of Travancore, whose troops had decisively defeated him only three weeks earlier. If Tipu had indeed written such a letter, he was likely exaggerating or fabricating his victory. Regarding the conversion of Hindus, he may have been lying or exaggerating as well. If the number of four lakh is inflated, then what was the true figure? Two lakh? One lakh? It is crucial to remember that Tipu was boasting about forcible religious conversion.

On 30 March 1790, Lord Cornwallis 'despatched, explicit instructions to the Madras Government not to allow a faithful ally to be overwhelmed by an insolent and cruel enemy'.[103] According to Bowring:

> [Tipu had provided Madras] a lame explanation of his attack upon the Lines, alleging that his troops were merely searching for fugitives, and had accidentally come into collision with the Travancore army. But he had no intention of desisting from his purpose, and ... he ordered siege guns to be despatched at once from Seringapatam, and recommenced the attack. Batteries were erected close to the defences in the early part of March. Yet although Tipu spoke with derision of the 'contemptible wall', nearly a month elapsed before the ramparts were destroyed. A breach being then effected, the Travancore troops were compelled to retreat, and Tipu directed the immediate demolition of the fortifications, sending off as spoil to his capital 200 pieces of cannon, and a vast quantity of ammunition.[104]

Despite heavy losses suffered by his army due to the determined resistance of the Nairs, Tipu was not one to give up easily. After all, warfare was his core competency.

Bowring further states:

> The Mysore army, flushed with success, now began to lay waste the country with fire and sword, desecrating and despoiling temples, and burning towns and villages, whose wretched inhabitants fled to the hills, where many were seized and made prisoners ... The ruins to be seen at the present day testify to the ferocity of the invaders, while all the records of antiquity and the archives of the Travancore State were consumed in the burning pagodas, public offices, and houses. These atrocities were perpetrated with the express sanction of Tipu Sultan, who himself marched with his main army southward to Alwai.[105]

A letter of 9 January 1790 from Van Angelback and Council to the British governor of Madras stated:

> Tipu pretends to say, that we have paid rent or tribute for Aycotta and Cranganore: this is an invention of his own, and a frivolous untruth. The Dutch East India Company in an open war became masters of those places, have retained the sovereignty over them, and have never paid for Aycotta or for Cranganore a single cash either to the Zamorin, or the Aumildars of Calicut, or to the King of Cochin, or to any other person; this is notorious, and the inhabitants in general of the Malabar Coast can vouch for it.[106]

Indeed, the Dutch had held these places for a significant 127 years. Mackenzie explains, '[The] Sultan, under the pretence that neither the Dutch had a right to sell, nor the Rajah to purchase Cranganore, without his consent, not only threatened to invade Travancore, but actually assembled fifteen thousand chosen men to put that threat in execution.'[107]

On 18 April, when the Mysore army appeared within a mile of Cranganore, the garrison fled. Two Madras battalions under Col Knox were stationed at Shandamagalam. On the 23rd, Col Hartley arrived with reinforcements from Bombay.[108] By 26 April, 'the Sultan ... made rapid progress with his approaches; and by the 7th of May, he had demolished the defences and silenced all the guns in the fort'.[109]

'Aycotta, Parur, Curiapilly, with various other inconsiderable forts, surrendered successively to the [sultan] without opposition.'[110] The repeated bombardment resulted in the destruction of Cranganore, and the surrounding countryside was left devastated. The Nairs sought refuge in the forests and mountains, while all cultivation came to a halt.[111]

Eventually, Tipu would pay a heavy price for his unprovoked assault on Travancore. He would not only lose the entirety of his Malabar territories but also a significant portion of his holdings in present-day Karnataka and Tamil Nadu.

Hearing that the British were regrouping at Trichinopoly, Tipu marched south, 'but finding the Coleroon river so swollen that to cross it would be impracticable, he changed his course. He proceeded due north through the heart of the Coromandel country, burning and destroying all the villages on the road, and exacting heavy contributions from the people'.[112]

While reconnoitring Dindigul, Captain Oram observed that it had undergone considerable repairs and improvements since the previous war.[113] He sent a messenger to the killedar, Hyder Abbas, demanding the surrender the fort. The killedar's response was defiant, 'Tell your Officer, that it is not possible to account to my Prince for the surrender of a fort like Dindigul, therefore, if any other person comes on that errand, I will blow him from a cannon.'[114]

Undeterred, the English bombarded the fort, eventually breaching its defences. Despite the killedar's brave defence, a spate of defections occurred during the night, compelling him to seek truce the following morning.[115]

Mackenzie points out, 'Pyny, Collumbrum, Colaveram, Animally ... surrendered without opposition.'[116] Undoubtedly, he meant Palani, Sholavaram and other places. Thereafter, 'the detachment that had reduced Dindigul marched against Palligautcherry [Palghat] by the route of Daraporam'.[117] The bombardment of Palghat began on 21 September. The garrison surrendered the following day, resulting in the English acquiring massive supplies of grain.

On 21 July 1790, Captain Meadows entered Coimbatore, having marched through many of Tipu's Coromandel (Cholamandal) territories unopposed. The British quickly gained control of Coimbatore, Palghat and Sathyamangalam, but struggled to retain their positions. On 2 September, Tipu led a 40,000-strong army to counterattack the British positions. The British contingent at Sathyamangalam was forced to retreat to Coimbatore. However, another force from Bengal had entrenched itself at Kaveripattinam. Unable to dislodge them, Tipu moved south towards Trichy. Pursued by the British armies, he continued southward, ravaging the towns and villages in his path. Upon reaching Pondicherry, he attempted to enlist the support of the French, who were preoccupied with their own revolutionary challenges at the time. (The French Revolution had erupted in 1789.) Tipu found himself isolated and without allies.

The Mysore garrisons stationed at various locations in Malabar were thoroughly demoralized, offering little resistance to the invading British armies and their Nair allies. When Colonel Stuart besieged the Palghat Fort on 21 September 1790, the defenders hastily capitulated. According to Mackenzie, 'The Killedar Yanin Khan surrendered. Among the papers captured in the fort was an order from Tipu which enjoined the Killedar that he should "by every exertion of judgement and policy whether by force or by consent make a Mussalman of every infidel in the district".'[118]

In December, a British force under Robert Abercromby landed in Tellicherry. Panikkar reveals:

> The Rajas of the neighbouring countries who had been in a perpetual state of revolt joined him. Among them was Kerala Varma of Pazhassy, who was for a long time the leader of the guerrillas against Tippu and who was destined till his death 15 years later to be the leader of the national revolt against British authority.[119]

Soon, Colonel Hartley, assisted by the Nairs, achieved a decisive victory at Tiruranagadi. Abercromby routed the Mysore–Arakkal alliance at Cannanore a few days later. By the end of 1790, Kerala had been cleared of the sultan's army, marking the end of the 25-year Mysorean occupation of Malabar. Although many rulers and princes had fled to Travancore following Haider Ali's 1766 invasion, the Nair militia remained to wage a guerrilla war from their hideouts in the mountains and forests. Panikkar opines, 'Without support from outside, with nothing but their love of freedom to guide them, the Nayar population kept up for a period of 25 years a resistance which is unparalleled in Indian history.'[120] While Cochin had submitted meekly to Haider Ali in 1766, '[the] Iruvanad [Iruvazhinad] Nambiars whose boast it was that they were not subordinate to any Ruler, and the Nayars of Kottayam [Cotiote] vied with each other in the fight against the invader'.[121]

In January 1791, the Cochin raja, Sakthan Thampuran, concluded a treaty with the 'Honourable' East India Company, agreeing to pay tribute to them instead of to Mysore. Meanwhile, a 30,000-strong Maratha army, under Parsuram Bhau, was advancing towards Mysore. It reached Dharwar in September 1790, having accepted the surrender of many minor outposts along the way. Following a seven-month-long siege, the garrison surrendered on 3 April 1791. Badar-uz-zaman Khan, commanding about 10,000 men, bravely resisted all attacks. However, due to the scarcity of provisions, he ultimately had no choice but to surrender.

After the fall of Dharwar, 'Parasu Ram Bhao crossed the Tungabhadra and marched towards Seringapatam, while another force under Hari Panth proceeded by a more easterly route by way of Sira in the same direction. The two armies effected a junction with Lord Cornwallis' troops at Cherkuli.'[122]

Bowring states:

> Nizam Ali's contingent, aided by a small British force, assembled near Haidarabad in May 1790, and, after protracted delays, invested the stronghold of Kopal. The fort held out until April 1791, a period of five months, when intelligence of the capture of Bangalore in the previous month induced the garrison to surrender.[123]

The nizam's troops then marched to recapture Kadapa and the adjoining districts. 'A large force of his cavalry also proceeded to join Lord Cornwallis' army, on its way to Seringapatam.'[124]

In February 1791, as the Bombay British army advanced towards Coorg, Tipu Sultan dispatched a formidable force under Bahadur Khan to intercept it. Balakrishna says, 'On 24th February 1791, the Kodagu Raja attacked Bahadur Khan's contingent. The valorous Kodava warriors badly mauled Bahadur Khan's force and killed 400 of his men. Bahadur Khan was effectively hemmed in from all sides and frozen in place without a drop of water.'[125] Khan surrendered to the Kodagu raja, but he explained his inability to accept the terms proposed by the latter, fearing certain death at the hands of Tipu. The raja, personally acquainted with Bahadur Khan from his earlier incarceration in Priyapattana, reciprocated Khan's previous kindness by allowing him and his troops to depart unharmed.

Cornwallis had assumed direct command of the British army at Vellore in January 1791. Anticipating Tipu's scorched-earth strategy of destroying crops to starve his enemies, Cornwallis had stockpiled grains and provisions. Additionally, he commissioned elephants to transport supplies and armaments.

Bowring tells us, 'The fortress of Bangalore, constructed in the 16th century by Kempe Gauda [the Red Chief], was originally of mud, but in 1761 it was, by order of Haidar, enlarged and strongly rebuilt in stone.'[126] Tipu made significant efforts to recapture Bangalore from the British. 'The Sultan made a desperate effort to recover the town … but after a prolonged contest his troops were repulsed on all sides.'[127] Bowring adds, 'The carnage had been great, and upwards of one thousand bodies of Tipu's troops were buried, while the casualties in the British army during the whole siege amounted to about five hundred.'[128] Tipu was now compelled to focus on defending his capital. A week later, Lord Cornwallis marched to Devanahalli to join a body of 10,000 cavalry dispatched by the nizam.[129] On 13 May, the combined forces reached Arikere, about 9 miles east of Srirangapatna. Here, on 15 May, the British encountered stiff resistance from Tipu's forces. Despite initial resistance, the Mysoreans were soon defeated and forced to withdraw to Srirangapatna Fort. However, Cornwallis decided to retreat as his army was on the brink of starvation, despite the elaborate precautions he had taken. He reckoned that the Maratha army would not arrive soon enough, and Abercromby was too far away. (The cunning Tipu Sultan had successfully intercepted all the messages intended for the British.) On 22 May, the British retreated to Bangalore, and three days later, the Marathas arrived.

With the English in close pursuit, a nervous Tipu Sultan ordered his people to 'remove from the walls of the houses of Seringapatam the caricatures of the English, with which his artists had ornamented them'.[130] There was considerable confusion and indecision in the British camp as well, likely due to severe shortages of food and fodder. Cornwallis ordered Abercromby to march to Malabar. Bowring states:

> These instructions were carried out, most of the cattle died on the way, and it was found necessary in consequence to bury the battering train at the summit of the pass into Coorg. The Mysore cavalry keenly pursued the retiring force, plundering the baggage and killing several men, while our gunpowder, having been deposited in a temple, was set fire to. The explosion destroyed the temple itself and a great part of the town.[131]

Bowring's account suggests that the gunpowder belonged to the British, while others have asserted that it was Tipu who had placed the explosive substance inside a Jain temple. It is possible that Bowring may have been referring to a different temple or there could have been confusion or misinformation regarding the incident. It is also conceivable that both parties engaged in such actions during the conflict.

Bowring informs us:

> Tipu, in contravention of the engagements he entered into at Mangalore in 1784, had retained in captivity no fewer than one hundred English men and boys, most of whom had perished

> through ill-usage. About nineteen of the youths, who had been trained to dance and sing, still survived, and were now cruelly put to death, lest their detention should be brought to light.[132]

He wonders why the Madras government had allowed these unfortunate individuals to remain in captivity for such an extended period.[133]

Bowring adds:

> Lord Cornwallis, finding his position no longer tenable, and all communication cut off, destroyed his siege train, threw his shot into the river, and burning his carts and tumbrels, retired on May 26 towards Bangalore. Tipu Sultan … fired a royal salute from his ramparts and illuminated his capital.[134]

Tipu's army attacked Coimbatore on 11 June. The garrison commander, Lieutenant Chalmers, made the decision to resist, despite being vastly outnumbered. This action went against the orders of Lord Cornwallis, who had instructed him to retreat if faced with a significantly larger force. Chalmers commanded only 300 men and had limited firepower. Despite these challenges, he managed to hold out until 6 November when he and his men were taken prisoner, in violation of the terms of surrender.

Parsuram Bhau's Maratha army marched on Shimoga. Commodore William Cornwallis fought the naval battle at Tellicherry. The governor-general himself effortlessly captured Nandidurg and Savandurg.

On 25 January 1792, Cornwallis carefully approached Srirangapatna. On 5 February, when the British launched their attack, they faced a barrage of Mysorean rockets. After intense fighting, Tipu retreated into the town. A week later, Abercromby arrived with the Bombay army. Tipu Sultan sought peace on 14 February, realizing the inevitability of defeat. The nizam's army, assisted by British contingents, had already seized Koppal, Gurramkonda, Ganjikot and Kollegal. The Marathas had captured Dharwar, Shimoga and other territories, while the British had control over the entirety of Malabar. Coorg had slipped from Tipu's control, and Cornwallis had captured Bangalore. Tipu Sultan found himself cornered, with Srirangapatna as his last stronghold.

Nandi Hills, then known as Nandidurg, served as Tipu Sultan's summer retreat. When seeking respite from the summer heat and the chaos of battle, the sultan would retreat to Nandi Hills, where he maintained a modest two-storeyed private residence. On the southwest side of the hill lies a steep cliff known as Tipu's Drop, from which many hapless prisoners were pushed to their deaths on the sultan's orders. The British assault on Nandidurg is described by Bowring in detail: 'A spirited defence was made by Lutf Ali Beg, the commandant, the garrison using their guns with effect, and rolling down huge masses of rock on the assailants.'[135] Three weeks later, two breaches were made, and on 19 October, the fort was captured.[136]

Cornwallis marched towards Srirangapatna and set up camp 6 miles away from the capital on 5 February 1792. He was accompanied by the main army of the nizam. Bowring remarks, 'The Maratha hosts under Parasu Ram Bhao were engaged in the congenial occupation of plundering the northern and eastern part of Mysore. Only a small portion of their troops under Hari Panth marched with the British army.'[137]

Cornwallis quickly 'succeeded in establishing himself on the eastern part of the island'.[138] Tipu sought refuge in the fortress. 'In the confusion that ensued, vast numbers of the Coorgs, who had been made to serve compulsorily in his army, contrived to escape to their own country.'[139] On 7 February 1792, Tipu Sultan made a desperate effort to expel the British from the island but was unsuccessful.

Cornwallis prepared to attack Seringapatam from both sides of the Kaveri. Bowring describes:

> On 19 [February], General Abercromby took up a position on the south-west of the river. The movement was sharply contested by the Sultan's troops, who were, however, driven back.... On the

> 22nd, Tipu received an intimation of the preliminary conditions which the allies offered for his acceptance. They specified the cession of half his dominions, the payment of over three million rupees, the release of all prisoners, and the delivery of two of his sons, named Moiz-ud-din and Abd-ul-Khalik, as hostages.... Tipu, after consulting his principal officers, assented to the general tenor of these terms, and duly signed the contents of the document submitted to him, remitting shortly afterwards a million of rupees in part payment of the sum stipulated. But when he found that the province of Coorg was mentioned in the detailed list of the territory which was to be severed from his control, his rage knew no bounds. For a long time, he refused to sign the final treaty, and it was only when he saw indications of the siege being recommenced and was told that the negotiations would be broken off, unless he at once accepted the proffered terms, that he at last gave way.[140]

The terms of the Treaty of Seringapatam were heavily weighted in favour of the British. Tipu Sultan agreed to pay a war indemnity of 3.30 crore rupees and hand over two of his sons as hostages to be held in British custody until the entire sum was paid. On 26 February 1792, the two minor boys were ceremoniously handed over to Lord Cornwallis with gun salutes and elephants on display. The Maratha general Hari Pant and the nizam's deputy Azmi-ul-Omrah witnessed this event. On 18 March, after much hesitation, Tipu signed the treaty, relinquishing half of his territories.

Malabar and the coastal areas were ceded to the British, along with Salem, Bellary and Anantapur, thus becoming part of the Madras Presidency. Coorg effectively came under British control, although formal annexation did not occur until 1834. Cochin and Travancore retained some degree of autonomy, albeit under British influence for the following 150 years. Kadapa was initially ceded to the nizam but later came under British control in 1800. Kirkpatrick writes about Kurnool:

> Runmust Khun was a Patan chieftain, who possessed the district of Kurnool. Hyder Ali compelled him to agree to an annual tribute; though he was, at the same time, a feudatory of the Nizam, to

> whom, when required, he was bound to render military service. By the partition treaty of 1792, his son and successor, Alif Khan, was released from his dependence on Tippoo Sultan, and the tribute payable to the latter transferred to the Nizam; by whom (If I mistake not) it was ceded to the East-India Company, by the treaty of 1800.[141]

Mackenzie provides the full list of districts ceded by Tipu Sultan to the allies. He mentions Dindigul, Salem, Namakkal, Palghat, Calicut, Coorg and other places.[142] What is noteworthy is that Wayanad is not included in the list. Nonetheless, the British would claim overlordship of this region and wage a long struggle to subdue Pazhassi Raja, who was the rightful ruler.

Cornwallis calculated that if they killed Tipu and captured Srirangapatna, they would either have to surrender the Mysorean capital to the Marathas or take on its administration themselves, both options fraught with danger. Thus, Tipu was spared, a decision that Cornwallis perhaps later regretted. Subsequent events indicated that it might have been wiser if the British had dealt with Tipu decisively in 1792. The following seven years would witness numerous casualties and inflict horrible suffering on countless helpless people.

Tipu grew increasingly desperate after the 1792 setback. He commissioned the construction of the massive star-shaped Manjarabad Fort in Sakleshpur (near Hassan in Karnataka) with the help of French engineers. Tipu also sent emissaries to Constantinople and Paris, seeking aid. He contacted Zaman Shah of Afghanistan, inviting him to invade India. Although Napoleon endorsed Tipu's ambitious plan of dividing India between the French and the Mysoreans, his defeat at the Battle of the Nile dashed his Indian aspirations. When Napoleon attacked Egypt, the Ottoman sultan severed ties with the French, aligned with the British and advised Tipu to follow suit. Zaman Shah did attack India in 1797, but he was repelled by the valiant Sikhs.

The Fourth Anglo–Mysore War ultimately spelled Tipu's downfall.

# 7

# THE COMPANY DEVOURS THE TIGER

Haider Ali died in camp during the Second Anglo-Mysore War. Despite enduring prolonged suffering due to a cancerous tumour, he continued to wage war without rest or recuperation. Haider Ali was a real conqueror, who laid the foundation for the mighty Mysore sultanate, a meticulous effort he had commenced long before his initial attempt to seize power in 1759. It was under his leadership that Bidanur, Malabar and other places were captured. It is ironic that despite Haider Ali's incomparable achievements it is Tipu Sultan who receives greater recognition as a conqueror, freedom fighter and patriot.

The climax of the Fourth Anglo-Mysore War on 4 May 1799 was marked by the fall of Srirangapatna and the death of Tipu Sultan. However, Tipu died not on the battlefield, but within the confines of the Srirangapatna Fort. The exact time of his death remains unknown. He was fatally shot by an unknown soldier, and his body was later discovered among a heap of corpses.

Haider Ali once escaped from Srirangapatna, leaving his family behind, when the dowager queen conspired to eliminate him. In contrast, Tipu Sultan actually surrendered two of his minor sons to the British in 1792 at the conclusion of the Third Anglo-Mysore War, besides ceding half of his territories and agreeing to pay a hefty tribute. Lord Cornwallis took custody of Tipu's sons to ensure the payment of the agreed sum. They were returned in 1794, after the British had secured their 'pound of flesh'.

The Treaty of Seringapatam was shameful and humiliating for one who called himself a 'Tiger'. Why did Tipu sign the treaty? Why didn't he continue fighting until the end? In the years following the signing of this humiliating treaty, Tipu made desperate attempts to garner support from France, Turkey, Afghanistan and other regions. He called for a jihad against the 'infidels' and requested Sultan Selim III of Turkey and Zaman Shah of Afghanistan to help him establish an Islamic state in India. The Muslim rulers in his immediate vicinity, such as the nizam of Hyderabad and the nawab of Arcot, did not share his jihadist zeal.

Tipu made derogatory remarks about the Mughal ruler in Delhi and openly alleged that he was in the pay of the Marathas. In his neighbourhood, Tipu Sultan alienated everyone. The Coorgis, the Nairs, the Marathas, the British and the nizam shared one common desire – they all sought Tipu's downfall.

One might question whether Tipu was, in fact, delusional. How could he have expected military assistance from a place as distant as Turkey?

While the Afghans did launch attacks on northern India, the Turkish sultan wisely kept his distance. He even wrote to Tipu Sultan, advising him to cultivate friendly relations with the British and sever ties with the French. However, a young Napoleon, upon reaching Egypt, penned a letter filled with bravado to Tipu, vastly raising his hopes and setting him on the path to total ruin.

## Napoleon and the Malartic Proclamation

Napoloen Bonaparte wrote to Tipu Sultan, 'You have already been informed of my arrival on the borders of the Red Sea, with an innumerable and invincible army, full of the desire of releasing and relieving you from the iron yoke of England.'[1] He was replying to Tipu's missive urging him to collaborate with Mysore to expel the British from India.

Unknown to Tipu Sultan, Napoleon had long been harbouring ambitions of reaching India. In the margin of a book on Turkish warfare, the Corsican general had scribbled sometime before 1788,

'Through Egypt, we shall invade India, we shall re-establish the old route through Suez and cause the route by the Cape of Good Hope to be abandoned.'[2] A decade later, he would receive a formal invitation from the Tiger of Mysore.

Chetti's account informs us:

> On the 18th of June, 1798, a letter was despatched from the Court of Directors in England to the Governor General, informing him, that a large French armament of ships and troops under the command of General Buonaparte, had been lately fitted out at and had sailed from Toulon, and that its destination was supposed to be India, by way of the Red Sea.[3]

Napoleon captured Malta and invaded Egypt. However, in early August, the French navy suffered a decisive defeat at the Battle of the Nile against the British navy led by Admiral Horatio Nelson. Napoleon's fleet was decimated, he found himself stranded in Egypt, and his Indian fantasies vanished into thin air.

The letter written by Napoleon to Tipu Sultan from Cairo was intercepted en route. Copies of the intercepted letter were forwarded to the governor of Bombay, and subsequently passed on to the governor-general Richard Wellesley.

In the meantime, yet another skeleton tumbled out of Tipu's cupboard, when the Malartic proclamation came to light. It was the proverbial last straw for the British. General Malartic was the French governor of Isle de France (Mauritius). Tipu sent an appeal to him asking for '10,000 French troops, and 30,000 Habshis (Negroes)'.[4] His envoys were transported to the island by a French privateer named François Ripaud. They arrived on 19 January 1798. The French did not maintain a standing army in Mauritius. So, the resourceful governor came up with an idea: Why not call upon citizens to volunteer? He issued a public proclamation on 30 January, calling for volunteers to fight on Indian soil under the banner of Tipu Sultan of Mysore.

The proclamation outlined Tipu's specific requirements:

1. He desires to form an offensive and defensive Alliance with the French, and proposes to maintain, at his charge, as long as the War shall last in India, the Troops which may be sent to him.
2. He promises to furnish everything necessary for carrying on the war, except wine and brandy, with which he is wholly unprovided.
3. He declares that he has made every preparation to receive the succours which may be sent to him, and that on the arrival of the troops, the Commanders and Officers will find everything necessary for making a War to which Europeans are little accustomed.
4. In a word, he only awaits the moment when the French shall come to his assistance, to declare war against the English, whom he ardently desires to expel from India.[5]

The proclamation further announced:

> We invite the Citizens, who may be disposed to enter as Volunteers, to enrol themselves in their respective Municipalities, and to serve under the banners of Tipu. This Prince desires also to be assisted by the Free Citizens of colour; we therefore invite all such who are willing to serve under his flag, to enrol themselves.[6]

The public response to the proclamation was lukewarm. Approximately a hundred men, under the command of Louis Auguste Chappuis, travelled to India on the French frigate *La Preneuse* on 7 March 1798, landing at Mangalore in April. Tipu was deeply disappointed by this meagre turnout.

While no substantial French army came to Tipu's aid, the Malartic Proclamation did make its way into a Calcutta newspaper. Chetti mentions:

> The proclamation issued in the Isle of France first appeared in one of the local newspapers at Calcutta on the 8th of June 1798, and an authenticated copy of the same was despatched by his

> Excellency Lord Macartney to the Governor General of India on the 18th of June, 1798.[7]

Lord Mornington arrived in Calcutta in May 1798, and in June, he received intelligence of the Malartic Proclamation. The British now had concrete evidence of Tipu's true intentions. It gave them a perfect pretext to invade Mysore. The nizam and the Marathas willingly allied with the British to eliminate their common enemy.

Wellesley carefully prepared for the war against Tipu. He avoided attacking until he had accumulated the necessary resources and ensured that neither the nizam nor the Marathas would support Mysore. The British extended peace overtures to Tipu and sent warning letters urging him to sever his ties with the French. Despite these clear signals, Tipu failed to see the writing on the wall. On 30 January 1799, he wrote to the Afghan king to inform him that he was aware of the impending British attack. Earlier, Zaman Shah had apparently informed Tipu of his intention to march on Delhi.

Following Napoleon's invasion of Egypt, the Ottoman sultan Selim III came to the conclusion that France could no longer be trusted. He forged alliances with Britain and Russia, and wrote to Tipu, advising him to ally with the British and abandon the French. His letter dated 20 September 1798 unequivocally stated, 'It has been discovered from several letters which have been intercepted that the further project of the French is to divide Arabia … to attack the whole Muhammadan sect … and extirpate all Muslims from the face of the earth.'[8] The Ottoman ruler held the esteemed title of caliph or khalifa, making him a revered religious leader among Muslims worldwide. However, Tipu found his advice unacceptable, and his response clearly indicated his stance. From that date, the caliph did not dignify any of Tipu's subsequent letters with a response.

By then, the British had already sanctioned the attack on Mysore. The governor-general issued an order on 14 December 1798 to all British area commanders in southern India. The company directors approved a sum of 5 crore rupees for the purpose of 'prosecuting' Tipu. The sultan's fate was sealed.

## The Final Assault

The governor-general took the initiative 'to negotiate with the nizam for the dismissal of a French contingent amounting to 14,000 men, well-disciplined and ably commanded by the officers that had succeeded De Bussy'.[9] The nizam reluctantly complied. 'On one side he regarded with apprehension the risk of disarming his French troops, and on the other the hostility of Tipu, with whom he had openly waged war, and whose advances towards a matrimonial alliance between the two sovereigns he had haughtily repelled.'[10]

'The disarming was successfully effected, the Sepoys being taken into the English service, and the French officers sent, by way of England, to France.'[11] Bowring opines that the French commander, Raymond, 'carried on a secret correspondence with the Mysore sovereign'.[12]Lord Mornington prepared the Madras army for action. On 12 August 1798, he recorded a minute in which he declared:

> The act of Tipu's ambassadors, ratified by himself, and accompanied by the landing of a French force in his country, is a public, unqualified, and unambiguous declaration of war, aggravated by an avowal, that the object of the war is neither explanation, reparation, nor security, but the total destruction of the British Government in India.[13]

On 5 March 1799, upon hearing of the approach of the Bombay force, the sultan suddenly appeared a few miles from Siddheshwar. Lieutenant Colonel Montresor, commanding three battalions of sepoys, found himself faced with an unexpected crisis. Bowring states:

> 'This brigade was completely surrounded, and would have been annihilated had it not been for the opportune arrival of General Stuart. The enemy then gave way and retreated, after losing many

> men and one distinguished general, named Muhammad Raza, commonly called the Benki Nawab or 'Fire' Nawab. General Stuart was accompanied on this occasion by Viraraj, the Wodeyar of Coorg, who had rendered every assistance in his power to the British troops, and was present personally in the action.'[14]

The Benki Nawab had a most unusual claim to fame. 'It is stated of him that on one occasion he shut up certain rebellious Nairs, with their wives and children, in a house, and burned them alive.'[15]General Harris arrived at Kellamangalam in Mysore on 9 March and was joined by a Hyderabadi contingent under Colonel Arthur Wellesley. 'Together they moved to encamp near Bangalore.'[16] Tipu was positioned near Maddur, midway between Bangalore and Srirangapatna, and 'he proceeded to encounter the British near Malvalli'.[17] However, his army was routed.

Bowring explains:

> Tipu then withdrew his guns and troops, having lost 1,000 men killed and wounded in the engagement, while the British loss was trifling.... Tipu had ordered the destruction of all forage on the more direct route.... But the English general, by marching to the south and crossing the Kaveri at Sosile, not only found ample fodder, but effected the passage of the ford without opposition. He was now within fifteen miles of Seringapatam, and Tipu found out that all his efforts to prevent the enemy from reaching within striking distance of his capital had been completely frustrated.... All his Sardars vowed to sacrifice their lives if necessary in the expected combat, and Tipu sending his two eldest sons into the fort to defend it to the last, crossed the river with his army to take up a position at Chendgal to meet the expected foe.[18]

He further states:

> On the 20th [April], Tipu again expressed a wish for a conference to adjust the terms of a peace. General Harris forwarded the draft of a preliminary treaty for his acceptance. This document stipulated that the Sultan should at once dismiss all Frenchmen in his service;

> that he should cede half his territory to the allies; pay two millions sterling, half immediately, and the remainder in six months; release all his prisoners; and finally make over as hostages two of his eldest sons besides four of his chief officers, whose names were given.[19]

He adds in a footnote that another letter dated 22 April mentions four sons, 'namely Sultan Padshah, Fatah Haidar, Moiz-ud-din, and Abd-ul Khalik'.[20] No response was received, and the siege continued. 'On the 26th and 27th hard fighting took place, in order to dislodge the Mysore troops from an exterior entrenchment still held by them.'[21] The Mysore troops were forced to retreat beyond the river.[22]

Bowring explains:

> The Sultan, now in despair, again attempted to open negotiations, and on the 28th wrote intimating his wish to send ambassadors to confer with the English general. He was told in reply that the allies would only treat on the basis of the conditions already forwarded to him, and that no envoys would be received unless accompanied by the hostages and specie required.[23]

He includes a footnote, stating, 'It was about this time that thirteen English soldiers, who had been taken prisoners, were killed by the sultan's orders, their necks being twisted by the professional executioners called Jettis.'[24]Tipu, despite being an orthodox Muslim, now turned to prayers and incantations performed by his group of Brahmin priests.[25]

According to Bowring:

> [With] a talisman on his right arm, he proceeded early on the 4th to his headquarters in a gateway on the northern face, called the Kalla Diddi, or private sally-port. Shortly after his arrival at this post, he was informed of the death from a cannon shot of Sayyad Ghafur, one of his most trusty officers, who was struck down while gallantly heading the troops in the breach ... The command of the storming party had been entrusted to General Baird, the same officer who had languished for more than three years in the dungeons of Seringapatam, having been taken prisoner after Bailley's defeat at Perambakam in 1780.[26]

On 2 May 1799, a British shot struck a magazine of rockets within the Srirangapatna Fort, causing it to explode, with thick black smoke rising from the battlements. On 3 May, a breach was made, and the Mysoreans responded with a flurry of rockets and musket fire. Baird led the final assault on the afternoon of 4 May. The fall of Srirangapatna occurred within a few hours. Following the victory, the victors engaged in a looting spree. As darkness descended, it occurred to the triumphant English to search for the sultan's body.

According to Chetti:

> Tippu's horse was shot down under him in attempting to get through the gateway…. But as he was proceeding into the inner fortifications by the narrow dark gateway, he was surprised to find that his men were retreating and flying before the flank companies of H.M.s 12th Regiment.[27]

Chetti further explains:

> Tippu Sultan severely wounded, though not [fatally], was put into a palanquin by his adherents, who begged him to proclaim his rank, but he disdained to do so, and in the thickness of the desperate fight they forsook him. While he was gasping for life, an unknown soldier with the object of snatching the rich diamond-hilt sword belt worn by him, pierced the Sultan with his bayonet, and when he struggled shot him dead.[28]

Chetti elaborates:

> Tippu's palanquin was discovered and beneath it lay a person wounded, but not dead, and who was afterwards found to be Raja Khan, one of the Sultan's most confidential servants, who had attended on his master during the whole of that fatal day. This person pointed out the spot where the Sultan had fallen and related that one of the soldiers seized his sword belt [which was very richly ornamented]and attempted to pull it off; that the Sultan, who still held his sword in his hand made a cut at the soldier with all his remaining strength and wounded him about the knee and that the

> soldier then shot the Sultan through the temple, when he instantly expired.[29]

Bowring's version states:

> [Tipu]was implored to make himself known to the English troops, from whose commanders he would no doubt have received the attention due to his rank, but he absolutely refused to comply with the suggestion. Soon afterwards some European soldiers entered the gateway, one of whom attempted to take off his richly jewelled sword belt, when Tipu, sorely wounded as he was, made a cut at the man and wounded him in the knee... The enraged soldier levelled his musket and shot him in the head, causing instantaneous death.[30]

Thus, the British were aware that the sultan had worn a jewelled belt, and they realized that it had been stolen.

Bowring states that once the British had firmly secured the fort, they began to wonder what had become of the sultan. 'Major Allan, Deputy Quartermaster-General, was accordingly sent to the palace with a flag of truce to demand the surrender of Tipu, and after some delay ascertained that a report had been received there that he had been wounded at the gate abovementioned.'[31]

According to Dalrymple:

> Baird was later taken to Tipu's body by one of his courtiers. It lay amid a heap of dead and wounded, with three bayonet wounds and a shot through the head. Tipu's eyes were open and the body was so warm that for a few moments, in the torchlight, Baird wondered whether the sultan was still alive: but feeling his pulse he declared him dead.[32]

Bowring adds:

> His turban, jacket, and sword belt had disappeared, but the talisman on his right arm, containing an amulet with Arabic characters on the manuscript inside, was at once recognized. The body was placed in his palankeen, and, by General Baird's orders,

> conveyed to the palace for the night. The next day the funeral cortege, escorted by four companies of Europeans, proceeded from the fortress to the Lal Bagh, where the remains of the ambitious and unfortunate sovereign were interred by the side of his father, Haidar Ali.... The bier was borne by his personal attendants, and followed by Prince Abd-ul-Khalik and the principal officers of the court, the streets through which the procession passed being crowded by Mussalmans, who prostrated themselves, and evinced every sign of grief.... In this memorable siege no fewer than 8,000 of the Mysore troops are said to have perished.[33]

After the death of Tipu Sultan, the British had no interest in governing Mysore. They decided to restore the kingdom to the Wodeyars. The truncated territory granted to the Wodeyars was larger than the area seized by Haider Ali almost four decades earlier. The last of the royals, Chamaraja Wodeyar, had died in 1796, leaving behind an infant son. The British transferred the kingdom to him on the following conditions:

> [An] annual subsidy of seven lacs of star pagodas should be paid to the British Government, that a general control over the affairs of Mysore should be exercised by a Resident at his court, and that the island of Seringapatam should be ceded to the British Government in perpetuity.[34]

Bowring opines, 'These liberal conditions were gratefully acknowledged.'[35] Thereafter, '[t]he Commissioners appointed to carry out the Governor-General's instructions allotted handsome pensions to the Sultan's principal officers.'[36]

Hoover explains that when the British occupied Sriranagaptana, Tipu's eldest son, Fateh Haider, was encamped on the north bank of the Kaveri and could have easily fled to safety.

> Fateh Haidar's officers urged the eldest prince to follow his father's last orders to retreat to Chitradurga, from which the fight against the British could be carried on from a network of formidable hill forts in northern Mysore. However, Tipu Sultan's Brahmin *diwan*,

Purnaiya, advised Fateh Haidar to leave the army and throw himself on the mercy of the British, who then might be inclined to recognize him as Tipu's successor. It did not take long for Fateh Haidar to suspect that Abdul Khaliq's surrender had been a ploy to gain British support for his own bid for power. Indeed, Purnaiya may have planted the seed of this idea in Fateh Haidar's mind. Throwing caution to the wind, the eldest prince abandoned his troops and gave himself up to the British.[37]

## Arthur Wellesley's Tryst with Destiny

Colonel Arthur Wellesley, who later achieved fame as the Duke of Wellington after defeating Napoleon at Waterloo, was the brother of the governor-general. He led a column of the British army during the Fourth Anglo-Mysore War. Initially, his forces suffered a setback when they were defeated by the Mysore army led by the Dewan Purnaiya at the Battle of Sultanpet on 5 April 1799.

Bowring states:

> The second column, under Colonel Wellesley, on advancing into the tope [or grove], was at once attacked in the darkness of night by a tremendous fire of musketry and rockets. The men, floundering about amidst the trees and the water-courses, at last broke, and fell back in disorder, some being killed and a few taken prisoners...In the confusion, Colonel Wellesley was himself struck on the knee by a spent ball, and narrowly escaped falling into the hands of the enemy.[38]

William Dalrymple emphasizes in *White Mughals* that Wellesley's role in the siege of Srirangapatna was exaggerated, as it was Baird and Harris who led the final assault. The author's description of the action is vivid and grounded: 'But by 3 May, after the guns of the Nizam's contingent had been brought up to within 350 yards of the weakest west corner of the walls, a substantial breach was made, and Harris set the following day for the assault.'[39] General Harris and the nizam's guns succeeded in causing the breach. It was Harris who decided that the island fortress of Srirangapatna would be stormed precisely at 1 p.m. on the fourth of 4 May, when the Mysore troops were expected to take their afternoon siesta.

Dalrymple explains:

> In the Company trenches, David Baird, who had spent forty-four months in Tipu's dungeons, roused himself and gave his troops 'a cheering dram and a biscuit'. He then drew his sword, jumped out of the trench and led a storming party - which included two hundred of Mir Alam's best Hyderabadi sepoys – over the River Cauvery and straight into the breach.[40]

A pitched battle ensued, and within a couple of hours, the fortress and the sultan fell.

Stephen Chetti declares:

> Colonel Wellesley, after an unsuccessful sortie on the 5th April 1799 at the head of the 33rd Regiment against the elephant batteries at Sultanpett, was struck on the knee with a spent ball, when it is said, he was confused, advanced into the woods and followed the enemy, mistaking the crowds who were flying for refuge into the fort to be the British, but fortunately recognizing them in time to be the enemy, quietly stole away and having wandered for some hours in the darkness regained the British camp in safety.'[41]

Arthur Wellesley would later achieve renown for winning numerous battles overseas. However, he failed in his repeated attempts to subdue Kerala Varma Pazhassi Raja, the courageous ruler of the Cotiote kingdom of north Malabar.

## Intrigues and Secret Communications

There were hidden manoeuvres, plots, intrigues and undercurrents, as every power tried to gain ascendancy over the others. Bowring reveals:

> In 1795 [Tipu] entered into a covert engagement with Ali Jah, son of the Nizam, then in rebellion against his father…. [The deal

> was in] case he succeeded in dethroning the Nizam, he should make over to Tipu Sultan all the territory lying south of the Tungabhadra and Krishna rivers.... This scheme was, however, foiled by the prompt action of Raymond, commanding a body of French troops in the Nizam's service. Ali Jah was taken prisoner. Tipu next deputed an embassy in 1796 to the court of Zaman Shah, the Afghan ruler, seeking his aid as a co-religionist, and making magnificent promises of cooperation, with a view to the subjugation of the Marathas and the expulsion of the English from India. Nor did he confine himself to these overtures. He also used every means in his power to foment misunderstandings between the Peshwa, Sindhia, and the Nizam on the one hand, and the English on the other.[42]

The British had signed a secret treaty promising to restore the Wodeyar dynasty. When the war ended, Purnaiya quickly switched sides and became a loyalist of the infant Wodeyar raja. To this day, many people in South India consider Purnaiya a traitor.

Chetti refers to a February 1799 letter addressed to Lord Mornington and Lord Clive by Rani Lakshmammani, wherein she states:

> Recently, when Hyder, who was in our service, proved a traitor to us, put to death many of our relatives and dependants, plundered the palace four times, and with the means obtained there, conquered countries and began to defy us, we unable to bear Hyder's persecution, thus reasoned with ourselves: The English are a just and wise people. By cultivating their friendship, we may enjoy happiness and safety for a long time... We communicated our intention through Mohamed Alli, to the then Governor of Madras. Mohamed Alli in reply said: If you will cancel the stipulations for the cession of Trichinopoly and surrender the bond given by me to Nanjaraj for the loan taken from him at Srirangam during the strife with Chanda Saib, we will restore liberty to Katti Gopal Rajaiyya, your father and with him send English troops to put down Hyder and re-establish your rule.[43]

She describes the various stages of the prolonged negotiations with Muhammad Ali and the British. The next part of the letter reveals, 'The design to capture Tippu and restore our rule was revealed to him by some wicked persons, when it was about to be executed, and the revenge he took resulted in the massacre of seven hundred men, women and children.'[44] This was apparently a reference to the Melkote massacre, which may have occurred in 1790. The rani further states:

> When peace had been concluded with the English, Tippu listening to the words of his French advisers, by some secret means brought about the death of the Raja, plundered the palace and drove us out from thence, stripped us of our apparel, leaving us only with the cloth we have on, and now keeps us in close confinement...We, therefore, seek your protection. Take pity on us; look to Fame, Justice and God, rid us of this enemy, and restore our country to us according to former agreements.[45]

Mr Webbe replied to this letter on 16 April 1799, stating:

> The three letters you sent, one to me, one to His Lordship of Bengal, and one to His Lordship here, your Pradhan Tirumal Rao, delivered to me, and they gave us much pleasure. Your Pradhan Tirumal Rao has for a long period continued to give us every information respecting you, and their Lordships solemnly promise to serve you - a fact which your Pradhan must have mentioned to you. You may rest assured that there will be no end to our friendship. We have now declared war against Tippu. But we know not what will be the result. God only knows it. I cannot write much on that head, but after the war is over, they will attend to your business. There is no doubt.[46]

## Transfer of Power

The victorious British restored Mysore to the Wodeyar dynasty and installed a resident commissioner at Srirangapatna to exercise indirect control. Mysore's territory was truncated, with Canara and Coimbatore transferred to the British. (Malabar had already come under British control in 1792 at the end of the Third

Anglo-Mysore War.) The nawab of Savanur's domain was divided between the Marathas and the British, while the nizam received minimal territory.

After the fall of Srirangapatna, the Mysore commissioners wrote to the governor-general on 25 June 1799 stating:

> We proceeded to His Highness' residence accompanied by Purnaiya, whom we thought it proper should be present at this first interview. Although every preparation was made for our reception, it is not easy to describe to your Lordship the state of misery in which we found this persecuted family.... We have the honor to inform your Lordship, that the partition of the country, and the elevation of the Rajah to the musnud was duly proclaimed. [Signed at Seringapatam by Arthur Wellesley, Henry Wellesley, William Kirkpatrick and Barry Close.][47]

On 30 June, the commissioners communicated once more with the governor-general:

1. We have the honour to inform your Lordship, that Purnaiya having reported to us, on the 25th instant, that the Brahmins had fixed on the 30th of June, as the most auspicious day for placing Kistna Rajah Wodeyar on the Musnud of Mysore, we resolved that the ceremony should accordingly be performed on that day.
2. We at the same time communicated to Lt General Harris our wish that he would, if possible, assist in person on this occasion.
3. His Excellency, in consequence came hither from camp yesterday morning, attended by his suite, and an escort of European Cavalry for the occasion.
4. The Rajah and his family [were]removed some days ago from Seringapatam to the old town of Mysore, where the best preparations were made for the accommodation which circumstances would admit.
5. This morning, the members of the Commission, accompanied by Meer Allum and his son Meer Dowran...proceeded to the

residence of the Rajah, who was placed on the Musnud about noon, under three volleys of Musketry from the troops on the spot and a royal salute from the guns of Seringapatam.

6. The ceremony of placing the Rajah in the Musnud was performed by Lt General Harris as Senior Member of the Commission and by Meer Allum, each of them taking a hand of His Highness on the occasion. His Excellency the Commander-in-Chief, sometime after delivered to the Rajah, the Seal and Signet of the Raj.
7. The deportment of the young Prince during the ceremony was remarkably decorous, considering the untoward circumstances which had [preceded] his elevation, and confirmed the opinion which we had formed of him at our first visit to him.
8. We have great pleasure in informing your Lordship that Gholam Alikhan, Ali Reza, Budruz Zeman Khan, and Syed Mohamud Khan spontaneously attended on this occasion. The Meer-Suddoor was prevented, we understand by indisposition.
9. After taking leave of the Rajah, we partook of an entertainment which had been provided for us in an adjoining choultry.
10. The inauguration having taken place under an open Pendal, the spectators were very numerous; and it would be difficult to describe the joy which was visible in the countenance of all the Hindus present.[Signed by Geo: Harris, Arthur Wellesley, Henry Wellesley, Willaim Kirkpatrick, Barry Close at Seringapatam, 30th June 1799.][48]

## Tipu's Treasures

Tipu's huge family was confined in the Vellore Fort. Seven years later, in 1806, a massive sepoy revolt erupted at Vellore. Following this event, Tipu's sons were shifted to Calcutta, where they lived in exile for many generations. Today, Tipu's descendants lead ordinary lives, devoid of royal privileges and wealth. It appears that for three or four generations, they lived comfortably, supported generously by the British. Interestingly, one of Tipu's sons even moved to England, accompanied by Mir Hussein Ali Khan Kirmani's priceless Persian manuscript. None of the treasured valuables of the sultan remained in the hands of his descendants.

Bowring's account informs us:

> The discovery of a private entrance into the treasury enabled marauders to carry off a vast amount of coin and jewellery before they could be stopped. Nevertheless, what remained was of priceless value. A magnificent throne, a superb howdah, curious and richly-jewelled matchlocks and swords, solid gold and silver plates, costly carpets and chinaware, a profusion of fine gems, and a valuable library, were among the treasures found in the palace.[49]

He adds in a footnote, 'With the exception of one precious Koran, which was forwarded to Windsor Castle, the greater part of this library was transferred to the newly-founded College at Fort William, Calcutta.'[50]

What happened to the sultan's designer throne is anyone's guess. It had been commissioned sometime after 1785, three years after Tipu Sultan succeeded his father. Wilks informs us that Tipu never sat on it. Perhaps his astrologers had issued some dire warnings.

According to Bowring:

> The principal ornament of his throne was a tiger's head of life-size, wrought in gold, which served as the support of the throne. The bas-reliefs of the throne, which was approached by silver steps, were decorated with tigers' heads worked in gold and adorned with precious stones. Over it was suspended a huma, or bird of Paradise, whose brilliant wings, encrusted with diamonds, rubies, and emeralds, hovered over the Sultan. The huma formed the apex of a canopy, fringed with pearls, which was attached to a gilt pillar seven feet high.[51]

He explains in a footnote:

> At Windsor Castle are preserved thc royal footstool of Tipu and the richly-jewelled bird which adorned the canopy of the throne. Among other relics of the Sultan are portions of his tent with silver

> poles, ivory chairs, elephant and horse trappings, a palankeen, two richly ornamented field pieces, and various weapons, including the sword and shield which were found with his body after the siege. In the library of the castle is a copy of the Koran, formerly belonging to the emperor Aurangzeb, which was found among Tipu Sultan's treasures.'[52]

Eventually, the throne of Tipu Sultan was discovered in Britain, albeit in many pieces, and became part of the heirlooms of various families. In 2021, one of the throne finials made of gold and precious gems, adorned with an exquisite tiger-head design, was put up for auction in England. Ironically, the auctioning agency stipulated that bids from outside the country would not be accepted.

Denys Forrest provides an inventory of relics that were transferred from Srirangapatna to England in the immediate aftermath of the British victory over Tipu Sultan and mentions the current locations where they now reside:

> Scattered up and down the British Isles to this day, in extraordinary profusion, is the loot of Tipu's storehouses and armouries.... At Windsor Castle and the Tower of London, and in the Victoria and Albert and countless other museums, in clubs and army messes, and in a quite remarkable number of private houses, rest labelled and dated relics of Tipu Sultan.[53]

The jewelled huma bird (bird of paradise) that once adorned the throne of Tipu Sultan is now housed in Windsor Castle as the private property of the royals. According to Forrest, 'Queen Charlotte, to whom it was sent by Lord Wellesley, bequeathed it to her four daughters.... They transferred it in turn to their brother, King George VI, on condition that it should never be separated from the Crown of Great Britain and Ireland.'[54]

Forrest adds, 'Windsor Castle also has "Tipu's turban ornament", and possibly even the very turban or war helmet which, according to other accounts, fell off or was lost in the struggle.'[55] He also mentions, 'The sun banner of Tipu's Mysore which was hoisted during the Vellore Mutiny and presented later to the Windsor Collection by Major General Sir Robert Gillespie.'[56]

Tipu's sword is another heirloom that has garnered global attention time and again. In fact, it is said that Tipu possessed thirteen such swords, and one of them was seized by the Nairs of Travancore in 1789, but later returned.[57]

The flamboyant Indian industrialist, Vijay Mallya, purchased Tipu's sword at an auction in 2003 for 1.57 crore rupees, but he relinquished it, claiming it had brought him bad luck. (Mallya currently lives in exile in London after fleeing the country to avoid legal proceedings.) In 2023, the sword was sold for a whopping sum of 143 crores rupees. The identity of the buyer remains unknown. The sword was discovered in the bedchamber of the fallen sultan and was handed over to David Baird as a token of appreciation for his leadership.[58]

Tipu Sultan's ring was recovered from his body (or rather, stolen) after the fall of Srirangapatna. In September 2022, Indiatimes.com reported, 'The jewelled ring is inscribed with the name of the Hindu deity Ram in raised Devanagari script and was sold for €145,000 [nearly 1.42 crore rupees] by Christie's auction house in 2014.'

## The Wodeyar Boy and Others

Lachhmi Ammani (Lakshmammani) and Dewaji Ammani (Dewajammani), the widows of Chikka Krishnaraja Wodeyar and Chamaraja Wodeyar, respectively, wrote an evocative letter expressing undying gratitude to the EICo on 24 June 1799, six weeks after Tipu Sultan's death.

> Your having conferred on our child the government of Mysore, Nagar, and their dependencies, and appointed Purnaiya to be the diwan, has afforded us the greatest happiness. Forty years have elapsed since our government ceased. Now you have favoured our boy with the government of this country and nominated Purnaiya to be his Diwan. We shall, while the sun and the moon continue, commit no offence against your government. We shall at all times consider ourselves under your protection and orders. Your having

> established us must forever be fresh in the memory of our posterity, from one generation to another. Our offspring can never forget an attachment to your government, on whose support we shall depend.[59]

The British believed they had little to gain by taking over the reins and administration of Mysore. They had already looted treasures from Nagar (Bidanur) in 1783 and Srirangapatna in 1799. Additionally, they had acquired the precious pepper-producing Malabar territories in 1792 through a treaty with Tipu Sultan. With their sworn enemy now deceased, they saw no further need for Mysore.

The Wodeyars (now spelled 'Wadiyars') remained faithful and obedient to the British. The young raja Krishnaraja Wodeyar III was married in 1805 at the age of twelve to Devajammani, also twelve years old at the time. She later made history by becoming the first royal woman to receive the smallpox vaccine, an event commemorated by a classic painting. This painting was auctioned by Sotheby's in the 21st century for an undisclosed sum. The raja's grandmother, Lakshmammani, had lost her husband to smallpox. This might have influenced the decision of the Mysore royals to embrace the vaccination programme advocated by the British.[60]

Raja Krishnaraja Wodeyar III passed away in 1868, having had the good fortune to occupy the throne of Mysore for nearly seven decades. Today, his successors reside in Mysore.

While the British restored the Mysore kingdom to the Wodeyar dynasty, they adopted an entirely different approach towards Pazhassi Raja, who was then resisting the EICO's encroachments in Wayanad and Kottayam-Malabar. They confiscated his territories, tracked down and killed his loyalists, and finally hounded him to his death in 1805. The reasons for this aggressive stance are not difficult to discern – pepper, pepper, pepper!

The Malabar boys did not share the good fortune of the Mysore boy. Their kingdoms were completely absorbed by the white occupiers, who maintained a firm grip on Malabar until India finally gained freedom in 1947.

## Simply Gumbaz

Visiting Srirangapatna 224 years after the demise of Tipu Sultan, I found no signs of grandeur, nothing to indicate that this was once the capital of a powerful kingdom. My first stop was the Vaishnavaite temple of Sriranganatha. I was surprised to see that the sultan had not demolished it. I wondered why.

With the echoes of 'Govinda! Govinda! Govinda!' still resonating in my ears and prominent red kumkum on my forehead, I made my way to Tipu's tomb, simply described as 'Gumbaz' by the locals. Here, the two sultans and Tipu's mother lie in state – Haider Ali's tomb in the middle, flanked by the tombs of Tipu Sultan and Fakhrunissa on either side. Each tomb is adorned with elegant, colourful, rich cloths and carpeted with flowers. Tipu's tomb stands out with its unique striped cover that resembles a tigerskin.

The premises are meticulously maintained, with spotless black pillars adorning the corridors surrounding the central hall where the tombs are located. The ceiling and walls are intricately decorated. Initially, the caretaker informed me that photography was forbidden, but eventually, he relented and obliged me by taking my picture alongside the tombs. He mentioned that the doors of the building were originally made of gold, as Tipu Sultan had decorated his father's tomb with utmost reverence. However, after the fall of Srirangapatna, the British looted everything valuable, including the doors. Subsequently, the Wodeyar king generously provided wooden doors with intricate ivory inlay work. While historical records indicate that the doors were repaired by the British, I am inclined to believe the caretaker's account. The doors remain in perfect condition and appear quite un-British. Chetti avers, 'The doors [of the mausoleum] are inlaid with ivory which were renewed by Lord Dalhousie in 1835.'[61]

The tomb had hardly any visitors – only a few Mappilas from Kerala and a handful of local tourists. For the Mappilas, Tipu was a benefactor who had once bestowed largesse upon their forefathers. He was an ardent promoter of their religion, a brave fighter who had fiercely resisted British colonization.

Other tourists visit Bailley's Dungeon, where the unfortunate English prisoners, including Bailley, had been chained to the wall by Haider and Tipu and kept for several years until death released them from their agony. Tipu's opulent Lal Mahal Palace has disappeared without a trace, with only a few stones and bricks remaining at the ground level. (I suspect the English even took away the bricks as souvenirs; otherwise, a magnificent palace cannot disappear so completely.)

The Summer Palace, also known as Daria Daulat Bagh, is well maintained. '[It is] outside the walls of the fort and stands as a memorial built by him [Tipu] in 1784 of the narrow escape Hyder Ali had from the hands of the assassins of Kande Rao.'[62] Chetti informs us:

> Its walls are decorated with paintings representing the daily life of various Nabobs, Rajas and Ranis of Southern India, as well as the victory over Colonel Baillie's little band by the combined armies under Hyder Ali and Tippu at Pollilore on the 10th September, 1780. The reservoir in the garden was Tippu's favourite bathing place. Before the siege of 1799, the picture of the defeat of Colonel Baillie was effaced from the walls by order of Tippu, but it was renewed by Colonel Wellesley's order, who occupied the building from 1799 to 1801. In 1855, Lord Dalhousie ordered that, the palace should be put into a state of thorough repair, and the paintings were once more renewed and the roof and walls of the building gorgeously decorated.[63]

The Srirangapatna Fort lies in ruins and is overgrown with weeds. One can see the Water Gate, near the spot where the English first managed to breach the defence. My cab driver told me it was the treacherous Purnaiya who had revealed to the English the weakest part of the defences and ensured there were fewer defenders there.

According to Chetti:

> The water gateway is pointed to by local tradition as the place where Tippu Sultan fell, mortally wounded.... Another account, as advanced by most travellers, points to an arch-way in the inner fortifications as the spot where Tippu fell [since destroyed] about 100 yards to the right of the sally port known as *hole-diddi-bagalu*.[64]

The British called it the Hoally Gateway. The location where Tipu's body was found is marked by a humble, roofless memorial, a short distance from the Water Gate but outside the fort walls. Historical anecdotes state that his body was discovered inside the fort, so this site may have been specifically designed for tourists. Given that the entire structure has fallen into ruin and the area is overrun by weeds, the only practical alternative may have been to choose a site outside the fort walls.

# 8

# FIRANGI TALES

Historians and military figures of various nationalities have written detailed accounts of the Mysore sultans and their military manoeuvres. Chronicles were written by English, French, Portuguese, Dutch and Persian authors, along with narratives in several Indian languages. Together, they paint a convincing portrait of the two sultans and their thirty-eight-year reign of terror.

While Dr Francis Buchanan, Mark Wilks, Colin Mackenzie, Alexander Beatson, Charles Warre Malet, Charles Stewart, William Kirkpatrick, James Scurry, James Bristow, Maistre de la Tour, Eloy Joze Correa Peixoto and Fra. Bartolomeo were contemporaries of the sultans, later authors include William Logan, Lewin Bowring and others. It is reasonable to expect that later authors drew upon the narratives of men who lived in the age of the sultans. British officers serving the EICo knew each other, and they were exchanging notes and consulting one another during their work. For instance, Wilks acknowledges Colin Mackenzie and William Kirkpatrick for sharing valuable information and documents. On the other hand, non-British authors like Bartolomeo, Peixoto and De la Tour probably relied on their own independent sources and firsthand experiences. It is important to remember that uncorroborated accounts are not necessarily untrue.

### James Scurry

The memoirs of the British sailor boy, James Scurry, who was originally illiterate, were published in London in 1824. They recount his capture by the French in 1781 and his decade-long captivity under the sultans. Titled *The Captivity, Sufferings and Escape of James Scurry, Who Was Detained a Prisoner during Ten Years, in the Dominions of Hyder Ali and Tipoo Saib*, Scurry's first-person account was written after his return to England in 1793. His words convey the raw emotions of an uneducated man. Since it was a posthumous publication, it is impossible to attribute any ulterior motives to the author.

Circumcised and renamed Shamsher Khan, Scurry endured countless brutalities but eventually managed a daring escape and returned to England. Hailing from Devonshire, James Scurry began his maritime career at a very young age, probably accompanying his father. His ordeal in India began at the age of fifteen when he was captured by the French off the Coromandel Coast and handed over to their ally, Haider Ali. In his memoirs published in 1788, William Thomson, an EICo official, mentioned that Haider Ali paid rupees 50,000 to the French Admiral Suffrein to hand over 400 English sailors and 60 Royal Navy officers captured at sea in 1782. Yazdani notes, 'He [Thomson] identified between sixty-two and sixty-seven circumcised Europeans in Mysore by 1784.'[1]

Scurry recalls his voyage from Plymouth Sound aboard the ship 'Hannibal', which eventually found itself near Ceylon (Sri Lanka) where they were attacked by the French. He dived into the shark-infested waters, attempting to swim to safety, only to be captured by the French and subsequently handed over to Haider Ali at Cuddalore.[2] After enduring two months of imprisonment in the fort of 'Chillembroom', amidst a raging famine, the prisoners were forcibly marched off to Bangalore. 'No butcher ever drove oxen with more cruelty than we were driven.'[3]

Eventually, a group of fifty-two boys aged twelve to seventeen years were gathered together and told that they were now considered the 'sons' of Haider Ali. They were then marched off to Srirangapatna, where their heads were shaved in preparation for the rite of circumcision. A European, dressed in Mahomedan attire, delivered the news to them. 'He addressed us in the most endearing, though hypocritical, language, and gave us to understand, that we were to be circumcised, and made Mahomedans of, by the express order of Hyder.'[4] Scurry reveals that a boy named James Murrell died as a result of the circumcision.

Months passed, and Haider Ali 'Cawn' passed away. Scurry discloses that 'towards the close of his life when the ulcer was rapidly spreading, he, by advice, ordered several criminals at different times to be killed, in order to apply their livers to his sore'.[5]

Haider Ali's death occurred roughly a year after Scurry's capture. Scurry makes an intriguing observation: 'Hyat Saib was the rightful successor, but Tipoo proved the more powerful.'[6] It is uncertain whether Haider Ali had officially nominated Ayaz Khan to succeed him or if Scurry was merely echoing palace whispers.

Scurry vividly describes Tipu's initial visit to his father's tomb, an event accompanied by a gruesome ceremony:

> A curious and tragic circumstance took place on his first visit to his father's mausoleum: in his going [through] the Gangam gate, a bullock's head on one side, and a man's head on the other, were lopped off, at one time. The real meaning of this ceremony we never could learn.[7]

The testimony is unmistakeable. It was human sacrifice indeed!

Tipu's accession aggravated the misery of the English captives, who were forced into slave battalions. 'Our ears were bored and a slave's mark was put in each of them.'[8] They were compelled to participate in a mass wedding, with their brides being female captives, probably from Arcot. Scurry thus found himself married to an Indian girl, with whom he had two children. Tragically, one of the infants died, and when Scurry eventually made his escape, he had to leave his wife and surviving child behind. Faced with the agonizing decision between freedom and family, he chose the former. Upon returning to England, he tirelessly sought to locate his Indian family but in vain.

Among the English officers under Tipu's custody, Scurry mentions that Colonel Bailley was confined in leg irons, while

Captain Rumney, Lieutenant Fraser and Lieutenant Sampson 'had their throats cut at Mysore'.[9] Additionally, 'Lieutenants Rutledge and Spiedman were Mohammedanized'.[10] Scurry also recounts the tragic fate of 30,000 Malabar (Mangalore) Christians who were 'driven to Seringapatam, where all who were fit to carry arms were circumcised, and formed into four battalions'.[11] Tipu wanted their daughters for his harem, and when they refused, they were all imprisoned. 'The chumbars, or sandal-makers were then sent for, and their noses, ears and upper lips were cut off; they were then mounted on asses, their faces towards the tail and led through Patam [Seringapatam, the anglicized name for Srirangapatna].'[12]

Scurry observes:

> The principal street in Seringapatam, on each side, was ornamented with paintings, such as, elephants whirling Europeans in the air—tigers seizing whole battalions of English sepoys—five or six English officers supplicating for mercy at the feet of one of his troopers.[13]

Scurry asserts that Tipu was not only a coward and a tyrant but probably suffered from mental instability. He recounts Tipu's gruesome methods, including keeping nine large tiger cages outside his treasury. Three of his top officers were 'thrown to the tigers, and devoured in an instant'.[14] The tigers themselves did not survive long either; Tipu would go hunting and replace them. Scurry describes in detail Tipu's unique torture devices. '[His] most common mode of punishment was that of drawing to death by the elephant's feet.'[15] This corroborates accounts from other writers in Malayalam and English. Scurry also describes Tipu's barbaric 'games' which would have shocked even the ancient Romans.

When Tipu signed a peace treaty with the British in 1784, concluding the Second Anglo-Mysore War, and the customary exchange of prisoners occurred, Scurry and around a hundred other boys were sorely disappointed. They had hoped for their freedom but were left waiting in vain. They began to question whether their own government had abandoned them. Scurry reveals that he fell into deep depression for three months. After enduring a decade of captivity, he eventually managed to escape into Maratha territory and returned to England in 1793. By then, Tipu had lost the Third Anglo-Mysore War and forfeited half of his territories to the British.

Scurry provides a description of Tipu's appearance, stating, 'In his person he was majestic, about five feet nine inches and a half in height, with large eyes, an aquiline nose, and remarkably broad shoulders; his complexion was about two shades lighter than quite black.'[16] He adds that Tipu's preferred mode of transportation was the palanquin. Scurry never witnessed the sultan riding a horse. Nevertheless, whenever Tipu was in the capital, four Arabian mares and two elephants would be kept on standby.

Scurry remarks:

> Since our arrival in England, we have oft times heard him extolled for a brave prince; but those who have thus stated, we presume know little of him. That he was a coward we could easily demonstrate, and that he was a tyrant … is a fact of which we had ocular demonstration.[17]

Scurry's language and spellings are quaint. He refers to speaking the 'Moorish' language, the 'Canary' language and the 'Tellingey' language. Additionally, he recounts 'seeing the Bramin women ascend the funeral pyre with the dead bodies of their husbands, apparently with as much composure as we would sit down to our breakfast'.[18]

### James Bristow

Bristow's memoir, first published in 1792 in Calcutta, is titled *A Narrative of the Sufferings of James Bristow, Belonging to the Bengal Artillery, during Ten Years Captivity with Hyder Ally and Tippoo Saheb.* Bristow embarked for India at the age of fourteen as an EICo recruit, landing in Bengal after a six-month voyage. His travails began when he accompanied Eyre Coote to Madras aboard the *Kingston.* Coote, a veteran commander, had been assigned the task of halting Haider Ali's military advance in the Carnatic. They landed at Fort St George in November 1780.

Bristow's narrative is indeed rich in detail. He reveals that Haider Ali was adept at engineering defections. 'On the very day our detachment left the fort, Sergeant Dempster deserted and went over to Hyder.'[19]

The 8,000-strong 'grand army' took the field in January 1781, led by their legendary commander, and advanced to the relief of Wandiwash. Upon hearing of their approach, Haider Ali abandoned the siege.[20] The army continued its march, and Bristow accompanied Lieutenant Doxat to Pondicherry. Their objective was to destroy the French boats to prevent the landing of military supplies brought by a fleet under M. D'Orves.[21] They successfully spiked several guns buried in the sand by the French and set fire to several boats before sunrise. However, as they returned to their camp, located 2 kilometres outside the town, they were attacked by Haider's troops. Within minutes, poor Bristow found himself captured.[22] 'Having bound my arms behind me, they hurried me almost naked before Hyder, on the 6th of February.'[23]

'Hyder's tent exhibited nothing very extraordinary and magnificent except a rich Persian carpet,' the prisoner observes.[24] Several French officers were in attendance. Bristow underwent interrogation by an English speaker, aiming to extract information about the British army's numerical strength and the details of their arms and ammunition. He provided some false information and was promptly accused of lying. Bristow states:

> Hyder was so much exasperated at my attempt to deceive him that he kept me three days without any food, tied down on the ground in the rear of his tent, which was the station I constantly occupied during the seven days I remained in his camp.[25]

Later, he was lashed to Sergeant Major Rickman and marched off to Gingee Fort, from where he was transferred to Arcot. Bristow reveals that it was only the compassion of the guards that prevented him from dying of starvation.[26] 'On my arrival at Gingee, I was handcuffed, and from thence, the succeeding day, removed to Arcot, whence my handcuffs were exchanged for heavy leg irons.'[27] Bristow mentions that 'Colonel Baillie, Captain Rumley, Lieutenant Frazer, and a Mr Skardon were at this time confined in Arcot. The latter of these gentlemen had been the English Resident at Pondicherry, and was treacherously delivered up by the French inhabitants'.[28]

Bristow and the other prisoners commenced their march to Srirangapatna on 1 March. Bristow discovered that Bailley, Frazer and Rumley were among those on the journey, along with Lieutenant Brumpton and M'Neal.[29] Upon reaching Srirangapatna, approximately 300 European prisoners were housed in a common prison, while Bailley, Frazer and Rumley were held separately. Sergeant Dempster, despite his defection to the Mysorean side, eventually found himself in the common prison as well.[30]

Bristow recounts the story of twelve circumcised European officers who were appointed to command over other slaves. However, when four of them successfully escaped, the remaining eight faced severe punishment. Their hands were tied behind their backs, and they 'received three lashes with a bunch of tamarind twigs from each of the chaylahs (chelas), which, from the number composing the battalion, consisted of fifteen hundred lashes'.[31] Bristow encountered one of the four escapees, Richard Higgins, a decade later at Machilipatnam, following his own escape to freedom.[32]

Meanwhile, '[the] whole of the officers and men of Colonel Braithwaite's detachment in the Tanjore country arrived in captivity and spread a gloom of despondence through the several prisons'.[33] Bristow elaborates, 'The number of Chaylahs that were confined in the fort together, without sufficient room to breathe in, and totally disregarded and surrounded by filth which was never removed, created at last epidemical diseases, which were fatal to great numbers.'[34]

Bristow narrates the harrowing ordeal of Lieutenants Speediman and Rutledge, also mentioned by James Scurry, who had been left wounded at Vellore for several months. Afterward, they marched with an escort to join the grand army but were ambushed by Tipu's forces and compelled to surrender. They were then brought to

Srirangapatna in July 1782, where they were treated more harshly than the other prisoners.[35] The poor men 'were almost rendered speechless when the horrid design of circumcising them became evident. They were marched to the village of Gunjam Pet, and secured in a large square building, where they found nine Europeans that had already undergone this abominable operation'.[36] On 1 September, these men were also circumcised.[37] Soon afterward, seven circumcised Europeans, including Bristow, were taken into the fort to discipline hundreds of Indian boys who had been captured from the Carnatic.[38] Bristow states:

> I had not been many days in the fort before fifty seamen arrived from Bangalore, being a part of those given up to Hyder by Admiral Suffrein at Cuddalore in June. These were all chosen young men, picked out from about three hundred that the Admiral gave up, and destined for Hyder's army.[39]

The author names Wilson, Ediman, Austin, Whiteway, Drake, Cadman and Lesage.[40] It is likely that James Scurry was among these unfortunate Englishmen. Cadman later escaped along with Bristow and others, eventually reaching Madras safely. This innocent narrative unveils a long saga of slave-raiding, slave-trading, forced circumcision, forced conversion and prisoner abuse.

Bristow reports that the youngest and most handsome boys were accommodated in Haider Ali's palace and received preferential treatment. They underwent training tailored to the roles they were expected to fulfil.[41] 'Some of these, after the peace, were intended for dancing boys, and sent among the *Notch* people to be instructed in the manoeuvres belonging to that art.'[42] Other authors have also noted that young boys were trained as dancers, presumably for the amusement of Tipu Sultan, who had ascended the throne well before the peace was concluded in 1784.

'Wilson, Ediman, Austin, Whiteway lost their lives in the tyrant's dominions some years ago.'[43] These unfortunate seamen were circumcised and met their deaths due to harsh treatment. They were not regarded as prisoners of war but rather as the exclusive property of Haider Ali, as he had received them as a gift from a French comrade.[44] 'It was the opinion of the wretched sufferers that Suffrein had sold them to the tyrant.'[45] Suffrein had attempted to recruit their services due to a shortage of manpower, but they had adamantly declined the offer. Perhaps this refusal had provoked him to sell them into slavery.[46]

In November 1782, '[the] universally esteemed and beloved Colonel Baillie fell a victim to long illness, and fatigues of mind as well as body, and died in the prison of Seringapatam'.[47] Bristow reveals that no medical treatment was provided to the colonel despite his terminal illness.[48] Within days of the colonel's demise, Haider Ali himself would also pass away.[49] Bristow notes:

> His son Tippoo Saheb, since called Tippoo Sultan, took undisturbed possession of all his father's territories.... No open attempts were made to oppose his accession.... The customary mournings were observed at Seringapatam, but the people seemed not to regret the loss of their ruler. His remains were not brought to the capital till three months after his death.[50]

In December 1783, 'all the circumcised Europeans in Seringapatam were moved to Mysore'.[51] Bristow continues, 'On our arrival here we were closely confined, and in the same room where Captain Rumley and Lieutenants Frazer and Sampson ...were murdered shortly before, by the order of Tippoo.'[52] They gleaned the details of the English soldiers' final moments from a slave. Bristow states:

> Captain Rumley, when he found that he would be constrained to swallow poison, put an end to his own existence rather than submit; and Lieutenant Sampson, having snatched up a large piece of wood that chanced to be within his reach, laid so furiously and resolutely about him, that the cowardly murderers, afraid of approaching, threw a stone at him from some distance, which met his head with a mortal blow. Lieutenant Frazer alone was secured, and had poison forced down his throat, of which he soon after died.[53]

For four months, Bristow and others were detained in Mysore before being marched back to Srirangapatna after peace was established in 1784. 'Our numbers at this time amounted to eighty, being the survivors of such as from time to time had been dragged out of the Seringapatam prisons, and circumcised. The seamen, except those selected for the palace, are included in this list.'[54] Bristow mentions receiving whispered information indicating that throughout Tipu's dominions, English captives had met a similar fate.[55]

The Englishmen were assigned to various Chela battalions as havildars, while Lieutenant Speediman and Rutledge were appointed as subedars. Lieutenant Brunton, who arrived in Srirangapatna around the same time as Bristow, and Ensign Gordon, who had been imprisoned at Chitradurga for an extended period, were finally released.[56]

Bristow mentions, 'Malabar Roman Catholic Christians, consisting originally of about 40,000 unfortunate wretches, men, women and children, forced away from the Bednore and Mangalore countries in 1784, and compelled to embrace Mahometism.'[57] He was assigned to their battalion, providing him with direct, firsthand information.

Soon after peace was established with the British, Tipu's formidable army advanced towards Mohabbat Jang's capital, Adoni. Jang fled to Hyderabad with his family and treasures, leaving Tipu to seize control of Adoni. Tipu completely demolished the fort.[58] Bristow discloses that he 'collected this information from the Europeans whom Tipu had carried along with him, four of the Malabar Christian battalions having being employed on this occasion'.[59]

Referring to Tipu's invasion of Adoni (which he spells 'Hydona'), Bristow avers:

> It was said that Tipu alleged the Nizam's refusal of his daughter, and Mouberjung [Mohabbat Jung] of his sister, for his son, as a pretext for the war. The proposal had been rejected with contempt, the young Mysorean being of too mean an origin to aspire at

> mixing his blood with that which flowed in the veins of such high descent.[60]

Other historians have mentioned this, but it was generally believed that the proposal was for the sultan's legitimate son Abdul Khaliq, who was less than ten years old at the time.

Bristow goes on to say:

> Soon after the tyrant's return we were divided into three parties and dispersed; one was sent to Bedanore, the other was sent to Chittledroog ... and the third, to which I belonged, remained in the city. Those that went away were in irons; we that were reserved were at first posted to a battalion of Coorikies [Coorgis] ...We were later subdivided anew into four parties, one of which remained with the Coorikies, another was posted to a battalion of Moplas (Mappilas), and the other two incorporated with the Malabar Christians.[61]

Thus, it is evident that Tipu had enslaved the Malabar Christians, the Coorgis, as well as the Mappilas, who were Muslims.

Bristow describes how Tipu would deceive his troops. He would delay payment of wages for several months on some pretext, then offer loans to the distressed soldiers at exorbitant interest rates. When the wages were finally paid, these advances would be recovered with interest. Additionally, soldiers were forced to receive one-fourth of their wages in grain. They would also be provided with damaged military stores that needed to be discarded. These deceitful methods of extortion ultimately enriched the sultan's coffers.[62] Bristow opines that only fear, lack of unity and the absence of leadership had prevented the soldiers from revolting.[63]

He recounts the escape of two Europeans who were quickly recaptured near Tellicherry. As they were being transported back to Srirangapatna, one of the men managed to escape again by swimming across a river, while the other, unfortunate enough to be brought back to the capital, had his ears and nose severed.

Subsequently, he was paraded on a donkey with his face towards the tail.[64] Scurry's narrative also includes a similar story.

'In the year 1788, six of Tippoo's chiefs and a Brahmin were hanged at Seringapatam for being suspected of carrying on a treacherous correspondence with the English.'[65] A letter addressed to Lieutenant Rutledge was discovered on the Brahmin, arousing the suspicion of the sultan. 'Lieutenant Rutledge was, in consequence of this discovery, loaded with fetters and sent to Nundidroog.'[66] There, he endured two years of misery, surviving on nothing but ragi and chillies, until he was ultimately shot dead for a minor transgression.[67] Bristow, having learned this from a farrier who had been chained on the same rock but was later summoned to attend to one of the sultan's Arabian horses, observes that this man is the only person ever known to have returned from any of Tipu's fearsome forts.[68]

Bristow further states:

> In the beginning of 1789, six men, whom we had not heard of before were brought from Chittledroog to Seringapatam; this sufficiently evinces that many more Europeans than what are suspected are concealed in Tipu's dominions. These men were, soon after their arrival, carried out of the fort in irons, into a wood near the island, where they were hanged. They had belonged to the Bedanore garrison which capitulated: what induced the barbarous conqueror to murder these men in cold blood I was never able to discover.[69]

The prisoners executed on this occasion were probably among those captured in 1783.

Soon thereafter, in 1789, Tipu marched down the ghats with a massive army. At Srirangapatna, nobody seemed to know his intended destination. Bristow testifies that after a significant period had passed, Tipu sent orders

> to prepare for the nuptials of his son, a stout boy about seventeen years of age, who was now to espouse the daughter of the Queen of Cannanore, since the Nizam had disdainfully rejected him for a son

> in law; orders were also received at the same time to arrange matters preparatory to the father's inauguration as 'Sultaun of the East', the title which he in future intended to assume.... He likewise issued a proclamation prohibiting all marriages in the kingdom of Mysore until such time as the wedding of his son should take place, being determined to celebrate that day by the consummation of 25000 marriages at his own charge.[70]

Bristow obviously refers to Tipu's eldest son, Fateh Haider, whose mother was a concubine. His second son, Abdul Khaliq, was barely ten years old in 1792 when he was offered as a hostage to the British. It is unimaginable that the boy's marriage could have taken place in 1789.

The author adds that when Tipu announced his intention to convert 100,000 of his Hindu subjects to Islam on the day of the wedding, their 'admiration changed into merited detestation'.[71]

'The palace of old Hyder was demolished and in the rear of it was begun a more extensive and magnificent one of a triangular form and fronting a famous pagoda in the centre of the fort.'[72] Bristow also reveals that 'four large and curious crystal pedestals' had arrived from France, presumably to support his throne.[73] When Bristow left Srirangapatna neither the palace nor the throne had been completed.[74] There is also no further mention of Tipu's son's wedding; perhaps it never took place.

'Tipu cut down last year a forest of beetle-nut trees,' writes Bristow.[75] He adds:

> Opposite the fort, at the distance of about half a mile, stands another forest, where Tipu is erecting a powder manufactory, with mills upon European principles, and where he has a foundry for casting cannon, constructed by one of the mechanics, lately arrived from France.' When Tipu's embassy had returned from France, they had brought about thirty mechanics with them.'[76]

Bristow's account also reveals that Srirangapatna housed a silk manufactory.

'On the 22nd of September 1790, I finally left Seringapatam. Tippoo had no sooner marched us out of the fort than we were divided into three parties and separated.'[77] Each party was assigned to a different fort. It was Outradurg (Uttaradurga), a fort near Bangalore, that fell to Bristow's lot.[78]

The terrain was rocky and steep, yet the prisoners were compelled to climb with their legs in irons. 'We all suffered dreadfully in travelling barefooted up this rough and difficult ascent, being very much hurried, notwithstanding the weight and encumbrance of our irons.'[79] Upon arrival, they were presented before the killedar, and Tipu's order was read aloud, specifying that the prisoners must be fettered and denied any food. The sultan's intention was clear; they were meant to die.[80] Bristow recollects at this juncture, 'He had often declared, that none of the European prisoners should be saved, for sooner than part with them he would murder them.'[81] Perhaps Tipu had begun losing the war, and he was relocating the English prisoners to places where they would suffer miserable deaths. Outradurg surrendered to the British in December 1791; however, by then Bristow had escaped.

Bristow expresses his profound gratitude to Tipu's Hindu subjects and asserts that every one of the English prisoners owes his life to them. 'They constantly commiserated the situation of the unfortunate European prisoners, and saved the lives of many by their timely humanity and assistance, when the unfeeling conqueror denied us food.'[82]

The English prisoner recounts a prison break in vivid detail, describing how he led eleven other Europeans to freedom in November 1790. After enduring the torturous journey from the interior of the prison to the bottom of the hill, Bristow discovered that the others had vanished. He pondered whether they had intentionally left him behind, considering his frail constitution and fearing he might hinder or delay their escape. He never encountered them again.

Bristow writes about the hardships endured during his solitary journey towards the nizam's dominions, where he finally found deliverance. It is a tale of grit and determination, and one cannot help but admire the perseverance of the courageous Englishman.

Reaching the Tungabhadra River on 1 January 1791, Bristow finally found himself among the Marathas by mid-February. Later, he managed to extricate himself from their midst and arrived near Koppal, from where the nizam's people conveyed him to Mohabbat Jung. Bristow finally reached Fort William, Calcutta, on 11 June 1791 after spending 'nine years, nine months and twenty-two days in slavery'.[83]

### Eloy Joze Correa Peixoto

The Portuguese captain Eloy Joze Correa Peixoto wrote *Memoirs of Hyder Ally from the Year 1758 to 1770*. Serving for nearly twelve years in Haider Ali's army, he witnessed the dramatic usurpation of the Mysore kingdom. Departing from the nawab's service in 1770, he travelled to various places within India before leaving for Lisbon. The book was written the same year, and at Tellicherry, he had the manuscript translated by an unnamed Englishman. A summary of Peixoto's narrative is found in the 'Annual Report of the Mysore Archaeological Department for the Year 1937', published by the Government Press, Bangalore, in 1938.

Peixoto provides explicit details of several military campaigns, making his book one of the earliest contemporary accounts of the initial phase of Haider Ali's rise to power. He appears relatively unbiased, shedding light on some of Haider's major faults while also revealing his admiration for the man. Peixoto equally praises and criticizes both Europeans and Indians.

Peixoto began his military career as captain of infantry in the Portuguese state of Goa. In 1758, he entered Haider Naik's service when the latter held the position of the faujdar of Dindigul. Peixoto remained with Haider until the end of November 1767, participating in almost all his campaigns. Despite attempting to return to Portugal, he seems to have encountered difficulties and wandered around India for over a year. Peixoto rejoined Haider's service in May 1769, following the conclusion of the First

Anglo-Mysore War. However, he left in August 1770, ostensibly to recruit more Europeans for Haider's army.

Peixoto informs us that Haider Ali arrived at Srirangapatna on 15 April 1758 with 5,000 men, when he was summoned to tackle a threatened Maratha invasion. It was at this juncture that Peixoto joined his service.[84] In December 1758, Haider sent Kabir Khan to recapture Channapatna, which was then held by the Marathas. Kabir Khan succeeded, and several Maratha soldiers joined Haider's army. However, the Marathas returned in strength, leading to two months of relentless warfare. Finally, peace was negotiated, and the Marathas withdrew on 23 February 1759. Upon his return to Srirangapatna, Haider Ali was received with 'much grandeur and honoured with the post of General in Chief'.[85]

Peixoto refers to Nanjaraj as the 'second Raja' who had relocated to Mysore following a misunderstanding with the 'first Raja' (the Wodeyar). Haider was instructed by the Wodeyar to march against Nanjaraj, despite Nanjaraj having been his original mentor. Nanjaraj commanded a 6,000-strong army and had two European commanders, Manoel Alves and Bento de Campos. Peixoto played a role in intriguing with these foreigners to persuade them to join Haider's cause. Although he succeeded in winning over one of them, Nanjaraj strongly defended his position for over three months, but eventually he was forced to reat to Konanur (Cunur).[86]

According to Peixoto:

> Hyder when he returned to Seringapatam, was well rewarded for his success and given the title of Hyder Ali with the injunction that whosoever should address him as Nayak thenceforth should have his tongue cut off. A poor man's tongue was actually cut off the very next day for his having, perhaps in ignorance, disobeyed this proclamation.[87]

Peixoto sheds light on the Khande Rao affair, describing him as a trusted Brahman servant of Haider, who, in addition to his administrative responsibilities, was also entrusted with spying on the raja.[88] It was Khande Rao who alerted the Wodeyar to the potential threat posed by Haider Ali to the throne of Mysore. He masterminded the conspiracy to eliminate Haider by inviting the Marathas to invade Mysore in 1760. While the bulk of Haider's forces were away in Pondicherry, the Marathas advanced toward Srirangapatna. Haider was caught unawares when the firing on his palace commenced. Khande Rao had initiated the firing in anticipation of the arrival of the Maratha army. Peixoto states:

> [Haider]commanded the inmates not to make even the slightest noise. A ball however rolled and struck his old mother on the leg. She cried out in pain and Hyder at once smote off her head making thereby an example of her for others to keep rigidly still. For three days and nights he remained in this manner and then fled away leaving his whole family, taking with him 30 horse and 11 camel with some money and jewels. Manoel Alves was killed and the other Europeans entered the service of Khande Rao.[89]

The matricide anecdote is not corroborated by any other author or historian. The English would not have had access to such information as they had no presence in the Mysore kingdom at that time. It is certain that Haider's staunch loyalists and the women of the household would not divulge such details. Undoubtedly, Peixoto wrote this based on hearsay, but the story certainly provides food for thought.[90]

On 18 August 1760, Peixoto, who was away from Srirangapatna at the time, received orders from Haider to join him at Anekal, which he promptly did.[91] The Marathas surrounded Anekal, but Haider managed to evade them and reach Bangalore before daybreak. The struggles with the Marathas continued for three months. At one point, Makhdum Sahib found himself besieged by the forces of Khande Rao and the Marathas at 'Tellemangal'. In response, Haider dispatched an army under Faizulla Khan, Ismail Sahib and Mir Sahib to relieve him, with Peixoto among its members. Haider sustained significant losses and was compelled to seek peace. Disappointed by the Marathas' departure, Khande Rao harboured deep regret.[92] Haider then sought Nanjaraj at Cunur and acquired his seal, which he used to issue orders to sow confusion among Mysore's citizens and divert their loyalty from the Wodeyar and his supporter Khande Rao.[93] Methodically, Haider conquered the provinces, replacing resistant governors with loyalists. Those who opposed him were ruthlessly eliminated. Soon, the whole kingdom, except Srirangapatna, was under his control.[94] When Haider marched on Srirangapatna, the Wodeyar submitted meekly, shifting blame for the fiasco onto Khande Rao, though he pleaded for the man's safety.[95] Haider initially offered benign assurances, but later he dealt severely with all those who had opposed him. Khande Rao was confined in a cage in Bangalore, where he remained until his death.[96]

When Basalat Jung, the brother of Nizam Ali, besieged Hoskote, which was held by the Marathas, he sought Haider's help. Peixoto mentions:

> Haider accomplished the task so soon that Basalat Jung in appreciation of his ability, gave him the title of Nawab Hyder Jung Bahadur, and asked him to take the fort of Sira which was also in the possession of the Marathas. With little difficulty this place was also conquered and garrisoned.[97]

Peixoto provides detailed accounts of Haider Ali's capture of Chickaballapur and Kodikonda. He then proceeds to describe the siege and eventual fall of the mountain fortress of Madakasira. He states:

> It took four days for Haider to effect a breach in the walls. His first commandant Joze Raiz [a Portuguese] died, at which he was very sorry. The other commandant Bento de Campos also died three days later, and had it not been for the presence of Hyder and the French Bishop [Noronha], the troops would not have made bold to mount the breach. The author of the manuscript was ordered to garrison the citadel and the hill and not to stir without a second order from Hyder himself. In the meanwhile, the gate at the citadel was fired at by the Marathas themselves, which incident caused

> great injury to the troops. Even Hyder was covered with blood, but in spite of the reverses, he persisted and eventually effected a breach in the fort wall at which those within retreated to the top, where the mountain is divided into three parts. Hyder intimidated them and eventually compelled the governor to deliver the place.[98]

Peixoto furnishes details of the annexation of Bidanur on 10 January 1763 and the subsequent developments.[99] Haider's attack on Savanur is also described extensively. When it became evident that Savanur was on the verge of surrendering, 'the old mother of the Nawab herself came to Haider and was received with great respect. Haider agreed to raise the siege if her son would consent to his terms and come to his camp.'[100] An agreement was reached for tribute, but it remained unpaid, causing Haider 'to waste several days in the expectation of men and money from the Nawab'.[101] The nawab had pledged 6,000 troops for the siege of Bankapur, Haider's next target. Haider finally sent Brahmins led by Bhima Rao to press his demands. When they tried to intimidate the Pathans, they retaliated, killing some guards and injuring Bhima Rao.[102] Haider, angered by this, threatened to massacre everyone in the fort if the amount was not paid within three days. The threat worked, and the tribute was soon paid. When the nawab of Savanur visited Haider, he was kept waiting for several days, and 'when finally he admitted him into his presence he scolded him by saying he was not a worthy son of his mother'.[103]

Peixoto continues, 'After this Haider captured Bankapur from the Marathas, and returned to Bidanur in September 1763... Until March 27, 1764, he remained at Bidanur, making military preparations.'[104] Then he received intelligence that the Marathas were approaching, and he marched to counter them. The encounters with the Marathas inflicted heavy losses on Haider's army, but with the onset of the rainy season, Madhav Rao returned to Poona. Once the rains subsided, Haider commenced plundering the Maratha territories near Anekal. Madhav Rao returned with Malle (Murari)

Rao and the nawab of Savanur, establishing their camp at Anavatti within sight of Haider's camp on 16 November 1764. On the 18th, the battle began in the open plain, resulting in significant losses on both sides. 'In the meanwhile, Raghoba arrived to help Madhav Rao.'[105] Five days later, peace talks commenced, but the Marathas refused to accept the offered tribute. War persisted until a treaty was reached on 23 May 1765.[106] As soon as the Marathas crossed the Tungabhadra, Haider ordered the invasion of Coorg. Mir Faizullah Khan led the march to subdue Coorg, while Haider himself moved to conquer Malabar.

The following year, when the Marathas arrived to collect their annual tribute, Haider learned that Nizam Ali was also marching towards Srirangapatna.[107] He quickly recalled Mir Faizullah Khan from Coorg and resolved to resist the invasion. With the Wodeyar's demise, Nanjaraj demanded recognition as king. He attempted to meet Haider on his way to Srirangapatna, but Haider skilfully avoided a meeting. The Maratha invasion compelled Mir Sahib to relocate to Sira, where both he and the fortress were captured. 'The news disturbed Hyder who was thus constrained to treat for peace with them.'[108]

By the end of April 1767, Haider made peace with the Marathas, paying 36 lakh rupees.[109] The inhabitants of Srirangapatna began to speculate that Haider Ali intended to designate his son as the future king of Mysore. To silence these rumours, Haider placed a son of the late Wodeyar on the throne. However, he retained control as the de facto ruler.[110]

In 1767, Haider Ali and the nizam jointly attacked Muhammad Ali's forces at Ambur, Kaveripatnam and Arcot. When the two forces clashed at Thiruvannamalai ('Trinamally'), 'there was great loss on both sides and the Nawab himself was wounded a little'.[111] Haider suffered considerable losses due to Nizam Ali's cavalry failing to follow orders. Colonel Smith put up a valiant fight, attacking both armies simultaneously. The nizam's army fled first, followed by the Mysorean army. According to Peixoto, 'Nizam Ali beat a shameful retreat in the night. Many were killed on the side of Haider who now retired to Changama. The enemy thus gained the battle on the 26th and 27th of September.'[112]

He further states that the cavalry sent under Tipu to invade Muhammed Ali's territories advanced very close to Madras and caused much damage. 'At St. Thome, they robbed, destroyed and broke all that was possible and even brought some prisoners with them some of whom were European ecclesiaticks.'[113] On 27 November 1767, when Peixoto left Haider Ali's service, he was entrusted with the return of these Jesuit priests to Madras. He explains that his departure was delayed as he awaited instructions from Goa.[114] (Perhaps he had intended to sail to Lisbon from there.)

Peixoto reached Madras on 4 December and stayed there for a month, during which the British governor extended an invitation to join their service. Politely declining, Peixoto expressed his reluctance to work against Haider Ali. On 13 December, he boarded a ship bound for Bombay, but it encountered a leak and sank off the coast of Ceylon on the 18th. Spotting the port of Galle, distress signals were sent, and two boats arrived to offer assistance. As the ship sank, Peixoto, the captain and six seamen jumped into the boats and tried to help other passengers. They managed to save only about 14 of the 116 individuals on board.[115] The local governor urged him to participate in the war against the Sinhalese, but Peixoto declined. On 5 February 1768, he embarked on a Dutch vessel bound for Cochin, reaching there on the 18th. Thereafter, he visited Padmanabhapuram, the capital of Travancore, and noted, 'The king was a Nair who knew the Portuguese language and sometimes dressed in European style.'[116]

Peixoto returned to Cochin on 29 April and subsequently visited Cannanore and Tellicherry. From there, he took a ship to Calcutta and had a brief sojourn in the Andamans. He observed that the 'Deanes' (Danes) were building a factory in Nicobar. 'Almost all were sick with bad colour and swelled legs. The natives had now become civilized but their actions were more apish than human. They went about naked.'[117] He reached Calcutta on 27 November and stayed there until the end of the year (1768). Peixoto then boarded another ship and reached Madras on 17 January 1769.

The First Anglo-Mysore War was in progress, and the English grew suspicious of Peixoto, considering him a supporter of Haider Ali. Consequently, he was placed under observation, and feared arrest if he ventured outside the Black Town. To avoid this, he departed for Pondicherry, arriving on 5 February. Peixoto noted that Pondicherry, once known as the Garden of Asia, had been razed to the ground by the British during the war. Reconstruction efforts were underway, including the construction of the governor's palace and fortifications. Leaving Pondicherry on the 10th, Peixoto travelled to Tranquebar and then to Nagapattinam, a flourishing Dutch town. There, he received news that Haider Ali was near Pondicherry.[118]

Peixoto returned to Pondicherry, likely facing financial strain after a prolonged period without employment and eager to rejoin the Mysore army. He claims that the French persuaded him to rejoin Haider, although he needed little persuasion.[119] Later, he accompanied a few French officers to Kolar, where Haider was encamped. These officers recommended Peixoto's reappointment, which Haider eventually agreed to after keeping him waiting for two months. Thereafter, he appointed Peixoto at half his former pay.[120] That Peixoto accepted this humble offer speaks volumes about his situation. This decision may have also been the primary reason for Peixoto's departure the following year.

Peixoto observes:

> Haider had now made many kingdoms tributary to him. Even the powerful Nawab of Kadapa had become subordinate. The sum that Hyder received as tribute was enormous. The destruction that Hyder caused in the territories conquered by him was also considerable. It resulted in the greatest ruin of these countries like Kadapa, Kurnool, etc. Only the fort of Bellary had held on.[121]

He continues, 'The Nawab's son now diverted the Marathas in the vicinity of Chikkaballapur and retired to Bangalore with the loss of

4,000 men.'[122] It appears that Tipu gained battlefield experience at a significant cost. Subsequently, he arrived at Srirangapatna, followed shortly by Haider Ali.[123] At that time, approximately 900 prisoners were present. Initially, Haider ordered that their noses be cut off, but due to the intervention of some good Samaritans, he reduced the punishment to chastisement with rods.[124]

We learn that the Europeans assisted in repelling the Maratha incursions that occurred several times during the year 1770.[125] Peixoto reports that 'the Marathas captured this year a number of forts', including one defended by Sardar Khan. Haider remained at Srirangapatna and avoided any direct confrontation.[126]

Peixoto recounts an anecdote regarding the suicide of the governor of Bidanur:

> Haider demanded an exorbitant sum from the Governor of Bidanur, by name Cunganur La, who is said to have even received chastisements. As it was not possible for him to pay this amount, he committed suicide saying that it was better to die than to suffer affronts from such an ungrateful man as the Nabob. The whole city of Bidanur, moreover, was oppressed under orders of Haider.[127]

On 27 February 1770, eleven days after his arrival at Srirangapatna, Haider Ali visited the Wodeyar and pretended to fall at his feet, but the latter prevented him from doing so. The queen mother (Maharani Lakshmammani) appeared very solemn. Peixoto states:

> Haider reported of the Maratha invasion and of the havoc committed by their force and also informed that they were demanding a great sum of money. The king replied that he was not afraid of such invasions as long as Haider guarded the country's interests ... The Marathas divided their army into three principal places – 30,000 at Adi Anantapur, 20,000 at Bankapur, Dharwar and Savanur, and 30,000 at Sira. Madhav Rao retired to Poona with the remainder of the force... A terrible war was expected in the month of November [1770] till the end of May [1771]. Haider had been sending out his men to enlist the services of Europeans and also of natives for

> the army. In fact, it was rumoured that people were being forced to join the army.... The Nawab's youngest and favourite son was Carim Saib, then about nine years old [in 1770]. He was sent for from Bangalore and received at Seringapatam in all state ... With Hyder's leave to procure Europeans for the army, the author left Seringapatam on the 6th [August] intending not to return again to the army on account of its present incapacity.[128]

Peixoto may have sensed that Haider's army was ill-prepared to face the Marathas and staying would be suicidal. He was a soldier of fortune after all.

## Charles Warre Malet (1752–1815)

An excerpt from the journal of Charles Warre Malet, the British Resident at Poona (Pune) reads as follows:

> 17th February [1787] Mahrattah Camp. The Mahrattas having accepted Tippoo's last offers his ambassador has left camp, and is returned to his master to settle the conditions. It is announced that Tippoo is to pay three crores of rupees for all arrears due, the country he has taken from the Mahrattahs for these ten years past, and for the expenses of the campaign.[129]

The Resident's diary reveals that Tipu procrastinated for months before eventually signing the treaty. It also notes that Tipu paid four years' arrears of tribute to the peshwa, indicating that he had become a tributary of the Marathas shortly after Haider Ali's death. Adoni was returned to the nizam of Hyderabad, while Nergund, Kittoor and Badami were ceded to the peshwa. From the terms of the treaty, it can be inferred that Tipu suffered significant losses in his war with the Marathas.[130]

Some of the entries in Malet's Poona diary are reproduced in the Appendix portion of Kirkpatrick's translation of Tipu Sultan's hukumnamas. An extract from the journal dated 7 March 1787 mentions that on 26 February, 'This day, between the hours of twelve and one, Tippoo's Vakeel returned, with three elephants and several camels, loaded with money. It is reported, the army will shortly march to the Kishna (Krishna) to await the second payment.'[131] A week later, on 14 March, he remarks, 'The treasure that arrived with the ambassadors is thought to be no more than fifteen lacks.'[132] Days pass, and then on 10 April, he writes to the governor-general from Poona, 'On the 8th instant I received intelligence from Behro Pundit that half of Tippoo's stipulated payment had arrived in camp, but that the ratified treaties were not yet exchanged.'[133]

Malet sends a message to the governor-general on 8 May 1787 from Poona stating:

> On the 30th ultimo the minister formally acquainted me, that after much prevarication on the part of Futtah Ali Khan [Tippoo], peace was at length made with that prince, and the ratified treaties exchanged, including, in one part, the Paishwa and Nizam Ali Khan, and on the other Futtah Ali Khan. The conditions of which were, that Futtah Ali Khan was to pay four years arrears of tribute due to the Paishwa, part of which had been already paid, the balance to be discharged in six months; that Adoni was to be restored to Mohabut Jung; Nergund and Kittoor to be surrendered to the Paishwa, who is also to retain Badamy.[134]

It is significant that Tipu is named Fath Ali Khan or Tipu, with the word 'sultan' never making an appearance.

Malet's communication to the governor-general on 3 June 1787 is more specific about Tipu's titles. It states:

> In reply to my enquiries relative to the late discussions on Tippoo's titles, the minister has informed me, that hitherto the Paishwa used to address him by the name of Futtah Ali Khan, that he had now desired to be styled Tippoo Sultan Khan Behadur. To the first of which, as it had no relation to royalty, but was actually the name given to him at his birth by his mother, in consequence of a vow to name her child, if a male, after a famous Mahommedan Peer, at Colar, in the Carnatic, whose name was Tippoo Sultan, no objection could be made. That Khan, as it had formerly joined to Futtah Ali, was nothing new, and, in fact, did away any royalty

> that might otherwise be imputed to the word Sultan; and that the appellation of Behadur was the only word of additional dignity to be used in the Paishwa's future addresses to this prince, who is not even styled Nabob by this Durbar.[135]

Malet arrived in India in 1774 and departed in 1798, a year before Tipu was killed. He played a crucial role in negotiating the British alliance with the peshwa and the nizam in 1789, upon the request of Lord Cornwallis, following Tipu Sultan's attack on Travancore. This diplomatic move was masterful, especially considering that Tipu was simultaneously seeking to ally with the Marathas.

## Colonel Mark Wilks (1759–1831)

Mark Wilks held the position of town major at Fort St George, Madras. Following the fall of Srirangapatna, he was appointed as acting resident at Mysore, where he served until 1808. This role granted him access to a wealth of firsthand information. Additionally, Wilks was a competent historian. The first volume of his work, *Historical Sketches of the South of India in an Attempt to Trace the History of Mysoor, From the Origin of the Hindoo Government of that State, to the Extinction of the Mahommedan Dynasty in 1799*, was published in London in 1810, followed by volumes II and III in 1817.

Wilks began his career in Madras as a cadet in April 1783, coinciding with Tipu Sultan's accession to the throne of Mysore. He actively participated in the Third Anglo-Mysore War, serving under Colonel Stuart during the siege of Srirangapatna in 1792. As secretary to Lord Clive during the Fourth Anglo-Mysore War, he gained insight into many significant events. Upon his return to England, he was posted as the governor of the island of St Helena, where Napoleon was held captive. Wilks maintained close contact with Colin Mackenzie, who provided him with many valuable papers and information. He also received inputs from Kirkpatrick and various others.

Wilks states:

> From my friend, Sir John Kennaway, I have received the communication of numerous and valuable facts, connected with his own diplomatic services from 1788 till 1792: and a voluminous collection of documents in the Persian language, bequeathed to him by the late Colonel William Kirkpatrick, comprising, among others, a variety of original compositions, in the handwriting of the late Tippoo Sultaun; and consultations, authenticated by the original signatures of his ministers.[136]

In 1790, the British captured Palghat and discovered a remarkable order under the seal and signature of Tipu. This order unequivocally stated that every individual in the district, without exception, must be converted to Islam. Wilks mentioned in a footnote:

> An officer of the staff, in searching the records, of the place for military intelligence, found one of the circular orders for conversion under the Sultaun's seal and signature, which was at that time deemed a curiosity of the highest order… [It directed] that every being in the district, without distinction, should be honoured with Islam, that the houses of such as fled to avoid that honour should be burned, that they should be traced to their lurking places, and that all means of truth and falsehood, fraud or force, should be employed to effect their universal conversion.[137]

Wilks elaborates, 'Before leaving this quarter [Dindigul], [Tipu] laid waste with fire and sword, the countries of such of the poligars dependent on Dindigul and Coimbetoor, as had recently failed in obedience.'[138]

He adds:

> Arshed Beg Khan … had been appointed by Hyder, shortly before his death to the office of civil and military Governor of Malabar…. His urgent entreaties to his master to avert the destruction of Malabar by his own presence had caused the Sultaun's visit to that country in the beginning of 1788. He found the conduct of Meer Ibrahim to have really placed the province on the verge of rebellion, and he removed and confined him, but he also removed

> and disgraced Arshed Beg Khan…. This venerable man… was still in prison … and he soon afterwards [in 1789] died of grief and disgust.[139]

Wilks further states, 'The measures of conversion in Malabar had been obstructed in the north by the escape of the Nairs to the English settlement of Tellicherry, whence they embarked for Travancore.'[140] He speaks of 'the Sultaun's coarse assertion that the English chief of Tellicherry had taken bribes for the protection of fugitive Nairs, and for permitting them to embark for Travancore'.[141] Tellicherry was placed under a 'blockade, by a cordon of the Sultaun's troops, during the whole period from the peace of 1784 till the war of 1790'.[142]

Wilks' three-volume book holds immense academic value, and subsequent authors have heavily relied on his narrative. His work has been extensively quoted in this text as well.

## Professor Charles Stewart (1764–1837)

Charles Stewart joined the Bengal army in 1781 as a cadet and advanced to the rank of major. Upon the establishment of Fort William College in 1800 in Calcutta, he was appointed assistant professor of Persian. After Tipu's death in 1799, his extensive library of over 2,000 manuscripts was transferred to Calcutta. Subsequently, several volumes were shipped to London and gifted to various universities, libraries and private individuals, including the king.

Stewart returned to England in 1806 and authored numerous publications, including *A Descriptive Catalogue of the Oriental Library of the Late Tippoo Sultan of Mysore, to Which Are Prefixed Memoirs of Hyder Aly Khan and His Son, Tippoo Sultan,* which was published in Cambridge in 1809. He drafted this catalogue of 1,090 manuscripts in Tipu's library during his tenure as professor of Arabic, Persian and Hindustani at the East India College in Haileybury. Stewart opines that Tipu acquired the bulk of the manuscripts through plunder during his military campaigns. However, it is true that Tipu was an active buyer as well as a looter.

Stewart states:

> During the years 1787 and 1788, the attention of the Sultan was principally engaged in the subjection of the Curg [Coorg] Raja, and the Nairs or Chiefs of Malabar. The former, who had been his prisoner for four years, made his escape and caused a successful insurrection; but the latter were either extirpated, forcibly converted, or obliged to fly for refuge into the territories of the English or their allies.[143]

When Tipu's ambassadors returned from France empty-handed in 1789, the sultan was sorely disappointed. However, when they began singing praises of the glory and splendour of the French court, Tipu became truly incensed. Citing Michaud's *Histoire de Mysore*, Stewart reveals:

> He therefore severely reprimanded the Ambassadors and forbade their ever again speaking of France. Disappointment and envy, however, continuing to rankle in his perturbed mind, he one day, while walking in private with Akbar Aly Khan and Mohammed Osman, ordered his attendants to put them to death, saying they had disobeyed his commands and betrayed his interests.[144]

In 1780, Haider Ali launched a massive assault on the Carnatic, beginning with the capture of the fort of Chittor from where a significant collection of Arabic and Persian manuscripts were taken to Srirangapatna. In August, villages around Madras were plundered, and in September, Bailley's contingent was slaughtered at Pollilur, with the survivors thrown into dungeons at Srirangapatna. After a long siege, the citadel of Arcot surrendered on 3 November. Soldiers were sent throughout the Carnatic 'to collect the cattle and sheep and to burn and destroy the villages and crops on the ground. The banks of the ponds or reservoirs were also broken down or cut through, and the wells filled with the putrid bodies of murdered fugitives.'[145] Haider proclaimed himself as the instrument of God's wrath. Stewart's account reveals:

> The boys were made Mussalmans, formed into battalions, and disciplined by the English prisoners, who were not only compelled to do this hateful service, but many of them were also circumcised, and every means used to make them embrace the Mohammedan religion. The girls were either married to the young soldiers or distributed as slaves.[146]

This account is corroborated by the personal testimonies of two English prisoners, James Bristow and James Scurry.

Stewart opines:

> Hyder Aly Khan was doubtless one of the greatest characters Asia has produced; and if his success cannot be compared with that of Tamerlane [Timur]or Nadir Shah, it must be attributed more to the competitors with whom he had to contend than to any want of ability on his part. Without the advantage of education, he acquired an extensive knowledge of the sciences of war and of politics; and by his superior talents, raised himself from a private station to the sovereignty of a powerful kingdom.[147]

Stewart adds, 'He is accused by the Mohammedans not only of putting great faith in astrologers but also of reverencing the Hindu deities.'[148] Haider Ali passed away, leaving behind a treasury brimming with wealth, a domain spanning 80,000 square miles and an army of 150,000 men.[149]

### Dr Francis Buchanan

Buchanan, a contemporary of Tipu Sultan, spent two decades in India from 1794 to 1815 as an employee of the EICo. Though primarily a medical doctor, he is chiefly remembered for two meticulous surveys conducted in British India, the first, in the Mysore territory in 1800, and the second in Bengal between 1807 and 1814. Following Tipu's death, Buchanan travelled extensively in the sultan's erstwhile dominions, including parts of present-day Tamil Nadu, Kerala and Karnataka. He meticulously maintained a daily diary, vividly detailing the people and places, religious practices, crops and cultivation, flora and fauna, culture, history, geography and living conditions. While his perspective is quintessentially British and reflects the colonial mindset, his elaborate descriptions provide valuable insights. In 1807, he published *A Journey from Madras through the Countries of Mysore, Canara and Malabar*, which remains a veritable goldmine of information.

Buchanan states:

> About fifty years ago the Moplays of this place [Ponnani] were very rich and possessed vessels that sailed to Surat, Mocha, Madras and Bengal; but the oppression of Tippoo has reduced them to great poverty, and most of them are now under the necessity of acting as agents to Mousa, a Mussulman merchant of Tellicherry.[150]

He mentions that 'Panyani' or 'Punany Wacul' contained 500 houses, 1,000 huts and 40 mosques, and adds, 'The huts are inhabited by boatmen and fishermen, who were formerly Mucuas, a low cast[e]of Hindus; but now they have all embraced the faith of Mahomet.'[151]

Buchanan's remarks about the Thangal family of Malappuram shed light on the local religious dynamics, 'Panyani is the residence of the Tangul, or chief priest of the Moplays, who says that he is descended from Ali and Fatima, the daughter of Mahomet.'[152] Tipu attempted to establish his own Thangal, whom he designated as Arabi Thangal. On 14 December 1800, nineteen months after Tipu's death, Buchanan notes:

> The late Sultaun, who wished to make innovations in everything, did not respect this descendant of his prophet; but appointed another head for the priests of his faith in Malabar. This person, called Arabi Tangul, resides at Panyani; but his followers are now reduced to five or six families, and he has lost one half of the property that Tippoo bestowed on his new favourite.[153]

The doctor penned this note on 14 December 1800, roughly nineteen months after Tipu's death. It appears that although

Tipu Sultan tried to replace the Thangal and bestowed many favours on his chosen substitute, soon after Tipu's exit, the people reverted to their belief in the original Thangal. Today, the eldest male member of the Panakkad Shihab Thangal clan is the president of the Indian Union Muslim League (IUML), a political party. I tried to find out if any Arabi Thangal family exists in the Malappuram district, but my Muslim friends expressed ignorance.

Buchanan further states that some of the rajas who had gone into exile in Travancore returned in 1790, and 'a little before the battle of Tiruvana Angady [Tirurangadi], they joined Colonel Hartly with 5000 Nairs'.[154] The combined army achieved a decisive victory over the forces of Tipu Sultan.

Buchanan opines that Calicut's prosperity stemmed from two factors– first, the victories achieved by the Zamorins in warfare, and second, their encouragement of commerce. Tipu's arrival tilted the scales dangerously. The town was destroyed in 1788, and its inhabitants were relocated to 'Nelluru', which was promptly renamed 'Furruck-abad'. Buchanan notes, 'Fifteen months after this forced emigration, the English conquered the province, and the inhabitants returned with great joy to their old place of residence.'[155] Before Tipu's assault, there were approximately 6,000–7,000 houses in Calicut. Despite the devastation, about 5,000 houses were soon re-established, with more residents gradually returning. Buchanan adds that the majority of Calicut's inhabitants were Mappilas, indicating that Tipu Sultan showed no mercy to his Muslim brethren.

Buchanan reports that the raja of Palghat resided in a humble dwelling. He notes, '[The raja] is now engaged in rebuilding the temple of Bhagawat[y], at Callay Colum; which was pulled down by Tippoo; but that bigot did not venture to destroy the image, which is in the form of a human hand.'[156] The Bhagavathy temple described by Buchanan is the Hemambika Temple at Palghat. Legend has it that Prime Minister Indira Gandhi visited the Hemambika Temple (Kallekulangara Kaipathi Kshethram) at the instance of the then chief minister of Kerala, K. Karunakaran. Thereafter, she decided to adopt a new symbol for the Congress Party; out went the 'cow-and-calf', and in came the 'hand'!

## Maistre de la Tour (M.M.D.L.T.)

Monsieur Maistre de la Tour, who headed the French troops in Haider Ali's army, later rose to command the artillery, overseeing 10,000 troops. He authored *The History of Hyder Shah, alias Hyder Ali Khan Bahadur and of His Son, Tippoo Sultaun*. The original version was published in London in 1784, followed by a Calcutta edition in 1848. Later, this work was edited and revised by Prince Gulam Muhammad, one of Tipu Sultan's sons.

'The countenance of Hyder, though not handsome, is open, and calculated to inspire confidence,' writes De la Tour.[157] He stands at five feet six inches tall and is clean-shaven. He is unadorned, easily accessible to all, and capable of conversing on any subject. He goes to bed after midnight and rises at 6 a.m. He takes an afternoon siesta from 3 p.m. to 5.30 p.m. 'If he has leisure, he appears at a balcony, and receives the salute of his elephants that are led before him, as well as his horses,' De la Tour observes.[158]

It is evident that the writer had close proximity to Haider Ali. His perspective is distinctly French, and he discloses certain facts that none of the English authors have mentioned. The documents included in the Appendix, mostly dated after 1784, are of high value. It is possible that they were attached with the reprinted edition of 1848.

M.M.D.L.T. states that Haider Ali is the son of 'Nadim Saeb', which adds to the mystery surrounding the man's origin. Other authors mention his father's name as Fath Muhammed. The author adds that Haider Ali was 'born in 1717 at Divanelli (Devanahalli)'.[159] Moreover, 'Hyder Ali claimed the honour of being by descent a Coreishy [Qureishi], and consequently of the same tribe as the Arabian Prophet Mohumed.'[160]

De la Tour states:

> After the death of Nizam El Moulouc [Nizam ul Mulk, Nizam of Hyderabad, Grand Vizier of the Deccan], Nadim Saeb retired to

> Divanelli, with his two sons, Ismael Saeb, and Hyder. Ismael Saeb was much older than his brother. He entered into the service of the king of Mysore.[161]

Here, Haider's brother also has a different name. (According to other authors, he was Shahbaz.) M.M.D.L.T. does not mention the early death of Haider Ali's father. On the contrary, he states that the man was alive in 1750 when Haider was thirty-four years old. Additionally, he writes that Bangalore was granted to Ismael, Haider's elder brother, by the king of Mysore after he successfully repelled a Maratha invasion.

The author points out that Haider Ali was involved in the battle where Nasir Jung lost his life. That was when he realized the superior skill and bravery of the French troops, who defeated a more numerous army in the face of severe odds. Subsequently, Haider Ali proceeded to Pondicherry, where he was impressed with the architecture, culture, armaments and especially by the French governor, Monsieur Dupleix. Thus began his French connection. Upon his return to Mysore in 1751, he persuaded his brother to send men to Bombay to purchase European cannon and muskets with bayonets, thus modernizing his private army. The governor of Bombay sold 6,000 muskets and 6 pieces of cannon to a Persian agent who delivered them to Mysore. This agent also recruited sixty European sailors of different nationalities from the Malabar Coast to serve as cannoniers. De la Tour opines that 'Meer Ismael Saeb, brother to Hyder, was thus the first Indian who formed a core of Seapoys, armed with firelocks and bayonets, and who had a train of artillery served by Europeans.'[162]

Haider Ali learned extensively from the French, even recruiting some of their officers and relocating them to Mysore, where his brother made full use of their expertise. The author notes that a soldier who joined him at the siege of Trichinopoly in 1753 remained in his service until 1770.

In 1755, Nanjaraj returned to Mysore having accomplished little in his Trichinopoly campaign. During his absence, Salabat

Jung of Hyderabad succeeded in extracting tribute from Mysore. By that time, Dupleix had been replaced, and his successor had issued orders to lift the siege of Trichinopoly.

The author narrates how the name Haider Naik evolved into 'Andernec' for the French. As his power grew, his name expanded, ultimately leading to his being known as Haider Ali Khan Bahadur.

De la Tour intricately describes the palace intrigues at Srirangapatna. In 1756, following the death of his brother, Haider Ali returned to Mysore. He had commanded 6,000 soldiers at Dindigul. As his brother had no male heir, Haider Ali inherited his contingent of 9,000 men and was appointed commander of the Mysore army in his brother's place. According to M.M.D.L.T., the raja appeared in public only twice a year, with the brothers Nanjaraj and Devaraj acting as de facto kings of Mysore. Haider Ali was content to retain his position as army commander. However, a Brahmin named Canero (Kanhere Rao or Khande Rao) exerted sinister influences at the court, even inviting the Maratha army to oust Haider Ali. The Marathas invaded Mysore during the rainy season, catching Haider off guard as he had virtually disbanded his army assuming no invasions would occur at that time.

Haider Ali retreated to the island of Srirangapatna and set up camp outside the fort. The Marathas arrived and encamped on the opposite bank of the Kaveri River. Upon discovering the gates of the fortress locked against him the next day, Haider suspected foul play. He learned that Khande Rao had demanded his surrender, threatening to starve the soldiers if he refused. In the dead of night, Haider Ali, along with a trusted band of thirty men, swam across the river, eluding the Maratha army. He then proceeded to Bangalore, where his uncle Ibrahim Ali Khan was in command. Soon thereafter, Makhdum Ali arrived with almost his entire cavalry, the 3,000 troops having crossed the river and sustained few casualties in a minor skirmish with the Maratha army.

In 1760, Makhdum was dispatched with a 7,000-strong army to defend Pondicherry at the request of M. Lally. Upon his return, he brought along carpenters, artisans and workers, together with 'all the French cavalry under Alain and Hugel',[163] which was a highly valuable acquisition. However, Makhdum had been unsuccessful in his attempt to compel the British to lift the siege of Pondicherry. Meanwhile, Haider Ali had managed to make peace with the Marathas.

As the time came for Haider's contingent to confront the Mysore army on the outskirts of Srirangapatna, they camped across the Kaveri. Haider demanded the surrender of Khande Rao. De la Tour reveals that Haider had an aristocratic lady friend in the palace with whom he maintained a systematic correspondence. She interceded with the king on his behalf resulting in his appointment as regent. Haider then captured and took Khande Rao to Bangalore, where he was publicly displayed in an iron cage, eventually dying after two years. The author notes that his bones could still be seen there, because he was neither buried nor cremated but left to rot in the sun. (The anecdote of the 'caged parrot' is also recounted by other historians.)

Haider Ali captured Sira in alliance with Basalat Jung. Thereafter, an incident occurs that is not mentioned by other writers. According to De la Tour, '[The] Marathas having collected their forces against him, he, by the pusillanimity of his allies, had nearly lost his life, having received a stroke on the head with a sabre, in a battle in which neither side gained the victory.'[164] A few days later, Haider made peace and retained Sira after paying off the Marathas.

De la Tour provides explicit details of Haider Ali's conquest of Bidanur. He also mentions that when Haider subdued Karwar and advanced towards Goa, the French soldiers in his army refused to engage in combat against the Portuguese. Consequently, Haider opted for peace with the Portuguese, who acknowledged his control over Karwar in return. Thereafter, Haider grew sceptical of the loyalty of the French troops and decided to use them carefully.

When Haider visited Mangalore for the second time, he was visited by Ali Raja of Kannur. A delegation of Mappilas (referred to as 'Mapelets' by De la Tour) was received by Haider Ali, who appointed Ali Raja as his high admiral and his brother Sheik Ali as the head of all his ports and maritime commerce. Ali Raja reportedly received a substantial sum of money for the purpose of purchasing and constructing ships.[165]

Haider now declared Haidernagar as the capital of all his dominions. He shifted his entire family to Haidernagar, although his first begum, who was the sister of Makhdum Sahib and the mother of Tipu, preferred to remain behind in Bangalore. (In other accounts, she is referred to as the second begum.) Haider entrusted the administration of Bangalore and its surrounding areas to his uncle Ibrahim Ali Khan, while Makhdum Sahib, now titled Nawab Makhdum Ali Khan, was tasked with governing Mysore. Sira and Bisnagar were also assigned to close relatives.

Ali Raja soon conquered the Maldives and upon returning in triumph, he arrived in Haidarnagar to pay homage to his newfound mentor. He presented the king of Maldives, whom he had blinded, before Haider Ali. 'Hyder, whose character is far from cruel, was so irritated at the barbarity of Ali Raja that he instantly deprived him of the command of the fleet; which he afterwards gave to an Englishman named Stanet.'[166] The author mentions that Haider Ali profusely apologized to the Maldivian king, who was a Muslim, and provided him with a palace and a pension. With this, Haider Ali acquired another title: 'King of the Islands of the Sea'. The conquests of Canara and the Maldives greatly enhanced Haider Ali's standing among the princes of Hindustan.

At this time, Cannanore had two forts– one was in the possession of Ali Raja, and the other was held by the Dutch, who had previously acquired it from the Portuguese. Faced with the imminent threat of a Mysorean invasion, the Dutch hurriedly sold their fort to Ali Raja.

De la Tour asserts that Haider Ali indeed had plans to attack Travancore. However, upon receiving intelligence that the nizam and the British were conspiring to march on Mysore, he changed his plans.[167] Describing Haider's march to Srirangapatna at the head of a 50,000-strong army, the author devotes several pages to providing explicit details of the grandeur of the procession, with elephants, horses, et al. Upon arriving at Srirangapatna, Haider was informed by Makhdum Ali that a massive Maratha army under Madhav Rao was advancing towards Sira. The author suggests that the English envoy at Poona instigated the Marathas to attack Sira simultaneously with the planned march of the British and the nizam on Mysore. Mirza Ali Khan, Haider's cousin and brother-in-law, who was the commandant of Sira, had sent a Brahmin emissary to Poona seeking Maratha support to gain independence from Mysore. Makhdum Ali warned Haider that Mirza could no longer be trusted. Madhav Rao refused to negotiate with a traitor. Meanwhile, Haider's three-year peace treaty with the Marathas had expired and needed to be renewed, ostensibly by paying them a sum of money. He had tasked Mirza with this renewal. However, upon hearing that the Maratha army had reached Sira, and that Mirza had simply opened the fortress gates to them, Haider was aghast. His options were limited. If he rode out to Sira for an open confrontation, he would be risking defeat. If he waited at Srirangapatna, a British attack may compel him to abandon his capital and retreat to Canara.[168]

Haider Ali did something unprecedented –he divided his army into numerous small units and sent them across the countryside to gather the citizens and compel them to relocate to the capital with their valuable possessions. Soldiers were ordered to destroy everything that could be of use to an invading army. Consequently, even the thatched roofs of the houses were burnt down. De la Tour states:

> It is scarcely possible to form an idea of the promptitude with which this extraordinary order was carried into execution; and in how short a time one of the finest and most beautiful countries in the world was changed into a desert, for thirty leagues around Seringatanam.[169]

As a military man, De la Tour seemed pleased with this strategy, showing little concern for the environmental disaster or the agony of the people. He insists that the people complied willingly and gladly.

Haider Ali dispatched Makhdum to Bangalore to secure it against a possible attack from the nizam, employing the same scorched earth strategy. Mir 'Fisoolah' (Fazalullah) Khan was sent to Bisnagar to defend the passes to Canara from potential Maratha incursions. Eventually, the Maratha army and the British army under General Smith (assisted by the nizam's forces) arrived simultaneously outside Srirangapatna.

Haider managed to bribe the Marathas and avoid war. De la Tour states, 'On receiving six lacks [sic] of rupees in hand, and six lacks payable in six months, they engaged to retire out of his country, and to restore Sira; but the rest of the district intrusted to Mirza was abandoned to them.'[170] Haider then recalled the contingent from Bisnagar and ensured it camped within striking distance of the nizam's army. The nizam's advisors then urged him to seek peace. General Smith recognized he had few options.

De la Tour opines that it was the wanton destruction of Pondicherry by the British that drove many Frenchmen to seek refuge under Haider Ali and other Indian princes.

Haider Ali had meticulously crafted plans, but they did not unfold as expected. His alliance with the nizam proved short-lived, and Arcot did not remain in his grasp for long. Tipu would never ascend to the position of nawab of Arcot. Today, a nondescript structure known as Tipu's Pavilion within the Vellore Fort stands as a stark reminder of the meteoric rise and fall of the Mysore sultans, marking their formidable yet fleeting presence in Arcot.

De la Tour also recounts Haider's attempt to build a fleet. Haider purchased a small frigate from the Danes and appointed an English admiral to command it. However, when the ship went to Bombay for repairs and refitting, the British promptly seized it.

When Haider Ali besieged Kaveripatnam, the English chose to surrender even before the fort could be breached. Haider, taken by surprise, readily agreed to the terms offered. The English garrison marched out, and many Indian sepoys joined Haider's army. 'Hyder was soon informed of this unexpected march, by the repeated signals of rockets.'[171] This demonstrates that Haider Ali was indeed using rockets liberally, even for military communications. It is puzzling why later historians have given the credit to Tipu Sultan for the 'invention' of the Mysore rocket.

Haider decided to send Tipu Sultan towards Madras with an army, and Tipu proved to be successful. As the Mysorean army approached Madras, the local people mistook them for Marathas. 'A crowd of the country people ran past towards Fort St George crying *Maratta! Maratta!*'[172]

De la Tour reports, 'The garrison of Fort St George consisted of only two hundred Europeans and six hundred Sepoys; so that the Black Town, which is properly the town of Madras, was at the discretion of Tippoo Sultan, a youth of eighteen.'[173] Though commonly referred to as Black Town, Madras boasted several colonies of European merchants. It served as a bustling trade emporium, housing a colony of wealthy Armenians and numerous Gujarati businessmen. As the conflict unfolded, the fort became inundated with refugees seeking sanctuary. Colonel Call, the chief engineer, who took charge of the fort, later recalled that nothing could have stopped Tipu Sultan from capturing it. However, Tipu, being rather inexperienced, conferred with his senior advisors when faced with the discharge of English cannons from the fort. Ultimately, he decided to heed his father's orders and limit his actions to the surroundings of Madras.

'The Author of these Memoirs had advised Hyder to besiege and take the Black Town of Madras, and to burn it.'[174] Haider, however, estimated that this would be a formidable task. In the meantime, Colonel Call had mobilized and armed all the Europeans and stationed sepoys to defend the entrance of the Black Town. The British suffered heavy losses. When Tipu decided to withdraw from Madras, he remembered his father's instructions to capture and bring along a few notable Europeans. Tipu thus took along a few Jesuit priests.

The nizam and Haider Ali met in camp and reached an agreement that the nizam would return to his dominions and trouble the British at Machilipatnam, compelling them to divide their forces. Haider Ali would continue his conflict against the nawab of Arcot and the British. However, shortly after his return to Hyderabad, the nizam ceded Machilipatnam and the Northern Circars to the British and acknowledged Muhammad Ali as the nawab of Arcot.

De la Tour describes the visit of Haider Ali's mother to the army camp near Vaniyambadi and Kaveripatnam. Upon hearing of her arrival, Haider and his sons rode out to greet her and escorted her into the camp with great pomp and ceremony. She was accompanied by 200 women on horseback, all veiled in full purdah. 'They were enveloped in large pieces of thick Muslin, which prevented even the smallest part of their clothes from being seen.'[175] If Haider had indeed killed his mother, as claimed by Peixoto, this incident would have to be fictional.

In 1775, Haider Ali sent a small army led by Cina Cerrao, a Maratha warlord, to subdue the Zamorin and other princes of Malabar. The Zamorin had failed to pay the tribute promised to Haider Ali when he restored his kingdom in 1767, a year after its capture. Fearing retaliation from Haider, the Zamorin sought protection by offering to become a vassal of France. 'The commandant of Mahe accepted the gift of the Samorin, and came with a few troops to take possession of the fortress of Calicut, where he hoisted the French standard.'[176] Haider promptly lodged a complaint with the French authorities in Pondicherry. Subsequently, the Mahe commandant was recalled, and Haider regained control of Calicut.

De la Tour's account concludes after the fall of Chitradurga to Haider Ali in 1779, suggesting his departure from India thereafter. He seems to present a realistic and reliable narrative. Given his alliance with Haider Ali, his perspective naturally favours the Mysore sultans. De la Tour ends his narrative by comparing Haider Ali with Philip of Macedon, and Tipu Sultan with Alexander the Great. Little did he know that barely a decade after the publication of his manuscript, Tipu Sultan would lose half of his dominions to the British, meeting an ignominious death seven years later.

De la Tour's observations on the Nairs of Malabar are indeed quaint:

> The Nayres are the nobility of the Malabar Coast. We may affirm that they are the oldest nobility in the world; for the ancient writers mention them, and quote the law that permits the Nayre ladies to have many husbands; everyone being allowed four. Their houses, which stand single, have as many doors as the lady has husbands.[177]

The Frenchman's fanciful caricature indeed adds a touch of humour to his narrative. He remarks, rather tongue-in-cheek, that 'Hyder imagined that the Nayres, awed by his power, and contented with his moderation, would peaceably support the yoke he had placed upon them; but he was not yet sufficiently acquainted with the character of that haughty people, who, once offended never pardon their enemies'.[178]

## Lieutenant Colonel Russel

The 'memoires' of Lieutenant Colonel Russel concerning Mysore were translated by Jean-Marie Lafont, senior fellow CSH, French Embassy, New Delhi, and are included in the 2001 publication titled *State and Diplomacy under Tipu Sultan,* edited by Irfan Habib. The translator references five primary documents housed in the Service Historique de l'Armee de Terre at the Chateau de Vincennes in Paris. He observes that while 'most of the Frenchmen who served Hyder Ali and Tipu Sultan did not publish any memoirs', there were a few exceptions, including Le Goux de Flaix and Maistre de la Tour.[179] The former wrote a book covering the whole of India with a focus on economic affairs. He mentions in the preface that he served as a civil and military engineer under Haider Ali for many years. Ironically, he scarcely discusses his experiences in Mysore.[180] The English translation of Maistre de la Tour's *Histoire* was published in 1855.[181]

The Russel papers consist of 'five documents written by Russel, two letters and three [or two] memoirs [the *Memoires* covering 106 pages]'.[182] The first, a letter dated 26 May 1781, reveals that Russel was 'sent on a political and military assignment to Hyder Ali Khan' in June 1772, succeeding Hugel as the commanding officer of the French detachment. He remained with Haider until mid-1778 and participated in most of his military campaigns. Russel provides a list of the sieges and campaigns (with dates), presenting an inside view of the early successes of the Mysorean usurper.[183]

The second document states that 'Hugel died in 1772 from wounds received at the Battle of Melkota, but before dying he advised Hyder Ali to select Russel as the next commander of the French troops'.[184] Lafont states, 'There was a severe outbreak of dysentery in Mysore in 1772, and Hugel died from the epidemic.'[185] Thereafter, 'Haider Ali, who had a high regard for Hugel, ordered his mortal remains to be buried in front of his palace at Srirangapatanam.'[186] Russel could not have been unaware of the cause of death, but he may have preferred to give his predecessor a more dignified exit, thus referring to wounds sustained in battle.

Russell served for six years as lieutenant colonel of cavalry and was replaced by Puymorin in June 1778. Upon returning to Pondicherry, he found the town under siege by the British. Entering the town in the guise of a Muslim, he secured appointment as aide-de-camp to the governor-general, Bellecombe. When Pondicherry fell, Russel was taken prisoner, and by October 1780, he was back in France. [187]

The third document, dated May 1781, spans fifty-eight pages and provides interesting details of Haider Ali's military career. It refers to the 'brilliant action of Hyder Naik at Trichinopoly when he captured 400 muskets and an unspecified number of horses'.[188] On Dupleix's recommendation, Nandi Raja (Nanjaraj) allowed Haider Ali to raise a troop of 400 sepoys equipped with the seized muskets and horses.[189] This indicates that, besides Nanjaraj, the French were also impressed by Haider's prowess in battle.

Russel discloses that in February 1773, Haider had 15,000 infantry and 10,000 cavalry.[190] He also mentions that in June 1778, Haider had a total of 222,900 men, including 900 Europeans, with a detailed breakdown provided. The cavalry had increased to 30,000.[191] Seven years later, when Haider Ali launched the Second Anglo-Mysore War in July 1780, he had around 100,000 soldiers, which was a significant accomplishment. Russel gives his own estimate from his camp in Paris, suggesting 166,000 Indians and 1,400 Europeans.[192] Despite variations in the numbers specified by different historians and military figures, it is evident that Haider Ali systematically strengthened his army year after year. By 1780, when he initiated the Second Anglo-Mysore War, he had indeed become a formidable force.

The Russel papers reveal that in 1773, 'The French Hussars joined them (Haider's troops) for the conquest of Coorg, and then for the re-conquest of the places lost to the Marathas (1774–1775). Haider then moved against Basalat Jung who was besieging Bellary.'[193] Describing the sequence of events, Russel informs us that 'Basalat Jang's army was almost completely destroyed or captured'.[194] He was astonished to find several wounded French soldiers in Jung's contingent. Haider Ali had not informed him that Lally's corps was fighting on the Hyderabadi side. Russel took care of his injured countrymen.[195]

In December 1775, Haider besieged Gooty. On 10 January 1776, Russel 'led the storming party, climbing an ascent at the head of his Hussars'.[196] The citadel capitulated only after the ramparts were blown up and stormed by the Mysorean troops.[197] In July 1777, the siege of Chitradurga was a challenging endeavour, lasting 75 days.[198] On 1 January 1778, Haider's army was engaged in battle against the Marathas. In March, the Mysoreans were compelled to retreat when two Maratha armies and the army of Basalat Jung faced them across the Tungabadra.[199] Russel then describes the Raghuba affair and expresses the opinion that 'the extraordinary acumen of Hyder saved Mysore from a devastating invasion'.[200] By June, Puymorin arrived, and Russel handed over the charge to him.[201]

In the fourth document, Russel reiterates that the French government of Pondicherry sent a military mission to Mysore with the express aim of strengthening the hands of Haider Ali and using him against the EICo.[202]

Lafont points out that, 'Russel criticizes the anti-Hyder lobby in Paris and Versailles which was casting doubts on Hyder Ali's strong opposition to the English.'[203] Russel staunchly believed that 'Hyder Ali has been able to convince Nizam Ali as well as the Marathas that it is in their own interest to expel the English from India.'[204] An admirer of Haider Ali's military capabilities, he observes that 'Hyder is following a long-prepared plan to take over India, and reduce the English East India Company to its original size'.[205] A year after Russel wrote the last of the five documents, Haider Ali died of cancer.

Russel concludes his *Memoire* (the fourth document, which appears to be a continuation of the third document) with the words: 'Hyder Ali will certainly reduce the East India Company, and perhaps the French Compagnie des Indes, to a mere couple of trading posts, since he is an ambitious man who can be contained only by superior power.'[206] Russel cannot be faulted for this assessment, as in 1780–1781, Haider Ali appeared to be unstoppable. Ultimately, what stopped him was indeed a superior, supernatural power.

Russel's fifth document is a confidential thirty-seven-page missive sent in November 1781 to De Castries, Ministre de la Marine, who was responsible for the overseas colonies. It contains a dire warning about the dangers of relying on Haider Ali. While Haider was the only native power capable of assisting the French in India, his driving ambition prevented him from allowing any other power to gain the upper hand.[207] Lafont observes, 'In a footnote, he (Russel) strongly advocates banning the sale of artillery to Hyder by French merchants; and if the French felt compelled to sell them, let them take their time and sell only defective guns.'[208] Russel suggests sending 12,000 soldiers to India, but only landing 6,000 men initially, to avoid arousing Haider Ali's suspicion. French generals are advised not to accept any Indian troops provided by Haider Ali, as they might betray them at any moment.[209]

Russel reveals that Haider Ali harboured ambitions regarding the kingdom of Travancore, attracted by its wealth and strategic importance.[210] He mentions the construction of roads by Haider in the forests leading towards Cochin as an initial move towards the invasion of Travancore.[211]

Quite a few of Russel's suggestions possess a Machiavellian essence. Obviously, he operated with shrewdness, prioritizing France above all. Russel speculates that if Haider Ali were to defeat the British, the Marathas and the nizam might unite against him. 'In that case, if Hyder was reluctant to accommodate the French, they could play the Maratha card against him.'[212] Russel also devises a Plan B in case Haider Ali refuses to agree to a treaty with France. 'Russel even dreams of Tipu Sultan joining the French against Hyder, as he too was reeling under his yoke! If Tipu acted this way, most of the Mysore army, especially the cavalry would follow him.'[213] Was this merely wishful thinking or did Russel indeed sound out Tipu and draw conclusions? One can only speculate.

Russel advises that when a French general meets Haider Ali, he should present appropriate gifts and negotiate a treaty. He states:

> He should also request permission to meet Tipu Sahib and offer him state gifts, along with the personal gifts Tipu had requested: taffetas 'cire' of different shades to make coats, 'gold and silver water' from Danzig, looking glasses, and a toiletry set with good soaps. Other notables should also receive gifts: Prince Karim Sahib, one of Hyder's sons 'du serail' ['from the seraglio', as opposed to sons born 'outside' the harem] and his most preferred child.[214]

This casual mention of Karim Sahib implies the existence of other sons, both within and outside the harem. It also suggests that Tipu was not his father's favourite.[215]

'A short "Recapitulation" starts with the clear affirmation that the purpose of French military intervention in India must be the conquest of all of India.'[216] Once the British are expelled, Haider Ali would need to be addressed. 'He is in possession of immense treasures and is the master of one of the most beautiful parts of

India.'[217] Russel asserts that 'there will be no injustice done to Hyder Ali if the French deprive him of his possessions since they helped him so much in acquiring them'.[218] He concludes by noting that that the possibility of Haider Ali's death cannot be ruled out, which is why he had assiduously cultivated a friendship with Tipu Sahib.[219]

Lafont opines:

> Being a king's officer, Russel did his duty in transferring without reluctance, military technologies to Mysore, and in training the Mysorean forces according to the most modern European systems of warfare.[220]

Therefore, for a quarter century, beginning with Haider Ali's hostile takeover of the Mysore kingdom in 1761, we possess direct evidence of the close French association with both father and son. In fact, Russel, as a loyal French subject, tries to warn his government that bolstering the Mysorean army would ultimately undermine French interests in India.[221]

## Father Bartolomeo (Paulinus Paathiri)

Fra. Paolino Da San Bartolomeo came as a missionary to Malabar in 1774 and remained in India for fourteen years. A Carmelite friar of Croatian (or Austrian) descent, he was formerly known as Johann Philip Westin before taking his vows. He was renowned for his erudition and linguistic abilities. Among the people of Kerala, he was affectionately referred to as Paulinus Paathiri. The raja of Travancore held him in high regard. Bartolomeo eventually returned to Rome in 1789.

Bartolomeo authored *A Voyage to the East Indies (Viaggio alle Indie Orientali)*, with the original version published in Italian in 1796. A German translation followed in 1798. The English version I read was translated from the German by William Johnston. Bartolomeo published numerous books on the Orient, which garnered high praise during his time. Among these works was the initial printed European exposition of Sanskrit grammar (published in Rome in 1799), with another edition released under the title *Vyacaranam*

(Rome, 1804). He was among the first Europeans to notice the close connection between Sanskrit and the European languages.

Bartolomeo mentions:

> In India, a man can openly carry money with him on the public highway; without having occasion to be in any dread of robbers... This security prevails at least in the kingdom of Travancore, where I have travelled more than twenty times by day as well as by night, from Cochin to Cape Comari [Kanyakumari].[222]

Bartolomeo is known for his keen observations, candid expressions, humour and straightforwardness. He writes:

> Timur-Bec, Thamas Kuli Khan [Nadir Shah], the Moguls and Marattas, the English and French, all pretended to have just reasons for seizing the possessions of others; and no man was able to refute these reasons, which, while they had arms in their hands, were rendered sufficiently valid.[223]

Bartolomeo states that when the king of Madurai, Virabhanayaguen (Veerappa Nayakan), passed away, 'no fewer than three hundred of his wives ascended the funeral pile'.[224] Madurai was invaded by the Marathas, the nizam and ultimately the nawab of Arcot in 1742. The latter brokered a deal with the British at Madras, dividing the territories of Madurai between his allies and the British. Subsequently, the English stationed troops in Trichinopoly. Bartolomeo also mentions that the English maintain another army at Tirunaveli (Tirunelveli) and that the formidable fortress of Paliamkotta (Palayamkottai) belongs to the raja of Travancore.[225]

Bartolomeo provides an interesting anecdote about the English and the raja of Travancore, related in his inimitable style:

> Whenever the English are desirous of procuring money from this prince, they instigate their ally Mohamed Aly Khan to send an army against Tovala, in the neighbourhood of Cape Comari; and

> if the king of Travancor wishes to prevent this disagreeable visit, he must pay to the English whatever they choose to demand. When I was at the court of this prince in 1784 the army of Mohamed Aly Khan required him either to send them a certain sum, or to give them permission to march through Tovala, in order that they might obtain money from Travancor. Cumaren Cembaga Ramapulla, however, a man of talents, who was then prime minister, settled the whole business by paying to the English 200,000 rupees.[226]

This firsthand account carries a touch of subtle humour. In 1784, the Second Anglo-Mysore War had just ended, and the British were in need of replenishing their coffers. Mohammad Ali of Arcot acted as their hatchet man. Rama Varma, the raja of Travancore, thought it prudent to buy peace, a decision that ultimately proved wise. When Tipu Sultan invaded Travancore five years later, the British declared war on him, leading to the Third Anglo-Mysore War (1790–1792). In the end, Tipu suffered a significant defeat, relieving Travancore of the Mysorean threat.

Bartolomeo identifies Tipu Sultan of Mysore and Muhammad Ali of Arcot as the two dreaded enemies of the Travancore raja, 'Through a dread of these two dangerous neighbours, the king of Travancor found himself obliged to conclude a treaty of alliance with the English, and to make a common cause with them both in peace and war.'[227] He adds, 'The annual tribute which he is obliged to pay to the English amounts to half a lack of rupees.'[228] This sum may seem insignificant, considering the advantages of the alliance. However, it is possible that Paulinus Paathiri was misinformed.

The book provides insights into the progress and methods of Christian conversion. Bartolomeo says, 'In my time there were reckoned to be in Madura (Madurai) eighteen thousand Christians; in Carnada (Carnatic) twenty thousand; and in Tanjaur (Thajuvur or Tanjore) ten thousand.'[229] These are interesting statistics. However, the non-Catholic annotator-editor challenges these figures in a footnote, He adds:

> This estimation of the number of Roman Catholic Christians [48,000] is certainly too high, even if we should forget how the missionaries of the Roman church behave in regard to their so-called converts. They insinuate themselves as physicians into the houses of the Indians; draw a wet cloth over the head and forehead of a sick person, even when at the point of death; mutter privately to themselves the baptism service; and think they have made one Christian more, who is immediately added to their list.[230]

William Johnston, referring to a 1797 German publication, further informs us that '[the] protestant missionaries have in the course of the past nineteen years baptised 19,340 persons'.[231]

Paulinus Paathiri's description of Madraspatnam, with its segregation into the black town and white town, is vivid and informative:

> Near the noblest palaces are seen the most wretched hovels; broad streets and narrow crooked lanes occur in turns; and instead of cleanliness, filth and dirt are everywhere seen. Fort St George, in which none but English must reside, is called the white town; but the outer district, inhabited by Europeans, Armenians, Bengalians, Chinese, Peguans, Arabians and black and white Indians of all classes, castes, and religious sects, is called the black town.[232]

The author gives a dispassionate account of the slave trade conducted by Europeans in southern India. He informs us that they trafficked in male and female slaves from the Malabar and Coromandel coasts,[233] 'The slaves are treated exactly like cattle. A youth in full health without blemish costs, according to his age and makes twenty, thirty or forty rupees. The females are sold cheaper.'[234]

Bartolomeo provides other interesting insights as well. 'The Pagans are accustomed to drinking cow's urine, in order to purify them from their sins,'[235] he declares. One wonders whether Bartolomeo was referring to all Hindus or specific caste groups. He adds, 'In Malabar, and every other place where the pagans have superiority, any person who kills a cow is hung on a gibbet.'[236]

## Lewin B. Bowring

Bowring's book *Haider Ali and Tipu Sultan and the Struggle with the Musalman Powers of the South* was published in London in 1899, a century after the death of Tipu Sultan. It enjoys widespread readership and is extensively quoted by both historians and laymen today.

Bowring contends that Tipu was born in 1753 at Devanahalli. According to him, his mother, Fakhr-un-Nissa, was the daughter of Mir Moin-ud-din, the governor of Kadapa.[237] Kirkpatrick's translation of Tipu's letters also mentions his year of birth as 1753. However, contemporary historians seem to favour 1750 as Tipu's birth year.

When Tipu ascended the throne of Mysore, he inherited a formidable force of 90,000 troops and a sizeable treasure amassed at Srirangapatna.[238] Meanwhile, in Madras, the authorities hesitated for a month before sending an army to continue the war. This delay provided Tipu with enough time to consolidate his forces and strategize his next step.[239]

Bowring states:

> The strong hill fort of Nargund ... and Ramdrug, a neighbouring fort, relied upon aid from Poona, and refused to submit to Tipu. The Mysore army besieged both places, the latter falling speedily, notwithstanding Parasu Ram Bhao's attempts to relieve it. Venkat Rao, the chief of Nargund, valiantly defended that town for some months, but was at last compelled to capitulate.[240]

He was given an assurance of personal safety, but 'on his surrender he was sent in chains to die miserably at Kabaldrug'.[241]

Bowring mentions:

> One of the principal victims of Tipu's revenge was the Raja of Chirakkal, of ancient descent, who having been falsely accused of conspiring, was attacked and killed, and his body hung up after his death. In this raid the Mysore sovereign is said to have carried off large treasures plundered from the temples in Malabar. He crowned

his achievements by compelling the princess of Cannanore to marry her daughter to his son, Abd-ul-Khalik.[242]

Bowring remarks:

> [Srirangapatna has] a series of frescos representing the triumphs of Tipu over the English. The most remarkable of these designs [are] intended to delineate the defeat of Baillie at Perambakam, and is a most amusing caricature, that General being shown reclining helplessly in a palankeen, while Tipu on horseback is calmly smelling a rose and giving orders to his troops ... The perspective is ludicrous–legs, arms, and heads flying off in all directions, and considerable research is needed to find the corresponding bodies. These frescoes were effaced by Tipu before the siege [of Srirangapatna], but restored by Colonel Wellesley when he inhabited the building. In course of time, they again became hardly recognizable, when Lord Dalhousie, on his visit to Mysore in 1854, ordered them to be repainted by a native artist.[243]

He further adds, 'On his tomb at Seringapatam, it is recorded ... the Haidari Sultan died for the faith ... the light of Islam and the faith left the world ... that Tipu on account of the faith of Muhammad was a martyr.'[244]

## Alexander Beatson (1758–1830)

Beatson participated in the actions of 1799 as ADC to the governor-general, affording him access to extensive information regarding the progress of the war and its ultimate outcome. In 1800, he wrote a book titled *A View of the Origin and Conduct of the War with Tippoo Sultaun; Comprising a Narrative of the Operations of the Army under the Command of Lieutenant-General George Harris, and of the Siege of Seringapatam,* published in London. Following his time in India, Beatson served as the governor of St Helena from 1808 to 1813, during which he successfully quelled a rebellion in 1811. Additionally, he harboured a passion for agriculture.

According to Beatson:

> The possession of his [Tipu's] lost dignity, wealth and power, could not be recovered without the conquest of a great part of the Company's territory, nor effectively secured without the total subversion of the British interests in India. A French army was the only instrument by which such an enterprise could be attempted: an alliance with France was, therefore, the necessary consequence of Tipu Sultan's restless but natural desire to restore his empire to its former splendour and strength.... In addition to his correspondence with the French at Tranquebar, with those at the Isle of France, and with the Executive Directory at Paris, his embassy to Zaman Shah, his intrigues at Poonah and Hyderabad and his correspondence with Monsieur Raymond, furnish abundant evidence that his antipathy to the English was the ruling passion of his heart, the mainspring of his policy, and the fixed and fundamental principle of his councils and government.'[245]

He reckons, quite rightly, that Tipu's heirs 'must have been educated in the same principles, encouraged to indulge the same prejudices and passions, and instructed to form the same views of the interest and honour of the throne of Mysore'.[246] His argument that it would be dangerous for the British to place a son of the late Tipu Sultan on the throne of Mysore is understanable. Choosing the Wodeyar boy was obviously a safer bet. Moreover, being a Hindu, he would be more acceptable to the Hindu majority in Mysore and show greater compassion towards the people.[247]

Beatson states:

> Since the fall of Seringapatam, the conduct of the Marhattas has been of the most conciliatory nature: and there was not the least appearance of their giving an interruption to the settlement of Mysore. Whatever may be the secret inclinations, either of the Peshwa or of Scindia, their mutual weakness and reciprocal jealousy, are sufficient securities against any danger from that quarter.[248]

He estimates the annual income expected from the newly acquired territories and provides many useful insights into the true value of the British acquisition.[249]

Beatson considers the possibility of an attack by Zaman Shah, although he acknowledges that the loss of an ally like Tipu Sultan would significantly impact Zaman Shah's aspirations.[250] He also predicts that the threat of a French invasion will diminish once news of Tipu's death reaches Europe.[251]

The British carefully studied the manuscripts found in Tipu's palace, thereby gaining insight into the history of Mysore. Beatson gives elaborate details in his book. He opines that Haider Ali seized control of Mysore in 1759 after imprisoning Nanjaraj.[252]

The appendices hold special interest as they contain some of Tipu's dreams, the Malartic Proclamation, the correspondence between Lord Mornington and Tipu Sultan, and various other intriguing documents.

### Denys M. Forrest

In his 1970 publication *Tiger of Mysore: Life and Death of Tipu Sultan,* Denys M. Forrest offers an interesting account of the lives of the Mysore sultans.

In 1756, significant events unfolded in Mysore. The twenty-seven-year-old puppet ruler Krishnaraja II began displaying signs of independence. Nanjaraj, who had earlier married his daughter to the ruler, suggested to the pregnant queen that she poison her husband so that the unborn child could inherit the throne. Nanjaraj's elder brother, Devaraj, opposed this violent scheme, leading to a major conflict between the brothers. Subsequently, Devaraj left Mysore in disgust. 'Nanjaraj besieged and stormed the Raja's palace and turned all his servants out into the street with their noses and ears cut off.'[253] It is therefore evident that this tradition of mutilation did not begin with Haider Ali.

Soon thereafter, Peshwa Bajirao I invaded Mysore, demanding a hefty ransom in cash, jewels and territory.[254]

In 1760, the dowager queen conspired with Khande Rao, hiring 6,000 Maratha warriors to confront Haider Ali. 'There was a fight round the walls of Seringapatam [12th August] which ended with Khande Rao tacitly allowing Haider to escape by night.'[255] Haider abandoned his family, but 'Khande Rao at once took charge of Tipu and also of his baby brother, Abdul Karim, born during the battle'.[256] Following the Marathas' defeat at Panipat five months later, all Maratha contingents were recalled from southern India, including the 6,000 men under Khande Rao's command. Haider seized the opportunity, ultimately defeating Khande Rao in battle and capturing him.[257] He then moved his zenana to Bangalore for increased security.

When Haider sent Tipu on a diplomatic mission to Hyderabad, it was led by Mahfuz Khan, elder brother of Muhammad Ali. Tipu, still a teenager, presented lavish gifts to the nizam, including '5 elephants, 10 splendid horses and a load of treasure'.[258] In return, the nizam bestowed upon Tipu a robe of honour and promised to disband the English troops. Forrest states:

> But the real heart of the treaty which was now signed was an alliance between Haidar and the Nizam to eject Muhammad Ali from the Carnatic and to replace him by his brother Mahfuz Khan; the latter would, however, at once resign in favour of Tipu, who was to be married to his daughter. According to some authorities the Nizam actually invested Tipu as Nawab during his State visit.[259]

The author adds that in 1780, Haider Ali declared himself nawab of the Carnatic, although he struggled to unseat Muhammad Ali from power.

In August 1767, the nizam and Haider Ali 'descended the Ghats as allies at the head of 60,000 men of all arms, and what is usually known as the First Mysore War began'.[260] Forrest elaborates:

> Tipu's task force ... laid waste the Arcot country [up to] the very gates of Madras ... Governor Bourchier himself had a narrow escape: he was with Muhammad Ali, Colonel Call, and others in the Company's garden house near the beach when Tipu's men galloped up; and he only just managed to get away in a small vessel lying offshore.[261]

Nizam Ali switched sides, joining hands with the British. According to Forrest, 'On February 23rd, 1768, he signed a treaty with Muhammed Ali and the English, by which he acknowledged the former as lawful and independent nawab of the Carnatic, and confirmed the latter in possession of the Northern Circars' with the exception of Guntur, which was held by Basalat Jung.[262]

Forrest mentions:

> When on May 10th, 1781, all the [English] officer prisoners at Seringapatam were placed in irons, Captain Lucas volunteered to wear a second pair to save his friend Baird who was wounded in the leg. Baird himself was put into irons on November 10th, 1781, but they were removed again the following April because of his sickness. Lucas died in prison on July 3rd, 1782.[263]

This happened during Haider Ali's reign. Despite this adversity, Baird survived and later played a prominent role in leading the final assault on Srirangapatna in 1799.

### William Logan (1841–1914)

The Scotsman William Logan served as the collector of Malabar from 1875, following over a decade of service in the region as a judge and magistrate. He arrived in India in 1862 as a member of the Madras Civil Service, demonstrating a remarkable ability to quickly learn Malayalam, Tamil and Telugu. His celebrated 1887 guide to the Malabar district, although titled 'Malabar' is popularly known as 'Malabar Manual' or 'Logan's Manual'. This comprehensive volume covers all aspects of Malabar, including history, geography, society, culture, agriculture, geology, economy, architecture, religion and more. Logan's meticulous documentation ensures that his work remains unparalleled to this day. In honour of his contributions, the main road in Thalassery (Telicherry to the British), a bustling town in Malabar, is named Logan's Road.

Logan states:

> The martial spirit of the Nayars in these piping times of peace has quite died out for want of exercise. The Nayar is more and more becoming a family man. Comparatively few of them even nowadays engage in hunting. With a large increase in their numbers, and with comparative poverty for the large body of them, the race is fast degenerating.[264]

Logan was correct in making this observation, but he was mistaken about one thing–a future he could not possibly have foreseen. The Nairs did not deteriorate or fade into oblivion. In the 21st century, they are still thriving. One of them is writing this book.

# 9

# CHRONICLES OF NON-EUROPEAN WRITERS

Mir Hussein Ali Khan Kirmani wrote the *History of Hydur Naik* and the *History of Tipu Sultan* in Farsi during the early 19th century. Among contemporary native chronicles recounting the exploits of the Mysore sultans, Kirmani's account stands out as undoubtedly the most renowned. Authored by a camp follower or court chronicler seeking favours from Tipu's descendants, this narrative likely presents a best-case scenario. The depictions of the Mysore sultans in Kirmani's works might thus paint a rosier picture than reality.

Here, I have opted to introduce (briefly) six authors alongside Kirmani – P. Stephen Basappa Chetti, a relatively lesser-known 19th-century writer from Mysore; C. Hayavadhana Rao, whose 1948 publication *History of Mysore* serves as a storehouse of credible information; Mohibbul Hasan, who authored the erudite work *The History of Tipu Sultan* in 1951; K.M. Panikkar, whose widely acclaimed *A History of Kerala, 1498–1801* was published in 1960; C.K. Kareem, who published *Kerala under Haidar Ali and Tipu Sultan* in 1973; and Sandeep Balakrishna, whose book titled *The Tyrant of Mysore* was published in the early 21st century. Among these writers, Kirmani stands out as the sole contemporary of the sultans. Thus, we find a diverse array of perspectives on the same events and individuals.

### Mir Hussein Ali Khan Kirmani

Kirmani's account presents a laudatory exposition marked by abundant exaggerations and poetic embellishments. It is plausible that either he was commissioned by Tipu Sultan's sons to write this story, or he anticipated some reward upon its completion. According to the website of the Royal Collection Trust, UK, 'Although not written as a commission, the author confidently asserted his "hope and trust" that Tipu's sons would reward his scholarly labours.' Kirmani, originally from Persia, served at the court in Srirangapatna from 1781 to 1786, and thus he was acquainted with both the sultans. His biographical account of their lives was published in Persian six years after Tipu's death. Written around 1802 in Vellore, where Tipu's sons were kept in luxurious confinement, Kirmani's work holds value as a contemporary account of the Mysore sultans' lives. Interestingly, Kirmani was apparently receiving a pension from the British at the time of writing the book. However, the circumstances of his presence at Vellore Fort and who induced him to undertake such a monumental task remain unknown.

A manuscript copy in the Royal Collection is dated 17 July 1805. Inscriptions indicate that it was originally owned by Muhammad Shukrullah Khan Sultan (1785–1825), purportedly Tipu's seventh son. His name was partially erased and replaced with that of Jami al-Din Muhammad (1792–1842), Tipu's twelfth son. Jami al-Din emigrated to Europe in 1832 and presented the manuscript to William IV that same year. H.S. Reid prepared an English translation of Kirmani's manuscript, which was published in 1834. The renowned translation by Col W. Miles was published in two parts – *History of Hydur Naik* in 1842 and *History of Tipu Sultan* in 1864.

Kirmani provides a detailed account of the events following Haider Ali's death. The body was discreetly transported in a casket to Srirangapatna. Karim Sahib was appointed dewan, wages were disbursed to the soldiers, presumably to forestall any possibility of a mutiny in case news of the regime change leaked out. Maha Mirza Khan was tasked with informing Tipu, who was bracing for an attack on the British army at Ponnani. Kirmani attests to Tipu's agitation upon learning of Karim Sahib's unexpected appointment to the office of the Dewani.[1] Upon his arrival, Karim Sahib and other nobles prostrated themselves at his feet and swore allegiance to him.[2]

Kirmani mentions the stirrings of rebellion at Srirangapatna and names certain conspirators who allegedly colluded with the British. It appears that Tipu's accession to power was far from smooth. Upon Tipu's arrival at Srirangapatna, Anchi Shamia, a key conspirator, was captured. Kirmani states, 'The next morning, with the sanction of the Sultan's mother, some of the rebels were blown from a gun; the companions of Shamia impaled, and he himself loaded with irons and confined in an iron cage – a fit punishment for his villainy.'[3]

Some accounts depict Karim as an imbecile, but there is no indication that he ever tried to seize power. Had he made such a move, Tipu may not have spared his life. Following Tipu's death, Karim was initially exiled to Vellore and later to Calcutta along with Tipu's sons.

Tipu proceeded to Bidanur and besieged the fort, which had been captured by the British. Despite holding out for eighteen days, the garrison was forced to surrender due to the depletion of water supplies. It seems that a mortar, thrown into the fort caused severe damage to a wall, leading it to collapse into the main well and fill it up. Consequently, the occupants of the fort depleted their water supply, leaving General Matthews with no choice but to surrender. Kirmani describes this event as a stroke of luck for the sultan.[4]

Tipu besieged Mangalore for three months until the garrison surrendered due to scarcity of provisions. Subsequently, the victorious Mysore army marched back to Srirangapatna via Coorg and Balam. Along the way, Tipu callously executed the commandant Muhammad Ali, a faithful follower and staunch supporter of Haider Ali and Tipu himself. Kirmani presents the entire story from a highly prejudiced perspective. 'In the course of this journey, the brave Muhammad Ali, commandant, for a trifling fault, and for showing too much obstinacy and presumption threw away his life.'[5]

Muhammad Ali's crime was his insistence on protecting Kasim Ali, the deputy governor of Bidanur under Ayaz Khan and later lieutenant-governor under the British. When Kasim Ali was sentenced by Tipu to be impaled for surrendering the fort without resistance, Muhammad Ali tried to intercede on Kasim Ali's behalf. Unfortunately, this proved to be a fatal error. To cut a long story short, Kasim Ali was impaled, and Muhammad Ali was sent to Srirangapatna in chains. Those who had supported Muhammad Ali faced severe consequences, with many being killed and the rest having their hands and noses severed. Distraught by the events, Muhammad Ali, in Kirmani's words, 'cut out his tongue, or rather drew it out by the root; and like a lamp at the approach of morning, died'.[6] Some claim he swallowed a diamond, while others suggest he was poisoned. However, there is no doubt that this loyal soldier of the Mysore sultans was driven to suicide by Tipu Sultan's cruelty. Many other loyalists would soon meet similar fates.

Tipu's rage did not subside with Muhammad Ali's death. He ordered the commandant's body to be dragged outside the camp and discarded. The commandant's sons were enslaved, and his widow was handed over to one of the soldiers to serve as a concubine. However, the good soldier treated her with kindness, regarding her as his own mother and caring for her. Kirmani reports, 'The mother of the Sultan, on hearing of these events, which arose entirely from misunderstanding, was much grieved and cursed the hasty anger of her son.'[7] She sent for Muhammad's Ali's widow and provided her with accommodation in the zenana, the protected women's quarters where she herself resided.

What Kirmani's account reveals is a long saga of incessant warfare. The Mysore sultans found themselves surrounded by enemies on all fronts, many of whom they had assiduously cultivated. They had few allies apart from the French.

While the Marathas and the nizam sent congratulatory letters to Tipu upon his accession to the throne, the former reminded him of his obligation to pay one-fourth of his revenue as tribute, as stipulated in the treaty signed by his father. Tipu replied that his treasury was currently empty. He added a seemingly casual remark, that he had inherited a few guns and muskets from his father, which he had kept prepared. He pledged to settle his dues as soon as he could stabilize his affairs. Simultaneously, he accused them of violating the treaty by failing to help his father in his war against the British.

This communication was perceived as an act of intimidation, and the Marathas were truly incensed. They negotiated a deal with the nizam of Hyderabad and resolved to attack Mysore. When Tipu sent his emissaries to Poona with 10 lakh rupees in cash as well as many presents, the peshwa and his minister, Nana Phadnavis, rejected the offering.

The nizam marched to Badami via Bidar with 40,000 men, while the Marathas, with 80,000 horse and 40,000 foot-soldiers, also reached the place. (The numbers appear to be exaggerated.) Badami surrendered following a nine-month siege, with additional forts such as Dharwar, Jalihul and Nargund also falling. Kirmani denounces the commanders of these forts as 'treacherous scoundrels', who succumbed to bribery.

In 1785, Tipu seized control of Adoni. Monsieur Lally accompanied him on this campaign, as did Kirmani.

## P. Stephen Basappa Chetti

In an 1897 publication titled *A Guide to Seringapatam and Its Vicinity: Historical and Traditional*, P. Stephen Basappa Chetti, a hospital assistant in the Mysore Medical Service, reveals that Srirangapatna had about 500,000 inhabitants during Tipu Sultan's reign. However, this number declined to 150,000 by 1800 and further fell to 31,895 in 1811, following the relocation of the British military headquarters to Bangalore. Chetti states, 'In 1837 the place was entirely deserted as a military garrison owing to its unhealthiness. According to the latest census, the population has been reduced to 12,560 inhabitants.'[8]

Chetti further reveals, 'The town of Ganjam ... was founded and colonized by Nawab Haider Ali Khan, with the deported inhabitants of Sira and other places.'[9] Srirangapatna had been under the control of Vaishnavite priests for 400 years until it became part of the Vijayanagar kingdom around 1510 CE and was ruled by viceroys. By 1610, a raja of the Wodeyar dynasty took over the town, and it remained in their hands until Haider Ali's usurpation in 1761.[10]

During the reign of Dodda Krishnaraja Wadiyar, the dalawai Devaraj Urs wielded absolute power. Upon the raja's death in 1733, Devaraj deposed his successor Chamaraja Wadiyar and 'after treating him with great indignity, sentenced him to a cruel death at Kopaldrug'.[11] Then, he installed Chikka Krishnaraja Wadiyar on the throne. (It is worth noting that Chetti uses the spelling 'Wadiyar' instead of the more commonly known anglicized 'Wodeyar.')

Devaraj's brother, Nanjaraj Urs, served as the commander-in-chief of the Mysore army. Together, the brothers succeeded in annexing Dindigul and Devanahalli to the kingdom.[12]

Chetti supplies specific information about the exchange of prisoners at the conclusion of the Second Anglo-Mysore War, 'Not less than 180 officers of all grades, 900 English soldiers and nearly 2,000 sepoys were rescued from the dungeons of Seringapatam on the 10th of April 1784. From this eventful date Tipu Sahib assumed the title of Tipu Sultan.'[13] The latter statement raises interesting questions. Chetti, like many others, suggests that 'sultan' is an assumed title rather than Tipu's given name.

Chetti recounts that the Srirangapatna Fort featured two major gateways and four sally ports. Among the latter, the *hole-diddi-bagalu* was nearest to the location where Tipu Sultan's body was discovered.[14]

Chetti testifies that the tower of the Narasimhaswamy Temple was demolished during the era of Tipu Sultan.[15] He further notes:

> The palace of Tipu is a very large building surrounded by a high stone wall. The only relic of that mighty edifice is a square building

> of stone now a depot for sandalwood. The elephant gateway of the palace now stands in silence, and on either side of this gateway are placed two elephants cut out of black stone.[16]

Today, there are no elephants, no stones, no building. Only a desolate ruin.

Chetti's account is filled with intriguing anecdotes. Concerning the origin of Masjid-Aulah, or the Great Mosque, Chetti writes:

> When Kande Rao, the Pradhan or Minister, plotted to check the growing power of Haider Ali and the leader fled to Bangalore to escape his assassins, the minister imprisoned Tipu [then a boy of seven years], along with Haider Ali's zenana in a house near the Ganjam gate, facing a Hindu temple dedicated to Anjaneya. Tipu used to play with some Hindu boys in the spacious compound of that temple; while so engaged it happened one day that a fakir passing that way and seeing Tipu, addressed him as follows: 'Oh! fortunate child, when thou art made king of this country, raze this temple to the ground and erect a mosque in its stead, and future generations will honour thee, and it will stand a memorial of thee.' Tipu with a smiling face said that whenever, by his blessings, he should be made king he would do so. And when Tipu did become king, he pulled down the temple and a mosque was raised on the site in 1790.[17]

Chetti states that the Delhi bridge over the northern branch of the Cauvery was constructed by the viceroys of Vijayanagar and was destroyed by Tipu Sultan in 1799 to prevent his enemies from crossing the river.[18] He also mentions:

> The Roman Catholic Church at Ganjam was erected during the administration of Hyder Ali by the Jesuit priests who followed Count De Lally, for the benefit of those natives who embraced Christianity. Monsieur Lally, it is said, adopted the simple plan of making converts to Christianity by branding the foreheads of those natives [who were sent to him by the orders of Tipu to work in the gun carriage factory] with a mark of the cross.[19]

Thus, Tipu was not the sole practitioner of dubious conversion methods; the French were also involved.

Chetti further explains:

> The curious traditional version of the circumstances of the siege [of Srirangapatna] current among the Mussalman inhabitants of Seringapatam is that the fall of the fortress was due to the treachery of Muhammed Mir Sadak, and of the Hindu Minister Purnaiya.[20]

He elaborates:

> Mir Syed Gaffur was Tipu Sultan's best and bravest officer, or rather he shared this distinction with Mir Sadak, only the former is esteemed a martyr, while the latter unfortunately has had the stigma of a traitor attached to his name, when the treachery myth was invented.[21]

The story goes that Purnaiya was on the ramparts with Syed Gaffur just before the assault, and through a scheme pre-arranged with the British, he ordered a green umbrella to be held over Gaffur's head, ostensibly to protect him from the heat of the midday sun. However, in reality, it was intended for the enemy gunners to identify their prime target. Consequently, Gaffur was killed, and the fall of the green umbrella signalled the commencement of the attack. Chetti opines that this is one of the imaginative stories circulated by the Muslims of Mysore to explain the defeat of their champion. He remarks:

> Kamaruddin Khan, on the 11th May 1799, came with great pleasure to offer his services to General Harris and obtained from the General a treaty entitling him to a jagir. Fateh Haider, with bright hopes of being placed on the throne of his father, surrendered himself to General Harris on the 13th of May 1799.[22]

Of the fate of Tipu's principal officers, Chetti writes:

> Mir Sadak was Tipu's go-to man. While attempting to get through the Bangalore gateway, he was killed by a sentry on the 4th of May.

> His body was exposed for nearly three days to the insults of the people, who it is said, spat on it as they passed by, and tied a shoe to it as a mark of contempt.[23]

The name 'Mir Sadak' is commonly used to refer to anyone who betrays or deceives. Purnaiya held the greatest authority in the country, second only to Mir Sadak. Following the downfall of Tipu Sultan, he was appointed regent during the minority of the child maharaja. In December 1811, upon the raja reaching maturity, Purniaya relinquished his position. Chetti says, 'He was a man of extraordinary abilities, eminent public zeal, integrity, judgment and energy. Purnaiya died on the 29th March 1812.'[24]

Chetti presents the view that neither Purnaiya nor Mir Sadak were traitors. They simply became scapegoats because the common people needed to identify some villains to explain the defeat of their supposedly invincible hero.

## C. Hayavadana Rao

Conjeevaram Hayavadana Rao was a competent historian and anthropologist, who served as the curator of the Madras Museum for several years. Proficient in multiple languages, he possessed the capability to examine and interpret a vast array of documents concerning Mysore. He even chaired a committee that revised and republished the Mysore Gazetteer compiled by the Englishman, B.L. Rice, in 1927. His three-volume compendium, *History of Mysore*, published in 1948 (posthumously), provides interesting historical details and is frequently cited by modern historians. It is an invaluable text, as the erudite author meticulously studied and analysed innumerable documents relating to the subject, striving to present an unbiased view.

Rao observes:

> Haidar, the Sarvadhikari of Mysore; Madhav Rao, the Mahratta Peshwa; and Nizam Ali, the de facto Nizam of Hyderabad, had each aimed at domination in the South.[25]

Rao states that Haider wished to annex Travancore and extend his dominions southward, using the Travancore raja's support for the rulers of Malabar as an excuse for preparing to attack that kingdom.[26] He sought assistance from 'the English, the French, the Dutch and the Portuguese in turn to aid him in his ambitious designs'.[27] Responding to Haider's looming threat, Rama Varma took proactive measures to defend his kingdom 'by constructing the historic Travancore Lines, stretching in an almost straight line from the shore of the Cochin backwater, opposite the town of Cranganore, to the foot of the Ghats'.[28] Moreover, 'He strengthened his position with the English at Madras, who assembled troops on the Madura-Travancore frontiers in anticipation of hostilities.'[29] Haider, in turn, tried to woo the English at Madras and simultaneously 'opened negotiations with the Mahrattas, with a view to prevent their incursions into Mysore during his absence'.[30] However, his attempts proved futile.

Rao mentions Haider's early attempts to cultivate favour with the British in the 1760s. In February 1764, Haidar wrote a letter to the governor of Madras expressing his desire 'that everything that will conduce to the increase of our friendship may be done by us both'.[31] During his wars with the Marathas, he corresponded with the British at Tellicherry, requesting them to provide arms and ammunition. Rao states, 'During 1766–1767, the friendly relations between Haidar and the Hon. Company continued, except that he came into conflict with the Factors at Tellicherry on their refusal to help him with powder and shot during his invasion of Malabar [1766].'[32] A year later, Haider Ali found himself at war with the British. Apparently, the Tellicherry factors were keenly aware of the dangers associated with supplying arms to Haider.

Rao narrates the tragic tale of Chikkappa, the palayakkar of Nandidurg, who was compelled to surrender to Mir Ali Raza Khan when provisions became scarce. He and his family were imprisoned in Bangalore under Haidar's orders. Rao remarks,

'Here Chikkappa died, some say leaving no issue, while others state that he left a number of sons, of whom two were made Mussalmans, according to the directions issued by Haidar.'[33] This conversion is also mentioned by Robson and Kirmani. Kirmani states, 'The Meer [Mir Ali], agreeably to Haider's orders, despatched the captive Poligar and his family to Bangalore; and of his sons two were made Mussalmans. One of them died, but the other Sufdar Khan is now living.'[34]

The province of Balam is represented by the present Belur taluk and the surrounding region. It constituted the core of the Hoysala kingdom, with its capital, Dorasamudra, located at Halebid, northeast of Belur.[35] The nearby Manjarabad Fort is an exotic octagonal structure containing a pond. Krishnappa Nayaka, the palayakkar of Balam, had asserted his independence from Bidanur around 1682, and he and his descendants had ruled until Haidar turned against them in 1765. Venkatadri Nayaka, a descendant of Krishnappa, had, in fact, attacked the dependencies of Mysore while Haidar was engaged in his campaigns, plundering goods and cattle.[36] Soon after, Haidar led an expedition against him. Rao notes:

> Being unable to stand the onslaughts of Haidar, Venkatadri abandoned his fort [probably Manjarabad] and fled with his property and family to the safety of the forest, and in confederacy with Chikka-Virappa, the Raja of Coorg, prepared for war. [37]

At Arkalgud, a major battle ensued, and Haidar's army was nearly overwhelmed. However, Haidar, with a few brave men, attacked the enemy's rear, causing their lines to break and their forces to be scattered. Venkatadri was forced to flee, and his dependents and women were captured by Tipu Sultan. Thereupon, 'Venkatadri made peace with Haidar by offering a large sum of money [fifty camel loads, it is said] and elephant's tusks.'[38]

Rao further mentions that Haidar Ali attempted to introduce mulberry cultivation and silkworm rearing in and around Bidanur but was unsuccessful.[39]

## Mohibbul Hasan

Hasan's book, *The History of Tipu Sultan*, published in 1951, is undoubtedly an erudite work, reflecting extensive research. However, many of its conclusions may be considered questionable, precisely because the author seems to be excessively reverential towards the subject. There are unmistakable indicators of paradigm blindness, especially in the analysis of fundamental issues such as religious persecution and wanton destruction of life and property.

Hasan declares:

> If [Tipu] crushed the Hindu Coorgs and Nairs, he did not spare the Muslim Moplahs. His conversion of some Coorgs and Nairs was not due to religious but to political motives. He had warned them several times that they should remain peaceful. But they ignored his warnings and repeatedly rebelled. He therefore converted them as a warning to others.[40]

Tipu Sultan doled out injustice to all, and sometimes Muslims were also at the receiving end. Since the Mappilas were already Muslims, they could not be converted and thus, faced different penalties. However, the real question remains – *who was the aggressor and who was defending their territory?* Tipu was the aggressor, and he was 'punishing' the Hindus through forced conversion – a horrendous process involving circumcision and beef-eating. One is led to conclude that Hasan's scholarship is not entirely unbiased.

Referring to Tipu's reputation for forcible conversions, Hasan writes:

> Tipu has also been accused of having forcibly converted the prisoners to Islam. But this again is a false charge. Those who became Muslims did so willingly. They changed their religion for the sake of rewards or for securing their liberty from the boredom of prison life.[41]

By this statement, the author concedes that inducements were offered for conversion, and those who converted to Islam were promptly released from prison.

Hasan insists that not all conversions were forced, '[thus], for example, Ranga Nair, one of the Coorg leaders, who had escaped, returned on Tipu's invitation and embraced Islam'.[42] This sounds quite improbable. The motive behind this conversion is almost impossible to discern. Context is crucial in understanding such situations.

It may be pertinent at this juncture to consider some of the reasons behind the conversion of Hindus to Islam in the face of a conquering Muslim army. A person might convert to save their own life, to save someone they cared about, to avoid or mitigate the agony of brutal circumcision, to evade imprisonment or deportation, to secure a prestigious post or receive gifts or privileges, to marry someone they desire, or because they suddenly see the wisdom of embracing Allah and the Prophet. There could be other reasons as well, such as breaking the caste barrier, for instance. However, it is reasonable to assume that such conversions were truly voluntary only in the rarest of cases.

Hasan also ventures to list some temples that received land grants from Tipu. These include the Guruvayur Temple and the Trikkantiyur Vettakkourumakan Kavu in Kozhikode taluk. Regarding the Canara Christians, Hasan says that many were exiled to Cochin and Goa, while others were marched off to Srirangapatna and Chitradurga.[43] He opines that they had been disloyal to Haider Ali, who had treated them well. In 1768, the Canara Christians had helped the English in capturing Mangalore. In 1783, when the English attempted to capture Bidanur, they supplied Matthews with rice, demonstrating disloyalty to Tipu as well. 'Under Tipu also they committed treason, so they were exiled.'[44] Moreover, '[the] Kanara Christians were punished not because they were Christians but because they were traitors'.[45] This reasoning is absurd. Hasan claims that Tipu treated Syrian

Christians well, but I have yet to meet a single Syrian Christian willing to vouch for Tipu's benevolence.

Hasan opines:

> Tipu Sultan was not a bigot but an enlightened ruler who raised Hindus to high positions in his government, granted them complete freedom of worship, conferred grants on temples and brahmins, gave money for the consecration of images, and on one occasion even ordered the building of a temple. There is no doubt that he sometimes ill-treated his non-Muslim subjects, but this was not due to their religion; it was because they were guilty of disloyalty.[46]

The choice of words is crucial. 'Sometimes ill-treated' is a ridiculous way to describe mass murders, forced conversions and the deportation of large populations. 'Guilty of disloyalty' is another term that is grossly misleading. Why would anyone be loyal to an invader who occupies their land and continuously oppresses them? How could anyone expect the Nairs, the Coorgis and the Mangalore Christians to be loyal to Tipu Sultan? Hasan's contention is that these people were indirectly responsible for the harsh treatment they received at the hands of the sultan – an argument that lacks any semblance of truth.

According to Hasan:

> In 1789 when he [Tipu] marched towards the Travancore lines, he stayed at Trichur from the 14th to the 29th December, and borrowed from the temple of Vadakkunnathan vessels for cooking food for his army. On leaving Trichur he not only returned the vessels to the temple but presented a large bronze lamp.[47]

This account sounds implausible, if not ridiculous. Which Hindu temple would willingly 'lend' its cooking vessels to a Muslim invader? It is widely known that Tipu's massive army camped at Thrissur and terrorized the helpless locals. The remainder of the story seems to be a product of someone's fertile imagination. A friend of mine, Uma Rao, now a dignified senior citizen, has been a regular visitor to the Vadukkunathan Temple since her school days. She told me she had never heard of Tipu Sultan's brass lamp. I visited the temple and spoke with a key functionary who gave me detailed information about the history of this ancient temple. When asked about the story of the cooking vessels and the brass lamp, he replied, 'It is pure fiction. This temple somehow escaped the notice of the sultan. Pujas were not disrupted because there was a secret passage from the palace to the temple.'

Hasan opines:

> The wars which he waged were none of his own making; they were fought in self-defence. He was more interested in the arts of peace than in the arts of war. He was a great soldier, but he was a much greater administrator ... Every day he consulted astrologers attached to his court about his stars. He fed Brahmins, bore the expenses of Hindu religious ceremonies performed to invoke success for his arms.[48]

This aspect has been noted by several authors. Evidently, Tipu was highly superstitious, and believed the Hindu gods could help him win his battles.

Hasan argues, 'After Tipu's death Beatson, Kirkpatrick and Wilks vied with each other in their campaign of vilifying the Sultan, and their statements were blindly accepted by subsequent historians, both English and Indian.'[49] Referring to Kirkpatrick's translation of Tipu's letters, Hasan even suggests, 'It is not unlikely that he might have himself forged some letters to damage Tipu's reputation.'[50] However, there is not a shred of evidence for any forgery on Kirkpatrick's part. When thousands of letters written by Tipu were retrieved after the fall of Srirangapatna, where was the need to fabricate more letters? Ironically, Hasan's views have been blindly accepted by many unsuspecting scholars, historians and laymen.

Nonetheless, it is Hasan's objective analysis of Tipu's legacy that is most noteworthy:

> Tipu has been regarded by some writers as the first Indian nationalist and a martyr for India's freedom. But this is a wrong view arrived at by projecting the present into the past. In the age in which Tipu lived and ruled there was no sense of nationalism or an awareness among Indians that they were a subject people. It will, therefore, be too much to say that Tipu waged war against the English for the sake of India's freedom. Actually, he fought in order to preserve his own power and independence.[51]

## K.M. Panikkar

Kavalam Madhava Panikkar was an Oxford-educated diplomat, professor, author and historian. He represented a newly independent India at the UN General Assembly in 1947 and served as ambassador to China, Egypt and France, later becoming a member of the Rajya Sabha. In this book *A History of Kerala, 1498–1801,* first published by Annamalai University in 1960, he incorporated two of his earlier publications titled *Malabar and the Portuguese* (1928) and *Malabar and the Dutch* (1931), to which he added a third section relating to the era of the Mysore sultans.

Panikkar provides a detailed description of Malabar's condition when the British acquired it. He observes, 'Twenty-five years of Mysorean occupation had practically reduced this fertile country into a wilderness.'[52] Lawlessness and anarchy were rampant as the feudal system collapsed. The primary aim of the British at this juncture was fourfold – settling land revenue, determining compensation for dispossessed chieftains referred to as *malikhana*, administering justice and controlling the pepper trade. Despite promising to return the territories to the local rajas, they had no intention of doing so. 'The Kerala Rajas had fought as allies on the understanding that their territories would be restored to them.'[53] But after the war concluded, they discovered that, based on a legal technicality, the British calmly seized from them the pepper-rich dominions they had possessed for over a millennium. The legal argument was that Tipu being in possession of Malabar before the war, he had formally ceded the territory to the British through the Treaty of Seringapatam. Consequently, the Malabar chieftains were left high and dry.

Panikkar emphasizes, 'When the Mysoreans left it after 25 years of occupation the countryside was a scene of terrible desolation.'[54] Many temples had discontinued their daily pujas, cultivable land had been reclaimed by the forests, pepper vines destroyed, commerce collapsed, ports deserted and peasants faced imminent starvation. The rajas were reduced to mere agents of the British for land revenue collection, a task made exceedingly difficult by decades of continuous warfare that had considerably impoverished the land and the people. Panikkar explains, 'The Nayar Chieftains, unable to meet the demands, fell into debt to the Mohammedan merchants and the Brahmin money-lenders.'[55] By 1800, even the privilege of collecting revenue was revoked.

The author reveals, 'In Murdoch Brown's (British commissioner) report dated 25th June 1798, it is noted with considerable surprise that gold and silver which the country had accumulated by centuries of trade had disappeared.'[56]

Panikkar points out that the Mappilas had enjoyed three decades of dominance under the rule of the Mysore sultans, making it challenging for them to accept their diminished status following the British takeover. He further notes that although the Mappilas had gained political power under Tipu Sultan, their economic interests had been systematically undermined. In 1788, Tipu Sultan monopolized the pepper trade, leading to the impoverishment of many prosperous Mappila traders. The price of pepper sharply declined due to the absence of competition among European powers for the precious commodity. With the French and the Dutch no longer on the scene, the British assumed complete control over the trade.

The Nairs bore the brunt of the suffering, losing not only their lands but also their occupation when the British seized control of Malabar and disbanded the troops. They were left without the means of sustenance through agriculture, trade or their fighting skills.

## C.K. Kareem

In his 1973 work *Kerala under Haidar Ali and Tipu Sultan*, C.K. Kareem tries hard to absolve the Mysore sultans of any blame for any wrongdoing. He contends that the British deliberately portrayed them in a negative light. Guided in part by Mohibbul Hasan, who was the dean of Aligarh Muslim University while Kareem was working on his PhD thesis on the same subject, Kareem dismisses all allegations as fabrications. He states, 'Stories of forced conversions, of the circumcision of thousands of Hindu subjects and of other manifold brutalities were invented and spread carefully. Historical writings by unidentified authors appeared in large numbers.'[57] With this broad assertion, Kareem unequivocally condemns nearly all British writers, offering commendation to only a select few. He criticizes Col Wilks' *History of Mysore,* written between 1810 and 1814, as a classic example of 'the English historian's bias'. He bemoans the fact that Bowring and Logan heavily relied on this 'highly prejudiced rendering of facts'. He condemns Beatson and Kirkpatrick, particularly denouncing the latter for 'dexterous manipulation of facts'. He further alleges that the memoir of Tipu Sultan is a forgery.

M.M.D.L.T. is deemed non-existent, and Kareem voices the suspicion that this account was written by the British with the deliberate intent of misguiding the gullible public. He notes, 'This book by the unnamed French author has been used by W. Logan as a source book in writing his Malabar Manual in the year 1885.'[58] However, there is ample evidence to contradict Kareem's claim that Maistre de la Tour was a fictitious character. Wilks references his military exploits,[59]and Bartolomeo mentions M. de la Tour's Map of the Coromandel, published in Paris in 1770. De la Tour's narrative unmistakably establishes he was not English. Despite this evidence, Kareem remains sceptical of his existence.

Fullerton is dismissed outright by Kareem as he fought in the Second Anglo-Mysore War, participated in the capture of the Palghat Fort, and had ample reason for harbouring animosity towards the Mysore sultans. K.M. Panikkar is devalued as he is considered to be 'guided by Logan's judgement'.[60] Kirmani is also denounced for his eagerness to present Tipu as a champion of Islam, which significantly wrecked the sultan's image.

Interestingly, Kareem speaks favourably of Dr Buchanan, noting, 'Eager to take in everything, Buchanan travelled extensively, always displaying keen curiosity and capacity for intelligent observation.'[61] He also certifies that 'the economic and commercial conditions of Kerala are well described in his work'.[62]

Kareem's reasoning is evidently flawed, as he effectively concludes that anyone who holds a negative view of the sultans cannot be a credible historian. Ironically, he extensively cites the very sources he condemns for their prejudice and partiality. Consequently, his conclusions must be taken with a pinch of salt.

In the first chapter of the book, Kareem states that Haider Ali 'was waiting for an opportunity to interfere in Kerala politics'.[63] He provides further proof of this in the appendix. Additionally, he lists several pretexts that Haider apparently cited as reasons for the Malabar invasion, including collecting war indemnity from the Zamorin, claiming dues owed by the raja of Chirakkal to the Canara rulers (after Haider had captured Bidanur, he believed this amount was owed to him) 'to punish the Raja of Travancore for evading payment of compensation for military preparations Haidar Ali had made on his behalf'[64] and obliging 'Aly Raja of Cannanore and Capu Thamburan, one of the scions of the Kolathiri family',[65] who had invited him to invade Malabar. Kareem does not question or analyse any of these dubious reasons.

Regarding the murder of Hari Singh, the Rajput confidante of Devaraj, who was tasked with collecting the indemnity from the Zamorin in 1758, Kareem acknowledges, 'Hari Singh met with his death at the hands of Mukhdum.'[66] However, he tries, rather unconvincingly, to absolve Haider Ali of involvement in the dark conspiracy. In truth, there is ample evidence that Makhdum Ali, Haider Ali's brother-in-law and trusted lieutenant, acted under his instructions at all times and could be counted upon to execute any order without question. It is unimaginable that such an unprovoked murder could have happened without Haider's connivance.

Kareem gives interesting details of the Cochin raja's stance regarding the Mysore sultans. He observes that while the raja feigned friendliness towards Haider Ali, he secretly conspired with the Dutch and the Travancore raja to free himself from Mysorean control. The raja wrote several letters to the Dutch at Batavia, seeking military support against Haider Ali. Additionally, he permitted the Travancore raja to extend the Travancore Lines to Cranganore by building fortifications through Cochin territory.

Kareem also examines the relationship between the Travancore rajas and Haider Ali. In 1766, when Haider conquered Malabar, he threatened to invade Travancore, prompting the Dutch to intervene to prevent such an invasion. The Cochin raja's agreement to pay tribute was a part of this arrangement. Haider demanded 15 lakh rupees and 30 elephants from Travancore, but Rama Varma, the successor of Marthanda Varma, pleaded inability, citing his status as a tributary of the Arcot nawab.

During the Second Anglo-Mysore War, the raja of Travancore sent two battalions to aid the British cause. When peace was established in 1784, the Treaty of Mangalore recognized Travancore as 'a friend and ally' of the EICo. Kareem rightly surmises, 'The attitude of Hyder Ali and later, of Tipu Sultan had driven the Raja closer and closer to the British camp.'[67]

The Cochin raja wrote to Batavia in 1789, expressing concern that '[if] necessary help is not forthcoming, Tipu Sultan will commit atrocities in all Malabar'.[68] The reply he received was not encouraging.

On 24 December 1789, Tipu arrived at the Travancore Lines and sent a message to Rama Varma, demanding the surrender of the Nair princes who had sought asylum in his territory. In response, the raja explained that he had offered protection to the rulers of

Chirakkal, Calicut and Kadathanad because they were his relatives. Understandably, Tipu was displeased with his reply. What is surprising, however, is Kareem's alignment with Tipu's perspective. 'We have seen that from the time of Hyder Ali a number of complaints were launched against the protection given by the Raja to the rebels belonging to the Mysore territory. Therefore, what Rama Varma had written was a gross misrepresentation of real facts.'[69] The erstwhile rulers of the occupied territories of Malabar were 'rebels belonging to Mysore'. According to this viewpoint, an invader who captured lands belonging to others is justified in demanding that refugees be handed over to him by a neighbouring ruler who offered them refuge. Kareem does not delve into the reason behind Tipu's demand for the refugees. Was it to convert them to Islam, subject them to torture or kill them? Such considerations are overlooked. Furthermore, Kareem accuses Rama Varma of distorting facts, despite the well-known inter-relatedness of all the princes of Kerala. Many rulers of small principalities within the Travancore kingdom were descendants of the Attingal ranis, who had been adopted from the royal house of the Kolathiri in Kannur in the14th century. Besides, was it a crime to offer protection to refugees, even if they were not related by blood ties? Kareem, in his eagerness to whitewash Tipu Sultan's misdeeds, attempts to tarnish the image of 'Dharmaraja' Rama Varma by painting him in poor light.

When the Mysore army attacked the Travancore Lines on 29 December, they suffered heavy casualties, a fact corroborated by several contemporary historians, including Kirmani and Wilks. The Travancore raja reported this event to Hutchinson on 2 January 1790, while George Powney, the British resident at Travancore, conveyed the news to Holland on 3 February 1790, 'Tipu has met with a repulse from the Raja's troops... Near a thousand were left dead within the Lines.'[70] Kareem, however, dismisses this as a mere 'frontier skirmish' and challenges the historical accounts that suggest Tipu had 15,000 men at his disposal, claiming instead that he had only 6,000 soldiers. He also challenges Wilks' suggestion that Tipu sustained wounds during this battle, refuting the ideas that they caused his subsequent lameness. According to Kareem, Tipu was neither wounded nor present at the battle scene, and did not lose his dagger and seal. He describes the battle as 'a foolhardy venture of a small portion of his army',[71] and suggests that the Travancore army had 'over a hundred thousand men'.[72] This appears to be a weak attempt to rationalize the defeat suffered by Tipu Sultan's army.

Kareem fails to provide a convincing explanation for Tipu's *tapas* at the Travancore Lines from December 1789 to April 1790. Speaking of the subsequent encounters that occurred four months later, Kareem states:

> Before the actual hostilities commenced [on] April 14, 1790, the Travancore forces repeated the same provocative attack twice and on both these occasions they were beaten back. Therefore, it can be rightly presumed that the first shot might have been fired by the Travancore army.[73]

Kareem indulges in various assumptions in his attempt to absolve Tipu of responsibility for starting what became the Third Anglo-Mysore War. However, the reality is that Rama Varma of Travancore was not encamped on the outskirts of Srirangapatna. It was Tipu Sultan of Mysore who was stationed in the vicinity of the Travancore Lines. In such circumstances, who fired the first shot becomes irrelevant; the pertinent question is: *who was the aggressor?* A historian cannot overlook fundamental facts. Kareem argues that Tipu sought to resolve his disputes with Rama Varma amicably through negotiations and did not desire conflicts. Only two other encounters occurred during the three and a half months that his army remained in the area, on 1 March and 9 April. This too is convoluted logic. The author fails to consider that the prolonged presence of an army cannot by any stretch of imagination be perceived as a peaceful gesture or negotiation strategy.

On 9 April, the bombardment began, quickly resulting in a wide breach. Tipu's army stormed the Travancore Lines on 15 April and 'with little or no resistance occupied it'.[74] Soon after, Tipu moved to capture Cranganore Fort, Aiyakota and Parur. In response, Cornwallis declared war on Mysore and directed British troops towards Srirangapatna, prompting Tipu to withdraw from Kerala.

Cornwallis quickly forged alliances with the nizam and the Marathas, while also attempting to woo the princes of Malabar. The British published a paper stating:

> In the name of the Honourable English East India Company, I Robert Taylor, Chief for transacting all affairs of the English nation at Tellicherry, do hereby assure you [here enter the Raja's name and titles] that provided you will enter heartily into the war against Tipu Sultan, and act vigorously against him, the English East India Company will assist and protect you and do everything in their power to render you independent of Tipu Sultan...In witness whereof I have hereto set my hand and the Company's Seal and you have affixed your seal at Tellicherry, this 4th day of May 1790.[75]

Soon thereafter, Taylor informed the Secret Committee of the Court of Directors that 'the Chirakkal, Cattinadu (Kadathanad), and Cotiote rajas are with us here. The Coorg raja is well inclined towards us but the Beebi of Cannanore has not declared herself'.[76]

Kareem's account testifies that Tipu Sultan was not an adept statesman. In his effort to portray Cornwallis as a scheming manipulator, Kareem inadvertently portrays Tipu's negotiation skills in a negative light. He states:

> All the efforts of Tipu Sultan to counteract the machinations of Cornwallis, through his vakils at Poona and Hyderabad, proved futile. Likewise, his effort to secure the help of the French bore no fruit, whereas Cornwallis could successfully induce Tipu Sultan's tributaries like Beebi of Cannanore and Rama Varma of Cochin to throw off their allegiance to Tipu Sultan.[77]

If Kareem's analysis is accurate, then it follows that Cornwallis was the superior statesman, and Tipu was despised by his neighbours, allies and tributaries, including the Muslim rulers.

Kareem also attempts to absolve Ali Raja of Cannanore of guilt and deftly shifts the blame for the ongoing conflicts onto the Kolathiri raja. He suggests, 'This perpetual enmity of the Kolathiris against the Aly Raja drove him to seek assistance from elsewhere. Hence his deputation to Haider Ali inviting him to conquer Kerala.'[78]

Kareem also gives a unique interpretation of Tipu's actions concerning the Guruvayur Temple. Citing the Inam Registers preserved in the Kozhikode Archives, he states:

> A number of religious heads and scholars of Kerala were recipients of Tipu Sultan's gift of land and cash. The *Satrams* where religious learning was imparted and Brahmins were fed received his financial help. All the known temples of Malabar obtained from him lavish presents in money and rent-free lands. Guruvayoor Temple, the most esteemed of all temples in Kerala, was to benefit most. Apart from the rent-free lands, this temple received 8000 pagodas in cash annually for the expense of ceremonies.[79]

Kareem fails to mention that temples were typically subsidized by the regional kings, and any new ruler had the option to maintain, discontinue, reduce or increase the customary grants. Was Tipu giving a new grant? Was the previous grant larger or smaller? These questions are not addressed. Kareem continues:

> The money was regularly paid every year by Tipu Sultan's agent Nalakathu Chandipurathu Aurasooty [Hydrose Kutty] Mooppan of Manthala. Even now the Hindus of this locality frequent the tomb of Aurasooty Mooppan for thanksgiving. This amount was reduced to 5000 pagodas by the English.[80]

This statement suggests that Hydrose Kutty may have been the true benefactor, rather than Tipu Sultan. In fact, there is no evidence to suggest that Tipu was even aware of this arrangement. The reduction of the grant by the British is ample evidence that grants to temples by the ruler was standard operating procedure. This is reinforced by the fact that even today, democratically elected governments in our country regularly provide grants to temples, with the present communist government in Kerala being no exception.

**Sandeep Balakrishna**

A modern, 21st-century debut publication titled *Tipu Sultan: The Tyrant of Mysore* by Sandeep Balakrishna vociferously presents the voice of the far-right, labelling Haider Ali as 'a mercenary for hire'[81] and Tipu Sultan as a bigoted tyrant. The author figuratively goes for the jugular.

Balakrishna rightly points out that Haider Ali had never nominated Tipu as his successor. Come to think of it, no writer seems to have mentioned whether Haider Ali had any sons by his first wife. Like so many other details about Haider Ali's early life, this too is unknown to us. What is generally known is that he had two sons, Tipu and Karim.

Tipu drafted a treaty of alliance with the French and passed it on to Pierre Monneron, who took the draft with him when he went to Paris in 1796. Balakrishna delineates the contents as follows:

> 1. The French are to send 10,000 troops to attack Tellicherry. After burning it they are to join forces with the Mysoreans with Tipu in supreme command and march towards Cochin, Madura, Trichinopoly and Tanjore.
> 2. With these [regions] placed firmly in their hands, there is to be a joint advance on Pondicherry and Madras, and thence by land to capture Calcutta. From there follows a sweep across the sub continent to Bombay which, said Tipu, the French may have for their own.
> 3.Tipu on his side promises to provide 5000 troops to every 1000 French troops.[82]

The French governor of Pondicherry, Monsieur de Cossigny, apparently concurred with Tipu's plans. Balakrishna cites a draft agreement that Tipu dictated to his munshis on 2 April 1797, wherein he laid out his plans for the bifurcation of territory between the French and Mysore. It states inter alia:

> Half of the country and the forts and stores, shall be taken over by our Sarkar and the other half made over to the French...the country and the forts of our Sarkar which the English wrested in 1792 are not to be included in the partition between the French and our Sarkar ... the fort of Goa shall be possessed by our Sarkar and that of Bombay shall be made over to the French.[83]

Balakrishna refers to the shifting of the sacred idol from the Guruvayur Temple to Ambalapuzha, and its reinstallation after the death of Tipu Sultan. He states:

> If no signs of destruction are visible today, it is because of the intervention of an officer called Hydrose Kutty, a Hindu who had been forcibly converted to Islam by Haider Ali, he helped repair and renovate the temple and reinstated the land grants and exemptions that had historically been given to it by various kings.[84]

Hydrose Kutty's name is mentioned in Logan's Manual (spelt Haidros Kutti) along with that of Mohidin Muppan (Moopen).

Balakrishna opines, 'Tipu's February 1782 victory against the British army led by Colonel Braithwaite was perhaps the only major milestone in his military career.'[85] He also suggests that a major share of the credit for this victory must go to the French general, M. Lally.

It is not easy to concur with Balakrishna's proposition that Tipu was a bad general. He did lead armies and he did win battles, even when his father was alive. At eighteen, he successfully besieged Madras. His capture of Colonel Bailley was certainly a feather in his cap. When Haider Ali died, Tipu rushed from Ponnani to take control of the Mysore kingdom. Though he had not been nominated as the successor, and despite the fact that his brother had been promptly installed as Dewan, Tipu did manage to seize the kingdom and enthrone himself in an apparent bloodless coup. Tipu's move to recapture Bidanur from the British was swift and successful. He managed to put down rebellions in Malabar and Coorg, and torpedo all palace intrigues at Srirangapatna, though his extreme brutality could well have contributed to his successes.

The face that launched a thousand protests. Source: AP

Mysore Palace today – magnificent interiors. Photo by Pushpa Kurup

Mysore Palace – Private Durbar Hall. Photo by Pushpa Kurup

Painting in Kowdiar Palace, Thiruvananthapuram, showing a wounded Tipu Sultan in his palanquin being carried away to safety. Photo by Pushpa Kurup

Tomb of Dewan Purnaiyya's daughter at Vellore, Tamilnadu.
Photo by Pushpa Kurup

Tomb of Bakshi Begum, Haider Ali's wife (died 1804), at Vellore, Tamilnadu.
Photo by Pushpa Kurup

Cannon balls abandoned, Vellore Fort. Photo by Pushpa Kurup

Cannon balls re-used, Vellore Fort. Photo by Pushpa Kurup

Thirunavaya Navamukunda Temple of Mamankam fame, Malappuram district.
Photo by Pushpa Kurup

Thazhekkad St Sebastian Church, Thrissur district – burnt down by Tipu and rebuilt by believers. Photo by Pushpa Kurup

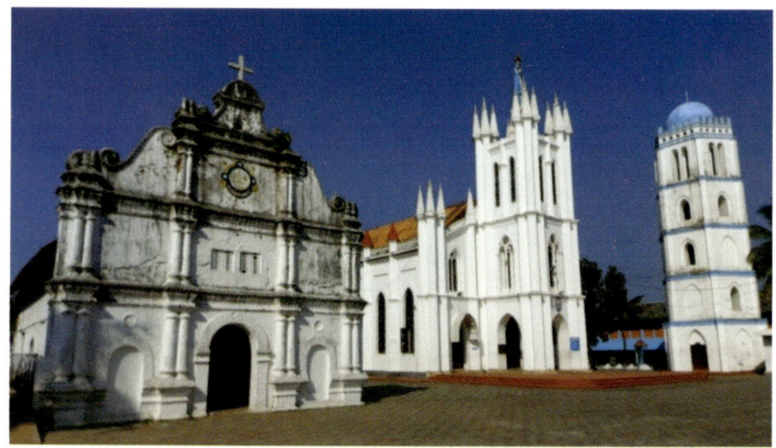

Ancient church, modern structure and watchtower with a blue dome – Manjumatha Church, Pallipuram. Photo by Pushpa Kurup

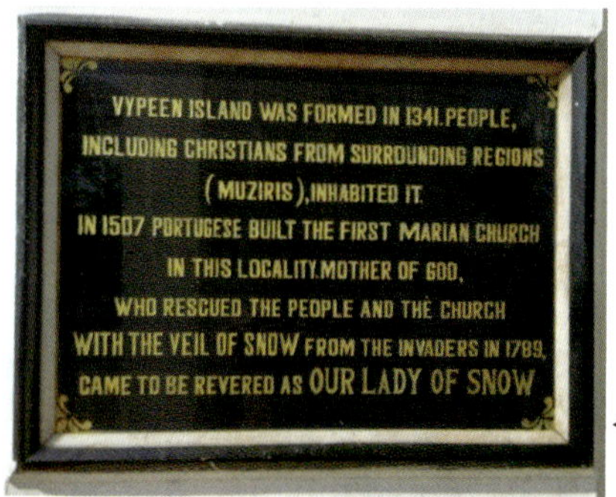


◀ Manjumatha Church, Pallipuram. Photo by Pushpa Kurup

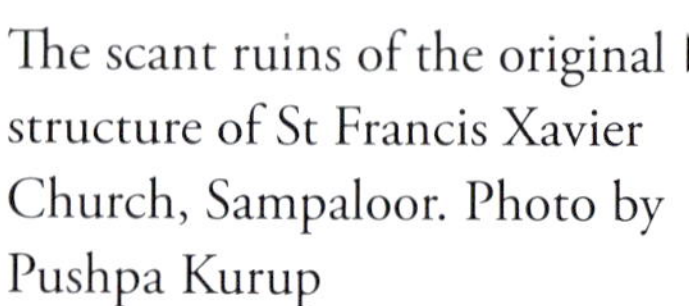

The scant ruins of the original ▶ structure of St Francis Xavier Church, Sampaloor. Photo by Pushpa Kurup

◀ Francis Xavier – the saint who came by sea. Photo by Pushpa Kurup

Church of St Francis Xavier, Sampaloor (Xavier's castle and the remains of the old church on the right). Photo by Pushpa Kurup

Painting in the museum adjacent to Sampaloor St Francis Xavier Church depicting the battle with the invading forces of Tipu Sultan. A cannon ball discovered at the site is displayed below. Photo by Pushpa Kurup

Christians and Nairs unite in the face of a Muslim threat – depiction on the exterior wall of Kanjoor Church. Photo by Pushpa Kurup

Christians fight Muslims – depiction on the exterior wall of Kanjoor Church. Photo by Pushpa Kurup

Tipu Sultan arriving on elephant back – mural at Kanjoor Church. Photo by Pushpa Kurup

Flood in the Periyar River washes away Tipu Sultan's army – mural at Kanjoor Church. Photo by Pushpa Kurup

Palghat Fort spruced up by Haider Ali – the Western Ghats faintly visible in the background. Photo by Pushpa Kurup

Kirmani's manuscript. Source: www.rct.uk/collection/1005027

Tipu's ring. Picture courtesy Indiatimes

Where Tipu fell. Photo by Pushpa Kurup

Gumbaz – the final resting place of the Mysore sultans. Photo by Pushpa Kurup

Hyder Ali's tomb in the middle, flanked by Tipu's on the left and Tipu's mother, Fakhrunissa, on the right. Photo by Pushpa Kurup

Tipu's tiger toy, V&A Museum, London. Source: Wikipedia

◀Tipu Sultan's tomb at Srirangapatna – the colours of the tiger. Photo by Pushpa Kurup

The Water Gate. Photo by Pushpa Kurup

Inside the Water Gate. Photo by Pushpa Kurup

Ruins of Tipu's Palace – the remains of the famed Lal Mahal. Photo by Pushpa Kurup

Daria Daulat Bagh – resplendent reminder. Photo by Pushpa Kurup

Bailley's Dungeon – where the English prisoners were incarcerated. Photo by Pushpa Kurup

Raja's Tomb, Madikeri (Kodagu). Photo by Pushpa Kurup

A tiger-headed sword-hilt from Tipu Sultan's palace armoury. Source: interactive.net.in

◀ Statue of Tipu's descendant, Noor Inayat Khan, who was a British spy. Photo by Henk van der Wal – own work, CC BY-SA 3.0. https://commons.wikimedia.org/w/index.php?curid=29471055)

Elephant statues in Madikeri Fort. Photo by Pushpa Kurup

Statue of Kerala Varma Pazhassi Raja in the Mridangasaileswari temple complex, Kannur. Photo by Pushpa Kurup

1,000-year-old Ranganathaswamy temple, Srirangapatna – the one that got away. Photo by Pushpa Kurup

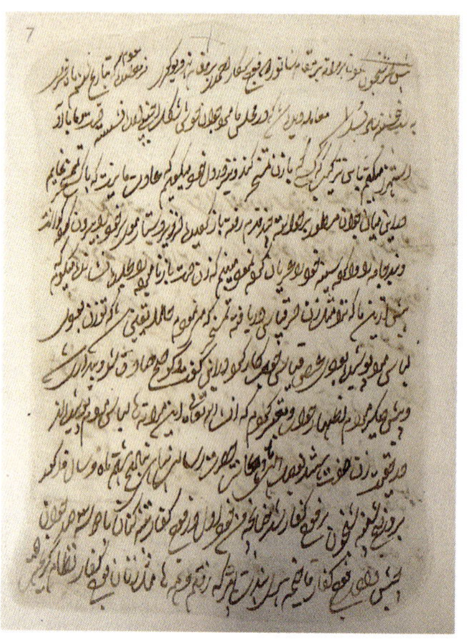

Dream 13: A woman in mans' clothes. British Library IO Islamic 3563, f. 7r

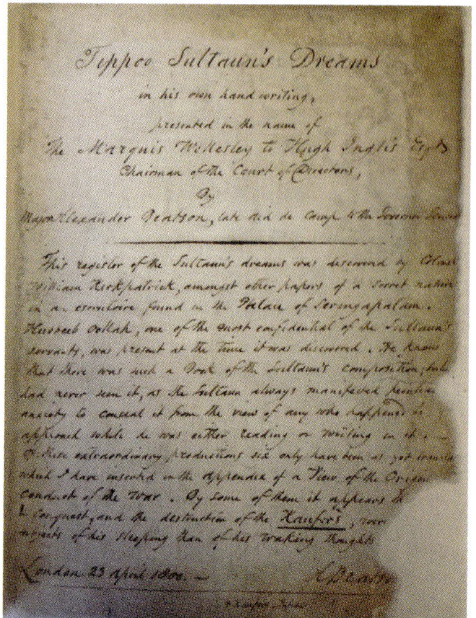

Tippoo Sultaun's Dreams
in his own hand writing,
presented in the name of
The Marquis Wellesley to Hugh Inglis Esq.
Chairman of the Court of Directors,
By
Major Alexander Beatson, late Aid de Camp to the Governor General

This register of the Sultaun's dreams was discovered by Colonel William Kirkpatrick, amongst other papers of a secret nature in an escritoire found in the Palace of Seringapatam. Hubbeeb Oollah, one of the most confidential of the Sultaun's servants, was present at the time it was discovered. He knew that there was such a Book of the Sultaun's composition, but had never seen it, as the Sultaun always manifested particular anxiety to conceal it from the view of any who happened to approach while he was either reading or writing in it. — Of these extraordinary productions six only have been as yet translated which I have inserted in the Appendix of a View of the Origin [illegible] Conduct of the War. By some of them it appears th[illegible] [illegible] conquest, and the destruction of the Kaufers, were [illegible] objects of his sleeping than of his waking thoughts.

London 23 April 1800. — A. Beatson

'Tippoo Sultaun's dreams in his own handwriting, presented in the name of the Marquis Wellesley to Hugh Inglis Esqr. Chairman of the Court of Directors, by Major Alexander Beatson, late aid de camp to the Governor General.' British Library IO Islamic 3563, f. 29v

Copper plate inscription in Paavali village, Virudhunagar, Tamilnadu. Photo courtesy *New Indian Express*

# 10

# THE TRAGEDY OF COORG

The Mysore sultans desired unimpeded access to the Malabar Coast and the Arabian Sea. The mountainous country of Coorg stood in their way, inhabited by the fierce Kodava warriors. Tipu found them exasperating, despising them almost as much as the Nairs of Malabar. He was determined to teach them a lesson they would not soon forget.

Tipu did succeed in leaving behind unforgettable, festering memories – memories of genocide. The Kodavas held onto these remembrances, passing them down from generation to generation by word of mouth. When Karnataka announced Tipu Jayanthi celebrations in the early 21st century, the Kodavas raised furious voices of dissent. More than two momentous centuries had passed since the downfall of the Mysore sultans, yet the people of Coorg had not forgotten. Like the Nairs of Malabar, they had their unrelenting memories.

'Coorg' is the Anglicized version of the original Kannada name 'Kodagu'. Dubbed the 'Scotland of India' by the British, Coorg lacked a formal standing army, relying instead on spirited bands of Kodava warriors. Constant Mysorean military interventions drove them into the arms of the British. Following Tipu's demise, they found themselves unable to break free from the vice-like grip of their British overlords.

On 15 March 1834, a proclamation was issued from Bangalore by Lt Col James Fraser on behalf of the governor-general. It stated inter alia:

> It is accordingly hereby notified, that a British army is about to invade the Coorg territory, that Vira Rajendra Wodeyar is no longer to be considered as Raja of Coorg, that the persons and property of all those who conduct themselves peaceably or in aid of the operations of the British troops shall be respected, and that such a system of government shall be established as may seem best calculated to secure the happiness of the people.[1]

Thus, in 1834, Coorg was entirely absorbed by the British.

## Historical Notes

When the mighty Vijayanagar kingdom collapsed in 1565 following their defeat at the hands of the Bahmani sultans, many of their feudatories gained sudden independence. Soon, the big fish began to devour the smaller fish. Among these big fish were the Ikkeri Nayaks, who quickly expanded their influence from Honavar in north Canara to Chandragiri in the south. By then, the Portuguese had established a strong presence in Goa. In Ullal, near Mangalore, the courageous queen Abbakka Rani Chowta fiercely resisted Portuguese incursions. The British and other European powers had yet to venture into India.

The Kodava warlords, who also referred to themselves as Nayaks, worshipped the forest god Ayyappa and the river goddess Kaveri. Initially, every village in the region possessed its own *devarakadu* or sacred grove. Temples and Vedic gods were later introduced by Brahmin settlers. The sultans of Mysore would soon enforce Islam through military conquest. Later, the British would introduce Christianity.

In 1600, Veeraraja, a Lingayat relative of the Ikkeri raja, seized control of Coorg and proclaimed himself king. His was succeeded by his son and grandson. It was Mudduraja, the grandson, who shifted the capital from Haleri to Madikeri in 1681. By the mid-18th century, Mudduraja's son, Siribai Veerappa, had expanded his domain significantly. He emerged victorious in battles against the Mysore raja and Veera Varma of Wayanad, whom he captured and executed.[2] Siribai Veerappa deemed his son unfit to rule and had him imprisoned, instead appointing his grandson, Chikka Veerappa, as his successor. Upon Siribai Veerappa's death in 1736 at the age of seventy-eight, two of his wives immolated themselves on his funeral pyre. Vedic Hinduism had firmly established its presence.

Mysore was still a relatively weak neighbour. By the time Chikka Veerappa's rule ended in 1766, the Haleri dynasty of Kodagu was over 150 years old. Then Haider Ali arrived on the scene.

## Coorg versus Mysore

Bowring states, 'When Haidar seized Bednur in 1763, he affected to regard Coorg as tributary to that principality, and in 1765 sent a force to reduce the country but was foiled in his attempt.'[3] In the same year, there were minor skirmishes at the northern border of Coorg between the forces of Haider Ali and Chikka Veerappa.[4]

Hayavadhana Rao notes that neither De la Tour nor Robson mentions Haider Ali's initial invasion of Coorg in 1765. Peixoto, the sole contemporary writer who refers to the invasion of Coorg under Fazalullah Khan, indicates that it occurred after Madhav Rao's campaign of 1764–1765. It is likely that the campaign extended until 1768, as the definitive treaty with Coorg was signed at that time.[5]

When Haider Ali marched from Bidanur to launch an attack on Coorg, Fazalullah Khan simultaneously marched on the northeastern frontier, catching the Kodavas off guard. Many battles ensued, resulting in Fazalullah Khan and his forces being routed and forced to flee the country. Haidar offered a compromise, proposing 'eternal peace' and the Uchchingi district, adjacent to Coorg's northern frontier, in exchange for a payment of 3 lakh pagodas. Chikka Veerappa agreed to the proposal, with a portion of the amount paid immediately and hostages provided for the remainder.[6]

Following Chikka Veerappa's death in 1766, his successors, Muddaraja and Muddaiya, ruling jointly, called on Haidar to fulfil the terms agreed upon with their predecessor. However, the negotiations failed, leading to a resumption of hostilities. Lingaraja,

Muddaraja's younger brother, attacked Fazalullah Khan near the Elu-Savira district and achieved victory. Fazalullah attempted to retreat towards Mangalore via the Bisale ghat, but Lingaraja pursued vigorously, routing his army. According to Rao:

> The whole camp, treasure, guns and ammunition fell into the hands of Lingaraja and his victorious troops. The campaign dragged on to 1768, when Haidar once again proposed peace. In place of the Uchchingi country, he ceded the districts of Panje and Bellare for the sum of Rs. 75,000 already paid to Fuzzul-ullah- Khan.[7]

In 1770, both of Coorg's joint rulers passed away, sparking a succession dispute. Lingaraja, accompanied by his three sons and nephew Appajiraja, fled to Mysore and appealed to Haider Ali for assistance in establishing his rule in Coorg.

Haider Ali now had a golden opportunity. In late 1773, with Haider's backing, Lingaraja invaded Coorg, causing the ruler Devapparaja (another of Lingaraja's nephews) to flee. Devapparaja sought refuge in the vicinity of Dharwar but was betrayed by informers and captured by Mysore forces. Haider Ali executed Devapparaja and his entire family in 1774. Lingaraja likely collaborated in this heinous act.[8] Thereafter, he became a vassal of Mysore and was obligated to pay an annual tribute. Lingaraja died in 1780, leaving behind three young sons.

In 1773, following the murder of Peshwa Narayan Rao, Haider Ali sent Tipu to recapture the northern districts from the Marathas. The Mysore army entered Coorg towards the end of 1773, encountering minimal resistance as they advanced to Madikeri. Thereafter, Haider Ali deployed a force through Wayanad to Calicut and 'speedily achieved the re-conquest of the whole of Malabar'.[9]

Lafont, a French embassy official, observes:

> Legoux de Flaix mentions as a spectacular achievement the road built by Hyder Ali in the mountains for the conquest of Coorg. My feeling is that he was involved in this engineering *chef d'oeuvre*, but I have no evidence of this. We know however that the French troops were involved in the conquest of Coorg by Hyder.[10]

Bowring adds, 'Some authorities state that on his first appearance on the frontier, Haidar offered a reward of five rupees for the head of every Coorg which was brought to him and that 700 heads were in consequence delivered.'[11] Beliappa states, 'The Kodavas were slaughtered indiscriminately and when Hyder saw the heads of minor boys being brought to him he was horrified and called a halt to the massacre.'[12] The survivors fled to the mountains and forests. Haider Ali imprisoned the ruler's family under the pretext of serving as their guardian. However, before he could annex Coorg, the British attacked Arcot, diverting his attention in that direction.

After Haider Ali's death, the Kodavas revolted and laid siege to the Madikeri Fort, but Tipu's forces quickly quelled the uprising.

Kirmani writes:

> [Zain-ul-Abedin, the foujdar of Coorg] regulated the affairs of the government according merely to his caprice and folly, insomuch that from the inherent vices of his disposition, he extended the hand of lust to the women of the peasantry, and compelled the handsomest among them to submit to his will and pleasure.[13]

He recounts that Momuti Nair and Ranga Nair, the ministers of the palayakkar of the place, united soldiers and peasants and 'surrounded and besieged Zafurabad'.[14] Thereafter, '[the] Sultan determined himself to punish the people of Coorg, who had frequently before rebelled against his government'.[15]

Initially, the Kodavas successfully repelled the Mysorean attacks, but soon they were overwhelmed. Kirmani states, 'The French under Monsieur Lally, and the Asad Ilahi Risalas, or regiments of Chelahs, made numbers of these pagans food for the musket and bayonet.'[16] He also highlights the enemy's bravery, noting, 'Notwithstanding all this, they still stood firm and made many vigorous attacks on the Sultan's army and dispersed them.'[17] However, the 'army of Islam' vastly outnumbered and outgunned them, and the Coorgis could not sustain their resistance for long. Tipu and Lally encamped in the region for several months. 'In the course of seven months and a few days, eight thousand, men, women and children, were made prisoners.'[18] The exact number of dead was not tallied. The fact that it took eight months for such a formidable army of Mysoreans and Frenchmen to subdue the Coorgis speaks for itself.

Kirmani records that all the prisoners were forcibly converted to Islam. The men were labelled as Ahmedis, given military training and constituted into eight regiments. Additionally, other puzzling details emerge from his accounts, 'Of the two chiefs, one Mumoti Nair in a short time died, and Ranga Nair was honoured by being circumcised and made a Mussalman by the Sultan, named Sheikh Ahmad, and appointed a Risaldar. The Sultan adopted him as his son.'[19] Another intriguing incident is when 'Ballia Banu the queen of Cannanore who was of the Mappila tribe, paid her respects to the Sultan while he was encamped at Talakaveri, and brought with her the tribute due for two years, with elephants, horses and other valuables as presents.'[20]

Kirmani further mentions that 6,000–7,000 men were sent to Coorg to repopulate it. Many succumbed to illness and were subsequently allowed to return, while others chose to remain and settle in the region.[21] This cycle of deportation, forced migration, depopulation and resettlement was a recurrent theme during the reign of sthe sultans.

Kirmani's poetic description of the natural glory of the Coorg region and the beauty of its women is rather interesting. The women are compared to the beauties of Turkistan, Persia and China, as well as the celestial 'houris' of heaven. 'In that wild country, which is however, beautiful as the garden of paradise, they move about gracefully as the divine Houris.'[22] Kirmani also mentions that when Haider Ali had conquered Coorg, he abolished the prevalent custom of polyandry, seized the women of the country and distributed them among his soldiers.

Buchanan reports:

> On Tippoo's accession, in order, I suppose to distress the inhabitants of Coorg, and thus to make their prince, Vir Raya, submit to his authority, he interdicted all communication with that country; and ordered, that all such of its inhabitants as might be found in his dominions should be instantly put to death. This restraint

> was severely felt by the people of Coorg, who, being entirely surrounded by the dominion of the Sultan, had no means of selling their produce, nor of procuring foreign commodities. The Vir Raya sent an embassy to the Sultan, and represented that it had always been customary for his merchants to trade with those of Mysore and Malayala.[23]

It was essentially an embargo, strategically designed to crush any form of resistance. The raja's appeal fell on deaf ears; Tipu remained relentless. The Kodavas were compelled to resort to guerrilla warfare.

The Second Anglo-Mysore War ended in 1784 with the signing of the Mangalore Treaty. Upon his return from Mangalore to Mysore, Tipu marched triumphantly through Coorg. He instilled fear among the Kodavas by accusing them of immorality and polyandry and issued threats of converting them to Islam. By this time, Veerarajendra, the 22-year-old eldest son of Lingaraja, was already in his custody, along with his brothers and others, imprisoned at the fort of Periapatna. With the raja in his custody, Tipu gained complete control of Coorg.

Buchanan's account indicates that Priyapattana (Periapatna) had 500 Brahmin households and 1,000 Lingayat households within the fort and its outskirts. However, 'Tippoo ordered the houses in both fort and suburb to be destroyed, and sprung some mines to render the fort useless to his enemy.'[24] There are also reports of Tipu ordering the destruction of a Jain temple, with Buchanan suggesting that destroying 'idolatrous' temples was one of Tipu's favourite pastimes. Regarding the current state of the fortifications, Buchanan stated, 'There are no inhabitants, and tigers have taken entire possession of its ruins.'[25] He further observed, 'Owing to the devastations of war, the people near Priya-pattana are at present so poor, that they are cutting off the unripe ears of corn, and parching them to satisfy the cravings of appetite.'[26] In other words, poverty and famine were rampant in the area.

Tipu's letter dated 12 October 1785, addressed to Mahommed Ghyas and Noor Mahommed Khan, states 'We, therefore, order, that, uniting your force with that of Meer Zynul Aabideen, the

Foujdar, you do together exert yourselves in the signal chastisement of the Koorgs.'[27] Kirkpatrick states, 'The appointment of this Zynul Aabideen to the Foujdary of Zuferabad is mentioned by the Sultan himself in his Memoirs. It took place on the first subjugation and settlement of that district, in the year 1784.'[28]

Tipu's letter dated 15 October 1785 addressed to Zynul Aabideen Shoostry (supposedly at Periapatna) states:

> At this rate, the expenditure of cartridges has been very great. We are curious to know, and desire you will inform us, how many of the enemy have been sent to hell, by the expenditure of such a number of cartridges. We also desire to be informed of the amount of the rebel force. One hundred of your men being wounded, no doubt great numbers of the enemy must have been killed and wounded.[29]

Kirkpatrick suggests 'Zynul Aabideen had received rather a serious check from the Koorgs'.[30] This inference appears to be correct, as four days later, on 19 October, Tipu dispatched another letter announcing his intention to personally lead a campaign against Coorg.[31] It is evident that subjugating the Kodavas was not a simple task for the mighty Mysore sultan.

In 1785, Tipu visited the Periapatna Fort and demanded that the entire royal family convert to Islam and spread the religion among their subjects. Veerarajendra courageously stated that they would rather die than renounce their faith. Tipu did not press the issue, perhaps because he was wary of antagonizing his Hindu subjects. However, he took a liking to Veerarajendra's sister Neelammaji and cousin Devammaji, whom he promptly added to his harem and renamed Mehtab and Aftab, respectively. The Hindu population of Mysore and the people of Kodagu were deeply offended, but their options for recourse were limited, leading to an uneasy peace. Buchanan mentions, 'One of his sisters was forced into the zenana of Tipu, and to her intercessions, the Raya probably owed his life.'[32]

Determined to secure the release of Veerarajendra, the Kodavas resorted to sporadic guerrilla warfare. In 1785, Tipu dispatched a formidable army of 15,000 men. After a fierce battle, the Mysore army was forced to retreat. Two months later, Tipu himself led an imposing army, which included French soldiers, into Coorg. In the ensuing battle, many Kodavas were martyred. Tipu seized Madikeri and proposed negotiations for peace. However, the outcome was the forced migration of thousands of Kodavas to Srirangapatna. Many men, women and children perished during the arduous journey.

Tipu renamed Madikeri as Zaffarabad and built a fortress where he posted a major garrison. He also renamed Bagamandala as Abjalabad; he seized the temple in Bagamandala and converted it into a military garrison. In response, the Brahmin priests secretly moved the idols to the safety of the forests.

In January 1786, Tipu wrote to Meer Moinuddin:

> By the favor of the Almighty and the assistance of the Prophet, we have arranged and adjusted the affairs of the Taaluk of Zufeerabad in the most suitable manner; the tribe of Koorgs, to the number of fifty thousand men and women, having been made captives, and incorporated with the Ahmedy class.[33]

Kirkpatrick notes that in a previous letter, Tipu had stated the figure as forty thousand.[34]

On 5 January 1786, Tipu had written to Runmust Khan:

> The exciters of sedition in the Koorg country ... conceiving vain hopes from the great distance of our victorious army, raised their heads, one and all, in tumult. Immediately on our hearing of this circumstance, we proceeded with the utmost speed, and, at once, made prisoners of forty thousand occasion-seeking and sedition-exciting Koorgs, who, alarmed at the approach of our victorious army, had slunk into woods, and concealed themselves in lofty mountains, inaccessible even to birds. Then carrying them away from their native country we raised them to the honor of Islam, and incorporated them with our Ahmedi corps.[35]

In a letter addressed to Budruz Zuman Khan on 4 March 1786, Tipu directs, 'Whatever number of Koorg women and children may, at this time, be at Nagar, Koonly-doorg, or elsewhere, must be collected together, and the allowance formerly assigned for their support be paid to them.'[36] The presence of Coorg women and children in Nagar suggests that they had been deported. It is plausible that they had been converted by this juncture, given the sultan's efforts to ensure their welfare. A day later, Tipu writes another letter acknowledging, 'What you write, concerning the death of five hundred Koorgs from the small-pox, is understood.'[37] There is no sign of compassion or remorse; the deceased are to be buried and forgotten.

Bowring observes:

> The Sultan in his memoirs gives the following account of his proceedings at Zafirabad, as he chose to call Merkara, the capital: 'It is the custom with you for the eldest of five brothers to marry, and for the wife of such brother to be common to all five: hence there cannot be the slightest doubt of your all being bastards. This is about the seventh time that you have acted treacherously towards the Government, and plundered our armies. I have now vowed to the true God that if you ever again conduct yourselves traitorously or wickedly, I will not revile or molest a single individual among you, but making Ahmadis [Muslims] of the whole of you, transplant you all from this country to some other'.[38]

The example of the 'five brothers' is indeed intriguing. Tipu may have been acquainted with the story of the Pandavas from the Mahabharata, and he likely used it to depict polyandry among the Coorgis and the Nairs, aiming to condemn them for what he perceived as sheer debauchery.

Four years after Veerarajendra's imprisonment, he was liberated by a group of twelve Gowdas, or village chiefs. On the night of 14 December 1788, Veerarajendra and his family managed to escape from the Periapatna Fort. His wife had recently delivered a baby girl named Rajammaji. As they fled undet the cover of darkness, the innocent baby was carried by Veerarajendra's brother

Appajiraja. Suddenly, the baby cried out, alarming Veerarajendra. In a desperate attempt to avoid detection, Veerarajendra signalled to one of his aides, Ismail Khan, to kill the baby. Khan took the child, administered a small amount opium and the child immediately fell asleep. With the baby now quiet, the group was able to escape without further trouble. They eventually settled in Kurchi village in the southern part of Coorg. To evade capture, the raja continued to move from place to place.

The Kodavas rallied behind their raja and began recapturing their villages one by one. In June 1789, they attacked the Kushalnagar Fort, and their commander Kuletira Ponnanna presented the head of Tipu's commander as a trophy to Veerarajendra.[39] This victory was followed by victories at Armeri in August 1789 and Bagamandala in 1790. The Kodavas subsequently managed to recapture all the villages of Coorg except the Zaffarabad Fort. Veerarajendra appealed to the British authorities in Bombay for help. In response, Tipu ordered the garrison to withdraw from Zaffarabad. However, during the retreat, the Mysorean forces were attacked by the Kodavas and suffered heavy losses.

By this time, Tipu had instigated the Third Anglo-Mysore War by attempting to attack Travancore in December 1789. He remained encamped near the Travancore Lines until May 1790, engaging in battles against the Nairs and the British.

Mohibbul Hasan states that Burhanuddin set out for Coorg with a large army, while Tipu also departed from his capital in early September 1789 with the determination to subdue Veerarajendra. He states:

> But Burhan did not succeed in defeating Vir Raja who captured the three Mysore forts [Bhagamandala, Beppunad and Kushalnagar]. Mercara still remained in the hands of the Mysoreans, but it was isolated and liable to fall at any moment. Tipu himself could not visit Coorg because he had to proceed to Malabar which was blazing up in revolt, and as soon as he had suppressed the rising in Malabar, war broke out with the English. Coorg thus remained unsubdued.[40]

In October 1790, Veerarajendra signed a treaty of friendship with the British at Tellicherry, wherein he agreed to allow British troops to pass through his territories at any time. In return, the British pledged to help him retain his independence and promised to facilitate his family's escape to Tellicherry in the event of an attack from Mysore. The kingdom of Travancore had firmly aligned with the British to counter the threats posed by the Mysore sultans. In fact, the kings of Coorg and Kerala allied with the British primarily as a defensive measure against the aggressions of the sultans.

By 1791, Veerarajendra had captured the Madikeri Fort, solidifying his position as the undisputed ruler of Coorg and earning the epithet Dodda Veerarajendra. The British sought passage for their troops from Bombay to Srirangapatna, and in April 1791, General Robert Abercrombie and his army were warmly welcomed and feted by Veerarajendra. Following the conclusion of the Third Anglo-Mysore War in 1792, British troops once again passed through the region on their return journey. Abercrombie and Veerarajendra developed a strong camaraderie during this time.

In his work, *Mysore and Coorg* (1878), Lewis Rice notes that Tipu was furious when the British insisted on the surrender of Coorg. He states:

> Coorg was in danger of being overlooked and sacrificed. It required the zealous intercession of Sir Robert Abercromby to induce the Governor General to make an after demand for the cession of Coorg, though not adjacent to the company's territory, in order to keep faith with Vira Raja and to save him from the fangs of Tippu, whose first move after the peace would no doubt have been to wreak his vengeance upon his former vassal.[41]

When the demand was communicated to Tipu, he flew into a rage and questioned why the British were not requesting the key of Srirangapatna instead.

The treaty hung in the balance during this critical period, but Tipu found himself in a precarious position, while Lord Cornwallis remained resolute. 'English guns, which had already been sent away, were ordered back, and Tippu began to prepare for defence. At the last moment he gave an unwilling assent to the demand.'[42] Thus, Coorg was spared from falling into Tipu's clutches thanks to Abercrombie's intervention. However, the raja was compelled to pay tribute to the British and return to Tipu the districts he had captured from him. Veerarajendra felt a sense of indignation, yet his options were limited. 'Tippu extended his claims also to Amara-Sullia, besides the districts of Panje and Bellare.'[43] Eventually, the raja conceded the last two districts while retaining possession of Amara-Sullia.[44]

In May 1792, a new settlement was established, and a fort was constructed to commemorate the alliance between Coorg and the British. This settlement was named Veerarajendrapette in honour of the Coorgi-British friendship. Over time, Veerarajendrapette evolved into a bustling market town. Today, it is recognized by the name Virajpet.

Due to the frequent conflicts with Tipu, Coorg faced depopulation, prompting the raja to undertake special efforts to repopulate his kingdom. Approximately 12,000 Kodavas who had been converted to Islam fled Srirangapatna during the war and returned to Coorg. While some reverted to their original faith, others retained their Muslim beliefs. However, due to the conservative stance of their clans, they were not fully accepted back into their communities, resulting in a loss of caste. These Muslims are now referred to as Kodava Mappilas.

It is reported that Tipu transported around 70,000 Christians from Canara, particularly Mangalore and its surrounding areas, to Srirangapatna, where he forcibly converted them to Islam. By 1792, only around 10,000 of them had survived. About 700 individuals escaped from captivity, and Veerarajendra invited them to settle in Virajpet. In November 1792, he ordered the construction of a church for their community. Additionally, during the late 18th century, Bengali migrants who had initially settled in Kannur following their nawab's defeat at the Battle of Plassey, relocated to Virajpet and established what became known as Bengali Street. Furthermore, Virajpet features streets named Telugu Street and Jain Street, reflecting its diverse population.

## British Takeover

In 1799, Veerarjendra facilitated the passage of the British army, led by General James Stuart, through Coorg as they journeyed to besiege Srirangapatna. He even offered to send troops to aid the British cause, but they declined the offer, saying that the Kodavas were better suited to guerrilla warfare than traditional regimental warfare.

Two weeks after the death of Tipu Sultan, General Harris 'sent a letter of thanks to Vira Raja, accompanied by a present of one of Tippu's own horses, one of his palkis and one of his howdas. The promise was also given that the country of Coorg would be restored to the Raja'.[45] However, despite their assurances, no such restitution took place.

Veerarajendra received a magnificently crafted sword from Governor-General Robert Wellesley. However, the British soon demanded that he pay them the same tribute previously paid to Haider Ali and Tipu Sultan. Veerarajendra adamantly refused, eventually reaching a compromise wherein he agreed to send them an elephant annually.

After Tipu's demise, the British reinstated the Wodeyar dynasty in Mysore and appointed a resident to oversee Mysore. Dodda Veerarajendra expected similar treatment, having cooperated extensively with the British. However, his expectations were not met, and despite his efforts, he found himself subjected to vassalage in all aspects, albeit without the cash tribute. While the elephant tribute may seem insignificant, it effectively solidified his status as a tributary to the British.

Veerarajendra felt he had been treated unfairly. However, he found himself powerless to resist the British. Over time, he became increasingly paranoid and despotic, ordering the murder of his brother Appajiraja and imposing capital punishment on those he suspected. He even attempted suicide, although some observers believed it was a ploy to gain sympathy from the British. Veerarajendra likely descended into madness and passed away in June 1809. Two months before his death, the governor-general, Lord Minto, acknowledged his last will and testament, in which he nominated his minor daughter, Devammaji, as his successor.

Veerarajendra's younger brother, Lingarajendra, assumed control as regent. On 9 September 1810, the eleven-year-old Devammaji wrote to the British governor of Madras expressing her desire to abdicate in favour of Lingarajendra. In 1811, Lingarajendra took over as absolute ruler and appointed his son Chikka Veerarajendra as the heir apparent.

Lingarajendra's rule was marked by despotism. On one occasion, he even took up his gun and shot down a pair of elephants for disturbing his sleep. He dealt with internal enemies through summary executions. Lingarajendra organized hunting expeditions for British dignitaries, maintained a harem of hundreds of women guarded by Siddhi bodyguards, and established a zoo in Madikeri Fort featuring an exotic collection of animals. Lingarajendra died in 1820, and he was succeeded by his son, Chikka Veerarajendra, who would eventually become the last ruler of Coorg.

Chikka Veerarajendra continued the legacy of cruelty and despotism. His dewan hanged his cousin Devammaji, who had willingly abdicated her throne in favour of his father, and also her half-sister Mahadevammaji, without apparent reason. In 1830, his own sister, also named Devammaji, and her husband sought asylum in Mysore under the British due to fear of persecution. By early 1834, relations between the raja and the British had deteriorated, and it became evident that a British attack on Coorg was imminent. Troops were mobilized from Cannanore and Mysore in preparation.

On 6 April 1834, Coorg was formally annexed by the East India Company, marking the end of the 234-year rule of the Lingayat rajas. The British confiscated valuables worth 16 lakh rupees, appointing a 'prize agent' to distribute the spoils among the soldiers and officers who had participated in the military campaign against Coorg. The raja was banished to Vellore along with his thirteen wives and many children, and relocated to Banaras with his large entourage the following year. He remained there under house arrest in a villa named Coorg Nest until his death in 1859.

The Kodavas were fierce warriors, but some of their rajas were flawed leaders, idols with feet of clay. The unstable and cruel nature of the last two rajas made it remarkably easy for the British to orchestrate a smooth takeover. It was essentially a bloodless coup.

## Social Change in Coorg

As explained earlier, the reign of terror under the Mysore sultans drove the Coorgis into the embrace of the British. Nine years before Tipu's demise, Coorg had already signed a friendship treaty with the East India Company at Tellicherry. With Tipu gone, the British effectively became overlords of Coorg, Mysore and Malabar. Coorg became their playground, summer retreat and hunting ground. The region underwent complete anglicization, with Kodagu renamed as Coorg and Madikeri as Mercara. The new white rulers did initiate some measures that improved the lives of the common people, such as establishing an Anglo-vernacular school in Madikeri and a Kannada school in Virajpet.

English education indeed brought significant advantages. Kodavas found employment opportunities in the armed forces and gained recognition as a martial race. Notably, Chonira Belliappa Muthamma, hailing from Virajpet, became the first Indian woman to join the IFS (Indian Foreign Service). She strongly resisted gender discrimination within the services, even taking the government to court over this matter.

The arrival of British planters from Sri Lanka introduced more scientific methods of coffee cultivation in Coorg, leading to significant economic rewards for the region. These planters constructed elegant estate bungalows, creating a sort of 'Little England' amidst the lush landscape. Additionally, three exclusive clubs were established, now counted among the top 100 elite clubs in India.

The first instance of Christian conversion in Coorg occurred in 1853 when Alamanda Somayya embraced Christianity and became Stephanous Somayya. Rev. Hermann Moegling, a German missionary based in Mangalore, officiated at the conversion. It was said that Moegling baptized Somayya at his own request and also assisted him in settling his debts. Shortly after, Moegling moved to Madikeri, where he set up a Protestant Church in 1855 and started the Basel Mission School.

The religious conversion stirred discontent among the people of Coorg, who lodged complaints with the British authorities, arguing that it violated the assurances given to them in 1834. The matter was taken to court, where the ruling favoured Stephanous Somayya. Subsequently, in 1854, a church was built on Somayya's land, leading to the simultaneous conversion of approximately 130 construction workers and their families to Christianity.

The people of Coorg were generally content with British rule, a sentiment that persisted for over a century.

## The Amara–Sullia Uprising

The Kodagu–Canara Mutiny is also known as Amara–Sullia Uprising. It occurred twenty years before 1857 and involved the residents of Kodagu and Dakshina Kannada districts of Karnataka, as well as the Kumbala region of Kerala. The primary goal of the rebels was to evict the British from their territory. The British had angered them by separating Amara Sullia from Coorg and merging it with the South Canara district, which was then part of the Madras province. Moreover, they had framed a rule stipulating that land tax must be paid exclusively in cash, refusing to accept grain and agricultural produce as payment. This policy was the immediate trigger for the rebellion.

The rebels successfully seized Mangalore, defeating the British forces stationed there, and raised the flag of the Haleri dynasty on 5 April 1837 at Bavutagudda. They maintained control of the town for thirteen days until reinforcements from Tellicherry were sent by the British to quell the revolt. The uprising was ruthlessly suppressed, with the rebels and their leaders captured and publicly executed. Guddemane Appaiah, who was hanged at the Madikeri Fort, is acclaimed as one of India's earliest freedom fighters. While many Kodavas fought against the British, there were also individuals who collaborated with them to crush the revolt, earning significant rewards for their treachery.

In 1857, amidst the massive uprising in northern India, Coorg staunchly supported the British. Recognizing this loyalty, the British issued a notification in February 1861 exempting Kodavas from the Disarming Act. In the 20th century, during India's struggle for independence, many Coorgis rallied behind Mahatma Gandhi's call for freedom, with several women generously donating their jewellery to support the cause.

# 11

# PAZHASSI RAJA'S UNCANNY RESISTANCE

Kerala Varma Pazhassi Raja, the ruler of Kottayam-Malabar (known as 'Cotiote' in its anglicized form), led a prolonged guerrilla war from his hideout in Wayanad, defiantly resisting the invasions of the Mysore sultans and the British until his last breath. He gained control of the principality in an age of political turbulence as his maternal uncle, Ravi Varma, the reigning raja, sought refuge in Travancore following Haider Ali's invasion.

When Malabar was ceded by Tipu Sultan to the British in 1792 through the Treaty of Seringapatam, Pazhassi Raja refused to acknowledge their overlordship. After all, vast swathes of territory were under his control, and he enjoyed the support of the tribals, peasants and local chiefs. He had never surrendered to the Mysore sultans. He considered himself the independent ruler of an autonomous kingdom. Neither the British nor Tipu Sultan had any right to trade away the dominions in his control. Bowring mentions that Lord Mornington 'had entered into a friendly correspondence with Tipu regarding certain claims preferred by that ruler to territory in Wayanad, which, after due examination into the facts, he ordered to be surrendered to the Sultan'.[1] It is likely that this land belonged neither to the British nor to Mysore. The territories in Wayanad were largely under the jurisdiction of Pazhassi Raja, and until his death in 1805, neither the Mysoreans nor the British exercised real authority in the area.

The British were displeased with Pazhassi Raja's insolence and labelled him a 'brigand'. Despite Arthur Wellesley's repeated attempts to subdue him, Pazhassi Raja continued to elude capture for five years. However, soon after Wellesley left India, Pazhassi Raja was ambushed near Mananthavady in Wayanad and killed in a gunfight on 30 November 1805.

## The History of the Region

C. Gopalan Nair, the deputy collector of Malabar, in his 1911 publication *Wynad: Its Peoples and Traditions*, provides interesting details about the history of this region. Nair states:

> According to tradition, Wynad was under the sway of *Vedar* [hunter] kings. These were conquered by the Kottayam and Kurumbranad Rajas who partitioned the country into Wynad and Parakkumeethil. Subsequently the Kottayam Raja, the ruler of Wynad proper, secured the sovereignty of Parakkumeethil also, and the whole country was under his sway when Tippu of Mysore exacted from the senior Raja of Kottayam a deed of relinquishment of his right over Wynad in 1786. On the fall of Seringapattam in 1799, Wynad became part of the British Empire. Kerala Varma Raja of Kottayam revolted against the British Power and was killed in 1805, after which peace reigned in the country interrupted only by a small rebellion of Kurichiyars and Kurumbers in 1812. This, however, was soon quelled.... An enquiry into the jenmam titles to lands in Wynad was commenced in 1884, and four years later, the properties that belonged to Kerala Varma Raja [the Pazhassi rebel] and his adherents were formally declared to belong to Government.[2]

In other words, the British seized the lands upon Pazhassi Raja's death and that of his brave band of warriors, with the seizure being officially legitimized eight decades later. Nair's account makes it clear that the land originally belonged to the Kottayam raja, was temporarily occupied by Tipu and ultimately acquired by the British through unfair means.

Nair's reference to 'a rock inscription in the Edakkal cave four miles southwest of Sultan's Battery'[3] testifies to the ancient human settlements in Wayanad. However, the region's history remains largely obscure. Oral traditions passed down through generations were formally recorded on 28 November 1810 following a court directive, shedding some light on its past.

According to these traditions, the Vedar kings, Arippan and Vedan, ruled Wayanad when the ruler of Kumbala (in the Kasargod district), embarked on a pilgrimage to the Tirunelli shrine. En route, he was captured and brought before the Vedar raja at the Velikumbam Fort (Veliyambam), who insisted he marry into the royal family. Reluctantly, the prisoner agreed, stipulating that the marriage adhere to Kshatriya rites. The condition was accepted and a date was fixed for the ceremony. In the meantime, the Kumbala raja sought aid from the Kottayam and Kurumbranad rajas, who promptly arrived with their forces, encamping near the Velikumbam Fort.

The Kumbala raja's Eradi attendant, an ascetic with matted locks, was assigned to beat the drum to herald the commencement of the marriage ceremony, serving as a covert sign to launch the attack on the fort. Subsequently, the fort fell, the Vedar king was killed and the Kumbala raja liberated. Refusing to abandon the bride-to-be, the Kumbala raja began the search for a substitute groom, settling on Nanthillath Nambiar, who hesitatingly accepted.[4] Nambiar was then made the ruler of Velikumbam, while the Kumbala raja returned home, and Wayanad was partitioned between the Kottayam and Kurumbranad rajas. The Eradi was rewarded with the fiefdom of Muttil, establishing the Bhagiya Svarupam, later known as 'Pakka' Svarupam. However, both the Velikumbam and Pakka clans soon became extinct, leaving the Kottayam and Kurumbranad rajas to maintain control in Wayanad until the arrival of the British.[5]

Nair observes that the Kottayam rajas were 'wise and capable administrators' who divided the country into 'Nads' and appointed Nair chieftains to govern each.[6] The administrative system operated democratically, with no single chieftain permitted to exercise absolute power. Nair notes, 'Every dispute had to be heard and disposed of by the assembly of chieftains.'[7]

Wayanad remained under the control of the western branch of the Kottayam family until Pazhassi Raja's death in 1805.[8] Despite Gopalan Nair's pro-British stance, he acknowledges that at the Theythal Bhagavathy Temple, 'the officiating priest even now places a burning lamp and flowers in the Raja's seat of honour, as doing homage to the ruler who during his reign used to attend the annual festival'.[9] This practice indicates the enduring respect the local populace held for the deceased king, despite more than a century having passed since his death.

## Malabar and Mysore

This idyllic atmosphere of Wayanad was disturbed by the incursions of the Mysore sultans.[10] Nair highlights:

> [Wayanad was] the only taluk in Malabar which never bowed its neck to the Mysore yoke and which defied the British power until its ruler fell fighting against the troops of the East India Company. Wynad remained undisturbed until 1773 when a Mysorean army passed through the country by the Thamarassery ghat on its way to Calicut.[11]

During the outbreak of the Second Anglo-Mysore War in 1780, Ravi Varma, the senior raja of Kottayam, who had earlier fled to Travancore, returned to assist the English forces besieged at Tellicherry. Around 2,000 Nairs participated in this effort. Later, 'in 1786 when Ravi Varma visited Tippu Sultan in Coorg, he – the Sultan – exacted from him a deed of relinquishment of all his rights over Wynad.'[12] The use of the word 'exacted' is significant, suggesting that no ruler would willingly relinquish any part of his territory without coercion or intimidation. The author opines that Kerala Varma, leading the western branch of the family, 'resented the action of the senior Raja and refused to submit to the Mysoreans, with whom he was engaged in desultory warfare from 1787 to the beginning of the Third Mysore War in 1790'.[13]

After Tipu's defeat at Tirurangadi in 1790, he was no longer a threat to Malabar. Following the conclusion of the war, a treaty was signed on 18 March 1792. Nair mentions:

> Malabar was ceded to the Company by Tipu Sultan. It was a disputed point whether Wynad was included in this cession, and it was not decided until the arrival of Lord Mornington in India in 1798 when it was finally settled that Wynad had remained part of Tipu's dominions.[14]

Decisions were primarily dictated by those wielding the guns, mostly unilaterally. Obviously, Pazhassi Raja remained unconvinced. He continued to fight until his last breath.

Robert Taylor, the head of the Tellicherry factory, had 'granted a cowle to Kerala Varma Raja that the English East India Company would assist and protect him and do everything in their power to render him independent of Tippu if he would enter heartily into the war against the Sultan'.[15] However, once the war was won, this promise was conveniently forgotten, and the British claimed that Wayanad now fell under their jurisdiction. Pazhassi Raja was labelled as a rebel when he refused to acquiesce.

Sreedhara Menon, in *Kerala History and its Makers,* points out:

> Kerala Varma Pazhassi Raja preferred to remain at his post of duty and serve his countrymen in their hour of trial. He collaborated with the British in fighting Tipu's forces, but when it was clear to him that the British had betrayed the faith he had reposed in them, he reacted sharply and fought against them to the bitter end, unmindful of his own personal safety.... During the Third Mysore War there was a tacit understanding between the English and Kerala Varma [1790] that the independence of Kottayam would be recognized at the end of the war in recognition of the latter's services in the fight against Tipu. However, the British failed to honour their commitment.[16]

Buchanan observes, 'The most vigorous steps would be necessary, as every Nair in Malayala secretly wishes success to the insurgents.'[17] The natives of the land were branded as 'insurgents', while the British perceived themselves as the rightful owners. When Tipu signed the 1792 treaty surrendering Malabar to the British, the latter conveniently assumed ownership of the entire region, including those parts that were not exactly in Tipu's possession.

The joint commissioners, appointed by the EICo to administer Malabar, initially erred by allocating Kottayam to the Kurumbranad raja, another uncle of Kerala Varma Pazhassi Raja. However, Pazhassi Raja refused to recognize the claims of the Kurumbranad raja as well as those of the British. He wielded considerable authority in Kottayam and expressed his resentment by stopping all revenue collections in the district.[18] When the British sent troops to subdue the raja, it resulted in the massacre of 1,100 company soldiers in the Periya Pass on 18 March 1797. Soon, the British cancelled their agreement with the Kurumbranad raja, leading to temporary restoration of peace. After the fall of Srirangapatna in 1799, Kerala Varma vehemently resisted all British efforts to take control of his dominions.[19]

Buchanan's account provides fascinating references to Pazhassi Raja, who was still alive at the time of his writing (although he died before the publication of Buchanan's three-volume magnum opus in 1807). He states:

> Of course, he is now in a state of open rebellion, and lives exactly on the same footing with the English as he did with Tipu; and a warfare has ensued, in which our loss has been very great, and the country has been terribly desolated. He is commonly called the Pychi Raja, from a house of that name, which was the principal residence of the family. He is also called the Cotay-hutty [Cotiote] or Wayanatil Raja, from the two districts that are now in his possession.[20]

This part of Buchanan's narrative highlights Pazhassi Raja's prowess and the grudging respect the British held for their elusive enemy. It also testifies that Kottayam and Wayanad remained under Pazhassi Raja's authority in 1800, eight years after Tipu ceded Malabar to the British. It would take another five years before the British finally managed to track down and eliminate the valiant 'rebel'.

On 31 December 1800, Buchanan recorded his visit to Koduvally:

> It is situated in Tamara-chery Nada, a district that formerly belonged to the Cotay-hutty or Pychi Raja. In this family, the four eldest males assume the title of Raja. The three eldest, like the other Rajas of Malabar, fled into Travancore, to escape from the violence of the late Sultan; but the fourth remained behind in defiance of the Mussalman, at times being forced to retire into the woods, and again at times issuing forth with a band of determined Nairs, overthrowing the troops of the Sultan.[21]

Buchanan also observes:

> Kerala Verma [Pazhassi Raja], the present Raja, is a younger branch of the family; but retains his country in absolute sovereignty, denying the authority of the Company, of the head of his family, and of all other persons. In the reign of Tipu, this active chief assembled some of his Nairs, and regained possession of the territories which the former reigning prince had, on Hyder's invasion, deserted. The [senior] Raja, who had so basely submitted to the Mussalman conqueror, succeeded afterwards to the territory of a relation, and now enjoys his share of the allowance which is made to the Rajas of Malabar by the Company, to whose authority he quietly submits.[22]

Buchanan does not hide his contempt for the senior raja while expressing his admiration for Pazhassi Raja. He recounts that the second and third rajas, at some point, likely after the death of Tipu Sultan, sought to negotiate with the British for the return of territory formerly owned by their family. It appears the British agreed to concede some of the territory to them, as Buchanan writes:

> This was accordingly granted, so far as practicable, and they are now in quiet possession of the fifth of the revenue in the Nadas, or districts of Curumbara and Thamarachery. This gave great offence to the fourth Raja, who considered himself entitled to the whole, by his seniors having deserted their country, while he stood gallantly on the defensive.[23]

Buchanan adds, 'The Waynad Raja has at present sent the Conga Nair, one of his officers, into the Mysore dominions, to cut sandalwood, and to plunder the villages.'[24] He was, of course, referring to Edachena Kungan, one of the valiant supporters of the raja.

Buchanan's perspective is undoubtedly biased and prejudiced, as one might anticipate given his circumstances. As an employee of the British East India Company stationed in India, Buchanan's account naturally reflects the company's interests. The company's primary objective in India was to make money. Having made considerable investments in military endeavours, they had an expectation of substantial returns. Throughout his writings, Buchanan often brands Pazhassi Raja as a 'dacoit' or 'thief', despite acknowledging repeatedly that the disputed territory rightfully belonged to the raja.

## Guerrilla Warfare

Pazhassi Raja engaged in battles against the forces of Tipu Sultan from 1786 to 1790. When the British tried to take control of Kottayam and Wayanad in 1793, as stipulated in their 1792 treaty with Tipu, Pazhassi Raja struggled to maintain his freedom. The First Pazhassi Revolt lasted from 1793 to 1797. The conflict arose when the British overlooked the claims of Pazhassi Raja and leased Kurumbranad to his uncle for one year. The following year, the lease was renewed for a five-year period.[25] Pazhassi Raja then declared open rebellion and prevented revenue collection, compelling the English to offer concessions, which were later withdrawn by the governor-general's order.[26] Thereafter, Pazhassi Raja adopted a more uncompromising stance. The British struggled to apprehend him as he was 'guarded by a contingent of five hundred well-armed

Nairs drawn from all over Wynad'.[27] He also defied them by sheltering one of the Iruvazhinad Nambiars (Narangoli), whom they had declared a rebel.[28]

On 19 April 1796, the British launched a concerted effort to capture Kerala Varma at his *kovilakam* at Pazhassi. Conducting a dawn raid with a 300-strong contingent from Tellicherry, they were dismayed to find that the raja had successfully escaped to Wayanad. They plundered the palace and decamped with much treasure.[29] Thereafter, Pazhassi Raja continued to wage guerilla warfare from the jungles of Wayanad. 'In June 1796 he blocked all traffic on the Kuttiyadi ghat.'[30] Alarmed by rumours of a potential alliance between Kerala Varma and Tipu, the British quickly patched up their differences with him and facilitated his return to Pazhassi. Peace prevailed for a while. However, tensions escalated when the Kurumbranad raja dismissed Kaitheri Ambu, a trusted confidante of Pazhassi Raja, from his service. Soon after, Pazhassi Raja resumed his activities in Wayanad, leading to a halt in revenue collection in Kottayam.[31] The situation reached a critical point in December 1796, with the British banning meetings in Wayanad and the 'rebels' defiantly resisting. On 7 January 1797, an 80-strong contingent of British troops under Captain Bowman was attacked and killed by forces led by Kaitheri Ambu. Bowman and several other officers and soldiers lost their lives.[32] The following day the guerrillas launched 'a daring attack on the Havildar's guard stationed at Pazhassi. The whole British party except one man was killed. The British detachments stationed at various strategic points in Wayanad were forced to withdraw under threat of annihilation.'[33]

In February, the British brought in reinforcements from Bombay and surrounded Wayanad, attacking from all sides. Menon states:

> In battles fought on three successive days [9th, 10th and 11th March] the British forces were overpowered by thousands of Nairs and Kurichiyas who had rallied under the banner of the Pazhassi Raja and they were even prevented from making good their escape to the plains.[34]

Thereafter, the governor of Bombay, Jonathan Duncan, came to Malabar on a peace mission. With the Chirakkal raja acting as an intermediary, a settlement was reached.[35] Menon opines, 'Pazhassi Raja's submission to British authority was only a tactical move, for in 1800 he again raised the standard of revolt with greater determination.'[36]

The Second Pazhassi Revolt bore all the makings of a revolution. Dubbed the Cotiote War by the British, it commenced in 1800. By then, an increasing number of individuals had joined the rebel ranks, and Pazhassi Raja had attained superstar status. His military force now comprised Nairs, Kurichiya tribals, Mappilas and Muslim soldiers who had been rendered destitute following the death of Tipu Sultan.[37]

## All the Raja's Men

Pazhassi Raja received steadfast support from Kannavath Sankaran Nambiar, Edachena Kungan, Kaitheri Ambu, Pallur Eman and other Nair and tribal chieftains, all of whom tragically lost their lives in the conflict with the British. Menon remarks:

> Several chieftains and nobles in Tellicherry who were apparently maintaining good relations with the British also extended their secret support to him. The prominent Muslim merchant of Tellicherry, Chovvakaran Moosa, supplied the Raja with rice and other provisions while keeping up pretence of friendly relations with the Company.[38]

In 1800, Arthur Wellesley assumed command of the British forces in Malabar. While he succeeded in cutting off all supplies to Pazhassi Raja's men, he failed to arrest the elusive 'rebel'. By May 1801, however, the British had captured all significant outposts in Wayanad, forcing Pazhassi Raja and his trusted followers to live as fugitives in the jungles. 'The Raja's supporters like Chuzhali Nambiar and Peruvayyal Nambiar were captured by the British.'[39] In August, the British proclaimed a general amnesty, hoping for the surrender of Pazhassi Raja and his supporters. However, their hopes were dashed as none surrendered.

Kannavath Sankaran Nambiar had previously rallied and organized the Kurichiya tribals against the forces of Tipu Sultan. In a battle with Pazhassi Raja's warriors in 1797, the British suffered heavy casualities, resulting in the deaths of Captain Bachelor and Captain William Brown. Sankaran and Ambu served as the raja's aides during this period.

In June 1800, Sankaran Nambiar led a group of warriors in an attack against the British, prompting the latter to announce a price on his head the following year. On 27 November 1801, Sankaran and his comrades were captured at Kuttiyadi after a traitor revealed their hideout to the British. They were transported to Kannavam for execution. When the British offered to spare their lives and reward them in exchange for divulging Pazhassi Raja's whereabouts, Sankaran staunchly refused. He asserted that their loyalty to their king would earn them a greater reward in heaven. Notably, faced with certain death, none of the prisoners agreed to betray the raja. Sankaran and his followers, including his brother, son and nephews, are believed to have placed the hangman's noose around their necks with their own hands. Today, a memorial known as 'Kuriti-Kalam' or 'Place of Blood Sacrifice' commemorates their martyrdom.

In 1801, a British force of 10,000 soldiers surrounded Kottayam and Wayanad, blocking all major passes linking the two regions. The raja and his men sought refuge in the forests, planning their next move. In October 1802, Edachena Kungan, led 150 Kurichiya tribals, armed with bows and arrows and headed by Talakkal Chandu, in the capture and destruction of the Panamaram Fort in Wayanad. The 70-member garrison stationed there met a grim fate at the hands of the attackers.

In 1804, during Thomas Harvey Baber's tenure as sub-collector, the British sent a huge army, along with 1,200 Kolkars, to suppress an uprising in Chirakkal led by Kalliat Nambiar and supported by Pazhassi Raja's warriors. The following year, a certain Chetti betrayed the raja and revealed his whereabouts to Baber. The raja and his faithful band were hiding at Mavila Thode near Mananthavady. Baber, leading a substantial force, arrived there and surrounded the guerrillas on the morning of 30 November 1805. In the ensuing gunfight, Pazhassi Raja and five others were martyred.

Baber wrote to the collector of Malabar a month after the event, providing a detailed account of the events that led to the defeat of the gallant Pazhassi Raja. In his letter dated 31 December 1805, he mentions deploying several agents to gather information about the whereabouts of the guerrilla leader, and 'three of them at last brought me intelligence of the Pyche [Pazhassi] Raja and all the rebel leaders, with the exception of Palora Jamen [Pallur Eman]'.[40]

Baber describes how he set out with a sizeable contingent of troops to vanquish the raja. In his own words, 'After proceeding about a mile and a half through very high grass and thick teak forests into the Mysore country, Charen Subedar of Captain Watson's armed police, who was leading the advanced party, suddenly halted and beckoning to me, told me he heard voices.'[41] To cut a long story short, they found around ten individuals on the banks of the Mavila Thode. A 30-man unit attacked the unsuspecting guerrilla group, sparking a skirmish. Kungan's party arrived and offered a token resistance but eventually fled. One of the raja's warriors, discovered hiding in the grass, revealed to Baber that Pazhassi Raja was among the first casualities. What followed has become the stuff of legend. Baber recounts:

> It fell to the lot of one of my Cutcherry servants, Canara [Karunakara] Menon, to arrest the flight of the Raja ... and it is worthy of mention that this extraordinary personage, though in the moment of death, called out in the most dignified and commanding manner to the Menon, not to approach and defile his person ... Aralat Cootty Nambiar, the only one remaining of those rebels proscribed by Colonel Stevenson and a most faithful adherent of the Raja, made a most desperate resistance, but at last fell.[42]

Thus, the raja and his followers displayed spectacular courage and met their end bravely. Baber mentions that four other men were killed, two were captured, along with the raja's wife and a few female attendants.

The only items of value they discovered were a gold dagger and a gold waist chain. Baber kept the dagger for himself and gave the waist chain to Captain Clapham. As the saying goes, 'To the victor belongs the spoils'. Nevertheless, it is important to acknowledge the conquering British for their respect towards the raja's remains and their courteous treatment of his wife. Baber writes:

> The Raja's body was taken up and put into my palanquin, while the lady who was dreadfully reduced from sickness was put into Captain Clapham's.... The following day the Raja's body was despatched under a strong escort to Manantoddy (Manathavady), and the Sheristadar sent with it with orders to assemble all the Brahmins and to see that the customary honours were performed at his funeral. I was induced to this conduct from the consideration that although a rebel, he was one of the natural chieftains of the country, and might be considered on that account rather as a fallen enemy. If I have acted injudiciously, I hope some allowances will be made for my feelings on such an occasion.[43]

Pazhassi Raja had defiantly resisted the company's forces 'for nearly nine years, during which many thousand valuable lives have been sacrificed and sums of money beyond all calculation expended'.[44] Baber's communication to his superior officer underscores the exhaustive measures the British had to employ to subdue the Kottayam raja, and the staggering cost involved. His comment that 'his annihilation became necessary for the stability and security of the Government and its subjects' carries a hint of remorse.[45] Baber observes that the locals displayed towards the fallen hero 'a regard and respect bordering on veneration, which not even death can efface'.[46]

Speaking of the formidable reputation of Pazhassi Raja, Panikkar avers:

> The resistance movement in the north produced at least one man of outstanding ability and character, Kerala Varma of Kottayam

> known as Pychy Raja to Wellington and his associates. Scholar, poet, and soldier, Kerala Varma who was a junior member of the Kottayam family organized an unrelenting resistance against Tippu. Later he led the rebellion against the British and the despatches of Wellington bear witness to the terror that his name inspired.[47]

After the death of Pazhassi Raja, the Kurichiyas experienced severe impoverishment. Chandran Vaidyar, a traditional healer from Thalassery belonging to the Kurichiya tribe of Mananthavady, describes the raja's death as a devastating blow to his people. 'Without our king, we were totally helpless,' he laments. 'We were forced deeper into the forests with no means of subsistence. We had no protector or saviour, and it is only by god's grace that our race has survived.'

## Buchanan's Observations

Among Buchanan's notable observations is a passage regarding the lineage of the Kottayath family of Pazhassi Raja:

> Another Kshatriya family called Cottay-hutty [Cotiote], who seem to have been descended from a younger sister of the Curumbara [Kurumbranadu] Rajas, seized on another portion of Coluta-nada [Kolathunadu] lying between Tellicherry and the Ghats. The Curumbara Nada Rajas became extinct in the Malabar year 954 (1778–1779), five years after Hyder invaded the country.[48]

The Kottayam family then staked a claim to the dominions of their relatives but later fled to Travancore. Upon their return, presumably after 1792, when the British had established authority in Malabar, the British allocated them some of the lands that previously belonged to their now-extinct kin.

Buchanan records that the senior members of the family returned after the English gained control of the region. The eldest surviving member was 'put in immediate possession of Curumbara Nada'.[49] Buchanan clarifies, 'The Company could not give him the original territory belonging to his family, as it had ever since been in the possession of the fourth Tamburan of the house, who assumes the title of Cottay-hutty Raja, and is in actual rebellion.'[50]

Buchanan also mentions that while the claims of the senior rajas were dubious, they had nevertheless been acknowledged by the East India Company. This was a consistent strategy employed by the English – support the weaker rulers and collect tribute, while suppressing the strong ones. Hence, Pazhassi Raja was labelled as a rebel, despite his efforts to retain his own territory. Kuttiady is identified as part of Pazhassi Raja's domain. According to C. Gopalan Nair's account, the original name of Sultan Bathery was Ganapathivattam.[51] The locals conferred the new name, which was not a part of Tipu's massive renaming initiative, and thus it has remained Sultan Bathery to this day. (Bathery is the vernacular version of 'Battery'.)

While travelling through Thamarassery, Buchanan wrote on 1 January 1801 that a significant portion of the land had been devastated:

> At Tamarachery there was a house belonging to the Pychi Raja; and as it was on the road to one of the principal passes leading up to Karnata, Tipu established in its neighbourhood a strong colony of the ruffian Moplays; and until lately, a constant petty warfare has been continued between them and the Nairs. A detachment of sepoys is now in possession of the house, and preserve the peace.[52]

Thus, when the British gained control, they proclaimed it as 'peace'. Buchanan conceded that the house rightfully belonged to Pazhassi Raja's family. However, the brazen British had no qualms about claiming it for themselves.

Buchanan's perspective is quintessentially British. He states, 'The rebellion in Wayanad had put a stop to all legal commerce. I believe, however, that there is much smuggling.'[53] Trade conducted without the British consent risked being labelled as 'smuggling', as they heavily relied on taxes for revenue. Hence, the 'Collector' wielded immense power in the district.

Buchanan's account suggests a significant decline in the production of pepper in Malabar, dropping to half of its earlier output following the attacks of the Mysore sultans. It appears that a substantial portion of the remaining production was situated within the territory of Pazhassi Raja, which Buchanan describes as 'the seat of a most bloody warfare'.[54] So, the enmity of the English towards Pazhassi Raja may not have been merely about territorial control and sovereignty but also about securing the crucial supply of pepper.

Buchanan extensively discusses various aspects of the trade in pepper, cardamom and sandalwood:

> The French having been expelled from Mahe [in July 1793], the company became immediately possessed of the whole pepper trade without a rival. As merchants it was then their interest to lower the price, which was undoubtedly in their power; but as sovereigns their interest was that the price should not be so low as to injure the revenue, or to discourage agriculture.[55]

The English displayed spectacular shrewdness and commercial acumen, with profit serving as their primary motive.

As for sandalwood, it was not native to Malabar but thrived on the eastern slopes of the Western Ghats. Typically, it was hauled by elephants, floated down rivers that flowed westward into Malabar and then loaded onto ships for export from the ports along the west coast. Buchanan states, 'Owing to the unsettled state of Malabar during the reign of Hyder, however, it was more convenient for the merchants to send this article to the eastern coast of the peninsula.'[56] The evolving dynamics of the sandalwood trade are depicted thus, 'Tipu on his accession having prohibited the exportation of this article, all that could be cut secretly was smuggled into the Coorg and Wayanad countries, and thence conveyed to Malabar.'[57] Buchanan mentions that the sandalwood trade also suffered setbacks during the reign of the two sultans. However, even after their demise, the confusion persisted. In the British view, only Europeans possessed the authority to export goods. Hence, Buchanan states:

> Since the overthrow of Tipu, the quantity brought down has been very small. The Coorg raja no longer can commit his depredations, and the rebellion of the Pazhassi Raja who possesses the Wayanad, and the principal passes up the Ghats, has thrown the trade back again towards the eastern coast. There can be little doubt, however, that, as soon as the communication is open, Tellicherry will be the principal port for the best sandalwood.[58]

The British held the belief that they were the masters of all they surveyed. In their eyes, whether it was the pepper trade or the sandalwood trade, they alone possessed the authority to dictate the terms of distribution and pricing. Pazhassi Raja and the Coorg raja were considered mere thieves.

## Company Control

On 11 January 1801, Buchanan wrote:

> Mr Wilson, the collector of a circle containing the two districts called Cotiote and Irvenaad (Iruvazhinad), conducted me to his house at Cadrur [Kathirur]. This formerly belonged to the Pychi Rajas, and was by the Nairs reckoned a superb building. It is in the form of a square, surrounding a court, in which there is a well and a small tank. The building is two stories high.[59]

The house was apparently a *naalukettu,* a stately mansion built in the unique Kerala-style architecture. The British appropriated all the notable buildings, as did Haider and Tipu. There is no record of either of the sultans erecting structures in Malabar.

The British astutely recognized the potential of the Kottayam-Malabar district as a lucrative venture. It is no surprise that they were determined to eliminate Pazhassi Raja from the equation. Buchanan's description of the Cotiote property is explicit, 'The plantations amounted to 37,440 acres, and the Parumba or hill-land under-woods contained 112,320 acres ... Cotiote formerly produced about 500,000 Rupees worth of pepper.'[60] The British had meticulously assessed the financial aspects, weighing profit and loss, costs and benefits. Buchanan remarks, 'Were it in a settled state, how valuable the Cotiote district might be made.'[61]

During his visit to the company's plantation at Anjarakandy, Buchanan laments the frequent attacks by the Nairs:

> The plantation has of late been much molested by the Nairs, and the eastern part of it has fallen into their hands; so that, for the protection of what remains, it has been necessary to station a European officer, with a company of sepoys, at Mr Brown's house. The Nairs are so bold, that at night they frequently fire into Mr Brown's dwelling; and the last officer stationed there was lately shot dead, as he was walking in front of the house.[62]

Thus, at the dawn of the 19th century, when Dr Buchanan made his memorable journey, Pazhassi Raja and his brave band of men were alive and fighting. Despite possessing superior weapons and larger forces, the British struggled to keep the Nairs and the tribals in check. Arthur Wellesley failed miserably in his attempt to vanquish Pazhassi Raja. Finally, after Wellesley had returned to England in 1805, the British in India succeeded in defeating and killing the 'Lion of Malabar' the same year. Years later, Wellesley would gain undying fame by defeating Napoleon Bonaparte at the Battle of Waterloo and go on to become the Duke of Wellington, later serving as the prime minister of Great Britain.

It was impossible to write about Pazhassi Raja without overshadowing the formidable image of Arthur Wellesley. Thus, only Buchanan and Logan provide detailed descriptions of his exploits. Buchanan's words occasionally reveal a grudging respect for the elusive raja. Logan, arriving decades later, viewed the local hero through colonial lenses, often labelling him as a 'brigand' or 'robber' or 'imposter', overlooking the fact that Kottayam and Wayanad were the raja's own lands, where he was revered and idolized by the populace. While Logan's assessments were mostly accurate, his portrayal of Pazhassi Raja's character was woefully inadequate. Wilks notes, 'Cotiote and the northern districts of Malabar were never thoroughly subdued by the Mysoor government, and it is only now that we are beginning to establish our authority there.'[63]

Denys Forrest affirms that when Tipu Sultan's letter of 10 July 1798 congratulated Richard Wellesley on assuming charge as governor-general, Wellesley's reply mentions Wayanad, which had been a point of contention between Mysore and the English since the 1792 treaty. Forrest states, 'On August 7th Wellesley responds with the good news that his Commissioners in Malabar have decided that the Wayanad was *not* ceded to the company under the treaty of Seringapatam, so Tipu is free to occupy it whenever it suits him.'[64] Tipu's response on 2 September reflects his dissatisfaction, stating that there is 'nothing there except forests and heaps of stones'.[65] This correspondence indicates that neither the British nor Tipu Sultan had effective control of Wayanad at the time, and it was Pazhassi Raja who had the upper hand.

After the fall of Pazhassi Raja, the British experienced a series of quick victories. They quelled the Vellore Revolt of 1806 with brutal force and crushed the Marathas in 1818. Following the death of the Lion of the Punjab, Maharaja Ranjit Singh, in 1839, the British capitalized on the ensuing chaos and swiftly annexed the Punjab. They compelled Ranjit Singh's eleven-year-old heir, Duleep Singh, to 'gift' the Kohinoor diamond to Queen Victoria in 1849 as per the terms of the Treaty of Lahore.

Sindh was annexed in 1843 by an army led by Charles Napier, while Lord Dalhousie formulated the infamous Doctrine of Lapse. Indian kingdoms were annexed one by one under various pretexts until the Revolt of 1857 led to a brief reversal of fortunes. The rebellion, however, could not be sustained, and it would be another nine decades before India ultimately freed herself from the British yoke.

# 12

# TIPU'S TEMPLE RUN AND JIHADIST ZEAL

Visible evidence of damage inflicted by Tipu can still be seen in many temples across Malabar. The famed Mridangasaileswari Temple in Kannur district, once the ancestral shrine of Kerala Varma Pazhassi Raja, stands as a prominent example. Logan's Manual names some of the notable temples destroyed by the sultan. In *Temples of Kannoor District,* S. Jayashanker meticulously compiles an exhaustive list, complete with explicit details, drawn from a census conducted in the late 20th century.

The website of the Kerala Tourism Development Corporation (KTDC) mentions:

> The Jain temple at Sulthan Bathery (Wayanad) is believed to have been built during the 13th century. Its design is strongly influenced by the architectural style of the then reigning Vijayanagar Dynasty. At one point in history, this temple also served as the ammunition store or battery of Tipu Sulthan's army.

In 1788, Tipu's army razed Calicut to the ground. Buchanan, writing in 1800, stated that 'Tipu destroyed the town, and removed its inhabitants to Nelluru, the name of which he changed to Furruck-abad'.[1] Ravi Varma of the Zamorin dynasty facilitated the flight of 30,000 Brahmins to Travancore. In August 1788, the ruler of Parappanad and a chieftain of Nilamboor, Trichera Thiruppad, were forcibly converted to Islam along with many nobles. The royal families of Chirakkal, Parappanad, Kadathanad, Kurumbranad, Balussery and Calicut sent their families to seek asylum in Travancore. Some princes fled, while several others perished in battle. Notwithstanding the risk of incurring the sultan's anger, the ruler of Travancore, Karthika Thirunal Rama Varma, provided sanctuary to the refugees.

As the Mysore army advanced towards the Koodali Thazathu *tharavad* in the Kannur district, the *karanavar*, Koran Gurikkalachan II, calmly entered the *kalari*, stood before the mother goddess, and instructed his aide to shoot him. After his death, the title of *gurikkal* ceased to be utilized by the clan. Buchanan's account narrates a similar incident involving one of the princes from the Chirakkal royal house:

> Seven chiefs of the house of Cherical managed the country and supported all the Rajas of the family. The last of these was Rama Varma, who being afraid that Tipu, then at Cotayangady near Tellicherry, would compel him to become a Mussalman, retired to Pazhassi, and procured a friendly Nair to shoot him dead... These events happened in the Malabar year 964 [AD 1788–1789].[2]

Before making the supreme sacrifice, Rama Varma ensured the safe evacuation of his sister and her two sons, the last surviving scions of the Chirakkal royal family. They embarked on a journey from Dharmadam to seek refuge in Travancore.

After the treacherous murder of the Kolathiri raja, Tipu Sultan tied his corpse to the feet of an elephant, dragged it through the streets and finally hung it from a treetop. The Palghat raja, Ettipangi Achan, following his surrender, was taken to Srirangapatna and subsequently vanished without a trace. Similar tales of horror are recounted by the Hindus of Coorg, the Iyengars of Melkote and the Christians of Mangalore.

Referring to the sacred shrine of Tirunelli in Wayanad, C. Gopalan Nair avers:

> There is a long blank in the history of the temple...The puja was naturally neglected during the Mysore invasion but subsequently, the Sannyasi – known as Samiyar – returned … After destruction by fire during Tippu's invasion the temple was first reconstructed with thatched roofs. The *Srikovil* [central shrine] has since been roofed with copper and surmounted by a gold spire.[3]

Of the Ganapathivattam Temple, Nair writes, 'When Tippu of Mysore overran the country his troops destroyed the temple and mutilated the granite idol. The town then took the name of Sultan's Battery.'[4] He also mentions, 'The Moplahs came in (to Wayanad) from Tellicherry, Kurumbranad and Calicut after the Mysore invasion.'[5]

The wanton destruction of places of worship recurred repeatedly across Malabar and along the borders of Travancore. In the southern regions, including Thrissur and Ernakulam districts, several churches were demolished, leaving believers waiting for several decades for the edifices to be rebuilt. Priests were scattered in all directions, sometimes returning after a few years, occasionally being replaced by newcomers, and at times seemingly disappearing without a trace.

Buchanan mentions that Tipu Sultan wanted to rebuild a dilapidated fort that had previously been erected by the Mysore rajas in the Pollachi region of present-day Tamil Nadu, 'Twelve years ago Tippoo gave it some repairs, and, to procure materials for the purpose, pulled down five large temples.'[6]

Among Tipu Sultan's letters translated by Kirkpatrick is one addressed to Nubby Shah in Bangalore, dated 14 September 1786:

> You write that agreeably to [our] orders, the Pagoda which was in front of the blessed Durgah has been demolished, but that the Aumil will not resign [to you] the ground [on which it stood]. It is known. The Aumil will make over the aforesaid ground [to you] when you must annex the same to the premises of the Durgah.[7]

Here, the sultan confirms the demolition of the temple and issues orders for the land to be attached to a nearby mosque.

Early in his reign, following his victory at Savanur against the Marathas and their allies, Tipu Sultan, in a letter dated 23 October 1786, addressed to Syed Ahmed Saheb, Boodhun Shah, Nubby Shah, Kuleem-ullah Shah and others (known as peer-zadehs or devotees), stated:

> By the blessing of God and the aid of the Prophet, the forces of the accursed having experienced a signal defeat and chastisement, have turned their faces to flight, leaving the troops of Islam victorious over the enemies of the faith. Thus has the army of the accursed infidels been trodden underfoot by the hoofs of the horses of Islam, and rendered vile and miserable; while the religion of Mahommed has been thereby made to flourish. You, Sir, are one of the elders [of the faith], and will therefore apply, with all your heart, to the best means of advancing the religion of Mahommed, and of administering to the support of Islam.[8]

The sultan's words are explicit and unambiguous, leaving no room for doubt about his intentions.

Charles Stewart expresses the view:

> Tipu's zeal for the conversion of his subjects was not however confined to the people of Malabar; he extended it to several of the inhabitants of Coimbatore, and to every other Hindu who incurred his displeasure, and had the misfortune to fall into his hands. It is said that had it not been for the remonstrances of his mother, who was a very sensible woman, he would have compelled his favourite Dewan Purnea to have forsaken the religion of his forefathers.[9]

In January 1788, 'the Sultaun, at the head of his army, proceeded by the route of Tamburcherry (Thamarassery), to visit and reform his possessions in Calicut'.[10] Wilks records that at a location called Gootipoor (Kuttipuram), approximately 2,000 Nairs along with their families had defended their fortified position for several days before being forced to surrender. They were presented with a Hobson's choice. In Wilks's own words:

> [The options being] a voluntary profession of the Mahommedan faith, or forcible conversion, with deportation from their native land. The unhappy captives gave a forced assent, and on the next day, the rite of circumcision was performed on all the males, every individual of both sexes being compelled to close the ceremony by eating beef.[11]

Tipu issued an ominous warning to the people of Calicut:

> From the period of the conquest until this day, during twenty-four years, you have been a turbulent and refractory people, and in the wars waged during your rainy season, you have caused numbers of our warriors to taste the draught of martyrdom. Be it so. What is past is past. Hereafter you must proceed in an opposite manner; dwell quietly, and pay your dues like good subjects; and since it is a practice with you, for one woman to associate with ten men, and you leave your mothers and sisters unconstrained in their obscene practices, and are thence all born in adultery, and are more shameless in your connexions than the beasts of the field; I hereby require you to forsake these sinful practices, and live like the rest of mankind. And if you are disobedient to these commands, I have made repeated vows, to honour the whole of you with Islam.'[12]

Tipu also complained that the cost of maintaining troops in Calicut far exceeded the revenues collected from the region, mainly due to the inhabitants' tendency towards rebellion and lack of cooperation. Given that the population was predominantly Muslim, it leads us to infer that the Mappilas resented the dominance of the Mysore Muslims.

Wilks recounts how the raja of Chirakkal was invited to meet Tipu Sultan, where he was entertained for several days and sent back with lavish presents. However, on his return journey, he was ambushed and killed in a skirmish. The aftermath of this event was truly horrific. Wilks states:

> The Nair raja of Chercul had been induced, by the most sacred promises, to pay his personal respects to the Sultaun, and was, for

> several days, treated with considerable distinction, and dismissed with costly presents to his little principality. Immediately after his departure, real or pretended information was received, of his being engaged in a secret conspiracy to revenge the cruel indignities of his countrymen; and Tippoo detached two brigades to effect his destruction, or ascertain his obedience, by directing him instantly to return to camp.... a skirmish ensued, in which the raja and some of his attendants were killed, and a few prisoners secured: and Tippoo, considering the accusation to be established, ordered the most base and unmanly indignities to be offered to the corpse, and that the dead and the living should afterwards be hanged on the same tree. These indignities recounted by the Sultaun himself, although free from his usual obscenity, are too brutal for translation.'[13]

Wilks elaborates:

> He (Tipu) states the destruction in the course of this holy war, of eight thousand idol temples, many of them roofed with gold, silver, or copper, and all containing treasures buried at the feet of the idol, the whole of which was royal plunder.[14]

Another account suggests that upon learning of Tipu's sinister designs, the raja sent a message to his family, instructing them to escape to Tellicherry for safety. After confirming their safety, he attempted to escape but, facing insurmountable obstacles, he shot himself. The more plausible story, however, indicates that he was intercepted and killed. Nevertheless, all accounts agree that his body was defiled. Thereafter, Tipu visited Cannanore and arranged for the betrothal of his son, Abdul Khaliq, to the daughter of the Arakkal Beevi.

Buchanan writes:

> *Tiruvana-Angady* is the place which in our maps is called *Tervanagary*, and is remarkable for the decisive victory which in the year 1790 Colonel Hartley gained in its neighbourhood over the forces of Tippoo. Near the *Angady*, or market, there is a small

> fort, which was erected by the Sultan around a *Colgum*, or palace, belonging to the *Tamuri Raja*. Both have now fallen into ruins.[15]

Buchanan's occasional misspellings can be excused, given the depth and significance of his narrative. He refers here to the Battle of Tirurangadi and recounts how the *kovilakam* (palace) of the Zamorin was ruined by the intervention of Tipu Sultan.

## Tipu's Trail of Destruction

S. Jayashanker details the destruction of temples by Tipu Sultan. Referring to the Thiruvillvaam Siva Temple at Kunnaru (in Ramanthali panchayat near Payyannur), he testifies, 'The idol (shivalingam) was broken during the invasion by the forces of Tippu Sultan. The broken parts of the idol then had to be joined by a bronze band. A portion of the nose and a hand of Lord Ayyappa's idol were also chopped by the invaders.'[16] Of the Perunthanniyoor Subramanyaswamy Temple, Korom (in Payannur town), the author states, 'This temple was also attacked by Tippu's forces and the holes on the compound walls testify his attacks.'[17] He adds, 'Tippu Sulthan's forces also attacked the Sree Maha Vishnu temple [Annoor, in Payannur town area] and desecrated the idol. The broken *vigraham* was changed thereafter and the entire temple was rebuilt.'[18] Of the Nambiathra Siva Temple at Payyannur, he notes, 'The original temple was completely destroyed by the forces of Tippu Sulthan and later the present temple was built.'[19]

The ancient Subramanyaswamy Temple at Payyannur, referenced in the Markandeya Purana, was torched by the Mysore army in March–April 1788.[20] A few precious items were salvaged as the locals were forewarned about the impending attack. According to Jayashanker, 'In this attack, the main *vigraham* was only broken but not completely damaged. The entire site was deserted for three years till one day… the senior lady of Thazhakkaat mana had a dream in which the God himself gave her directions to rebuild the temple.'[21] Jayashanker notes, 'The available parts of the broken vigraha were put together and fixed with silver clasps and then poojas commenced.'[22] He adds, 'The details of reconstruction are recorded by Vishnu Kanakka Pillai in one of the *pattolas*.'[23] The reconstruction efforts started in 1790, and it took forty-seven years to rebuild the temple. It was re-consecrated in April 1835. The author testifies, 'This could be achieved by the liberal contribution of the public including some Muslim brothers.'[24]

Of the (Kantotthidam) Someswary Temple in Payyannur, we learn, 'During the invasion of Tipu's forces, it is believed that the idol of the temple was taken to Patapenngaat temple and re-installed at the present temple site when the situation became normal.'[25]

The Sankaranarayana Temple, located at Chunta, Pulingom, in Kasargod district, was previously known as the Sree Sastha Temple, with the earlier structures dating back to the 14th century. Jayashanker avers:

> It is believed that the mosque at the east of this temple was previously a temple dedicated to Goddess Bhagavathi and even now some of the rites in the mosque are akin to the earlier rituals of the temple. The most common rite of *vaanku-vili* [the loud call to prayers] in a mosque is absent in this mosque.[26]

Of the Subramanyaswamy Temple at Pariyaram, Jayashanker writes, 'The forces of Tippu Sulthan ransacked the temple and destroyed its structures. For a long time, the temple was in a dilapidated condition. The original *oorulars* belonged to Ganga illam which later became extinct.'[27]

The Sri Krishna Temple at Trichambaram in Taliparamba town is now a highly favoured place of worship. Jayashanker informs us, 'Major renovations were done during 10th–11th century, 14th–15th century and 18th–19th century.'[28] This temple was also demolished by Tipu's army.

The Thiruvattoor Shiva Temple in Pariyaram village is a very ancient structure, featuring inscriptions in *vattezhuthu*. According to Jayashanker, 'This temple was also ransacked and damaged by Tippu's forces.... The *valiya-balikkall* is ruined. The *gopuram* which existed earlier is not there now. In short, all the structures in the temple are in a ruined state.'[29] Of the Someswary Temple at Panniyoor in Kurumathur Panchayat, Jayashanker writes, 'This temple was completely destroyed by Tippu's forces... The sreekovil was rebuilt in 1988.'[30]

The Maha Vishnu Temple at Kurumathur is an ancient temple believed to have existed since the 9th century, boasting considerable fame in its heyday. Jayashanker says, 'The forces of Tippu Sulthan tried to ransack the temple but the alert local people foiled their attempt.'[31] The temple showcases exquisitely carved *dwarapalakas* in granite, wood carvings of navagrahas adorning the ceilings, and mural paintings on the walls. Jayashanker adds, 'No festival has been held for the last ten years in this temple.'[32]

Regarding the Isaanamangalam Mahavishnu Temple at Cheleri in Kolachery panchayat, Jayashanker notes that during the Mysorean attack, 'this temple and the sub-shrines and *chuttambalam* were brought to the ground'.[33] In the 1970s, reconstruction activities started, and in 1977, Chinmayananda Swami's visit gave a boost to this initiative.

The ancient Raghavapuram Rama Temple at Cheruthaazham is believed to have been consecrated by Parasurama. During the Kolathiri reign, 'The temple was donated to Thulu Brahmins brought from Gokarnam for conducting *hiranya-garbham* (a ritual for transforming one as Kshathriya) as the Perinchelloor graamakkaars refused to do it for Kolaththiris.'[34] The author highlights an interesting method of social advancement and caste elevation through the performance of a special puja. He adds, 'This temple was also subjected to the attack of Tippu Sulthan and the Brahmins fled to Thiruvalla taluk [presently in Pathanamthitta district].'[35]

Regarding the Vatukunda Siva Temple at Madayi (near Pazhayangadi), Jayashanker states:

> Around 1789, Tippu descended on Malabar via Thamarasseri ghat in one of the attempts of his forces to occupy the Valapattanam fort

> of Chiraykkal Raaja from the northern side, his army had to stay sometime at Pazhayangaati. During this time, they destroyed the temple by using cannons. For about 180 years the temple complex was completely neglected.[36]

Reconstruction commenced in 1978 and was completed in 1992.[37]

The Vateswaram Siva Temple at Aroli in Pappinisseri panchayat was built by Vatakeswara or Vatuka Varma of the Mooshika dynasty and managed for centuries by the Chirakkal kovilakkam. This ancient temple was 'subjected to the attacks of Tippu's forces who shattered and leveled to the ground the massive structures including *chuttambalam, gopurams*, etc'.[38] Jayashanker also notes that *devadasis* used to sing and dance at this temple, with pujas performed thrice daily.[39] In 1975, the four sub-shrines underwent repairs, and following a *shuddhikalasam* or purification ritual, regular worship commenced.[40]

The famous Sree Krishna Temple at Kadalayi has a chequered history closely linked to the Mooshika kingdom.[41] The *Mooshikavamsa,* composed by Athula, the court poet of Srikantha, traces the origin of the dynasty and highlights several prominent rulers, notably Vallabha II. His capital, Vallabhapattanam (named after him), later known as Valapattanam, was anglicized to Baliapatam.[42] Jayashanker points out, 'The Mysorean invasions changed the history of the region. Though Haider Ali adopted a friendly attitude towards the Kolathithiris, Tipu Sulthan's policy was detrimental to the interest of the Hindu community. The second attack of Tippu's forces resulted in the desecration of temples and also forced conversions to Islam.'[43] Fearing a Mysorean invasion, the Kolathiri raja instructed his men to conceal the idol. The priest, Kallamballi Embraanthiri, and his assistants, Thalavil Vaaryar and Ezhothth (Kuttyaattoor) Maaraar, fled, and Vaaryar immersed the idol in his family well. The priest safeguarded the *uthsava-thitamb* in his illam at Cheruthaazham.[44] Tipu relinquished control of Malabar in 1792, after which the British became the undisputed rulers. In 1839, the Kolathiri raja formally ceded his sovereign rights to the British, retaining only the administration of the temples owned by him. 'Thereafter the Kolaththiri royal house came to be known as Chiraykkal.'[45] Nearly eleven years before this event, the raja constructed a small Krishna temple at the same site, and the concealed idol was retrieved from the Warrier's well and reinstalled.[46] If this account is accurate, the idol remained concealed for nearly half a century.

The Saasthaamkottam Siva Temple at Vaaram in Valiyannoor village of Chelora panchayat was once surrounded by several illams. Pallipram, situated west of the temple, was once the centre of great religious activity. In ancient times, the practice of *sathya-pareeksha* (trial by ordeal to ascertain truth) was prevalent in this temple. Accused persons were compelled to take a dip in the nearby Vaarampuzha, where a crocodile named Vaarathth Koonan lived. According to prevailing belief, if the person was truthful, the crocodile would spare him, but if he was dishonest, the crocodile would devour him.[47] Jayashanker avers, 'During the Mysorean invasions, the temple was demolished and they took away gold and precious metals beneath the idol. However, the idol remained intact.'[48]

The ancient Durga Bhagavathi Temple at Erannikkal in Edakkad panchayat had been under the stewardship of Brahmins for many centuries until the attack of the Mysoreans compelled them to flee. Jayashanker states, 'The temple was ransacked. Thereafter for some period, certain Nair families managed the temple.'[49] Similarly, the 11th-century temple of Mahavishnu (Narasimhamoorthy) at Edakkad was managed by Brahmin families until the appearance of Tipu's militia prompted their departure, leading to the temple's neglect.[50] Regarding the famous Oorpazhassi kavu or Durga Bhagavathi shrine at Nataal in Edakkad panchayat, it is reported that the imminent invasion by Tipu Sultan necessitated the relocation of the temple idols to the Thevaar-matham of the Akkara family of Thiruvangaat. Later, once peace was restored, the idols were returned and reinstated.[51]

Tipu's forces assaulted the Subramanyaswamy Temple in Makreri village of Peralasseri panchayat, resulting in the destruction of the idols.[52]

The Kuzhumbil Durga Bhagavathy Temple at Punnaat, near Iritty, is believed to be one of the 108 Durga temples consecrated by Parasurama and entrusted to Brahmins. Later, it fell under the control of the Kottayam rajas. According to Jayashanker, 'The temple was acclaimed as one of the *maha-kshethrams* of the past. However, considering its prominence and fame, Tippu Sulthan ransacked the temple, destroyed the structures and desecrated the idol by mutilating both hands of the *sila-vigraha* of the goddess.'[53] The remaining structures were destroyed by fire on three occasions between 1965 and 1972. Concerning the Keezhoor Mahadeva Temple at Iritty, Jayashankar notes, 'The forces of Tipu Sulthan ransacked, destroyed and desecrated the temple. However, the idol was not affected by the vandalism.'[54] Similarly, the Keezhoor Mahavishnu Temple at Iritty was also destroyed by Tipu's army, leading to the cessation of worship and the subsequent overgrowth of weeds and bushes. The temple underwent renovation and re-consecration in 1974.[55]

It took nearly 200 years for the temples in this region to regain their former splendour. The death of Pazhassi Raja in 1805 and the subsequent British rule undoubtedly marked the decline of many temples in the Kottayam svaroopam. In the post-independence era, with no kings in power, the responsibility fell on the common people to spearhead the revival of the temples.

The Itakkaanam Maha Vishnu Temple at Paayam in Keezhoor-Chavasseri panchayat also witnessed a royal visit from Tipu Sultan. 'All the structures of the temple were destroyed. Fearing the atrocities of Tippu's forces, the Brahmin families, particularly women, fled to other places for safety. There was no one to look after the temple and its lands.'[56] A century of neglect followed. Then, Christian migrants from the northern parts of Travancore began to settle in the region. 'Once the entire Itakkanam desam belonged to the temple but now the temple has only 32 cents of land.'[57] The murals had faded, the *bali-kallu* was in a dilapidated state, and the *sila-idol* of Mahavishnu lay shattered at the time the book *Temples of Kannoor District* was compiled. In 2015, however, a new idol was consecrated.

The (Paanunta) Siva Temple at Eruvatty in Pinarayi village is an ancient temple having four caves nestled amid picturesque surroundings 'Some years back pooja articles were obtained from these caves.'[58] The steps leading to the fourth cave exhibit intricate carvings, suggesting that this place may have been used by rishis for meditation in ancient times. Legend has it that after the Daksha yaga, Parasurama sought refuge here, and Kamadhenu, the divine cow, provided him with milk to quench his thirst. Later, a swayambhu idol manifested at this sacred spot. Originally, the land belonged to Brahmins but later came under the ownership of the Kottayam kovilakam.[59] 'The forces of Tippu Sulthan ransacked the temple and for some years the poojas could not be conducted.'[60] While the temple once possessed 8 acres of land, it now retains only 4 acres.[61]

The Eruvatty kavu or Vettakkorumkan Temple, located in the Kottayam–Malabar village of Kottiyoor panchayat, can be traced back to the 11th century. Eruvatty is the location where Sathi Devi encountered the *bhoothaganas* sent by Lord Shiva to escort her to the Daksha yaga, while Kottiyoor is renowned as a Shakti-peetha, where Sathi performed self-immolation. Such is the legend associated with this sacred site. 'The temple is believed to have been built by the chieftains of the army of Kottayam Rajas belonging to the Kurup family.'[62] Even before the temple's construction, Eruvatty was believed to harbour a divine essence. 'During the onslaught of Tipu's forces on the Sree [Paanunta] Siva Temple, the priest safely shifted the idol of Sree Vettakkorumakan to southern Kerala, as per the orders of the chieftain [Kurup].'[63] The idol was transported to Thiruvananthapuram, 450 kilometres away, perhaps the only place beyond the sultan's grasp, where it was installed in the fort area and worshipped. 'After the retreat of Tippu's forces, the *ooralars* decided to install a new idol which had already been made. When the consecration rites commenced the idol which was installed at Thiruvananthapuram was brought back.'[64] Now, the *thantri* (temple priest) faced a dilemma – which idol should he install? Seeking divination, it was decided to install both idols on a single *peedom*. In Thiruvananthapuram, a new idol was installed in place of the old one.[65] Princess Aswathi Thirunal Gouri Lakshmi Bayi mentions this in her book *Thulasi Garlands*.[66] Eruvatty Kavu is my father's *kudumba-kshethram*, yet I was blissfully unaware of its glorious past until I began tracing the movements of the Mysore sultans in Malabar.

The Suryanarayana Temple at Kathirur, situated on the Thalassery–Koothuparamba road, is an ancient shrine with a fascinating history. Legend has it that the idol was consecrated by Lord Rama himself while on his way to Lanka in search of Sita. After consecrating the idols of Subramanya at Peralasseri and Makreri, and of Shiva at Pinarayi, Lord Rama was worshipped by Vedic Brahmins, upon which he appeared before them and blessed them. Thereafter, he installed the Vaishnavite sankalpam of the Sun God as Suryanarayana at Kathirur. And then came the sultan.

According to Jayashanker:

> On 14th Meenam of 964 K.E. (March 1789 AD) Tippu Sulthan's forces plundered the temple. There was large exodus of Hindus and their attendants from the area. For months Kathirur was the temporary camp of Tipu's forces. As these forces had to urgently proceed northwards major portion of wealth plundered from this temple as well as from neighbouring temples was deposited in the temple tank with the intention of taking them back to Mysore on their return. But God's wish was different and Tippu's forces had to retreat without returning to Kathiroor. The general belief is that large quantity of wealth of all the temples still lie deposited at the bed of the tank.[67]

After the invasion, the temple administrators and priests fled, leaving the temple abandoned. Soon, the temple fell into disrepair and became overgrown with weeds as worship ceased.

'At that time Thomas Harvey Baber who was looking after the affairs of Malabar decided to annex Coorg with Malabar in spite of the resistance of the Kuricchyas.'[68] He sent a battalion to Coorg, led by his assistant Kappana Karunakara Menon. On the way, they passed Kathirur, where Menon offered prayers at the dilapidated temple and pledged that if they succeeded in their mission, he would renovate the temple. Upon their success, Menon convinced Baber that their triumph was aided by the supernatural assistance of the lord of Kathirur. Baber provided helpful support, Menon took over the administration, and the renovation was completed in 1835.[69]

Regarding the Sri Rama Temple at Thiruvangaat, Jayashanker writes:

> In 1766, when Haider marched with his army into northern Kerala, the members of Chiraykkal family had to take refuge in this temple. It is said that Tippu's forces directed the guns against the eastern gopuram and damaged its walls. The retaliatory fire damaged the cannon of Tipu and his forces had to stage a retreat. The place where Tippu's forces camped was known as Perumporkalam [large battlefield]. Its present name is Perumkalam, where the *palli-vetta* of the deity is held.[70]

Though Tipu was only 16 years old in 1766, the destructive activities in Malabar are often attributed to him rather than his father, who was the original invader. Moreover, there are curious legends related to the British overlords as well. Once, Thomas Harvey Baber, the sub-collector of Thalassery, rode into the temple premises on his horse, despite being advised against it. When he reached in front of the shrine, 'the horse suddenly stopped and fell'.[71] Baber witnessed a devotee offering a bunch of plantains to the deity. He questioned whether god would consume it, and upon being assured by the chief priest that it was indeed possible, the disbelieving Englishman requested that the bunch be weighed before and after offering. 'When it was returned after *nivedya* it was found that the same bunch of plantains had lost some weight.'[72] The chief priest explained that the

Lord had taken the essence and left behind the waste, leaving Baber intrigued. In appreciation, he constructed massive outer walls for the temple and installed a granite plaque inscribed with the words: 'The wall around this pagoda was constructed under the supervision and patronage of T.H. Baber Esq., in 1815.' Jayashanker mentions that 'on the valiya-balikkall there is an inscription datable to 826 CE'.[73] If the date is accurate, the temple would be at least 1,200 years old. 'The laterite compound wall [maryaada] built under the supervision of T.H. Baber has its top in the shape of an elephant's back.'[74] This design may have ancient origins, as similar walls can be found at the Eruvatty kavu.

In fact, the assault of the Mysore sultans left a lasting impact on several temples in Malabar. While some temples were rebuilt, the treasures looted during those times were never recovered, and many shrines struggled to regain their lost grandeur. Priestly families either perished or migrated elsewhere, and the sacred *theyyam* rituals were either discontinued or carried out in a subdued manner. However, today many of these temples have been renovated and rejuvenated, and the gods and goddesses continue to be venerated as they were in the past. The ancient *theyyam* tradition has also been revived. In hindsight, it can be said that the actions of the Mysore sultans did not significantly alter the course of these sacred traditions of Malabar.

Other authors have mentioned the destruction of temples located in Tamil Nadu and Karnataka. Meenakshi Jain, in *Flight of Deities and Rebirth of Temples: Episodes from Indian History* informs us that, 'The town (Srirangam) was twice burnt or laid waste by Tipu Sultan to prevent it from being used by the British army on its march to Seringapatam.'[75] The author mentions: 'Srirangam was twice attacked by armies from the north, first in 1311 CE by Malik Kafur, and second in 1323 CE by Ulugh Khan.'[76] The third and fourth assaults on the temple town were led by Tipu Sultan.

## Tipu as an Islamic Fundamentalist

Even the accounts of court chroniclers fail to mask the hideous face of the Tiger of Mysore. Kirmani makes every attempt to whitewash

Tipu Sultan's portrait but fails. Or perhaps, he genuinely aimed to be objective, choosing words of praise with care and precision, allowing the truth to be read between the lines. It is hard to discern how much was lost in translation or distorted by the translator. While every account must be taken with a pinch of salt, Kirmani's narrative needs two pinches and a liberal dose of imagination.

Quotes from Kirmani shed light on Tipu's character, although the author tries to mask his cruelty and mistakes by shifting blame onto others or attributing them to Fate. Tipu's epitaph at Srirangapatna contains words in Farsi composed by Kirmani and transcribed by Abdul Kadir. Hailing Tipu Sultan as the 'light of Islam', it leaves no room for doubt: 'Tipu on account of the faith of Muhammad was a martyr.'[77]

Bowring explains, 'Tipu directed the entire destruction of the old town of Mysore, in order to obliterate all associations with the deposed Rajas.'[78] He dismissed all Hindus from administrative positions, replacing them with uneducated Muslims. Only Dewan Purnaiya was spared. One wonders about the price he had to pay. Was his daughter's conversion to Islam voluntary, and did it influence his retention?

Tipu's fanaticism led him to implement drastic steps, eventually contributing to the collapse of his administration. Mark Wilks notes, 'There was indeed one novelty of a ludicrous description; offices requiring an exact knowledge of accounts, and formerly filled by Brahmins or Hindus, were ordered to be executed by Mahommedans.'[79] Wilks further remarks that upon learning that the new appointees were unable to write, the sultan calmly responded that they would learn!

Tipu's Islamic zeal did yield some desirable effects. His ban on alcohol may have had some positive impact. He also banned the cultivation of the white poppy and the hemp plant even in private gardens, ordering their destruction wherever they were discovered.

On 19 January 1786, Tipu wrote to Budruz Zuman Khan directing him to crucify Moona Kool and to bring his family to Srirangapatna in chains. If Moona Kool's nephew is found to be over twenty-five years old, he should also be crucified. Additionally, two hundred of Moona Kool's followers should be made Ahmedies and posted at Nagar.

Writing sometime between 21 and 24 May 1786 to Urshud Baig Khan, the foujdar of Calicut, Tipu advises, 'Getting possession of the villain Goorkul, and of his wife and children, you must forcibly make Musulmans of them, and then dispatch the whole under a guard to Putn [Srirangapatna].'[80] In another letter dated 13 June 1786, addressed to Abdul Kureem, the sipahdar of the Jyhse Kuchurry stationed with Urshud Baig Khan, Tipu writes, 'You write, "that the villain Goorkul, being wounded, had thrown himself, together with his wife and children, into a fire [kindled for the purpose] which had consumed them [all]". You add, "that the Mapilahs have all taken to flight".'[81] What makes the letter particularly interesting is the mention that even the Mappilas fled, fearing the fury of the sultan's men. The letter obviously refers to an unnamed Gurikkal of North Malabar who resorted to self-immolation to evade capture. Kirkpatrick observes:

> Knowing the fate that awaited himself and family if they fell into the hands of their tyrant, he had resorted to the final remedy and refuge from dishonour, so usual among the Hindoos. The studied indifference ... with which the Sultan mentioned this dreadful catastrophe, will not have escaped the reader's notice.[83]

Bartolomeo describes Paravur as 'formerly a very large and considerable town, which was however, reduced to ashes by the troops of Tipoo Sultan'.[84] Describing Thrissur (Trichur) as a place belonging to Brahmins, he mentions, 'This place was also destroyed by Tippoo Sultan; but rebuilt by the Brahmans after Tippoo's defeat.'[85] Speaking of the fortress of Palghat, he notes, 'The garrison always consists of the flower of Tipu Sultan's troops.'[86] Today, the fort houses a Hanuman temple, a tiny shrine with a formidable reputation. Those who wish to glorify Tipu Sultan presume that this temple existed during the *padayottam* days and insist that the very existence of the shrine is a sign of the sultan's religious tolerance. However, the temple appears rather new.

Describing Tipu Sultan's attack on Tiruvannamalai in Tamil Nadu during the Third Anglo-Mysore War, Roderick Mackenzie states, 'Their pagodas, breached with sacrilegious cannon, were forcibly entered, their altars defiled, their valuables seized, their dwellings reduced to ashes, and the devastation was rendered still more horrible by the scattered remains of men, women and children.'[87]

The EICo stationed a garrison at the Brihadeeswara temple at Thanjavur from 1771 to 1798 during the wars with the Mysore sultans. During this phase worship at the temple ceased and the structure was partially ruined. Later the Marathas were entrusted with the upkeep of the temple and a purification ceremony was performed. In 1855 the British annexed Thanjavur when the ruler died heirless.[88]

Meenakshi Jain avers:

> Tipu Sultan sponsored the construction of the Ala Mosque in Seringapatam fort, in which pillars of Hindu origin were clearly visible. According to the Mysore Archaeological Survey, at least three temples in his realm were destroyed on Tipu's orders. The Hariharesvara temple at Harihar was looted and a section of it converted into a mosque, while the Varahasvami temple in Seringapatam and the Odakaraya temple in Hospet were both destroyed.[89]

Kirkpatrick wonders why Tipu allowed Srirangapatna and Bangalore to retain their original names, 'especially as the former appellation, having been derived from an idol, might, on that account, be supposed to have been particularly offensive to a bigoted Musulman'.[90] The mystery remains.

## An Erratic Streak

Haider Ali maintained the pretence of showcasing the raja to his people once a year during the Dussehra festival, but Tipu abandoned that tradition and relocated the rani and the young king to a decrepit hovel, where they were discovered after the fall of Srirangapatna.

Haider Ali had built up a network of spies and a sophisticated intelligence system, but Tipu, while following in his father's footsteps, often received inaccurate information, probably due to his practice of administering indiscriminate and brutal punishments. Tipu's economic policy was short-sighted and reckless. He banned the consumption of liquor due to his religious fanaticism and ordered the cutting down of all palm and date trees. Fortunately, this order was not strictly enforced.

Bowring remarks:

> He deemed women of little account, with the sole exception of his mother whose influence over him was great. There is little to say about Tipu's revenue administration, which, owing to his frequent wars and his absence from his capital, naturally fell into the hands of his subordinates... The want of proper supervision led to numerous exactions and consequent discontent, of which he remained in ignorance.[91]

Buchanan records, 'Owing to the persecution of the Hindus by the late Sultan, and to the incessant warfare between them and the Moplays of Tamarachery, one-fourth of the rice fields in Curumbra Nada is estimated to be waste.'[92] The seeds of Hindu-Muslim discord were sown by Tipu Sultan, with tragic consequences for Malabar.

Tipu paid no heed to the Delhi royals, whose power had substantially declined by the time he ascended the throne. He minted his own coins and had the Qutba read in his own name in the mosques within his domain instead of in the name of the Mughal emperor as was the protocol at that time. The Mughals had lost control over the southern kingdoms after Aurangzeb's demise in 1707, so there was little they could do about this symbolic act of defiance.

Was Tipu a devout Muslim? Did he offer namaz five times a day? Was jihad simply a war cry? Was religion only a cover for greed and bloodlust? Tipu was apparently a devout Muslim, yet his belief in astrology was unshakable. Before the fall of Srirangapatna, Brahmin astrologers prophesied that a great misfortune would befall him unless propitiatory measures were taken. Tipu arranged for all the ceremonies to be duly performed. He even sacrificed two elephants with all their gold trappings as advised by the Brahmins.[93]

Was the inspiration for war the greed of profit or the urge to serve Allah and spread the religion? If it was the latter, why did Tipu appeal to Napoleon, a ruler from a faraway Christian nation? His entreaties to Napoleon and the governor of Mauritius had no religious overtones. However, when he appealed to the Ottoman sultan and the king of Afghanistan, he played the Muslim card. This tactic was at best opportunistic, at worst diabolic and sinister in its motives. The same strategy, however, failed with the nizam of Hyderabad and the nawab of Arcot, who were his immediate neighbours. Neither did the Mughal emperors in Delhi ever collaborate with the Mysore sultans. This speaks volumes about the credibility of the sultans. Even the Ottoman sultan advised Tipu to cut ties with the French and befriend the English. Tipu disregarded his advice, and a year later he was dead.

## Religious Conversions at Other Locations

There is ample evidence of widespread religious conversion by Tipu Sultan. His *hukumnamas* and memoir provide adequate testimony to this fact. Even if one were to ignore the anecdotes provided by other writers, both Indian and European, the conclusion would be unavoidable.

It was not limited to just Malabar, Mangalore and Coorg. The Tamil country also bore the brunt of Tipu's brutality. Describing the tragic plight of the *palayakkars* of the Coimbatore region, Buchanan notes:

> On Tippoo's accession, the Asoph or lieutenant of Coimbatore, Khadir Ali Khan, forced the Polygars to pay tribute for the lands which Hyder had allowed them to retain, and they were entirely disarmed, but they were allowed to retain over their vassals both civil and criminal jurisdiction. Ten years ago Tippoo endeavoured to seize them, in order, by circumcision, to make them Mussulmans;

> but they made their escape into the country of the Cochin Raja, and continued there until the fall of Seringapatam.[94]

Bowring observes:

> Haidar indeed put his captives in irons, fed them sparingly, and treated them badly, but he rarely took their lives deliberately. Tipu, on the other hand, had no compunction in cutting their throats, or strangling and poisoning them; while, as has been stated, numbers of them were sent to die of malaria and starvation on the fatal mountain of Kabaldurg. The English prisoners were specially selected as victims of his vengeance, not omitting officers of rank such as General Matthews; while, in direct contravention of the treaty made at Mangalore in 1784, he did not scruple to retain in captivity considerable numbers of Europeans. Many of these, particularly young and good-looking boys, were forcibly circumcised, married haphazard to girls who had been captured in the Coromandel districts, and drafted into the ranks of the army, or compelled to sing and dance for the amusement of the sovereign.[95]

Tipu wrote to Turbiyut Ali Khan and Rajah Ram Chundur on 27 February 1785:

> You write, that the European [formerly] taken prisoner in the Payen-ghaut, and whose original allowance of two fanams a day had been, in consequence of his misbehaviour, reduced to one, being skilled in the mortar practice, you proposed converting him to the faith, and wished for our orders on the subject. It is known [or understood]. Admitting the aforesaid to the honor of Islamism, you will continue to pay him, as before, two fanams a day.[96]

This letter makes it clear that Tipu made no distinction between Indians and Europeans, or between Hindus and Christians, when it came to the conversion of individuals to the Muslim faith. Besides, some consideration was shown to Muslim converts in terms of perks and allowances. This fact is corroborated by another letter dated 9 May 1785, instructing Ghulam Ahmed, Kazi of Nagar:

> You have written, that nine Frenchmen, together with their captain, had embraced the faith, and that the said captain humbly hoped to be honoured with the command of a Risala of Ahmedies ... our pleasure is, that ten rupees be given to each of them and that they be all dispatched, under an escort, to the Presence, where, on their arrival, the aforesaid captain shall receive the honor he solicits.[97]

The Ahmedies were a group of soldiers who were converted, whether forcibly or voluntarily, to Islam. In his *Memoirs*, Tipu himself provides a detailed, albeit puzzling, account of their origin:

> The Portuguese Nazarenes established themselves, about three hundred years ago, in a factory situated near the sea shore, and on the banks of a large river. This place they obtained of the Rajah of Soondah, under the pretext of trading: and here, availing themselves of the opportunities which arose in the course of time, they acquired possession of a territory, yielding a yearly revenue of three or four lacks of rupees, throughout which they equally prohibited fasts and prayers among the Mussulman inhabitants, and the worship of idols among the Hindus; finally expelling from thence all who refused to embrace their religion, which the Hindus were required to do within three days under pain, if they remained in the country after that time, of being forcibly converted to it. Some of the people, alarmed at this proceeding, abandoned their property and homes, and took refuge in other countries: but the greater part, considering the threatened danger as improbable, and not possessing the means of removing their effects, preferred remaining; whereupon these infidel Nazarenes, at the end of the appointed time, obliged them all to embrace their false religion.... [Such was the state of things here] when ... the port of Kurial [Mangalore] fell into our hands; on which occasion the odious proceedings of these accursed Padries becoming fully known to us, and causing our zeal for the faith to boil over, we instantly directed the Dewan of the Huzoor Kucherry to prepare a list of all houses occupied by the Christians, taking care not to omit a single habitation. The officers of the Kucherry ... soon prepared and delivered to us a detailed report on the subject. After this, we

caused an officer and some soldiers to be stationed in every place inhabited by the Christians.[98]

Tipu issued orders: 'On such a day of the week and month, and at the hour of morning prayer, let all the Christians, whatever their number may be, together with their women and children, be made prisoners and dispatched to our Presence.'[99] His memoir states:

> Accordingly our orders were everywhere opened at the same moment; and at the same hour [namely, that of morning prayer] were the whole of the Christians, male and female, without the exception of a single individual, to the number of sixty thousand, made prisoners, and dispatched to our Presence; from whence we caused them, after furnishing them duly with provisions, to be conveyed, under proper guards, to Seringapatam: to the Taalukdars of which place we sent orders, directing that [the said Christians] should be divided into Risalas, or corps, of five hundred men, and a person of reputable and upright character placed, as Risaldar, at the head of each. Of these Risalas, four (together with their women and children) were directed to be stationed at each of the following places, where they were duly fed and clothed, and ultimately admitted to the honour of Islamism; and the appellation of Ahmedy was bestowed upon the collective body.[100]

Kirkpatrick observes, 'This corps was not composed exclusively of converts from Christianity.'[101] It was soon bolstered by a significant influx of prisoners from Coorg, all of whom were compelled to embrace Islam and join the Ahmedy Corps.[102]

Chetti recounts the trauma of the Christians of Mangalore:

> On a certain new moon day in … February 1784, a strict injunction proceeded from the Imperial Sultan of Mysore to all the Faujdars and Amildars of the Barkur, Kundapur, and other taluks … ordering them to take a census of all native Christians in their respective Taluks, and to arrange them into batches of some ten thousand each. On that unfortunate day, their places of worship were destroyed, houses pillaged, property confiscated, and their gurus or priests were forced

> to take refuge in the Portuguese territory of Goa.... When these native Christians were numbered they were found to be 80,000. Each batch, or band, consisting of 10,000 persons, was placed under a military guard with strict martial orders, and were directed to proceed by forced marches by way of Nagar or Bidanur ... and from thence these poor wretches, ... were finally led on to Seringapatam. During their travels these desolate and miserable followers of the cross were grossly ill-treated. Their sick and weak relatives and friends, and their women in a delicate state of health, as well as those that were unfit to continue the journey, were left behind by the road-side to take care of themselves, and the main body was forced by the guards to push on their way. Thus these poor captives, who were left behind, were either devoured by wild beasts, or robbed, or starved to death or left to the tender mercies of nature, or to the inclemencies of the weather.[103]

Chetti goes on to explain:

> When the main divisions or batches arrived at Seringapatam, houses or places for their accommodation were given to those that could work in iron, brass, or wood, in Shahar Ganjam. The villages of Palhalli and Yennahole Koppala were given to those that were able to till the soil and cultivate the ground.... As soon as they were settled, orders were issued to the military department to recruit some 15,000 young or middle-aged men that could carry arms from among the captive Christians. A scrutinising search was made, and about 15,000 men were chosen for the army, and ultimately, they were formed into fifteen battalions of infantry and sent out to be drilled and disciplined. After a lapse of sometime, *these men were forcibly circumcised and made to embrace Islam...* The young women who belonged to the families of these unfortunate men were taken away by force from among them and given in marriage to Mohammedans, and some 200 of the most comely among them were sent to the Sultan's harem.[104]

Chetti also narrates another curious anecdote:

> On one occasion when Tippu Sultan gave orders to dismantle the Christian place of worship at Seringapatam one Serappal Chetty

> a gallant Christian Colonel in the Sultan's army, was bold enough to warn the Sultan that desperate efforts would be made by his people, if he resorted to such a sacrilege. After Serappal Chetty's death, the place of Christian worship was razed to the ground. Many of those Christians ... [secretly] kept up Christian worship. Amidst dangers and trials, they used to meet for prayer during the night in the underground vaults near their dwellings ...Those that were found at prayers in the underground vaults were very cruelly maltreated and beaten to death.[105]

With the fall of Srirangapatna, approximately 20,000 individuals managed to escape and journeyed back to the west coast to rebuild their shattered lives and reclaim their religion. The Christians who currently reside on the Canara coast are said to be the descendants of these liberated souls.

The fascinating story of the Maratha adventurer, Dhondia Waugh, is narrated by Stephen Chetti and several others. Chetti notes:

> Dhondiah Waugh, a Maharatta freebooter in the service of the Sultan, was a brave and dashing officer. He was forcibly circumcised and was named Mullik Jahan Khan and chained in one of the dungeons of the fort by order of the Sultan. He was released by the British after the siege...He collected marauders around him and committed great depredation and ravages in the newly acquired territories. At last, his gang was completely destroyed and dispersed by Colonel Wellesley and Dhondiah himself was slain at Conahgull near Raichur.[106]

## The Shringeri Anomaly

Bipan Chandra, in his book *History of Modern India*, examines Tipu's patronage of the Ranganatha Temple at Srirangapatna and the Sringeri Mutt and arrives at the simplistic conclusion:

> Though he was orthodox in his religious views, he was in fact tolerant and enlightened in his approach towards other religions. He gave money for the construction of the image of goddess

> Sarda in the Sringeri temple after the latter was looted by Maratha horsemen in 1791. He regularly gave gifts to this temple.[107]

However, this interpretation is far from accurate.

On the eve of Tipu's death, there were only two operational temples in his domain – the Sringeri Temple and the Ranganatha Temple. These were spared because the sultan depended on the Brahmin priests and astrologers associated with these temples to perform pujas for his success and to forecast his fate on a daily basis. The wealth of all other Hindu temples had been plundered by him before 1790 to compensate for the revenue loss caused by his liquor prohibition policy.

A bundle of letters, discovered in 1916 at the Sringeri Mutt, contained communications from Tipu Sultan to the acharya of the place. They revealed that the Marathas under Raghunath Rao Patwardhan had raided and pillaged the temple in 1791, displacing the idol of Goddess Sharada. The swami, who had sought refuge in Karkala, informed Tipu about the attack and requested his help to reinstall the idol at Sringeri. Tipu promptly ordered the *asaf* of Bidanur to provide the swami with cash, grain and other provisions necessary for the reinstallation ceremony. He requested the swami to 'pray for the increase of our prosperity and the destruction of our enemies'.[108] Mohibbul Hasan observes that the idol was duly reinstated, and 'Tipu received *prasada* and shawls and in return sent cloth and a bodice for the goddess and a pair of shawls for the swami'.[109] Hasan adds, 'His interest in the temple and friendship for the swami were not confined merely to the war period but lasted down to the fall of Seringapatam.'[110] One simply cannot ignore the fact that when push came to shove, neither the goddess nor the swami could save Tipu Sultan from the wrath of the foreign invader.

In 1793, Tipu wrote to the swami, who had embarked on a pilgrimage: 'You are the *jagadguru*. You are always performing penance in order that the whole world may prosper, and the people may be happy. Please pray to god for the increase of our prosperity.'[111] Having lost half of his territories to the British in 1792, Tipu was perhaps anxious to regain his domains, and he might have felt that he needed blessings from every quarter.

C.K. Kareem notes:

> In the Central Record Office, Ernakulam, there is a curious document – an eye-witness' report – of the Fourth Anglo-Mysore War. Tipu Sultan, knowing that he was passing through the last days of his life went to the Mutt, barefooted and received blessings from the *Jagathguru* as he addressed the Chief Priest. It is reported that the Guru gave a letter to the Maratta Chief requiring him to help Tipu Sultan instead of forming an alliance with the English.[112]

The Lakshmikanta Temple in the village of Kalale in Nanjangud taluk possesses four silver cups, a silver plate and a silver spittoon said to have been donated by Tipu. Similarly, the Narayanaswami Temple at Melkote houses jewels and gold and silver objects with inscriptions stating they were donated by Tipu. It is also understood that in 1785, Tipu gifted an elephant to the temple, followed by a kettledrum in 1786. Hasan notes:

> A jewelled cup, set with five kinds of precious stones at the bottom, in the Srikanthesvara temple at Nanjangud was a present from *Tipu Sultan Padasa*. Seven silver cups and a silver camphor burner in the Ranganatha temple at Seringapatam bear inscriptions stating that the articles were the gifts of *Tippu Sultana Pachcha*. And at Nanjangud in the Nanjandesvara temple, there is a greenish jadite *linga* called *pachcha* or *padshahlinga* which is said to have been installed by Tipu's orders.[113]

Whether Tipu actually issued these generous orders or whether the Brahmins in his inner circle took the initiative on their own remains uncertain. The sultan was engaged in battle most of the time, so it is highly likely that he was unaware of at least some of these gifts. Another possibility is that he was deeply superstitious and desperate to appease all the gods in the vicinity of his capital.

Stephen Chetti reveals the information:

> Haider Ali, knowing Tipu's fanaticism and passion for sacrilege of Hindu sacred buildings, it appears, left him strict injunctions not to meddle with the three most famous temples in his dominions, viz:
> 1. The idol standing [the temple of Chelva Raya Swami] at Melkote.
> 2. The idol sitting [the temple of Nanjundeswara] at Nanjangud.
> 3. The idol reclining [the temple of Sri Ranganathaswami] at Seringapatam.[114]

While Tipu did not forcibly convert the Hindu population of Mysore, he directed his cruelty and sadism towards conquered peoples. Following his defeat in the Third Anglo-Mysore War and the consequent depletion of his treasury, he made a sizeable grant to the Sringeri Sankaracharya Mutt, perhaps with the ulterior motive of gaining favour with the Hindu gods. Those seeking to portray the sultan as a secular and benevolent sovereign frequently laud this gesture as a stellar example of religious tolerance. However, his destructive and diabolic acts cannot be overlooked.

C. Gopalan Nair, in his 1911 book on Wayanad, makes some intriguing remarks regarding Tipu Sultan's destruction of the Ganapathivattam Temple, 'Who knows whether Tipu Sultan did not suffer for the sacrilege? That he repented to a certain extent at least is proved by the grant of lands to the Temple free of tax.'[115] If Tipu Sultan did indeed experience even the slightest tinge of remorse, it could only have stemmed from some form of superstition or been influenced by the machinations of certain Brahmin priests. Tipu had systematically destroyed many temples and churches, and no amount of regret or grants could have undone the evils he perpetrated.

# 13

# DREAMS, LETTERS AND ZENANA WOMEN

The sultan meticulously recorded, analysed and interpreted his dreams, wrote numerous letters and collected manuscripts in his library, as well as women in his zenana. His incomparable missives contained orders and instructions to his generals, agents and revenue collectors. His dream book was a closely guarded confidential document. The books in his collection were either looted or acquired through purchase. The women in his harem remained invisible once they entered, only to emerge in historical records after the sultan's death, when they were listed, catalogued and relocated to Vellore by the British conquerors.

Lieutenant Colonel William Kirkpatrick served the EICo from 1771 to 1812. In addition to his English wife, he had a brown *bibi*, and he was regarded by the British as an Orientalist. His father had also served as a colonel in the Madras army. Hence, it is not unreasonable to consider William Kirkpatrick as partially Indian.

During the Third Anglo-Mysore War, Kirkpatrick served as a Persian interpreter under Lord Cornwallis, and after the death of Tipu Sultan, he was appointed as one of the commissioners for the partition of Mysore. Kirkpatrick's English translation of Tipu's letters, titled *Diary and Letters of Tippoo Sultaun,* was published in London in 1811. Tipu is believed to have written more than 2,000 letters in Farsi in his own hand.

Irfan Habib acknowledges Kirkpatrick's invaluable contribution in collecting, translating and publishing Tipu Sultan's letters, noting that without his timely intervention and presence of mind, these documents might not have survived the siege of Srirangapatna. Among these documents was a manuscript believed to be the memoirs of Tipu Sultan written by the sultan himself. Kirkpatrick translated three portions of this manuscript. He suggests, 'It may be noted that Tipu Sultan, who must have composed this account sometime after the Treaty of Mangalore concluded in March 1784, wrote it as a private document and so is uninhibited in his expressions.'[1]Habib also, intentionally or not, absolves Kirkpatrick of any questionable motives, 'Kirkpatrick is careful to quote the original text in footnotes wherever he had doubts about his own rendering; his translation, is, however, usually found to be accurate enough in such cases.'[2] Kirkpatrick, who completed his work over 200 years ago, could not have received a better certificate of authenticity from a 21st-century scholar. However, other scholars, such as Mohibbul Hasan, have questioned his motives and accused him of bias against Tipu Sultan. In fairness, one must acknowledge that, in terms of translation, Kirkpatrick has done a commendable job. Readers may focus on the sultan's own words and choose to ignore Kirkpatrick's elaborate observations.

Kirkpatrick mentions that the letters began in February 1785, coinciding with Tipu's conflict with the Marathas, and concluded in November 1793. Given the sultan's meticulousness in his correspondence, it seems likely that there were additional letters written after 1793 that simply disappeared amidst the chaos following his demise.

Wilks opines that Tipu Sultan, 'although an incessant writer, was an exceedingly bad scribe'.[3] Tipu's letters were often fanciful, riddled with inaccuracies and designed to mislead. While he dangled the Indian carrot before the French, who likely had their own intelligence sources, he secretly corresponded with other foreign Muslim rulers such as the Ottoman caliph and Zaman Shah of Afghanistan, expressing his desire to establish Islamic rule in Hindustan with their support. Perhaps the French themselves had ulterior motives in encouraging Tipu in his grandiose designs.

Nevertheless, the French did share valuable intelligence with Tipu. In July and August 1798, General DeBuc wrote letters to Tipu warning him that the British governor-general was expected to reach Madras from Calcutta, 'for the purpose of entering upon a negotiation with your Majesty, which will be followed by a declaration of war'.[4] De Buc's letter of 15 December 1798 urged Tipu 'to convince the English of your good intentions'.[5]

Tipu was undoubtedly the sworn enemy of the British, so it is understandable that they would not paint him in favourable light. However, much of what was written about Tipu by the English is based in truth. While there may be some exaggeration, there is no evidence of falsification or fabrication. Regarding Tipu's letters, they are his own words, and Kirkpatrick simply acted as a translator. Kirkpatrick says in the preface to the collection:

> [Tipu] is here successively and repeatedly delineated, in colours from his own pencil, as the cruel and relentless enemy; the intolerant bigot or furious fanatic; the oppressive and unjust ruler; the harsh and rigid master; the sanguinary tyrant; the perfidious negotiator; the frivolous and capricious innovator; the mean and minute economist; the peddling trader; and even the retail shop-keeper.[6]

The translator also refers to 'the secret murder of his English prisoners, his dreadful slaughter of the Koorgs and Nairs, and his forcible conversion of so many thousands of the two latter tribes to the Mahommedan faith'.[7]

About the quality of Tipu Sultan's writing, Kirkpatrick comments:

> Even in his own Memoirs, which he did not begin to compose till he was past forty, we meet with nothing indicating capacity of any kind. He did not even write with facility. This is clearly [shown], by various memorandums in his hand-writing, which, though very short, and on subjects of no difficulty, abound in erasures and corrections.[8]

Of the sultan's memoir, Wilks remarks:

> The title of the work is *Sultaun u Towareekh* or the King of Histories; the substance was dictated by Tippoo Sultaun himself and the work composed by Zein-ul-ab-u-Deen Shusteree, brother of Meer Aalum, the late minister at Hyderabad.... The author then goes on for several pages to compare the Sultaun with the sun, the moon, the stars, and the planets; the prophets and apostles; and the most celebrated kings and philosophers of antiquity; in a style of accomplished extravagance and absurdity.[9]

Wilks adds that since some parts of the text are distinctly obscene, the scribe subtly conveys 'that many passages of the work are of the express dictation of the Sultaun himself'.[10] He also provides a few classic examples, such as 'Madras has the honourable name of the City of Hermaphrodites; and the Nabob Mohammed Ali Khan, the contemptuous designation of *the Christian*'.[11]

## The Sultan's Men and Methods

Burhanuddeen, married to one of Tipu's sisters, held the trust of the sultan and often received crucial military assignments. Revealing that he was killed in 1790 at the battle of Sathyamangalam, Kirkpatrick states, 'Of that battle, the Sultan has given a partial and exaggerated account in one or two letters; in which it is remarkable, that he speaks of the death of this gallant commander without a single expression of regard or regret.'[12]

Kirkpatrick cites a letter as proof that, despite his trust in Burhanuddeen, Tipu had deployed several spies to monitor his movements. Kirkpatrick observes, 'The Sultan had organized a very extensive system of espionage throughout his dominions, and in almost every department of his government.'[13] Espionage was a common practice worldwide, but Tipu Sultan, filled with suspicion and paranoia, ensured surveillance on even those closely related to him and deemed most loyal.

Tipu's letter of 18 June 1785 to Mahommed Ghous states, 'Nobody besides yourself is to be admitted to a knowledge of it;

and when you have anything of a particular or secret nature to communicate, you must write in this cypher.'[14] Kirkpatrick observes:

> At a subsequent period, the Sultan appears to have improved somewhat in the art of cyphering; for the Vakeels, who accompanied the hostage princes to Madras, in 1792, were in possession of a figure-cypher, in which a descriptive account of the works of Fort St George, written throughout in cypher, was discovered among the papers found at Seringapatam on the capture of that place.[15]

He also mentions, 'Tippoo Sultan occasionally sent his orders in the Hindi language, even to persons whom he usually addressed in Persian.'[16]Subterfuge was obviously a crucial part of military intelligence.

Kirkpatrick reveals:

> Budruz Zuman Khan was one of the principal men at the court of Tippoo Sultan, and seems to have possessed the confidence and esteem of his master in a considerable degree. He commanded at Dharwar when that place was besieged by the united English and Mahrattah forces, in 1791.[17]

He had apparently entered into the service of Haider Ali in 1762, a year after the latter seized power in Mysore. 'Budruz Zuman Khan, and his son, Mirza Bakir, were among the chiefs of Mysore who survived their sovereign; and who, submitting to the British authority, were liberally pensioned by the Company's government.'[18]

Meer Kamaruddin Ali Khan was the son of Meer Ali Raza Sahib or Meer Sahib, who was killed at the battle of Porto Novo in 178I. Meer Sahib's daughter, Fakhrunissa, was the wife of Haider Ali and the mother of Tipu. Kirkpatrick states that Haider Ali 'conferred all the honors and appointments enjoyed by his brother-in-law upon his son, Kumruddeen, then a young man, whom he, at the same time, committed in a very public manner to the especial care and favor of his cousin, Tippoo Sultan'.[19] He also mentions, 'Upon the death of the Sultan, the British Government, in conjunction with the nizam, provided for Kumruddeen Khan in the most liberal manner. He did not, however, long survive his cousin and master, dying very soon after he had taken possession of the Jagire bestowed upon him.'[20]

Kirkpatrick informs us:

> Meer Mahommed Sadik was the Sultan's principal Dewun, and, in that character, presided over the revenue department of Mysore. Europeans commonly considered him as Tippoo's prime minister, but Tippoo's government recognized no such officer...Meer Sadik lost his life in the assault of Seringapatam. He was believed by many persons to have been a son of the celebrated Bussy; nor was the uncommon fairness of his complexion the only circumstance that gave weight to the report.[21]

Kirkpatrick opines that it was Zynul Aabideen, the brother of Meer Alam of Hyderabad, who 'composed the Futhul Mujahideen, under the immediate direction of the Sultan himself. He was also the author of the Sultan e Tuwareekh, mentioned by Colonel Wilks ... but this work appears to have been little more than a rhetorical amplification of the Sultan's own Memoirs.'[22]

The sultan's letters reveal his ruthless and devious character. On 22 July 1785, Tipu wrote to Burhanuddeen to 'employ every means, fair or foul, which may induce the besieged to surrender the fort'.[23] A letter of 25 November 1785 to Budruz Zuman Khan stated, 'We some time ago wrote to you, desiring you would contrive some means of getting possession of the person of Moona Kool; and we now again write, to say that he must be secured, by stratagem or deceit.'[24] Kirkpatrick presumes that Budruz Zuman Khan was then stationed at Bidanur.[25] Yet another letter was sent to Budruz Zuman Khan on 25 November 1785 saying, 'Write a letter to Moona Kool, inviting him to come to you, and then seize upon his person.'[26]

Tipu wrote to Urshud Baig Khan, the foujdar of Calicut, on 8 December 1785:

> You must, on some pretence or other, send to Worm-raj, the Rajah of Kurtinad, to his brother Sabbabut, and to Unnund Kurp, his

> manager, to come and visit you; upon their doing which you are to secure their persons, and to report the same to us. You must keep this matter secret.[27]

The translator adds, 'All these names are somewhat doubtful.'[28] As Kirkpatrick was translating from Persian to English, many of his spellings do not reflect Indian names accurately and are open to interpretation. 'Worm-raj' might possibly be Varma Raja (an incomplete name), and 'Unnund Kurp' could be Ananda Kurup. 'Kartinad' is obviously 'Kadathanad'.

On 14 February 1787, Tipu wrote to Kutbul Mulk Mahommed Kutbuddeen Khan Bahadur:

> In consequence [of this treaty], we shall have to relinquish the possession of Adoni: but we will bestow some other country upon you in its stead... You must, moreover, completely encompass two or three towns, and getting together five or seven thousand people, report the particulars to us; as men are wanted [at this time] for the [Usud-Ilhye] corps.... Although the treaty, recently concluded between the Sultan and the Mahrattahs, would seem to have provided for the restoration of Adoni and its dependencies to the Nizam...Here, then, we see Tippoo, with his characteristic perfidy, eagerly endeavouring to avail himself of the short interval which might be expected to elapse before the completion of the general peace, in order to impoverish and depopulate, as much as possible, the country he was about to relinquish.[29]

## Tipu's Military Manual and Manoeuvres

Tipu authored a military manual titled *The Triumphs of Holy Warriors*.[30] While he may not have been regarded as the finest general, there is no denying that he rated himself as such.

On 25 December 1785, Tipu wrote to Burhanuddeen from Talakaveri:

> The Mahrattah forces are assembling. Vigilance and [due attention to] the safety of your army are necessary. We therefore write to desire, that you will encamp your troops in a secure situation; not

> far asunder, but [close together] in the form [or manner] of a rose-bud. You must also post piquets&c. on all sides of your army. Let it not happen that the enemy's army surprize you.[31]

On 24 August 1786, Tipu gleefully communicated to Burhanuddeen, 'The passage of the Tungbuddra is effected.'[32] This marked a great triumph. Kirkpatrick mentions that in his *Memoirs*, Tipu indulged in abundant self-praise while describing this near-impossible feat:

> Marching from thence [Adoni] I arrived on the bank of the Tungbuddra. It was now the rainy season, and the river was at a great height. I sent for boats from the country of Nugr and consulted with the commanders of the Usud-Ilhye army on the subject of crossing [the river], when all of them stated it to be their opinion, that the attempt was on no account advisable, inasmuch as Hurry Pundit Phurkia, and the commanders of the army of Nizam Ali Khan, to the amount of a hundred thousand horse, besides numberless foot forces, were posted on the opposite side, for the purpose of preventing our passage. To this, they added, that the river was at its greatest height; that the rains were extremely violent; and that, as the army of the Sircar would be obliged to cross in small bodies at a time, [it was to be feared that] the enemy, apprized of this circumstance, would bring a heavy [i.e., superior] force against [the divisions as they crossed] ... Just at this moment I arrived, and opened fire upon the enemy from some guns and rockets, which soon made them flee in disorder. After an interval of a day, the infidels once more advanced with the intention of attacking us: when the Usud-Ilhye army met them as before, and they, according to their usual practice, turned their backs and withdrew in confusion to their camp.[33]

Tipu continued to boast:

> The next day, in order to strengthen the hearts of my people, I distributed presents of horses, money, gold and silver wrist-rings, &c. to the value of near a lack of rupees, among the officers and

> men of the three Kushoons, according to their respective merits.... The following day the Mahrattah army, with a train of artillery, came and presented itself in order of battle before the Usud-Ilhye tygers, on whom they commenced a distant fire from two or three guns. The men of our victorious army hereupon placing themselves in a state of preparation, received the enemy, with the same kind of cry [or noise] that is employed to frighten [or drive away] hogs and the like; upon hearing of which, the enemy returned shamefully by the same road they had come.[34]

Writing to Burhanuddeen on 25 September 1786, Tipu advised, 'You must leave all the women and other rubbish, together with the superfluous baggage belonging to your army, at Unwutty[name uncertain], and crossing the river with the above-mentioned [Ghazy Khan], repair directly to the Presence.'[35] Ghazy Khan served as the chief Pindareh commander under Tipu Sultan.[36]

On 27 September 1786, Tipu Sultan wrote to Syed Mahommed, the kiladar of Srirangaptna:

> Buhauddeen and Kustoory Runga, who were sent [some time since] to Bengal, for the purpose of procuring silk-worms, are now on their return [to Seringapatam]...You must, moreover, supply for their food [leaves of] the wood or wild mulberry-trees, which were formerly ordered to be planted.[37]

Kirkpatrick observes:

> He was, at the date of it, not only deliberating on the measures to be pursued with respect to Shanoor; in planning the future operations of the war in which he was engaged; and in providing for the safety of Burhanuddeen's army; but he was, in fact, on the eve of a general engagement with the Mahrattahs. Yet all these important and urgent considerations united were not capable of diverting his attention from any of the minor objects of his interest. Thus, in the bustle of a camp, and in the face of an enemy, he could find leisure and was sufficiently composed, to meditate on the rearing of silk-worms.[38]

On 1 October 1786, Tipu sent a letter to Meer Ali at Bangalore, stating, 'You write, "that the Piadehs who arrived there [at Sevendoorg], wounded, from Badamy, are without arms". It is known. Direct the Kilaadar to buy arms for them, and let the price of the same be deducted, by instalments, from their pay.'[39]

In a letter to Monsieur Cossigny on 10 October 1786, Tipu brags:

> At this time, the rulers of Poonah, notwithstanding the innumerable favors [for which they are indebted to us], uniting with the forces of Nizam Ali Khan, came and confronted our victorious army. With the aid and power of God, we were enabled, in a single assault, to establish our camp on the ground which they had occupied, and to give them a signal defeat. Upon this they took to flight, and we are now engaged in close pursuit of them.[40]

A copy of a circular addressed to Mahommed Baig Khan Humdany and several others, announcing his recent military successes, was sent to the Mughal emperor, Shah Alam, on 6 November 1786.[41]

Tipu continues to blow his own trumpet:

> I next marched to chastise the ministers of Poonah, who, together with the forces of Nizam Ali Khan, had established themselves at [or near] Shanoor. On this occasion, I crossed the Tungbuddra with my whole army and artillery in boats, and proceeding with rapidity against the enemy, suddenly appeared before them.[42]

Describing a brief encounter on 1 October 1786, Tipu brags, 'the fire from our guns sent such numbers of the infidels to the abode of perdition [or hell], that leaving their camp standing, and abandoning great part of their baggage, they took the road of flight. Shanoor became, in consequence, a [easy] conquest.'

The bragging continues, 'I rushed forward into the camp of the infidels, and opened upon them a [brisk] fire from my artillery.'[43] Tipu proceeds to embellish his account with similies and metaphors, 'The flight of the unbelievers resembled that of kites and crows;

and, after some time, they stood viewing from the summits of the distant eminences, the plunder of their deserted camp.'[44]

On 22 October 1786, Tipu instructs Budruz Zuman Khan:

> Do you remain on the borders of Soandeh, Kittoor, Dharar, &c. and there apply yourself to the effectual chastisement of the turbulent wretches who infest those parts...Demolish the fort of Kittoor. Seize upon the disturbers of the country, and incorporate them with the Ahmedies [i.e., make Musulmans of them].[45]

On 4 November 1786, Tipu communicates to the Dewan of Cuddapah, 'Your letter, praying to be allowed the use of ten Bandars [rocketmen] for the services of your house and gardens, has passed under our view. Bandars are entertained for fighting, not for looking after houses and gardens.'[46]

On 15 December 1786, Tipu issued a circular to Monsieur Cossigny and several others, including the governor of Madras and the imam of Muscat, providing a detailed account of his recent victory over the Marathas and the nizam near Savanur on 2 December:

> The [main] body of the accursed ones joined by the forces of Nizam Ali Khan, and amounting together to nearly a hundred thousand horse and foot... the enemy, no longer able to support the fire from our guns, involuntarily took the road of flight; upon which they were closely pursued for two or three coss by our victorious army, who slew and took prisoners great numbers of the fugitives, besides obtaining possession of the whole of their baggage. In addition to this, three thousand camels, laden with various articles, twenty thousand bullocks, five elephants with canopies, twenty standards and kettledrums, and seven or eight thousand horses, fell into our hands.[47]

Kirkpatrick opines that Tipu's army won a spectacular victory on this occasion.

On 17 January 1787, Tipu sent a team to Srirangapatna to bring treasure. Kirkpatrick observes:

> The treasure here mentioned was, most probably, designed for the Mahrattahs; and appears, by a subsequent letter, to have consisted of 3,88,971 pagodas of sorts, and 72,000 Pondicherry rupees, making together about thirteen lakhs of rupees, which agrees pretty nearly with the sum ... he paid to the Mahrattahs at the conclusion of peace ... Budruz Zuman Khan was chosen to conduct the negotiations now pending with the Mahrattahs...an act of submission, as the deputation of a person of Budruz Zuman's rank to the Mahrattah camp would be.[48]

Tipu's memoir provides his perspective on the conflict with the Marathas and its resolution:

> In compliance with their desire, I sent Budruz Zuman Khan, Ali Riza, and other great men, to negotiate with them. On the arrival of the latter in the enemy's camp, the Mahrattah leaders addressed them, saying, 'Our master stands in the place of a son to yours, and we are servants. Pardon us for the evils which we have, by our own brought upon the country; and let your sovereign, by way of sweetmeat, present our master, according to custom, with a little money, and one or two villages: this being no more than such a favor as a son is entitled to claim of his father.'[49]

The memoir further elaborates:

> I agreed to an accommodation, and to give them twelve lacks of rupees. The treaty being concluded, I wrote [a letter] to Lewai Madhee Rao, which I sent to him, together with a Kulgy and Surpaish of precious stones, and an elephant. I also sent an elephant, with a dress and jewels, to Tukojee Holkar; and the same to Rao Rasta and to Hurry Pundit.[50]

Kirkpatrick says, 'The Sultan asserts that the Mahrattah chiefs themselves assured his Vakeels, that independently of those who had fallen in battle, they had lost near a hundred thousand men by sickness, since the commencement of the campaign.'[51]

## Letters to Malabar

On 18 September 1785, Tipu Sultan wrote to Ali Rajah Beeby (Arakkal Beevi) of Cannanore:

> What you have written, relative to your having paid twenty thousand rupees to Meer Zynul Aabideen, the Foujdar of Zuferabad, is understood, and meets our approbation. You must, in like manner, discharge the remaining balance due by you. Upon your arrival at the Presence, we will personally state all matters to you. Tillicherry is situated near the Taaluk of that refuge of chastity. You will, therefore, regularly transmit to us whatever intelligence you may be able to procure from thence.[52]

The letter clearly indicates that she was considered a tributary, with the sultan expecting her to pay her respects in person and to provide intelligence regarding the British at Tellicherry. Kirkpatrick observes:

> Ali Rajah Beeby was a Mahommedan; and on this account, perhaps, was treated by the Sultan with somewhat more distinction and lenity, than he was accustomed to show to his other tributaries in Malabar. He would not seem, however, to have succeeded in his endeavours to conciliate her good-will, or to inspire her with confidence in him. This fact is deducible from the constant repugnance, which she evinced to complying with his desire of seeing her at Seringapatam.[53]

On 16 December 1785, Tipu wrote again to the Beevi:

> We have received your letter by Fukhruddeen, who has also expatiated to us upon your situation. The custom of the world is this. Servants and dependants hold themselves [at all times] prepared for the performance of services; the execution of orders; obedience and fidelity. Many times have we written to that lady of chaste degree on the subject of repairing to our Presence; in reply to which you have continually brought forward evasions and excuses, and still continue to do the same. In this case, what is to be

> done? Be yourself the judge. Raja Wurm-raj, who presented himself before us, was honoured with a grant of the farm of the Taaluk of Cherkul, and with other gifts. If you [in like manner] had come [to us], agreeably to our orders, you [also] would assuredly have experienced our bounteous favour.[54]

The Arakkal Beevi evidently declined the favours of the Mysore sultan by choosing not to go. Three days later, Tipu wrote another letter, presumably in response to a communication from her:

> You write that the villages of Mutmail, &c. have, from days of yore appertained to you, and been [actually] in your possession; but that now the revenues of the said villages have been sequestered, on account of our Sircar. It is revealed; and, in consequence, we enclose a letter to Urshud Baig Khan, the Foujdar of Calicut, in which we have given him strict orders to relinquish the villages in question and the revenues thereof. Forward the same to him. We have repeatedly written to you, desiring you to repair to the Presence; but, instead of coming to us, you have excused yourself upon different pretences. For this reason, and in conformity with the policy of the moment, the settlement of the Taaluk of Cherkul, and the appointment of a separate Aumil, on our behalf, to the charge of the same, has appeared expedient to us.[55]

The Beevi appears to be facing consequences for avoiding a direct meeting with the sultan. On 4 May 1786, Tipu once again wrote to the Beevi requesting her 'to transmit incessantly intelligence of what passes at Bombay and Telicherry'.[56] On 11 June, he ordered her to join Urshud Baig Khan with her forces and assist him in chastising the rebellious Nairs.[57]

On 7 April 1786, Tipu wrote to Mahommed Ali, Aumil of Ufzulabady Nagar, 'In like manner as you have caused two thousand Samories (Samuthiris or Zamorins), inhabitants of Zuferabad, to flee [the country], even so must you send for them back [or cause them to return thither].'[58] It is likely that there was a paucity of workers to cultivate the land. The refugees are wrongly listed as 'samories'. More likely, they were farmers from south Canara.

On 28 December 1786, Tipu wrote to Urshud Baig Khan, 'Abandon your vain idea of proceeding [on a pilgrimage] to the Holy Temple, and apply yourself, according to custom, to the affairs of the Sircar.'[59] Kirkpatrick reveals:

> This officer appears, from other parts of the correspondence, to have formed some improper female connection, which the Sultan had insisted upon his renouncing. The lover resented this interference, by announcing his resolution to proceed on a pilgrimage to Mecca. This sort of declaration is often made under the influence of temporary chagrin or disappointment, and sometimes without any serious intention of fulfilling it, and with no other view than that of intimidation. Whatever the case might be with regard to Urshud Baig Khan, he ultimately relinquished his purpose [whether real or pretended], although the object of his irregular attachment had, by order of his sovereign, been publicly banished from the town of Calicut.[60]

On the same day, Tipu wrote to the dewans of Calicut:

> Dissuade Urshud Baig Khan from his vain purpose of repairing to the House of God [Mecca]. Try, at first, as far as you may be able, the effect of fair persuasion; and if this should not succeed, you must, of necessity, confine him. You must, likewise, imprison the courtezan, who has been the cause of this affair.[61]

Kirkpatrick notes that upon Urshud Baig 'coming again to his senses', he was restored to his position, while the poor woman was driven out from the city.[62]

On 31 January 1787, Tipu wrote to Meer Ibrahim, 'You must not, in future, form the design of chastising either the Nairs or Moplahs. This business appertains to the Foujdar of that quarter. Yours is to apply yourself earnestly to the collection of the revenue, and other fiscal matters.'[63]

On 2 February 1787, Tipu wrote to Urshud Baig Khan:

> You must give the most strict orders to all the merchants, and other inhabitants of that place [Calicut], neither to buy any goods of the English factor who is come thither, nor sell grain, or any other articles whatsoever, to him. How long [in this case] will the above-named remain? He will, in the end, despair of making either sales or purchases and depart from thence.[64]

Kirkpatrick observes that this order 'amounts to a gross infraction of the eighth article of the treaty of Mangalore, concluded between the English and Tippoo in March 1784'.[65]

## Sundry Letters

On 17 November 1785, a letter directed the nawab of Savanur to '[dispatch] to Nursia, the Dewan of Nugr, one lack of pagodas, on account of annual Paishcush'.[66] On 30 October 1785, Tipu wrote to the governor of Pondicherry expressing his interest in purchasing 7,000–8,000 firelocks.[67] On 27 November 1785, he wrote to Raja Ram Chundur regarding 'a manufactory of musquets to be established in the Fort of Khan-Khan-hulli: for which purpose, if it should be necessary to pull down forty or fifty houses belonging to poor people'.[68]

On 30 December 1785, Tipu wrote to Mohyuddeen Ali Khan and Urshudullah Khan, the Dewan and Bakshi of Cuddapah, informing them that Gurramkonda should henceforth be called Zuferabad, and directing them to disseminate this information throughout the territory. Kirkpatrick remarks:

> I cannot positively state, whether or not Merkerrah of Koorg continued to be called Zuferabad after the latter name was transferred to Gurramcoondah: but I am inclined to think in the negative; both because it is not probable that the same new name should have been applied to two different places, and because, whenever Zuferabad is subsequently mentioned, Gurramcoondah would constantly seem to be intended.[69]

This is just a small example of Tipu's erratic behaviour.

Tipu's letter dated 4 January 1787 instructed Ghulam Hyder, Aumil of Bangalore:

> The account, stating you had strictly prohibited the distilling and vending of spirituous liquors, and had, moreover, made the whole body of vintners enter into written engagements [to desist from selling such liquors], is understood. You must make the distillers execute a similar engagement, and then oblige them to take up some other occupation.[70]

On 2 February 1787, Tipu wrote to Karim Saheb, his half-brother:

> Your humble address, accompanied by a Nuzr on account of our chastisement of, and [late] victory over, the enemy, has passed under our view. What you write, respecting your intention of repairing to our Presence, and the re-establishment of your health, is understood, and has afforded pleasure to our mind. With the blessing of God, our special retinue will soon shed lustre on that place [Seringapatam] when we shall have a meeting.[71]

Kirkpatrick provides insights into the background:

> Kureem Saheb was the second son of Hyder Ali by a concubine, but was adopted by Medina Begum; who, I believe, was a lawful wife of Hyder, as well as Fukhurun Nisa Beeby, the mother of Tippoo Sultan. Kureem Saheb survived his brother, after whose death he came under the protection of the British government.... He is represented to be of weak intellects.[72]

He elaborates in a footnote, 'It was a daughter of Medina Begum, by Hyder, who was married to Abdul Khyre Khan, the Nabob of Shanoor.'[73]

A perplexing letter dated 29 January 1787, written from Hugly near Kopul, was discovered in the possession of the Poona Resident, Sir Charles Malet, who, according to Kirkpatrick, could not remember how it came into his possession. Kirkpatrick speculates that it was probably found among the belongings of Budruz Zuman

Khan when he was looted by the Marathas after the surrender of Dharwar in 1791.[74] The letter, apparently referring to some prisoners, contains an intriguing instruction:

> It is right that they have kept these people also for a breed. Doubtless, their offspring will be good. One Kishun Rao, likewise, has been detained by the above. He likewise, being old, I do not want. Let the Brahmens employ him in getting children: and as I have a great many other useless people, I will, if they please, send them also, who may be employed in the same way.[75]

The sultan's intent behind this order remains unclear and defies speculation.

## Father–Son 'Agreement'

After the fall of Srirangapatna, Kirkpatrick came across a beguiling document that seemed to be a form of father–son 'Agreement':

> It is certain, indeed, as I learn from Colonel Wilks, that Tippoo himself was once publicly bambooed [or caned] by order of Hyder, in whose good graces he would never appear to have stood very high. This opinion is strongly confirmed, by a most curious original document, which I met with at Seringapatam, in the year 1799.... I found it amongst a variety of other papers of the time of Hyder, deposited in a basket or box, where it had probably remained undisturbed and forgotten ever since his death. It is a narrow slip, about twelve inches in length: is entitled, at the top, 'an agreement' beneath which words are the impression, in ink, of a small square seal, resembling, in all respects, the usual signet, or ring-seal, of the Sultan, and bearing, together with the name 'Tippoo Sultan, the date 1184 (Higera)'.[76]

The document itself was undated, but Kirkpatrick presumed that it might have been drafted between 1769 (the year the seal was engraved) and 1782 (when Haider Ali passed away).[77] Kirkpatrick explains, 'The existence of this seal satisfactorily proves that Sultan was not a title assumed by Tippoo (as commonly supposed) upon succeeding his father, but made part of the name given him, probably, at his birth.'[78]

The so-called agreement stipulates as follows:

(1) I will not do one thing without the pleasure of your blessed Majesty. Lord of Benefits [or my bountiful Lord]: if I do, let me be punished, in whatever manner may seem fitting to your auspicious mind.

(2) If, in the affairs of the Sircar, I should commit theft, or be guilty of fraud, great or small, let me, as the due punishment thereof, be strangled.

(3) If I be guilty of prevarication, or misrepresentation, or of deceit, the due punishment thereof is this same strangulation.

(4) Without the orders of the Presence, I will not receive from any one, Nazzers, &c.; neither will I take things from any one [meaning perhaps forcibly]: if I do, let my nose be cut off, and let me be driven out from the city.

(5) If, excepting on the affairs of the Sircar, I should hold conversation [probably cabal or intrigue] with any person, or be guilty of deceit, &c., let me, in punishment thereof, be stretched on a cross.

(6) Whenever a country shall be committed to my charge by the Sircar, and an army be placed under my command, I will carry on all business regarding the same, with the advice, and through the medium of such confidential persons as may be appointed by the Sircar; and if I transact such affairs through any other channel than this, let me be strangled.

(7) If there should be any occasion for correspondence by writing, or to buy or give [away] any thing, or any letters should arrive from any place, I will do nothing without the concurrence and advice of the person appointed by the Sircar.

(8) I have written and delivered these few articles of my own free will: keeping the contents whereof in my heart's remembrance, I will act in each article accordingly. If I forget this, and act in any other manner, let me be punished, agreeably to the foregoing writing.[79]

This document is indeed baffling and mysterious, tempting one to draw conclusions. The description of severe punishments such as strangulation, crucifixion and nose-cutting is deeply disturbing, especially considering that the person signing and delivering this agreement is the son and heir of the de facto ruler of the powerful kingdom of Mysore. It would not be unreasonable to assume that this agreement was signed under duress. The explicit statement claiming it to be purely voluntary lends credence to this assumption. If the father trusted and respected the son, why would such an agreement be necessary? Likewise, if the son was loyal and trustworthy, why demand such a written agreement?

In any case, when Haider Ali's authority was absolute, such an agreement could only serve to intimidate and control the unruly heir. It is worth noting that Haider Ali had another son, Karim, who was rumoured to be slow-witted, and an adopted son, Ayaz Khan, who was a prime favourite. In this context, did Haider Ali harbour doubts about nominating Tipu as his successor? There is no evidence that he ever formally designated a successor, despite his serious illness in his final days. Moreover, immediately after Haider's death, senior nobles proclaimed Karim Sahib as 'Dewan' before Tipu Sultan's arrival from Malabar. Could there have been a clandestine plot to oust Tipu when Haider Ali passed away? It is a mysterious affair, to say the least.

Bowring reflects on Tipu's character:

> From his youth upwards he was deficient in stability and straightforwardness, so much so as to excite the wrath of his father. Haidar, besides publicly flogging Tipu at Chinkurali ... exacted from him an agreement...It is evident from the contents of this curious paper...that Haidar was well aware of the unstable and fickle temperament of his son. It was also asserted by many who knew Tipu in later life that his understanding was at times clouded over in a way that betrayed symptoms of mental aberration.[80]

The English prisoner James Scurry also expressed the opinion that Tipu appeared to be mentally unstable.

## Tipu's Memoir

Referring to 'a highly interesting manuscript, purporting to be a memoir of Tippoo Sultan, written by himself', Kirkpatrick reveals:

> This curious document was among the numerous papers discovered by Colonel Ogg. The copy with which that gentleman favored me was entitled Tareekhe Khodadady, i.e. the Khodadady Annals, or History of the Khodadad Sircar. The work was, from the beginning, in an imperfect state; the narrative being brought down to no later a period than the termination of the Mahrattah war, or the month of February 1787. My copy, however, has been rendered still more incomplete, by an unfortunate accident, which occasioned the destruction of several leaves of it.[81]

He adds, 'There can be little doubt, that there are other copies of the sultan's memoirs in existence, besides the mutilated one in my possession.'[82]

Wilks states:

> The memoirs of the Sultaun's reign found in the palace, and written in the first person, is supposed by Colonel Kirkpatrick to be the rough draft from which the Sultaun-u-Towareekh was prepared by Zein-ul-ab-u-Deen by the Sultaun's command.[83]

Simply put, Tipu Sultan was not a scholar. He repeatedly displays evidence of his coarse language, his practice of effecting forced conversions to Islam, his strategy of conscripting prisoners of war into his army and his penchant for causing the forced migration of large numbers of civilians.

The memoir commences with the siege of Bidanur in January 1783. It largely comprises bombastic content, glorifying and exaggerating Tipu's military achievements while ridiculing the actions of his adversaries. Although the actual or perceived obligations of the Marathas to Haider Ali and his successor are often mentioned in Tipu's letters, he writes in his memoir:

> Previously to the resolution of making war against the Nazarenes [i.e., before the commencement of hostilities against the English by Hyder Ali Khan] the Mahrattahs being reduced to great straits, and defeated by the English, had [actually] filled their houses with straw, and prepared to burn the city of Poonah. In this situation they dispatched four of their principal and confidential people to our late father, with letters, accompanied by oaths and deceitful engagements, soliciting the grant of a fort within our dominions, wherein they might lodge their chief [more worthless, in truth, than a horse keeper]. Accordingly, these trusty persons [who, in fact, were not to be trusted]arriving in the presence of our deceased father [whose place is in Paradise] represented, that being broken down [or discomfited] by the English, they were on the point of abandoning their country, within eight coss of [the capital of] which the Nazarenes were arrived: that, in these circumstances, they could look for help to no one but his Highness; that their master was a child, the preservation of whose life, honor, country, and wealth, by the UsudIlhye state, would confer an obligation, which would continue to be acknowledged, as long as any of the Madho Raos existed; and, finally, imploring his Highness to consider their chief in the light of a son. These representations were seconded, on the part of Nizam Ali Khan, whose country had also been threatened by the English, and whom the Mahrattahs had prevailed on, by promises and engagements, to espouse their cause, and to interest himself in their favour [with our late father] ...Our father [who reposes in Paradise]agreed to their propositions, and resolved on war with the English, notwithstanding the opposition made to the measure by the chiefs of the state, who represented that the war would prove arduous and tedious; that there was no necessity for his drawing the misfortunes of another's house upon himself; that these two impure ones [namely Madho Rao and Nizam Ali]were both of spurious origin, and neither their words nor actions entitled to the least credit or faith.[84]

Tipu references the terms of the treaty and the signatories in his characteristic irreverent style. He states that it was agreed between 'these two bastards and the Hydery state, that no peace should be entered into with the English, except with the knowledge of all three'.[85]

About the Coorgis, Tipu has this to say:

They laid siege to a fort newly erected by the Sircar, and in which the Governor [of the district] resided. The garrison being reduced to great straits surrendered on capitulation; but were all massacred, on marching out of the place. The fort was completely demolished by the rebels, who through enmity, i.e., to mark their hatred the more strongly, conveyed away every stone belonging to it, and threw the whole into the quarry from which it had been originally taken...When this occurrence came to our blessed hearing, we dispatched a commander, named Hyder Ali Baig, with a suitable force, to reduce the Koorg country. The aforesaid commander proceeding to the borders of Koorg had arrived near the fort of Periapatam when the rebels collecting together advanced to meet him. One or two battles ensued: but the aforesaid commander was not able to settle the affairs of that quarter.... Hereupon I detached another army, under the direction of the Rajah of Kunak-geery, to the aid of the aforesaid commander, and pursued my march to Nugr; after the recapture of which, the victorious army was engaged in the reduction of Mangalore. It was during this period, that the two before-mentioned commanders, having advanced, for the purpose of subduing Koorg, two or three coss into the woods, were attacked from all quarters by the Koorgs, who closed up every avenue [to their camp or position]. For three successive days was the conflict maintained; at the end of which time, my base commanders, consulting only the safety of their worthless lives, took to flight, leaving behind them their troops and guns. The Rajah of Kunnikgeery, however, with a few men, maintained their ground [for some time]; and after amply discharging the obligations of valor, and sending numbers of the enemy to hell, made an offering of their lives for the service of the Usudllhye Sircar. In consequence of these events, I proceeded, after the reduction [or subjugation] of Bul, as above related, towards Koorg. From Periapatam the army advanced in two divisions, by different roads, and in two days, by rapid marches, reached the residence of the governor [of the district], where the infidels had taken post. Here I made a great number of prisoners. Kutty Naik, however, the no-chief of the Koorgs, effecting his

> escape, with his family and children, through the woods and adjacent hills, concealed himself and followers in a glen, or valley, of the Elaichi mountains, which was inaccessible both to wild beasts and birds.[86]

Kirkpatrick mentions in a footnote that the name of the Coorg chief is uncertain.[87]

Tipu's narrative continues:

> Beyond this end of the glen was a small plain, where three houses of Kutty Naik stood. When we reached the spot it was sunset; so I took up my quarters in those houses, drawing up and encamping my followers on each side of Kutty Naik's dwelling. Here, telling my people that the enemy would approach in the night, and after discharging their muskets at a great distance, would set up a howl or noise, in the manner of dogs, swine, and jackals, I strictly forbad their standing to their arms on that account, directing them to sit still, and satisfy themselves with frightening the dogs away … When morning came, I set the pioneers and others to work upon making a road, fifty yards wide, through the glen, which was accordingly completed by the evening. The following day I sent for the whole army, with which I proceeded in three marches to the passes, spreading detachments, as I advanced, over the country, for the purpose of seizing on the thieves. The aforesaid Naik, fleeing into the woods, escaped with his family, by another road over the passes, to Tillicherry, a sea-port belonging to the English. Here dying a natural death, at the end of two or three days, he made his entry into hell: Whereupon orders were sent to his followers from the Presence, directing them to bring his family and effects to the Presence; and accordingly, the thieves, who had accompanied him, leaving Tillicherry, repaired with his family, two or three elephants, and his other effects, to the Presence. The special retinue returning from hence through the glen and other places [by which it had advanced], reached, after some marches, the fort of Merkerrah which the infidels had demolished. Here I halted.[88]

Kirkpatrick opines that the Marathas took up arms against Tipu in 1795 not only to support the Zemindar of Nergund, but 'they had claims on him for considerable arrears of tribute, the discharge of which he had hitherto refused or evaded; not less, according to some accounts, than forty lacks of rupees'.[89] He notes, 'The Sultan himself, in his Memoirs, states the sum at twelve lacks of rupees.'[90] While the exact amount of tribute may have been disputed, the fact that Mysore owed tribute to the Marathas was never disputed by the sultan.

## The Sultan's Dream Book

Written in secrecy and concealed from view, this mystifying compilation was discovered in Tipu's palace after his death. The sultan had recorded thirty-seven dreams in his own hand in the Farsi language, dating from April 1786 to January 1799.The book contained several spelling errors, and the dreams were not arranged in any chronological order, prompting scholars to deduce that only a few were recorded immediately upon waking. Perhaps the sultan was trying to comprehend the events rapidly unfolding around him. Many of the dreams revolve around his enemies and his preoccupation with warfare, while others feature religious figures such as Prophet Muhammed and his son-in-law Ali.

The manuscript was presented to the Court of Directors of the East India Company in 1800 by Alexander Beatson on behalf of Governor-General Richard Wellesley. The account of its discovery is documented in Beatson's signed and dated note at the end of the volume as follows:

> This register of the Sultaun's dreams was discovered by Colonel William Kirkpatrick, amongst other papers of a secret nature in an escritoire found in the Palace of Seringpatam. Hubbeeb Oollah, one of the most confidential of the Sultaun's servants, was present at the time it was discovered. He knew that there was such a book of the Sultaun's composition, but had never seen it, as the Sultaun always manifested peculiar anxiety to conceal it from the view of

> any who happened to approach while he was either reading or writing in it.[91]

Mahmud Husain, professor of history at the University of Karachi, who translated Tipu Sultan's *Dream Book*, mentions, 'In a few places the language is defective and ungrammatical, but what is even more astonishing is that it contains spelling mistakes. The following list which is not exhaustive will give an idea of the mis-spellings.'[92] Husain then provides a lengthy list of Tipu's literary errors.

One of these dreams is dated September 1786 and appears to have occurred during the Mysore–Maratha war when the Marathas had formed an alliance with the nizam and launched an attack on Tipu's dominions. Mahmud Husain's translation is as follows:

> At the place where I had halted, on the farther side of the Tungabhadra, I had this dream: It appeared to me as if it was the Day of Judgement when no one would be interested in anyone else. At that time a stranger of great strength and commanding stature with a bright face and red beard and moustache came to me and taking my hand in his, said to me: 'Do you know who I am?' I told him I did not. He then said to me, 'I am Murtaza Ali and the Messenger of God has said and is still repeating it that he would not set his foot in paradise without you and would wait for you and enter the paradise with you.' I felt so happy and woke up. God is all-powerful, and the Messenger is the intercessor.[93]

This dream certainly seems like the epitome of a grandiose fantasy. The notion that Prophet Muhammed refused to enter paradise without Tipu Sultan is indeed extraordinary and reflects the mindset of a consummate megalomaniac.

Another dream from the same year (1786) involves a woman dressed in male attire, and occurred at a time when Tipu was engaged in a battle with the Marathas. On 1 October, he launched a surprise attack on the military camp of Haripant Phadke, compelling the enemy to retreat. Husain's translation of the Sultan's dream narrates:

> Prior to the night attack upon the Marhattas at Shahnur.... I had a dream: It seemed to me as if a handsome young man, a stranger, came and sat down near me. I passed certain remarks in the manner in which one might, in a playful mood, talk to a woman. I then said to myself: 'It is not my custom to enter into playful discourse with anyone.' Shortly thereafter, the youth rose, and walking a few paces, returned to loosen his hair from beneath his turban, and opening the fastenings of his robe, displayed his bosom and I saw it was a woman. I immediately called and seated her and said to her: 'Whereas formerly I had only guessed you were a woman, and I had cut jokes with you, it is now definite that you are a woman in the dress of a man. My conjecture has come true.' In the midst of this conversation the morning dawned, and I woke up. I conveyed the contents of the dream to other people and interpreted it thus: That please God those Marhattas have put on the clothes of men, but in fact, will prove to be women. By the favour of God and the aid of His Messenger, on the 8th of the month and the year above mentioned, on the morning of Saturday, I made a surprise attack upon the army of the unbelievers. Advancing with two or three hundred men, I myself penetrated the camp of the unbelievers, crushing them as I went, as far as the tent of Hari Pant Pharkiah, and they all fled like women.[94]

The message is unmistakeable. The sultan's dream reflects his contempt for both the Marathas and women in general. However, why he chose to engage in a flirtatious conversation with a male stranger remains a subject of debate. In Tipu's own interpretation of this dream, he perceives the Marathas as women disguised as men, and assumes they could be easily defeated.

Another of the sultan's ambitions was the eviction of the British from India. As expected, his nocturnal flights of fancy reflected his heart's desire. In 1792, he surrendered half of his territories to the British, and since then, he had been plotting a comeback with the help of the French under Napoleon Bonaparte. In January 1797, he had a dream, which Husain translates as follows:

> [In] the early hours of the morning, I had a dream: Raghunath Rao, the Marhatta agent, who had been to me before, appeared before me and said, 'The English have suffered a crushing defeat in Europe and are now on the verge of leaving Bengal voluntarily.' On hearing his statement, I said, 'That is fine, I will despatch troops as well as money; if God wills, the Nazarenes shall be expelled from India.'[95]

This aspiration proved to be yet another pipe dream, as Tipu was killed two and a half years later, and the British went on to govern India for the next 150 years.

Tipu aimed to expel the Christians and convert the kafirs. A long-bearded maulavi frequently appears in his dreams, symbolizing his devout adherence to Islam. In another dream, Tipu goes on a pilgrimage to Mecca. His hopes and desires are mirrored in these nocturnal visions. He dreams of a 10,000-strong French army arriving to assist him in his fight against the British. Addressing the commander, he asserts 'Here too all the equipment for war is ready and the followers of Islam are eager, in large numbers to prosecute *Jihad*.'[96]

In his thirty-third dream, Tipu writes, 'My interpretation is that by the grace of God, all unbelievers would embrace Islam and the country would pass into the hands of the *Sarkar-i-Khudadad*.'[97] In another dream, Prophet Mohammed presents him with a green turban.[98] In yet another dream, the Chinese emperor sends him two white elephants, a gesture previously extended only to Alexander the Great, when the then Chinese emperor sent him a single white elephant.[99] In his twenty-second dream, Tipu encounters a large temple with slight damage, 'It contained several large idols. I went into the temple along with a few other men and noticed that the idols were seeing like human beings and their eyes were in motion.'[100] Observing two female idols in the last row, Tipu approached them, whereupon one spoke, revealing that only two were women, while the others were males or other objects. Tipu thereafter ordered his men to repair the temple.[101]

Kate Brittlebank, springing to the sultan's defence, says, 'There is a long tradition of dream interpretation in Islam, known as *ta'bir* and regarded as a science.'[102] Readers are expected to understand that dream interpretation is neither superstitious nonsense nor exclusively a Hindu activity. It is both Islamic and scientific.

Why did the sultan consider his dreams worth recording? Why did he conceal the book from others? Did he interpret them himself or with the help of his Hindu astrologers? These questions remain unanswered. However, it is an undeniable fact that Tipu's dreams reflect his obsession with war.

## The Zenana Women

After the fall of Srirangapatna, the inhabitants of the zenana were counted, classified and catalogued by the British. There were a total of 601 women, including wives, concubines and various others. Among them, 268 women belonged to Haider Ali, while the remaining 333 were associated with Tipu Sultan. They were guarded by eunuchs. According to Wellesley and Marriot, there were 193 concubines of the first rank and 100 slave women in Tipu's zenana. Marriot adds that many of the slaves were brought from Constantinople (Turkey) and Georgia.

Haider had initially desired Tipu to marry the daughter of the late Imam Saheb Bakshi and sister of Ghulam Hussain Khan, also known as the Pondicherry nawab. However, Tipu's mother, Fakhrunissa, favoured Ruqayya Banu, the daughter of Lala Mian and sister of Burhan-ud-din. Ultimately, Tipu married both girls on the same night in 1774.

Roderick Mackenzie, a lieutenant of the 52nd Regiment, in his 1799 publication titled *A Sketch of the War with Tippoo Sultaun*, which he seems to have written in 1792 at the conclusion of the Third Anglo-Mysore War, presents some interesting revelations. He writes, 'To the injuries and insults that the Marathas were necessitated to submit from Tippoo Sultan, Purseram Bhow could bear the most ample testimony; and some of his nearest female relations, still in the harem of the Sultaun, furnish woeful proofs in addition.'[103] This information was probably supplied by the Poona-Resident, shedding light on the manner in which Tipu Sultan assembled his harem. Chetti avers:

> Tippu had eighty ladies, many of whom were the sisters and daughters of the Brahman and other Hindu noblemen and princes, taken in war or in peace and forced into his zenana.... He, it is said, also forced one of the sisters of Vira Raja of Coorg into his harem.[104]

Though the evidence is overwhelming, Mohibbul Hasan expresses a more lenient view:

> How many concubines Tipu had is difficult to say. Kirmani, Mackenzie, Dirom, Beatson, and other contemporary accounts do not mention any concubine. In fact, according to them, the Sultan led a strictly moral life. But Arthur Wellesley and Marriott say that there were 193 concubines of the first rank and one hundred slave women in Tipu's *mahal*.[105]

The British had a practice of meticulously documenting and cataloguing everything they observed. After Tipu's death, every individual in the zenana was accounted for. If Tipu had only two or three legal wives, it is hard to imagine the roles of the other women found in the palace. It is improbable that all of them were merely cooks, serving maids and seamstresses, as Hasan would have us believe.

Ruqayya Banu passed away in February 1792, a day after the British stormed Tipu's position near Srirangapatna. In 1795, Tipu married Khadija Zaman Begum, the daughter of Sayyid Saheb. A son was born to her in 1797, but both mother and child died after a few days. A fourth wife, Buranti Begum, said to be from Delhi, is mentioned by the British officer who listed the residents of the zenana after Tipu's death.

Tipu reportedly had twelve surviving sons and eight daughters in 1799. Wilks asserts that Tipu left behind three legitimate children (Mohiuddin and two unnamed daughters) and seventeen illegitimate ones. He also mentions that twenty-four illegitimate offspring had predeceased Tipu.[106] By this account, Abdul Khaliq was considered illegitimate as well.

Tipu's eldest son, Fath Haider, was born to a concubine named Roshani Begum. Fath Haider claimed she was the principal wife, but Wellesley regarded her as a concubine. It is said that Roshani Begum, even after Tipu Sultan's death, continued to wield considerable influence and even organized song and dance parties in the Vellore Fort, where Tipu's descendants were confined.

# 14

# TIGERS, ROCKETS AND OTHER FADS

Tipu had many innovations to his credit. The fact that most of them were discarded after his death testifies to their uselessness. Tipu changed the language of business to Farsi, replacing Kannada and Marathi. He also introduced changes to the calendar, weights and measures. Among Tipu's 'innovations', the only one that endured beyond his lifetime is what later became known as the Mysorean rocket – although it was not originally his invention.

Tipu possessed an insatiable thirst for foreign products, particularly those with destructive potential. Bowing observes:

> He pronounced decided opinions on science, medicine, commerce, religious observances, engineering, military establishments, and a host of abstruse matters with equal facility but with little real knowledge. He seems to have written Persian with tolerable readiness, signing his name generally in a device or cryptogram, meaning 'Nabbi Malik', or 'the Prophet is Master'.[1]

Was it Tipu who first envisioned the construction of the Krishnarajasagar Dam? Was Visweswarayya merely the planner and executor of the project years later? Was Tipu a visionary? Was he a pioneer of rocket artillery and missile technology? Can he be credited with land reform and tax reform? Did he encourage or initiate sericulture in Karnataka? Was he a tech innovator? Did he emulate and adopt best practices from far and near? Well, ample evidence suggests otherwise.

### Tipu and the Mysore Rockets

Gunpowder-packed rockets were not Mysorean inventions. They had been around for centuries and were preceded by fire-arrows and flaming torches. Poisoned arrows and fire arrows are mentioned in our ancient epics. In the 16th century, Abbakka Rani in Ullal and the Kunjali Marakkars on the Malabar Coast launched flaming torches to set fire to Portuguese ships.

In the 18th century, rockets were widely used throughout the Deccan. The Marathas used them against the Afghans during the Third Battle of Panipat in 1761. It was said that Haider Ali's father once commanded fifty rocket-men for the nawab of Arcot. Haider Ali himself introduced a dedicated Rocket Corps into the Mysore army, beginning with approximately 1,200 men. The strength of this corps rose to about 5,000 during Tipu's reign. In the Third Anglo-Mysore War, Tipu fielded two rocket units, led by Kamaruddin Khan (comprising 120 men) and Purnaiya (comprising 131 men) respectively.

De la Tour, referring to the rockets used by Hyder Ali, remarks:

> These rockets are very well adapted for setting fire to towns and villages in which the enemy have magazines. A body of cavalry, not used to this kind of instrument, would be quickly thrown into disorder by it; for the rockets falling at the feet of the horses, emit a flame resembling that of a forge furnace, which frightens them; and when they burst they do considerable mischief.[2]

Hayavadana Rao reveals that Haider's army had 3,000 men equipped with iron rockets.[3]

Rocketmen were trained to launch the missiles at an angle calculated to inflict maximum damage on the enemy. Additionally, the Mysoreans possessed wheeled rocket launchers capable of firing five to ten rockets simultaneously. The use of iron cylinders to encase the propellant facilitated greater thrust and longer range for the missile.

However, despite this advanced rocket technology, Tipu Sultan was unable to win the third and fourth Anglo-Mysore wars. In 1792, he suffered a decisive defeat, and in 1799, he was killed. As the cliché goes, 'The proof of the pudding is in the eating'.

In 1763, Haider conquered Bidanur in Shimoga district, which was one of the wealthiest areas with access to the coast. To date, over 3,000 rockets have been recovered from this region. The first of these discoveries was made in 2002 during excavations for water in an abandoned well. Initially, 160 of the retrieved items were transferred to a local museum, where they languished in wooden crates for over a decade.

Bidanur, renamed Haider Nagar, fell into British hands in January 1793, barely a month after Haider Ali's demise, when Ayaz Khan surrendered to the British army. It is reasonable to assume that the rockets were already lying there before Tipu's accession to power. They may have been concealed in the well to prevent them from falling into British hands.

Nagar served as Haider Ali's secondary capital. It is likely that he anticipated ruling from Nagar if he ever lost control of Mysore and had to flee. Much of Haider's war loot and his 'adopted son' Ayaz Khan were positioned in the Bidanur Fort. So, it is not surprising that a major hoard of Mysorean rockets was discovered in the region.

Nagar could indeed have served as a hub for rocket manufacturing under the Mysore sultans. Turkanahully has been mentioned as a centre for rocket production. According to Nidhin George Olikara, an independent researcher, a location called Tadaknahally, situated 45 km from Shimoga, is highly likely to be this site of rocket production. This assumption is supported by the presence of parts of furnaces and tell-tale remnants of ancient gadgets scattered throughout the area.

Initially, wood, particularly bamboo, was used for making these rockets. At some point in the manufacturing process, iron casing came to be used – an innovation often credited to Tipu, although the evidence is inconclusive. It is just as likely that the use of iron casings for rockets started during Haider Ali's rule.

At the Battle of Pollilur on 10 September 1780, Hyder Ali's forces purportedly detonated Col William Bailley's ammunition stores with the help of a rocket, a stroke of luck that led to the surrender of the British army. Some sources attribute this success to French cannon instead. An ammunition wagon explosion ignited two other ammunition wagons, causing chaos in the British army. This allowed Tipu Sultan's cavalry to overwhelm the British forces and capture Col Bailley. If Mysore rockets were indeed responsible for Haider's victory in 1780, it becomes difficult to attribute the 'invention' of the rocket to Tipu.

The rockets used by Tipu Sultan were considered state-of-the-art or ultra-modern during their time. The Congreve rocket, developed in 1805 by William Congreve, was based on the Mysore model. Of Tipu's rockets that have survived him, two are located in Britain at the Woolwich Royal Armoury, while three are housed in the Bangalore Government Museum. The remaining rockets are possibly scattered throughout his former kingdom awaiting discovery.

Tipu Sultan employed two rocket units in the defence of Srirangapatna in 1792. He used them again in 1799 as he attempted to defend his capital against the invading British army.

During the assault on Srirangapatna on 2 May 1799, a magazine of rockets within the fort exploded when struck by a missile. On 4 May, during Baird's final charge, his contingent faced muskets and rockets, but the celebrated Mysore rockets could not alter the fate of the sultan. The fort fell less than an hour after the assault began, and Tipu himself was killed by an unknown soldier. He had lived and died by the sword, with rockets ultimately unable to alter his destiny.

After the fall of Srirangapatna, the attackers discovered 700 serviceable rockets and 9,000 empty rockets inside the fort.

The Mysore rockets were also used for ceremonial purposes. When the Jacobin Club of Mysore, formed after the French Revolution, sent a delegation to Tipu Sultan, 500 rockets were launched to greet them.

Tipu's Ordnance was reputed to be superior to that of the Ottomans. In the late 1780s, the French ambassador, Cossigny, sent 100 matchlocks to Tipu. However, Tipu returned the entire consignment, stating that those produced in his kingdom were of superior quality. According to Yazdani, 'In 1786, Cossigny (the French Governor of Pondicherry) was of the opinion that Tipu's locally produced musket – that was presented to him by the sultan himself – was comparable to any produced in Europe. The two pistols that Tipu gifted to Louis XVI were also rated favourably.'[4] Unfortunately, these pistols did not bring luck to the French monarch, who was guillotined in 1793 in the aftermath of the French Revolution.

Until the 19th century, Indian iron and steel were considered superior to similar European products. The superiority stemmed from an ancient tradition, advanced processes and a small-scale but widespread production. The militarization under the Mysore sultans gave a boost to the iron industry. However, both father and son employed methods based on coercion, intimidation and exploitation to develop the industry. Forced labour, extended working hours and harsh punishments were common practices. The industry primarily focused on the manufacture of destructive commodities such as cannons, firearms and rockets.

Tipu indeed made several attempts at modernization, but his primary focus was on war-making, and his modus operandi involved importing or capturing Europeans and employing them for his purposes. Sadly, circumcision was often part of the deal.

## Tigers, Leopards and Gadgets

Tipu loved tigers just as much as he hated the English. He is said to have declared that he would rather live two days as a tiger than two hundred years as a sheep. According to English prisoners, 'Several live tigers were kept in cages or chained up in front of his palace.'[5] Tipu supplied tiger-striped uniforms to his soldiers and adorned his guns, muskets, swords and other items with tiger heads and stripes. Kirkpatrick reports that Tipu ensured the tiger stripe was 'introduced into almost every article belonging to him. Hence it was found stamped on the binding of his books, engraved on his plate and his firearms...It even formed the watermark of the paper manufactured for his use.'[6] His Tiger Throne represented the pinnacle of this endeavour.

Around 1795, Tipu commissioned a life-size mechanical device showing a tiger pouncing on an Englishman. The poor man, dressed in uniform, is depicted lying on his back with a horrified expression as the tiger pins him down, its teeth menacingly poised on his neck. The wooden gadget is brightly painted, with the soldier wearing a black hat, a red coat and trousers, and black shoes. A crank on the tiger's side can be turned, causing the tiger to growl while the soldier emits a moan. A 36-pipe organ is also installed on the tiger's side, featuring push-buttons for play. This contraption is housed in the Victoria and Albert Museum in London and remains a popular tourist attraction.

It is believed that the sultan conceived the idea of creating this macabre toy following a tragic incident in 1792 when the son of General Hector Munro was mauled by a tiger during a picnic on a coastal island. General Munro had defeated Tipu Sultan's army twelve years earlier during the Second Anglo-Mysore War, and the sultan perhaps took pleasure in his enemy's personal misfortune.

Tipu sultan did not have the opportunity to enjoy his tiger toy for long. After the sultan's death, it was displayed in the Museum of the East India Company for half a century. After the company ceased to exist, it was put on display in the Victoria and Albert Museum.

Chetti states:

> Near the door of his treasury, an enormous tiger was found chained. There were other tigers in the edifice, and so numerous as to give some trouble to Colonel Wellesley. The history and character of the son of Hyder Ali, were in a manner, indicated by the barbarous big toy invented for his amusement, which was found in his palace, and which may now be seen in the Library of the East India House, London. This rude automation is a tiger in the act

> of devouring a European, who lies prostrate under the savage beast. There is likewise, in the palace of the Maharaja of Mysore, another automated figure of a tiger, life-size, so set on springs, that Tippu could make it take a leap and light on the person of any unsuspecting visitor, who of course imagined that he was assailed by a living tiger, to the great merriment of the monarch.[7]

Tipu not only collected tigers and kept them in his palace but also commissioned several paintings depicting himself tackling tigers with his bare hands. Moreover, he employed trained leopards for hunting antelopes. Historical records indicate that Haider Ali similarly possessed tigers and leopards. De la Tour gives an elaborate account, stating, 'Hyder himself gives each of them a ball of sweetmeats which they take very adroitly with their paws, being exceedingly tame. These are the spotted tigers, and their keepers lead them every day into those places where the greatest crowds are.'[8] The author also describes Haider Ali's method of tiger hunting, armed only with a knife. James Scurry testifies that Tipu Sultan had a fondness for hunting.

Tipu Sultan had a penchant for gadgets and acquired rare toys from distant lands. Guns, muskets, bayonets and rockets – all of these he purchased, collected and even manufactured. Wilks states:

> Royal tigers were chained in the court of the entrance of the palace, and the construction of the throne was made to conform to the same terrific emblem. A tiger, rather exceeding the full size, of pure gold, and well fashioned, the eyes and teeth of appropriate stones, was the support of the throne; and from a richly ornamented canopy, was suspended over the throne a fluttering humma formed of beautiful precious stones.[9]

This throne may have rivalled Shah Jahan's peacock throne – and perhaps met a similar fate. The peacock throne travelled to Persia and was dismantled. Tipu's throne arrived in England in many fragments. Chhatrapati Shivaji's throne vanished without a trace. History tends to repeat itself, especially concerning invaluable artefacts.

## Tipu's Coinage

On 23 June 1785, Tipu Sultan sent an unusual gift to the Mughal emperor Shah Alam along with a rather peculiar letter. He wrote:

> In acknowledgment of this magnificent donation, [I] respectfully offer [my] most humble obeisance. This steadfast believer, with a view to the support of the firm religion of Mahommed, undertook [some time since] the chastisement of the Nazarene tribe; who, unable to maintain the war [I] waged against them, solicited peace [of me] in the most abject manner. This is so notorious a fact, as not to require to be enlarged on. With the divine aid and blessing of God, it is now again [my] steady determination to set about *the total extirpation and destruction of the enemies of the faith.* In token of [my] sincere attachment [or devotion] to your Majesty, [I] send, by way of Nuzr, a hundred and twenty-one gold Mohrs to your resplendent Presence.[10] (emphasis added)

Kirkpatrick comments:

> The writer here does not once style himself, as is customary, 'the slave', 'the devoted servant' or even 'the dependent' of Shah Allum. The very manner in which he offers his Nuzr is lofty and unsuitable to the occasion, but is still less offensive and affronting than the Nuzr itself.[11]

Tipu had forsaken the imperial coinage and substituted the name of the Mughal emperor's with his own. According to Kirkpatrick:

> Not content, however, with putting this affront upon the aged monarch, he had the temerity to aggravate it in the highest degree, by sending the latter a Nuzr, consisting of a coin, from the inscription on which the name and titles of Shah Allum were entirely excluded.[12]

On the same day, 23 June 1785, Tipu jubilantly wrote a letter to Munzoor Ali Khan, the chief of the eunuchs at the Mughal court, and a confidante of Shah Alam:

> I have, on this account, devised and coined, and caused to be circulated, a new and superior kind of gold Mohr; in which the names of God, of the Holy Prophet, and of the august Prince of Sanctity and of Sages, are introduced. Of this new coinage is my Nuzr to his Majesty composed; and I have likewise sent, in token of friendship, twenty-five of the same sort of gold Mohrs for your acceptance.[13]

Bowring informs us, 'When he [Tipu[ found that the Great Mughal took offence at the inscription, he pretended that he had merely sent the coins in order to ascertain His Majesty's pleasure about them, and offered an apology for the affront.'[14]

Kirkpatrick describes the new coin in detail:

> On one side is the following legend, written here in the order in which I suppose it is intended to be read: which may be translated, 'the religion, or faith, of Ahmed [i.e., of Mahommed] is rendered luminous on earth by the victories of Hyder. Struck at Putn [i.e., Seringapatam] in the year 1785.'[15]

The Englishman notes, 'He [Tipu] ingeniously managed to impress his coin, not only with one of his own names but also with those of his father and grandfather.'[16] On the reverse of the coin appear the following words: 'He [i.e., God] is the only Sultan [or Lord] and dispenser of justice.'

Kirkpatrick observes, 'It is very remarkable, that the first word in this inscription and, consequently, that which immediately precedes the word Sultan, is so impressed, as to be susceptible, without any extraordinary licence or exercise of the fancy, of being read Tippoo.'[17] If indeed this was the Sultan's intention, the coin would read, 'Tippoo, the only Sultan, the just.'[18] The coin was minted on the anniversary of Tipu's enthronement, 'which took place on the 3rd of Behary of the year Sukh, corresponding, as nearly as I can calculate, to the 10th of May 1783; and being, therefore, somewhat more than five months subsequent to the death of Hyder'.[19] This is indeed an intriguing fact. Why was the coronation delayed for so long?

## Poetry and Panegyric

Tipu Sultan, like many other rulers of his time, revelled in praise. Among the documents discovered in his palace were numerous poems composed in his honour. Kirkpatrick, who translated some of them, reveals:

> [The] concluding distich of each ode, which is in Persian, the rest of the composition is in the Hindivy dialect, which is, indeed, denoted by the term raikhteh. These odes are ninety-six in number; and consist, on the one hand, of the most fulsome and hyperbolical praises of the Sultan, and on the other, of disparaging allusions to the English, the Mahrattahs, and the Nizam.... They are utterly destitute of every kind of poetical merit. Of these curious compositions, which were set to music, and sung, or recited, at appointed seasons and hours of the day, the following extracts may suffice as a specimen .... 'The flash of his sabre struck the army of Bailey like lightning: it caused Munro to shed tears'.... 'When the Mahrattahs behold this army of our King, the dread thereof causes them to flee like deer'.... 'The Fringy [i.e., the European] and Nizam ul Mulk pass night and day together trembling with fear of our King.'[20]

## Perverse Punishments

Kirmani narrates an episode that unfolded near Sathyamangalam in the year 1790 when Tipu was at war with the British:

> [Tipu's soldiers] having surrounded the followers of the British army in the forest of Dindigul, after killing and wounding many, took prisoners some of the soldiers with their women, muskets and baggage, the latter tied in bundles on their heads. Among these were some Muhammadan women, who from want of shame and fear of a hereafter, had gone aside from their religion, and had given up their impure bodies to the lust of men of other religions, and they according to the orders of the Sultan were impaled.[21]

In a letter to Budruz Zaman Khan dated 13 August 1786, Tipu writes about the punishment of the 'insurgents' of Soopah:

> Ten years ago, from ten to fifteen thousand men were hung upon the trees of that district; since which time the aforesaid trees have been waiting for [or been in expectation of] more men. You must [therefore] hang upon trees all such of the inhabitants of that district, as have taken a lead in [or been at the bottom of] these rebellious proceedings.[22]

Kirkpatrick reckons, 'The dreadful executions, here spoken of with so much levity by the Sultan, must refer to the time of his father, in the year 1776.'[23]

He notes:

> At the head of it [Tipu's embassy to Constantinople] was Mahommed Othman Khan, who had formerly filled the station of Hyder Ali Khan's Vakeel at Madras.... Major Stuart relates, on the authority of a French writer, that Othman Khan and one of his colleagues were put to death by the Sultan on their return from France.[24]

The sultan wrote to Mahommed Ushruf on 17 May 1785, 'You must scourge the defaulters severely, and speedily realize the dues of the Sircar.'[25] This was, perhaps, the simplest method of revenue collection. Tipu sent a letter on 15 December 1786 to Mahommed Ghyas and Noor Mahommed Khan, 'Your two letters, of the 23rd and 24th November, have been received, and what you state, respecting the misconduct of the Brahmens, is known...Let them be separately flogged.'[26] There were simple punishments for minor offences and gruesome ones for serious transgressions.

Another letter dated 30 August 1786 instructed Budruz Zuman Khan, 'The aforesaid captives must be dispatched to Nugr and incorporated with the Usud Ilhyes; to such of whom as are without wives, the females among the prisoners are to be given in marriage.'[27] Fixing marriage alliances was also a straightforward task for the sultan.

A circular dated 16 December 1786 was dispatched to the Seven Superintendents of the Post, at the seven capital cities of the sultanate, stating:

> We have fixed the Coss at six thousand Gvz, which distance must be travelled by the postmen in a ghurry and a half [or thirty-three minutes and forty-five seconds]. If the letters appertaining to your province are not delivered according to this rate, and any delay arises, you must flog the Hurkurehs belonging to you.[28]

Kirkpatrick states:

> I am not able to specify, with any certainty, the seven capital cities intended by the title of the present letter: but there can be little or no doubt, that Seringapatam, Nugr, and Bangalore, were among the number; while it is not improbable, that the other four were Chittledoorg, Gooty, Gurramcoondah, and Sera.[29]

Interestingly, Kirkpatrick does not mention any Malabar location. Can we conclude that the sultan's hold over Malabar was tenuous at best? Coorg is also absent. This could imply that either the sultan lacked administrative control over Coorg or had no intention of sending any posts there.

On 29 October 1786, Tipu wrote to the Bukhshy of Ehsham at Gooty instructing him 'to chastise the turbulent [or seditious] wherever they raised the head of the revolt; and after making them prisoners, to place those under age in the Ahmedy band, and to hang the remainder'.[30] Circumcision or execution was deemed appropriate punishment for disobedience.

To Mahommed Mehdy at Seringapatam, Tipu's instructions on 14 May 1786 were, 'You must not suffer anyone to come to your house; and whatever business you may have to do, let it be transacted in our Kuchurri. If, nevertheless, people should persist in coming to your house, they shall be deprived of their ears and noses.'[31]

Chetti recounts:

> Sabbl Rani Tittu, the elevated ground to the right of the high road leading to Ganjam on which a cenotaph now stands is said to have been the place where Tippu Sultan in order to enforce strictness of

> morals is said to have cruelly punished with a red-hot iron crow-bar a woman charged with adultery.[32]

He also describes the heartless manner in which prisoners of war were treated:

> The Killedar of Chitaldrug after threatening the 17 British officers who had surrendered themselves along with General Matthews at Bednore, in a most cruel manner, administered to them poison when they asked for drinking water to quench their extreme thirst. A list of the prisoners will be found in the Appendix.[33]

Bowring provides an account of Tipu's methods of torture:

> Those who conspired against him were put in a cage. This was an imitation of Haidar's treatment of Khande Rao. The unhappy victims were allowed half a pound of rice a day, with salt, but no water, so they soon expired under this frightful ordeal. There were other punishments nearly equally dreadful, such as making men bestride a wooden horse on a saddle studded with sharp spikes. On a spring being touched the horse of torture reared, and the spikes penetrated the unfortunate wretches.[34]

James Scurry also provides shocking descriptions of the sultan's unique implements of torture.
Bowring asserts:

> A more common mode of punishment was to bind tightly the hands and feet of condemned men, and then to attach them by a rope to the foot of an elephant, which, being urged forwards, dragged them after it on the rough ground, and painfully terminated their existence. Some again were ruthlessly thrown into the dens of tigers to be devoured, and it is said that three of Tipu's high officials met with this fate. Cutting off of ears and noses was a general practice, and was frequently inflicted on defaulters, thieves, and peccant subordinates.[35]

Tipu's orders to his revenue commissioners, as translated by Iqbal Husain, provide evidence of his perverse nature. Order No.20 explicitly states, 'Anyone who steals property worth more than two-and-a-half rupees shall be punished with the cutting off of his or her hands.'[36] Order No. 55a states, 'Let not the soldiers or anyone else distil alcohol in your territory. If any case is reported go out and verify the facts and then cut off the hands of the offender. Similar punishment is to be meted out to those who cultivate *bhang*.'[37]

## Dr Tipu's Prescriptions

If Tipu had not become a soldier, he could have been a successful physician or veterinarian, or so his letters would have us believe.

On 12 September 1785, he wrote to Syed Mahommed, the kilaadar of Seringapatam:

> It has been reported to us, that the Mutusuddy of the Jyshe, Kishna Rao, has been bitten by a mad dog... you will give the aforesaid [Mutusuddy] in particular charge to the physician, Mahommed Baig, who must administer to him the proper medicines in such cases, and restore him to health. He must also be told not to let the discharge from the wound stop, but to keep it open for six months.[38]

On 24 May 1786, Tipu wrote to Chishty Yar Khan I Zynul Aabideen:

> 'Your letter' ... has informed us of Dowlat Khan's being ill of the stone in the bladder: we have, in consequence, sent by the post an emetic [to be taken the first day], together with medicines for the seven subsequent days.... The way of taking an emetic is this: dissolving the powder in about four tolah weight of hot water, let him swallow it. After this, whenever he feels inclined to vomit, he must drink eight tolah weight of warm water. When he has vomited five or six times, let him, after an interval of six hours, have some broth mixed with rice. In the evening, before he eats his dinner make him take, in a little cold water, half a tolah weight of a seed of flea-wort softened with some oil of almonds. By the favour

> of God, in one or two vomitings, the stranguaiy, or obstruction of urine, will be removed. The following morning [after the vomit] a dose of the other medicine is to be taken in eight tolahs of syrup of ab-shakh and radish leaves. This course is to be pursued for seven days, during which the patient need not abstain from acids, but must avoid eating black and red pepper, and other heating and flatulent things. The diet should be curry of radishes with boiled rice, and his drink an infusion of musk-melon seeds, cucumber seeds, and dry thorn, of each half a tolah weight. By this means, if there should even be a stone [in the bladder] it will be passed.[39]

In a letter to Ghulam Ali Khan on 7 January 1786, from his camp at Talakaveri, Tipu stated:

> The camphor tree has been [recently] discovered in this part of the Sircar's country. We have sent two bottles of the essential oil made from it, for your use. You must rub your feet with it, and take it [inwardly] in meat-broth ... inform us what benefit you may receive from the use of it.[40]

Kirkpatrick notes, 'Ghulam Ali Khan was afflicted with some scrophulous or rheumatic complaint, which had rendered him a cripple.'[41]

Tipu's credentials as a doctor are highly suspect, especially considering that he often tried to play the role of a veterinarian as well. He wrote to Shah Noorullah on 4 February 1786:

> It is owing to the whoreson tricks and roguery of the elephant keepers that the elephants have been made to get hot: you must, therefore, flog them [the keepers] well. If, after all, one of the elephants proceeding with you [to Constantinople] should continue hot, you must separate him from the other [or others], by putting him on board a different vessel.[42]

Kirkpatrick observes, 'In a letter of the following day the Sultan repeats his orders for separating the must [hot] and tame elephants, with an addition, purporting, "that the proper medicines should be given to the hot elephant for expelling his heat".'[43] Tipu was not only planning to send an elephant in *musth* on a long voyage to Constantinople, but he also prescribed that the best way to keep the elephant under control was to whip the mahout.

## Jester Tipu

Tipu Sultan could at times exhibit a sharp wit. Wilks presents a quaint example of his sense of humour. Ghulam Ali Khan, upon his return from Turkey, was relieved of all his positions and ordered to remain in his house. This punishment was preceded by an investigation. After all, only 68 of the 900 men who had set sail on that ill-fated mission had returned to Mysore, with nothing to show for their troubles.

One evening, Tipu Sultan instructed one of his officers to 'call the man-eaters'. The confused man did not understand what the sultan meant. Tipu then clarified that he should 'call the men who had lately returned from Room [Constantinople], after eating their companions'.[44] This became a standing joke in the kingdom, and the hapless ambassadors to Turkey were soon nicknamed 'man-eaters'.

## Trader Tipu

Tipu regularly corresponded with Meer Kazim, the *darogha* or commercial consul of Mysore, who was stationed in Muscat. On 17 November 1785, he wrote, 'Juzeerah Diraz is in that quarter. Silkworms and their eggs are produced there. We wish you to procure some of both, and to dispatch them to us, together with five or six men, acquainted with the proper mode of rearing them.'[45] On the same day, he wrote another letter directing Meer Kazim to hire and dispatch ten individuals skilled in pearl fishing to Mangalore.[46] Kirkpatrick notes that 'Juzeerah Diraz [or Long Island] is the Kismish of our maps, and situated in the Gulf of Persia'.[47]

On 19 November 1785, the sultan's message to Meer Kazim stated, 'You must not be in haste to dispose of the cinnamon, sandalwood, black pepper, and rice, imported at Muscat from Mangalore and Khooshhdipoor. Keep them carefully, till they become dear, and will yield a [good] profit, and then sell them.'[48] A week later, on 25 November, another missive was sent, 'Having ascertained in what part of that country saffron is cultivated, engage two persons in our service, and send them thither to purchase one or two maunds of the seed, which [when procured] is to be dispatched to us.'[49] On the same day, another letter urged Meer Kazim, 'You are to buy yearly, and send to the Aumil of Mangalore, a hundred Utls of almonds, and thirty Utls of pistachio-nuts.'[50] The sultan meticulously oversaw activities such as identifying markets, procuring goods at optimal prices, hoarding and selling at opportune moments.

On 9 December 1785, Tipu sent another message to Meer Kazim, providing explicit instructions regarding the sale of commodities:

> The first sort of sandalwood you must sell at the rate of one hundred and twenty pagodas the candy; the second sort at one hundred pagodas; the third sort at ninety pagodas; the fourth sort at eighty pagodas; and black pepper at eighty pagodas the candy. You must not sell them at any other [i.e., not at less] prices than these.[51]

He further instructed, 'Go to Hurmuz, and buy there large rolling [i.e., perfectly round] pearls: small pearls are not wanted.'[52]

Mao Saith, Tipu's agent in Muscat, also received regular correspondence. On 16 January 1786, Tipu wrote to him:

> With respect to our establishing factories [as you propose] at Port Mundry in Kutch, and at the port of Jamnugr, our intention is, to dispatch, some time hence, trusty persons, with letters and the customary tokens of friendship to the Rajahs of both those places. On this occasion we shall require you to introduce our agents to the two Rajahs, and to procure the necessary permission for the establishment of factories.[53]

On 24 April 1786, Tipu wrote to Meer Kazim:

> You have done well, in buying and lading on our ships, rock-salt, instead of sapphires. For the future, you will, in like manner, send rock-salt instead of sapphires. The carpenters at Muscat construct very excellent Dows and Dingies. You must advance to four or five of these carpenters whatever money they may require for their expences, and dispatch them to the port of Mangalore.... You must take care and sell the sandal wood, black pepper, rice, and cardamums, belonging to us, to the best advantage, sending an account of your sales and purchases regularly to Ghulam Mahommed.... Procuring, moreover, some [pearl] divers from Bahrain and Hormuz; and making them whatever advances they may require for their expences, dispatch them hither, together with their families.[54]

On 12 January1786, Tipu informed Meer Kazim:

> Your letter, accompanied by a sealed packet of pearls, with a memorandum of the prices at which they were bought, has been received. The pearls you have sent have, on the whole, been purchased at a very heavy price. If they can be procured cheaper in Bahrain you must send thither for them. There is, at the same time, no objection to your buying them at Muscat, when they can be had cheap there. Making some advance to ten divers, dispatch them to the Presence, as they are wanted for the purpose of diving or fishing for pearls on the shore of Mangalore ... We want ten ship-wrights, acquainted with the construction of Dows. Get them together, and dispatch them hither.[55]

Kirkpatrick opines:

> [Tipu Sultan] not only exported rice to Muscat in his own vessels, and imported the commodities of that country into Mysore, but he also obliged the Muscat merchant to purchase all the government rice on hand, at a price fixed probably by himself, before he allowed him to buy elsewhere. In addition to these restraints, there is reason

> to believe, that the most profitable branches of the commerce of his dominions, namely sandalwood, betelnut, pepper and cardamoms, were entirely monopolized by the Sultan.[56]

He also opines, 'The Sultan's anxiety to establish a pearl fishery on the Coast of Malabar, as well as to introduce the culture of the silk-worm into his dominions, appears to have been very considerable; but I believe that he failed entirely in both attempts.'[57] Kirkpatrick's assessment was partially inaccurate, as the Mysore silk industry continues to thrive today.

## Miser Tipu

Tipu's correspondence with members of his delegation to Turkey reveals his frugal nature. In a letter to Mahommed Ghyas and Noor Mahommed Khan dated 27 July 1785, he wrote, 'You write for a supply of money and represent the dearness of everything there. Now that you are about to return hither, where is the necessity of making you a remittance for your expences?'[58]

Referring to Tipu's letter to Burhanuddeen dated 6 June 1785, Kirkpatrick writes:

> Parsimony, or perhaps, more strictly speaking, a rigid economy in his general expenditure, was always known to be a prominent feature in the character of Tippoo Sultan; and we have here a curious and striking proof of the fact. One of his principal generals, and his brother-in-law, is obliged to apply to him for the means of providing himself with wearing apparel.[59]

On 15 December 1785, the sultan wrote to Shah Noorullah, who was preparing to sail for Turkey:

> You are to proceed to Mangalore; and there obtaining from the Aumil of that place whatever supplies [or stores] may be required for the use of the ships, you are to dispatch the latter to Tidry. You write, proposing to take fifteen hundred wax candles, besides wax. Where is the necessity for so many wax candles? Get the Aumil to deliver what number may be [really] requisite.[60]

Tidry is a small harbour on the Canara coast, where Tipu's ships were anchored when not in use. Tipu continued, 'You moreover write, that the Aumil of Mangalore delivers to you "only old and black rice". It is known. That rice is good. You must take it, and not engage in improper altercation.'[61]

## Dreamer Tipu

It has been suggested that Tipu was a megalomaniac and a dreamer, harbouring numerous illusions that fuelled his grandiose plans. It is possible that he lacked effective advisors or that he chose not to heed their counsel. Perhaps, the wise men in his employ were terrified of him, leading them to withhold their opinions.

On 1 March 1786, Tipu wrote to Ghulam Ali Khan, Lutf Ali Khan, Shah Noorullah Khan and Mahommed Hunee, expressing his wish to obtain control of the port of Basra (located in modern-day Iraq).[62] He went on to add:

> From thence you must repair straight to Nujuf … where you will represent in the most respectful and submissive manner, that if it is agreeable [to the priests in charge of the holy shrine] to have an aqueduct brought to Nujuf the noblest [from the Euphrates] … we will, in the following year, send the necessary people and money for its construction.[63]

Tipu's seemingly impractical scheme to build a canal from the Euphrates to Najaf must have sounded preposterous to those contacted by his delegates. They might have even doubted his sanity.

Tipu dreamt of Mysore becoming a naval power on par with the European nations, but this dream never materialized. When Tipu lost Malabar in 1792, he lost access to the teak forests and the ports essential for ship building. Furthermore, Mysore, being a land-locked region, lacked individuals with sailing skills. How could Tipu Sultan have built ships without wood? Where would the sailors come from? The navy remained yet another of the sultan's unattainable aspirations.

Bowring states:

> In 1796 a Board of Admiralty, consisting of eleven persons, was nominated under the appellation of Mir Yam, or sea-lords, under whom were to be thirty Mir Bahar or commanders of the fleet. The Navy was to consist of twenty line-of-battle ships, and twenty large frigates, of which six of each class were to be stationed at Jamalabad or Mangalore, seven of each at Wajidabad near the Mirjan creek, and seven at Majidabad or Sadashivgarh.... The Sultan kindly sent a model to the Admiralty Board for their guidance in building the ships, ordering them to have copper bottoms, and prescribing where the timber for them was to be cut. Minute details were furnished as to the complement of the ships, and the pay of all grades. It was amusingly ordered that twenty of the Mir Bahar, or those highest in rank, were to receive a horse allowance and that when the Mir Yam visited the fleet, they should get a specially good dinner, with fruit, at the expense of the Government. This grand scheme for creating a navy came to nothing.[64]

Tipu dreamed of driving the British out of India and defeating the Marathas in battle, yet none of these ambitions materialized. He also envisioned Napoleon coming to India or sending French forces to aid him against the British, an idea that seemed far-fetched at the outset and finally came to nought. Even the French Revolution did not open his eyes. Tipu even imagined that the Afghan king and the Ottoman caliph could help him, but their distant locations and personal agendas made such alliances impractical. Thus, Tipu's attempts to forge international coalitions ended in tragic failure. In reality, his immediate neighbours, both Hindus and Muslims, turned against him. Poona, Hyderabad, Coorg, Malabar, Arcot – all sought the intervention of the British to counter Tipu's threats.

## The Sultan's Idiosyncrasies

Though a gallant soldier and an able commander, Tipu was conceited and prone to violent anger. He was brutal in meting out punishments for both real and imaginary offences. His behaviour was whimsical, impulsive and merciless, often bordering on insanity. His religiosity leaned towards fanaticism, and his concept of justice was tinged with sadism. By tampering with the calendar and zealously re-naming towns, Tipu caused chaos and consternation not only within his kingdom but also beyond its borders.

Bowring points out that the sultan also amended the standard measures of distance:

> The kos thus fixed was 2 ¾ miles, and if the letter carriers did not travel this distance in 33 ¾ minutes they were to be flogged. All the names of weights and measures were altered. But the most wonderful of his improvements was his new method of calculating time ... Tipu founded a new calendar on this basis, giving however fantastic names to the years, and equally strange ones to the lunar months. The year, according to his arrangement, only contained 354 days, and each month was called by some name in alphabetical order. From the year 1784, all his letters were dated according to the day of one or other of the months in this new nomenclature.[65]

Wilks recounts an incident when a commotion erupted in the bazaar at Srirangapatna. Foot soldiers grabbed stocks of rice due to its acute scarcity. Upon hearing of the incident, Tipu Sultan ordered the bazaar to open only one day a week. This decree was brutally enforced, leading to widespread suffering and the spoilage of perishable goods. After about a month of hardship, the rule collapsed under its own weight. Wilk avers, 'The most dreadful confusion and distress ensued; and at the expiration of about forty days, the shops gradually opened without orders and without notice.'[66]

In 1798, Tipu famously drained the Moti Talab (Lake of Pearls), a huge body of water formed by an embankment constructed in the gap between two rocky hills in the Tonnur area. His objective was to prevent its use by enemy forces coming to besiege Srirangapatna. This event is recounted by several authors.[67] The water flowed into another lake (Heroor), which was also drained. The impact on the environment and the local populace can be well imagined. The embankment was later rebuilt.

Chetti's version of this event states:

> Tonnore or Yadavapuri, once the powerful capital of the Ballala Rajas... is in ruins and has dwindled down into an insignificant village. The reservoir is so large as to deserve the name of a lake ...It was named 'Moti Talav' by Nazir Jung in 1746. The waters of the Yadava Nadi, a mountain stream, which forces its way through the valley between the two rocky hills, is said to have been stopped and filled by a mound 28 feet high, 225 feet long and 375 feet thick... The bed of this tank is about 15 miles in circumference...During the reign of the Sultan, on the unfounded report that a great treasure lay embedded in the mound as well as a golden vehicle of the god Narayana, he cut a trench through the mound in 1788; the velocity and the force of the water undermined and swept away the mound convincing Tippu Sultan of the absurdity of the report. The tank was afterwards repaired by Dewan Purnaiya.[68]

Buchanan's report reveals that both the British and Tipu cut down sandalwood trees, 'In the Coleagala (Kollegal) district are some sandalwood trees, which are now cutting by the collector, who employs a Mussulman agent. Fifteen years ago, the sultan cut the whole of the large trees.'[69] Tipu also ordered the cutting down of palm trees since they were used for making palm wine. Moreover, he was responsible for the large-scale destruction of pepper vines in Malabar.

Bowring remarks:

> In addressing even great foreign potentates, such as the King of France, he used expressions only suitable when writing to an inferior. The climax of his arrogance was reached when he ordered the Khutbah, or daily prayer in the mosques, to be read in his own name, instead of that of the Mughal Emperor.[70]

Tipu's management style was a combination of micro-management and severe punishments. His subordinates were naturally terrified of him. Wilks notes:

> Yet with all this parade of being the master of every detail, he was ignorant of the contents of his 'tosheckkhana' royal warehouse of the capital, to the extent of sending to Poona, on the occasion of a marriage, for a small quantity of old cloths, of which a ton at the least, was found in the store at the capture of the capital.... Spanish guns were found ornamented with the tiger stripe and inscriptions, purporting that they were cast at Seringapatam.[71]

The sultan was not averse to a bit of cheating here and there!

In 1788, when Tipu conceived the idea of sending his son to Paris for higher education, his ambassadors to the court of Louis XVI presented this proposal to the French king. The French expressed their willingness to entertain the idea but suggested it would be better for the boy to learn some French as well as arithmetic before moving to France. However, Fate had other plans in store for both Tipu Sultan and France. The outbreak of the French Revolution in 1789 tragically ended the lives of the emperor and his family. Additionally, Tipu was defeated by the British in 1792, resulting in him surrendering two minor sons as hostages, effectively putting an end to his aspirations for foreign education for his children.

Tipu's embassy to Turkey harboured several grand designs. Initially, the sultan dreamed of acquiring Basra from the Ottoman sultan in exchange for any port on the west coast of southern India. However, this absurd suggestion did not find favour with Sultan Selim. In a hukumnama issued on 17 November 1785, Tipu advised his ambassadors to persuade the sultan of Turkey to lease the port of Basra to him. Irfan Habib observes:

> Tipu's instructions required his envoys to send him the Sultan of Turkey's letter approving the lease of Basra to the Mysore government. Colonel Wilks appears to have derived information from the English factors at Constantinople as well as from Kirkpatrick, about the negotiations that took place between Sayyid Ghulam Ali and the Vazir of Turkey. He says that the proposal greatly annoyed the interpreter, who warned him against making such a proposal.[72]

The irony lies in the fact that all three ships dispatched for this grand mission met their demise in the vicinity of Basra.

Tipu's second offer was even more outlandish. Iqbal Husain's translation of Tipu's briefs prepared between 1785 and 1786 provides a clear insight into his grandiose plans.

This mighty south Indian ruler, who never constructed a single canal in his own kingdom but instead poisoned water bodies and drained up lakes, actually dreamed of building a canal in faraway Iraq.

Wilks reflects on the likelihood 'that an intellect too weak for such a giddy height occasionally tottered on the verge of insanity'.[73] Referring to a crazed military march ordered by the sultan, he observes:

> He [Tipu] was apprised by men of cooler heads that the monsoon had commenced; he determined to march through the depth of it to Coimbetoor, answering those who attempted to dissuade him, that he would order the clouds to cease discharging their waters until he should have passed.[74]

The result of this conceited stance was that '[the] clouds were not controlled, and the army suffered the greatest hardships, in their tedious march through the swamps, the floods, and the unceasing torrents of rain, until their arrival at Coimbetoor'.[75]

Wilks further states:

> The Sultaun's letters show that he had written to Louis XVI to send him three medical persons, a physician, a surgeon, and an apothecary, and on the return of his embassy [from France] … two of these gentlemen were presented to him at Coimbetoor. The physician after being introduced, demanded his dismission, but however strongly vouched … to Heckeem Wasil, the native physician-in-waiting, that he perceived in the Sultaun symptoms of incipient madness.[76]

According to De la Tour, 'He [Tipu] reduced his cavalry and augmented the infantry. He adopted Persian and Tartar terms for the words of command, which were formerly given in English or French, and gave new names to the different divisions of the army.'[77] Tactical blunders, one after another.

Habib notes that the sultan ordered '[workshops] of iron and steel should be established in the localities, their products to be sent to the government or sold in the market. And there should be no distillation of alcohol or cultivation of bhang.'[78]

Tipu, a Sunni Muslim, also harboured Shiite inclinations and beliefs. He held reverence for Sufism and provided grants to Sufi saints. He also entertained Hindu sadhus, fed Brahmins and funded certain Hindu religious ceremonies. His faith in astrology intensified after his defeat at the hands of the British in 1792.

Tipu named his kingdom Sultanat-i-Khudadad, meaning God-given kingdom. (Although, some might argue it was dad-given!) He is said to have performed namaz five times a day, carried his rosary at all times and observed the Ramadan fasts. His fervour for jihad is evident – at least he invoked the term 'jihad' whenever he found it expedient. As a ruler of Hindu subjects, he likely refrained from using it frequently at home.

Tipu appealed to Muslim sentiments whenever it suited his purposes. Whether attempting to sway the nizam to his side, placate the Ottoman sultan or the king of Afghanistan, he invoked Islam and jihad. However, when dealing with Napoleon, the emperor of France, or the governor of Isle de France, the focus shifted to the French–British rivalry and the sharing of Indian territories. Similarly, when appealing to the Marathas to oppose the British, he tried to arouse their patriotic sentiments. Undoubtedly, Tipu was a cunning strategist, if not an unscrupulous manipulator.

Tipu invaded not only the Muslim principalities of Hyderabad, Adoni, Savanur, Kurnool and Arcot but also targeted the Marathas, the Nairs of Malabar and the Hindu rajas of Coorg. Additionally, he conducted a conversion campaign targeting the Christians of Mangalore.

Mohibbul Hasan opines that theology and Sufism were Tipu's favourite subjects, although he also displayed a keen interest in science, engineering, medicine, sericulture, astrology, calligraphy and music. However, the undeniable truth is that the sultan's primary passion was warfare.

# 15

# VELLORE AND OTHER REVOLTS

The first major rebellion by Indian sepoys (an anglicized form of the Hindi word 'sipahi', meaning soldier) occurred on 10 July 1806, in Vellore in the North Arcot district of present-day Tamil Nadu. Referred to by the British as the Vellore Mutiny, today the Tamils recognize it as the First War of Independence, as this uprising predates the revolt of 1857 by half a century.

In addition to the Vellore Revolt, several other insurrections occurred across various regions of British India throughout the 18th and 19th centuries, leading up to the 1857 War of Independence, during which the British nearly lost their hold on the 'Jewel in the Crown'.

## Forgotten Rebellions

In 1757–1758, a hundred years prior to the 1857 War of Independence, a rebellion erupted among the palayakkars of the 'Madura' and 'Tinnevelly' districts. Pulithevar of Nelkettumseval village, situated in Tirunelveli district, led the revolt against the British and their ally, Muhammad Ali, the nawab of Arcot. Pulithevar refused to pay taxes, leading to the village being known locally as *Nel-kettadha-seval* or 'non-tax-paying village' for many years thereafter. ('Nel' referred to paddy; in those days, taxes were often paid in grain.)

The British had yet to establish themselves as a formidable power in India. Haider Ali held the position of faujdar of Dindigul, a territory recently conquered by the Mysore army. The Tamil country consisted of about seventy-seven *palayams* or military camps governed by palayakkars or military chiefs. These were breakaway factions of territories previously under the control of the Nayakas or provincial governors of the Vijayanagar kingdom, which had collapsed two centuries earlier. The confrontation between the palayakkars and the British persisted for over half a century and was labelled by the English as the 'Poligar Rebellion'. However, it was far from being a single event. Instead, it constituted one of the bloodiest chapters in the people's resistance to foreign domination, where the raw courage of the locals clashed with the superior firepower of the British occupiers.

Pulithevar hailed from a martial community then referred to as Maravas, but today they prefer to be known as Thevars. Engaging in the dangerous sport of *jallikattu*, where the participants bravely grappled with bulls, was a prominent aspect of their valorous tradition.

In 1755, the East India Company dispatched an army led by Colonel Alexander Heron to the western palayams for tax collection. Accompanied by the Arcot nawab's forces under the command of his elder brother, the army indulged in widespread looting. However, they faced stiff resistance at Nelkettumseval, where Pulithevar's stone fortress proved impregnable. Heron was forced to retreat and subsequently faced a court-martial, resulting in his dismissal by the company.

Soon, the Western palayakkars formed a confederacy under the leadership of Pulithevar. They recaptured all the forts occupied by the Arcot forces and re-established their control over Tirunelveli. Additionally, they forged a strategic alliance with the raja of Travancore, who commanded a formidable standing army trained by a Dutchman. After several years of armed conflicts, Pulithevar encountered a formidable adversary in the form of Yusuf Khan, a man with extraordinary capabilities and a newcomer to the military scene. Originally Maruthanayagam Pillai, he had converted to Islam and aligned himself with the Arcot nawab. Yusuf Khan gradually gained influence, attracting many powerful nobles away from

Pulithevar's camp, causing a decline in the latter's strength. With the Raja of Travancore joining forces with Yusuf Khan, Pulithevar's fate was sealed. When enemy forces besieged Nelkettumseval, Pulithevar had no option but to flee to the forests. It is said he died in exile in Ramnad, but rumours suggest that he was later captured by Yusuf Khan's troops, taken to the remote Kalugamalai (Vulture Hill) and secretly executed, probably around the year 1761.

The first mutiny by Indian troops occurred in Tellicherry in early 1780. Upon learning that they would not be relieved by the Bombay forces as promised, the Carnatic battalions from the Madras Coast Infantry raised the banner of revolt. The British response was brutal and instantaneous. One mutineer was executed by being blown from a gun, and two others received a punishment of 1,000 lashes each.

In October 1780, the Circars' battalions of the Coast Infantry mutinied at Visakhapatnam when they were ordered to sail to Madras. During the mutiny, they shot dead three British officers, marking the first instance of British soldiers dying at the hands of Indian mutineers.

On 16 October 1799, barely six months after the fall of Tipu Sultan, the gallant Veerapandiya Kattabomman was hanged in the village of Kayathar in Thoothukudi (Tuticorin) district, approximately 25 kilometres from Tirunelveli. Kattabomman, the palayakkar of Panchalankurichi, had consistently resisted British rule and was only thirty-nine years old when he attained martyrdom. He deserves recognition as one of the pioneers of India's freedom struggle.

Kattabomman's tale is a saga of determined resistance against a vastly superior force. After the Carnatic Wars, the nawab of Arcot gained control over extensive territories in present-day Tamil Nadu with British assistance. He owed substantial debts to the British, and eventually granted them the authority to collect taxes from his feudatories. However, certain palayakkars refused to acknowledge the supremacy of both the nawab and the British.

'Taxes' and 'tribute' were euphemisms for what was in fact 'protection-money'. Taxes were paid by the vulnerable to the powerful, ensuring they remained undisturbed. How could a group of foreign merchants collect taxes from indigenous populations if not by coercion? The British possessed a powerful standing army, equipped with muskets and cannons. Thus, kings and chieftains who aligned with them emerged as victors, while those who resisted found themselves on the losing side.

Kattabomman was among the palayakkars who staunchly refused to comply with the tax demands imposed by the East India Company. He argued that the prolonged drought conditions in the region warranted exemption from taxation for his principality. In response, the British promptly sent their army to Panchalankurichi to deal with Kattabomman. Initially, the British forces suffered heavy losses, but reinforcements soon arrived from Palayamkottai, compelling Kattabomman to retreat into the forests. A month later, he was captured and subsequently executed, while the Panchalankurichi Fort was razed to the ground.

An elaborate report of Kattabomman's hanging was prepared by Major John Bannerman and forwarded to Governor Edward Clive, the son of Robert Clive. The report commends the undaunted bravery and defiance displayed by 'Cataboma Naigue' until his final moments.

It was rumoured that the Ettayapuram palayakkar had aided the British, facilitating Kattabomman's capture. Today, a common Tamil slang for traitor is *ettapa* or *ettappan*. Bannerman's report mentions that Kattabomman frequently cast scornful glances at the Ettayapuram palayakkar and the palayakkar of Sivagiri, indicating his awareness of their betrayal.

It is plausible that Kattabomman may have intended to coordinate a joint operation with the Marudhu brothers of Sivaganga, Gopala Nayak of Dindigul and others. However, the sudden attack by the British likely forced him to abandon the Panchalankurichi Fort after a futile attempt at resistance.

Five days after Kattabomman's execution, Bannerman made an announcement to all the palayakkars, stating that Kattabomman was hanged because he had 'caused inconvenience to the Company' by joining hands with the palayakkars of Nagalapuram, Kolvarpatti, Ezhayirampannai, Kulathur and Kaadalkudi. All of them were punished by the confiscation of their posts and weapons. The populace was warned that anyone causing similar inconvenience to the company would face a similar fate. This announcement was pompously engraved on copper plates and installed at various locations across the region on 21 October 1799. One of these plates was unearthed in the 1960s in Paavali village in Virudhunagar, 114 km north of Thoothukudi. It is obvious that the British expected resistance from various quarters, as otherwise, such copper plate warnings would have been unnecessary. Additionally, the British arranged for several palayakkars from southern Tamil Nadu to witness the execution of Veerapandiya Kattabomman.

Another rebellion occurred at Coimbatore in 1800. K. Rajayyan in *The South Indian Rebellions: Before and After 1800,* a 2007 compilation by the South Indian History Congress, states, 'The period of struggle lasted from 1795 to 1806 but the effective period was from June 1800 to December 1801.'[1] Sporadic uprisings also occurred in the Konkan, Malabar, the Coromandel and coastal Andhra, with the struggle extending until 1806. These rebellions were brutally suppressed, with deliberate displays of extreme cruelty aimed at instilling fear among the populace. 'They slaughtered the fleeing population, executed the messengers, hanged grandfather, son and grandson upon a common gibbet, paraded the mutilated bodies of the patriots through the streets and piked the severed heads of rebels on the highways.'[2] The Southern Rebellion, characterized by a prolonged resistance led by a confederacy of palayakkars, abruptly ended with the brutal suppression of the Vellore Revolt in 1806.

In June 1801, Marudhu Pandian's proclamation was displayed on the walls of the Srirangam Temple and the nawab's palace in Trichinopoly. The proclamation urged individuals from all castes and religions to unite in rebellion against British rule. It warned the people of India that if they allowed British dominance to continue, the entire country would soon be enslaved by the British.

As explained earlier, Periya Marudhu and Chinna Marudhu (or Marudhu Pandiyan), had accompanied their widowed queen, Velu Nachiyar, into exile in 1772. They returned with her in 1780 to retake Sivaganga, successfully defeating the British. Thereafter, they wielded immense power and influence, and were sometimes regarded as the de facto rulers of Sivaganga. Following the martyrdom of Kattabomman, Marudhu Pandiyan provided sanctuary to his brother, Kumarasamy Nayak, also known as Oomadurai. This action angered the British, who launched a massive invasion of Sivaganga in 1801.

The Marudhu brothers fiercely resisted the British and simultaneously instigated many other palayakkars to unite and rebel against them. The rebellion spread like wildfire, but despite initial successes, the Marudhu brothers were finally captured and executed on 24 October 1801. Alongside them, their sons, grandsons and a large number of gallant patriots, including Oomadurai, met the same fate. Seventy-three individuals who were spared from the gallows were exiled to Prince of Wales Island in Penang, Malaya. Among them was Doraisamy, the youngest son of Marudhu Pandian, who managed to return to his homeland in 1821.

According to K. Gowri in the chapter titled 'Rebellion in the Dindigul Region' from *The South Indian Rebellions: Before and After 1800,* Gopala Nayak, the palayakkar of Virupakshi, was chosen as the confederate leader.[3] The rebels waged a valiant struggle, capturing Dindigul and the southern parts of Coimbatore, expelling the tahsildar from Udumalpet, and destroying the taluk office. However, they were ultimately overpowered. 'On 20th June 1804 the march of the Collector was intercepted near Dindigul.'[4] The British authorities subsequently executed all the rebels, including Gopala Nayak and his son Muthuvel Nayak. Others were banished to Penang.

The palayakkars of Chittoor staged revolts in 1804 as well as 1846. In Karnataka, several rebellions occurred, with Kittur Rani Chennamma's resistance in 1824 standing out. Another significant event was the Canara Revolt or Amara-Sullia Uprising of 1827.

After every rebellion in the south, the British and their allies adopted a scorched earth policy, reminiscent of tactics employed by the Mysore sultans in the past. This approach led to widespread famine and prolonged drought in the affected regions, ultimately consolidating British control for extended periods.

The 1959 Tamil film *Veerapandiya Kattabomman*, starring Sivaji Ganesan, Gemini Ganesan and the sisters Padmini and Ragini, was a box-office blockbuster. Sadly, outside the borders of Tamil Nadu, the names of Velu Nachiyar, Marudhu Pandiyan, Pulithevar and Kattabomman are hardly known, while mainstream historians have consistently and extensively lauded Tipu Sultan.

## Proximate Causes of the Vellore Revolt

The Vellore Fort, built by a feudatory of the Vijayanagar kings, witnessed numerous conflicts throughout its long history. Forces of Aurangzeb once occupied it, and in the 17th century, the Maratha chieftain Shivaji Bhonsle captured it. Robert Clive captured the fort in 1751, six years prior to his decisive victory at the battle of Plassey. In 1756, Muhammad Ali, the nawab of Arcot, gained control of the fort with the support of Clive's English forces. Subsequently, an English garrison was stationed at Vellore, and the nawab remained a staunch ally of the British. Later, Haider Ali and Tipu Sultan briefly held control of the fort.

Many royals were incarcerated within the imposing walls of the Vellore Fort. After defeating and killing Tipu Sultan, the East India Company officials decided that the fort was the most suitable location to house his numerous wives, sons and daughters. New mansions were built within the fort, and the massive retinue lived comfortably for nearly seven years until matters took a sudden and dramatic turn.

On 10 July 1806, preparations were underway for the marriage of one of Tipu's daughters, drawing many visitors from afar who entered the fort the previous day and stayed within the precincts. In the dead of night, the sepoys rose in revolt and attacked the sleeping Englishmen in the barracks and officers' quarters. Almost 14 British officers of the sepoy regiments and 115 white soldiers of the $69^{th}$ Regiment were killed. By daybreak, the fort was under the control of the sepoys, and a flag bearing Tipu Sultan's insignia was raised from the ramparts. There were rumours that the rebels proclaimed Fateh Haider, Tipu's eldest son, as their new king, but this version was rejected by the commission appointed to inquire into the incident.

The sepoys had numerous grievances. They were unhappy about their meagre wages and the treatment meted out to them. Moreover, the British officers' indifference to their social and religious sentiments further fuelled their discontent. The possibility of agrarian distress and animosity towards foreigners sowing the seeds of rebellion cannot be ruled out. In 1806, both North and South Arcot districts experienced famine, exacerbating the suffering of the poor. In this scenario, the insensitivity of British officers and their associates might have acted as the trigger, akin to a lit match igniting a dry haystack.

C.A. Bayly, author of *Empire and Information: Intelligence Gathering and Social Communication in India, 1780–1870,* informs us:

> Travelling puppet shows and theatrical performances also helped spread subversive political ideas. Thus in the months before the Vellore Mutiny of 1806, it was puppeteers that carried the message that Tipu Sultan's sons were about to regain their power, aided by the French.[5]

Vellore had a distinctive Muslim character around the year 1700. James W. Hoover in *Men without Hats: Dialogue, Discipline and Discontent in the Madras Army, 1806–1807,* observes:

> The character of both the town and many of the surrounding villages was decidedly Muslim; Vellore was an Urdu-speaking pocket in a predominantly Tamil and Telugu-speaking area.... During the Second Anglo-Mysore War, Haidar Ali had besieged British-held Vellore, but to his dismay local Muslims had aided the Company garrison with men and supplies. Haidar Ali's forces had retaliated against the people of Vellore by brutally torturing all civilians who fell into their hands – cutting off ears and noses.[6]

When John F. Craddock, commander-in-chief of the Madras Army, issued orders in November 1805 proscribing sepoys from wearing religious or caste marks on their foreheads and mandating the trimming of their moustaches and shaving of their beards, both Hindu and Muslim soldiers were incensed. To add insult to injury, they were given round hats instead of their traditional turbans. Moreover, the new headdress sported a leather cockade, which was offensive to Hindus. Additionally, they were ordered to stop wearing earrings. This sparked suspicion among the people that it was a ruse to gradually convert them to Christianity.

Craddock had indeed been warned by the military board against making any changes to the military gear without considering local sensitivities. However, he ignored this advice, and as a consequence many British soldiers paid with their lives for this decision.

When a few sepoys raised objections against these unpopular orders and refused to wear the new hats, they were taken to Fort St George in Madras and subjected to flogging. Among them, a Hindu and a Muslim, suspected by the British to be the instigators, received ninety lashes each and were dismissed from the army. Nineteen others were pardoned due to their repentance and sincere apologies.

In June 1806, the military auditor general, James Brunton, wrote to Cradock who was encamped in Nandidurg, warning him about the discontent prevailing in the Madras regiments due to the new regulations, and urging him to rescind the order. Craddock referred the matter to his superiors in Madras, whereupon Governor William Bentinck ridiculed him.

The Revolt erupted after simmering for over a month. During this period, there were several clandestine meetings of sepoys, attended by some retainers of Tipu's sons. W. Jones, who was contracted for manufacturing the leather cockades for the new hats, reported receiving death threats from locals. While there were other faint signs of unrest, the British remained complacent. They viewed the sepoys as docile and thus grossly underestimated their capabilities.

K.A. Manikumar, referencing W.J. Wilson, the author of *History of the Madras Army*, notes:

> A European woman, Mrs Burke, attempted to apprise Colonel Fancourt of what she had heard about the plan of murdering all the European officers in the Fort when she went to him to apply for the posthumous reward announced for her husband. But Fancourt damned her as a woman of easy virtue and sent her away.[7]

Colonel John Fancourt, the commander of the Vellore Fort, paid dearly for this mistake. When the rebellion broke out, he responded to the commotion by emerging from his house in his dressing gown. He was shot on the doorstep, and his life ebbed away within a few hours. Fancourt's wife, Amelia Farrer, was the sole surviving eyewitness who provided a detailed account of the progress of the uprising and the murder of her husband and other British soldiers. Lady Fancourt wrote her narrative barely two weeks after the massacre.

It is noteworthy that women and children were spared by the rebels, and only white-skinned males were targeted. James Frost later recounted to a Commission of Enquiry that he was spared by one of the sepoys because he was born in India, while his father, Sergeant Frost, was killed.

## Quelling the Revolt

The rebellion was brutally suppressed. Around 350 sepoys were killed, and an equal number were wounded. At least a hundred others were summarily executed without the pretence of a fair trial. Any brown-skinned soldier within the fort was considered guilty. Moreover, the British scoured the countryside and apprehended anyone found loitering. The number of innocents hanged, shot or executed by cannon fire remains uncertain. Some were sentenced to transportation for life.

The revolt was suppressed by a relief force comprising British soldiers and sepoys from nearby Arcot. A British officer, Major Coates, stationed outside the fort, sent a messenger to alert Colonel

Robert Rollo Gillespie in Arcot. Gillespie promptly left Arcot on receiving the message, and raced ahead of the main force with a small contingent of twenty men. It took only a few hours and some remarkable acts of bravery to quell the rebellion.

On reaching the Vellore Fort around 9 a.m., Gillespie found that about sixty men of the $69^{th}$ regiment, including two doctors, had survived. Despite running out of ammunition, they bravely held a section of the ramparts. Unable to breach the heavily defended gates, Gillespie scaled the massive walls with the help of a rope and promptly led the regiment in a bayonet charge along the ramparts. Upon the arrival of the remainder of his army, he ordered the gates to be blown open and spearheaded a second charge, quickly subduing the rebels and taking control of the fort.

After the British recaptured the fort, nearly a hundred Indian soldiers, who had sought refuge in the palace, were brought out. They were ordered to stand against a wall and executed in cold blood.

Lieutenant Colonel Marriot, the officer in charge of Tipu's family, told Gillespie that he would not allow British soldiers to enter the palace, as he would be held accountable by the British government if anything untoward were to happen to the members. Perhaps Tipu's descendants owe a huge debt of gratitude to Marriot.

In a letter to the commander-in-chief on 11 July, Gillespie wrote:

> I have great satisfaction in informing Your Lordship that none of them have made their escape and they are now in safe custody as I have strong reason for supposing that if not the instigators, they were at least abettors of this infernal plot. Moiz-ud-Deen in particular, the third son, actually sent his own flag to the insurgents and it was hoisted for several hours on the garrison flagstaff.[8]

The British had acted with lightning speed and singular determination. The exploits of Gillespie became legendary in the annals of British colonial history. His prompt and decisive response to the rebellion successfully ensured an epic victory and pre-empted the possibility of any further unrest.

Some of the mutineers were executed by being blown from the mouths of canons, while others were shot or hanged. Many others received life transportation sentences or were discharged from service. Eight of the retainers of the Mysore princes faced trial. Three were later acquitted, one was sentenced to ten years, and another to life imprisonment, while two were condemned to exile in a faraway land. One person received the death penalty.

Eventually, after numerous fact-finding missions, the British concluded that Tipu's sons were not the main instigators of the Vellore revolt. Similarly, half a century later, the enquiry into the Mutiny of 1857 would reveal that the Mughal emperor, Bahadur Shah Zafar, was not a key conspirator. The Mysore royals, as well as the Mughals, were essentially glorified pensioners of the British, accustomed to their cosy and lavish lifestyles. They lacked both the military strength to stage a revolt and the motivation to fight for liberation. In contrast, the common people, burdened by colonial oppression, had little to lose. Thus, the driving force behind many a rebellion was the common soldier.

Zafar was exiled to Rangoon (Yangon) in Burma (Myanmar), similar to Tipu's children who were exiled to Calcutta. After being relocated from Vellore, Muiz-ud-din and Mohi-ud-din spent seven years in jail before being released in 1813. The British possibly viewed them as being complicit in inspiring or instigating the revolt.

The rebellions in both 1806 and 1857 ultimately collapsed. In Vellore, it was swiftly crushed within hours. However, the revolt of 1857 endured for several months, spreading across various regions and culminating in the siege of Delhi, before British forces, with resolute determination, managed to suppress it. In both instances, while the sepoys may have been the initial instigators, they were unable to sustain momentum due to a lack of effective leadership.

## Repercussions and Ripple Effects

Tipu Sultan's sons were under a cloud of suspicion, especially since some of their followers had joined the Vellore rebels. The full extent of the conspiracy and the motives of the civilian conspirators were difficult to ascertain, and as the British executed anyone they even remotely suspected, further trials and collection of evidence appeared to be merely superficial. Perhaps the rebels expected that once they captured the fort, the Indians in the surrounding countryside would join in the revolt. This, however, remains a grey area. What is apparent is that Tipu's heirs did not actively participate in the uprising. It is doubtful whether they did more than offer moral support.

The three Madras regiments involved in the Vellore Mutiny were disbanded. Both Lord William Bentinck, the governor of Madras, and John Cradock were recalled to Britain. (Bentinck, however, returned as the governor-general of India eighteen years later.) The new dress regulations were rescinded, and flogging of soldiers was prohibited.

Half a century later, history was destined to repeat itself. The Revolt of 1857 was triggered by greased cartridges, resulting in a semi-revolution that lasted several months. It included the capture of Delhi and the re-installation of the Mughal emperor before being eventually suppressed with brutal force. The exile of the emperor and the death of Rani Laxmibai of Jhansi are matters of common knowledge.

There is no doubt that the Vellore Revolt of 1806 served as the precursor to the 1857 War of Independence. In both cases, the primary aim of the rebels was the removal of the British. The Mughal emperor in Delhi and Tipu's sons in Vellore were mere rallying points. Particularly in Vellore, there were likely few followers of the Mysore royals, as it was the stronghold of the nawab of Arcot, a staunch ally of the British.

Ferdinand Mount states:

> Even after Gillespie's prompt and brutal suppression, for weeks afterwards, minor uprisings broke out at intervals in towns and at forts within a radius of 50 miles and more. Gillespie had saved Vellore, perhaps, he had saved the Presidency.[9]

Gillespie had indeed secured the future of the British Empire.

During the Vellore Revolt the sepoys massacred the British, and in retaliation, the British massacred the sepoys. Finally, the empire prevailed. It would be a century and a half before the sun finally set on the British Empire. For Indians, there was a long wait ahead, but they did not wait in silence.

It has been suggested that the brutality of the punishments meted out by the British might have deterred the sepoys in South India from joining the rebellion of 1857. However, it is important to note that there was an uprising at Wallajahbad on 27 July, barely two weeks after the Vellore Revolt. This uprising was quickly suppressed by a force led by Gillespie. Further uprisings occurred at Bellary, Hyderabad, Bangalore, Nandidurg, Sankaridurg and Chittoor, all of which the British managed to quell rapidly. Later, alarm bells sounded from Palayamkottai, but the British were already on high alert. Major Welsh disarmed the Muslim sepoys, and reinforcements arrived from Ceylon and Trichinopoly even before any unrest occurred. In April 1807, hundreds of Muslim sepoys were dismissed from service for conspiring to overthrow the British at Palayamkottai.

Manikumar points out that at Palayamkottai many individuals had relatives who were slaughtered by British troops during the Vellore uprising. He explains:

> Towards the third week of November 1806, the Company government believed that the Muslim sepoys in Palayamkottai were about to rise and massacre all the Europeans. According to the plan, some buildings were to be fired at in the cantonment to draw the English officers from their homes, and in the melee, all the English officers were to be slain, the fort was to be seized, and the rebel flag hoisted on the ramparts.[10]

However, the plot was uncovered, and Major Welsh, along with British forces, took elaborate precautions. Despite this, on 6 November, bloodstains appeared on a church door, fuelling dark rumours throughout the town. Welsh 'ordered two prominent native officers to go on an errand to Tirunelveli town. One of the officers objected to going and his open defiance confirmed [his] suspicions'.[11] Thereupon, Welsh disarmed 450 Muslim soldiers pending investigation into the alleged plot.[12] He also sought assistance from the governor of Ceylon, requesting European troops, likening the situation at Palayamkottai to a full-blown revolt. Although troops arrived from Ceylon, they were not deployed, as reinforcements had already arrived from Trichinopoly.

Hindu sepoys received pay hikes and promotions as the British implemented their time-tested policy of divide-and-rule. Later, Welsh was court-martialled, and the Muslim sepoys were reinstated. Following detailed investigations into the alleged 'Mohammedan conspiracy' to overthrow British rule in India, Welsh was finally acquitted. Subedar Sheik Hyder was identified as the main conspirator and summarily dismissed from service. Additionally, two soldiers accused alongside him, Sikandar Khan and Sheik Nutter, were also dismissed. In a report sent to the Court of Directors, Bentinck remarked that 'conditions were ripe for a revolt'.[13]

In Hyderabad, 'Umar Ali, Qadir Beg, Sidi Hussain and Sheik Hussein were identified as ringleaders and transported to the prison at Penang for life'.[14] In Wallajahbad, Subedar Venkata Naik was dismissed from service, and an entire battalion was disarmed. An investigation conducted in Bellary concluded that two faqirs and two sepoys had attempted to incite a revolt. Subedar Mir Bakr was subsequently dismissed from service.

A year after the Vellore Mutiny, Marudhu Pandian's proclamation resurfaced in various locations, such as Trichnopoly and Triplicane in Madras. In Srirangapatna, a French flag was raised. The disturbances were numerous and diverse. The British authorities launched multiple investigations and commissions of inquiry to identify the source and perpetrators of these disturbances. Court-martials were held, resulting in both severe and lenient punishments. Hoover provides intriguing details.

One cannot help but ponder how many undiscovered conspiracies may have petered out due to other unidentified factors.

Bayly informs us, 'A large espionage operation was later established to monitor the contacts of Tipu Sultan's heirs who had been exiled to the British military station of Vellore.'[15] He further adds, 'Certainly, there exist Burmese intelligence documents which refer to multilateral links between the Ava court, Tipu Sultan's heirs, the Marathas, Nepal and an unidentified country in the northwest, possibly the Punjab.'[16]

It seems evident that the British Indian army in southern India was neither content nor tranquil in the early 19th century. The sepoys, though relatively powerless, were far from obedient and servile.

## Velu Thampi Dalawa and the Kundara Proclamation, 1809

Velayudhan Chempakaraman Thampi aka Velu Thampi served was as the prime minister (dalawa) of the Travancore state from 1801 to 1809 during the reign of Balarama Varma. Thampi maintained a good rapport with Colonel Macaulay, the British resident. Born to Nair parents in Talakkulam in 1765, Velu Thampi rose to prominence when he organized a mass revolt in Thiruvananthapuram to demand the removal of an oppressive triumvirate of ministers – Jayantan Sankaran Namboothiri, Sankaranarayana Chetti and Mathu Tharakan.[17] The raja not only dismissed the erring officials but also appointed the rebel leaders as ministers. Velu Thampi was appointed minister of commerce, while his comrade in arms, Chempakaraman Pillai of Chirayinkeezhil, became the dalawa.[18]

In 1801, Velu Thampi assumed the position of dalawa. He implemented reforms to streamline the administration and enhance the efficiency of various departments. However, his measures were often severe, leading to discontent among the soldiers, who eventually mutinied, triggering an unexpected crisis. Velu Thampi fled to Cochin, and Macaulay intervened to suppress the mutiny, thereby enabling the East India Company to strengthen its control over Travancore. A new treaty was negotiated in 1805, granting greater powers to the British and fixing the annual tribute at 8 lakh rupees.[19] As Velu Thampi persuaded the maharaja to sign the treaty, he faced severe criticism. Sreedhara Menon states, 'There was a general feeling that the Dalawa who had all along championed the rights of the people had now betrayed their interests to serve his selfish ends.'[20]

Soon, Velu Thampi clashed with Macaulay due to the latter's undue interference in the state's administration. Velu Thampi became convinced that armed aggression against the British was necessary to regain the kingdom's independence. Meanwhile, Govinda Menon, the Paliath Achan of Cochin, also found himself at odds with Macaulay.[21] In December 1808, Velu Thampi joined hands with Menon and the duo attempted to oust the British from Travancore and Cochin. They recruited soldiers, stockpiled ammunition, strengthened forts and meticulously prepared for an uprising. Soon revolts erupted simultaneously in Cochin and northern Travancore. 'In an outbreak at Alleppey some British officers lost their lives.'[22]

The duo planned to attack the Cochin Fort and assassinate Macaulay. However, on 28 December 1808, when their forces besieged the Bolghatty Palace, the resident managed to escape to a frigate anchored in the harbour.

On 11 January 1809, Velu Thampi issued what became known as the Kundara Proclamation, urging his compatriots to join him in expelling the British from India. However, at the Battle of Quilon (Kollam) on 15 January, Velu Thampi's forces suffered heavy casualties. Subsequently, on 19 January, they attacked Cochin but were repelled. On 30 January, they captured and executed three military officers and thirty English soldiers at Purakkad. Among the executed was the British surgeon Hume, who had once treated Velu Thampi.

Menon observes:

> The British army emerged triumphant in the campaigns against the Cochin forces and Paliath Achan was to ditch his ally Velutampi and extend full support to the British in putting down the insurrection. The defection of Cochin was a big blow to the Dalawa, but Velutampi did not lose heart.[23]

After facing successive defeats, Velu Thampi moved his forces to the southern border of Travancore near the Aramboly Pass. In response, the British sent a force from Trichinopoly to confront him. Following a brief encounter, on 10 February, Velu Thampi fled to Kottar near Nagercoil. His forces suffered defeat at the hands of the British army on 17 February, and shortly thereafter, Padmanabhapuram and Udayagiri fell under British control.

The British promptly demanded that the maharaja surrender the dalawa. Velu Thampi found himself cornered. He fled from Thiruvananthapuram to Kilimanoor after bidding farewell to his sovereign. On 18 March, the maharaja appointed a new dalawa with the approval of the British, and the resident assumed responsibility for the defence of the state. A reward of 50,000 rupees was offered for the capture of Velu Thampi. Thampi left his sword with the raja of Kilimanoor and continued his journey in disguise. The sword was later handed over to the President of independent India.[24]

After seeking refuge in the forests at Kunnathoor for a period, Velu Thampi found sanctuary in the Bhagavathy Temple at Mannadi. However, his hideout was soon detected, and finding himself surrounded, he committed suicide. His brother, Padmanabhan Thampi, was captured and executed by hanging on 10 April 1809. Velu Thampi's body was publicly displayed on a gibbet at Kannamoola. Their ancestral home was demolished, and many of their relatives were exiled to the Maldives, while others faced execution. The Paliath Achan surrendered and was exiled, first to Madras and then to Benares (Varanasi), where he died in 1835. Other leaders, such as Vaikom Padmanabaha Pillai, were hanged at various locations such as Quilon (Kollam), Purakkad and Palthuruthee.

Today, a life-size statue of Velu Thampi stands in front of the government secretariat building in Thiruvananthapuram. Interestingly, one of his descendants is employed at the Kowdiar Palace. This gentleman assisted me in locating the painting of Tipu Sultan, as requested by Princess Aswathi Thirunal.

## A White Mutiny

In 1809, three years after the brutal suppression of the Vellore Revolt, British officers of the Madras army staged their own revolt. This tragic event had been brewing for three years. In a dramatic turn of events, 90 percent of the 1,300 officers commanding native troops in the Madras Presidency refused to obey the orders of their superiors.[25] Mount observes:

> The mutiny spread across virtually all the garrisons and cantonments where the native regiments of the Madras Army were stationed: from Masulipatam, Samulcottah and Ellore in the north-east to Tanjore, Quilon and Cochin in the south, at Madras on the east coast and Goa on the west, through Seringapatam and Chittledroog in the middle and over the borders of the Presidency into Hyderabad.[26]

The initial outbreak happened at Machilipatnam. The first British mutineer was Major Joseph Storey. On 25 June 1809, Storey and a group of men proceeded to the bungalow of Colonel James Innes and placed him under arrest.

A major conflict took place approximately 30 miles from Mysore, where the Chitradurga contingent had assembled. Mount states, 'The official tally was nine dead and 281 missing, but most of the missing were thought to be killed. A realistic estimate might be around 300 dead. The British had no casualties to speak of.'[27] In other words, the mutineers were Europeans, while the casualties were Indians. He further adds:

> By August 22nd the great White Mutiny came to an inglorious end. And several hundred sepoys lay dead in the ditches of Seringapatam, gunned down by Dragoons who were supposed to be their comrades-in-arms. The sepoys had never had any quarrel with the Honourable Company. In marching, they were simply obeying the commands of their discontented officers.[28]

Stephen Chetti provides the following account:

> On the 11th of August 1809, an engagement took place near Seringapatam, where the 'Rana Kambha' known as Webb's Monument now stands. This action took place between a detachment of Mysore Horse under the command of Bakshis Rama Rao and Bhima Rao by order of Sir Arthur Cole, the British Resident in the Mysore Court, and two battalions of British Native Infantry under the command of Col Mackintosh marching from Chitaldrug to join the disaffected garrison at Seringapatam. Col Mackintosh was totally defeated and taken prisoner, with two guns and two colours and delivered into the hands of Col H. Davies commanding Mysore Division. This affair led to the spot being named the 'Rana Kambha' or the Pillar of Bloodshed.[29]

Mount elaborates:

> On September 25, Minto produced a General Order naming three officers – Colonel John Doveton, Major Joseph Storey and Colonel John Bell – to be tried forthwith by court-martial and 18 others to be given the choice between a court-martial and dismissal from service. The other 1,300 officers in the Madras army, loyal and mutinous alike, were forgiven and restored to their former rank and pay.[30]

Fourteen of the accused opted for dismissal without trial, while one officer died, and three others (from the Seringapatam garrison) faced trial. Eventually, no serious action was taken against any of the ringleaders. Many of them were re-employed. Mount emphasizes that this stands in stark contrast to the brutal punishments inflicted upon the Indian mutineers in Vellore only three years earlier.

Ironically, one of the white mutineers, Captain James Lushington, rose to the rank of lieutenant-general, later becoming a director of the East India Company. He eventually found a place among the Tory benches in Parliament.[31]

Mount points out, 'There is not a single firsthand account by a White Mutineer.'[32] The conspiracy of silence persists, leaving many in India unaware of this mutiny.

# 16

# TIPU SULTAN'S MODERN MAKEOVER

Mohibbul Hasan writes, 'Few Indian rulers have been so much maligned and misrepresented as Tipu Sultan.'[1] He contends that after Tipu's death, Englishmen like Kirkpatrick, Wilks and Beatson launched a campaign to vilify the fallen hero, and sadly, their views were accepted by subsequent historians. It is rather ironic that if we label these writers as 'prejudiced', we will logically have to dismiss Hasan's erudite work as part of a glorification effort. The reality is that, in the absence of other corroborating evidence, Tipu's own letters are enough to paint a damning portrait of the 'Tiger' of Mysore.

If Tipu is to be labelled a patriot solely based on his resistance against the British, how do we reconcile his French connection? It is an established fact that French mercenaries were integrated into the Mysore army during both Haider Ali's and Tipu Sultan's reigns. Tipu went as far as inviting Napoleon Bonaparte of France and Zaman Shah of Afghanistan to invade India.

What are we to make of Tipu's overseas delegations? He wished to lease the port of Basra (in modern Iraq) from the Ottoman sultan, offering any port under his control in exchange. He proposed to surrender either Mangalore or Calicut to the Turks. Such actions can be deemed quixotic and unpatriotic. Thankfully, the sultan of Turkey did not respond as Tipu desired. However, the Afghan king did undertake an unsuccessful invasion from India's northwest frontier.

In 1787, yet another Mysorean delegation approached French emperor Louis XVI, offering to cede Madras and other ports on the Coromandel Coast to the French in exchange for the supply of 10,000 troops to assist Tipu in his battles. However, the delegates returned empty-handed in 1789, as the monarchy was overthrown during the French Revolution. Meanwhile, Tipu suffered defeats at the hands of the Marathas and was forced to pay tribute. He also became entangled in conflict with the British, leading to the disastrous outcome of the Third Anglo-Mysore War in 1792.

Tipu, however, remained undeterred. He reached out to Napoleon. In 1798, Napoleon wrote to Tipu, informing him of his arrival in Egypt and declaring his intention to free him from the threat of the British. At this time, Napoleon was merely a military commander in his late twenties. Although he would soon seize power in France through a coup, by then, Tipu would already be dead.

Tipu's embassy to Mauritius in 1798 ultimately led to his downfall. When he sought French assistance to evict the British from India, the governor of Mauritius issued a proclamation urging volunteers to help the sultan by enlisting in his army. This proclamation quickly found its way into the *Calcutta Gazette*, sealing Tipu's fate.

In May 1799, Tipu's major enemies – the Marathas, the nizam and the British – converged upon him. Governor-General Richard Wellesley had meticulously planned the assault. His brother Arthur Wellesley, the future duke of Wellington, commanded one of the battalions, with Baird and Harris leading the charge. The Mysoreans found themselves completely encircled, and Tipu's resistance crumbled within minutes.

## Tipu Sultan's Descendants

For nearly seven years, Tipu's extensive family was confined within the Vellore Fort. Despite their internment, they were kept in comfort and well-provided for. A substantial sum of 2 lakh pagodas was allocated for their maintenance. Records indicate that Tipu's family included twelve sons and eight daughters, as well as numerous mothers, wives, concubines and their attendants.

Fateh Haidar and Abdul Khaliq, the two eldest of the twelve princes, harboured deep animosity toward each other.[2] Tipu had placed considerable trust in Fateh Haider, as the eldest, and many believed he would inherit the throne after his father's passing. Fateh was born to a concubine, whereas Abdul Khaliq's mother was Tipu's legitimate wife.

Fateh Haidar experienced profound depression upon his arrival at Vellore. It is possible that he regretted surrendering, considering that he was outside the fort of Srirangapatna during the British assault. He could have escaped and lived to fight another day, but he was persuaded by Purnaiya to surrender.

After the revolt of 1806, the British authorities suspected the direct involvement of two of Tipu's sons, Moin-ud-Din and Moiz-ud-Din, in the conspiracy. Consequently, they transported the male scions of the clan to Calcutta, where large estates were provided for their accommodation. However, despite the comfortable provisions, they remained virtual prisoners. The transferred retinue included 10 sons, 2 daughters, 3 begums of Tipu, his brother Karim, his nephew Hyder Hussein Khan and a contingent of 300 relatives and attendants. One of Tipu's sons, Jamaluddin Haidar, later moved to England. Accompanying him was Kirmani's precious manuscript, which has since remained in British possession.

It appears that for three or four generations, the descendants of the Mysore sultans lived in relative comfort. Some drank themselves into oblivion and others were mired in scandals, while some lived a dignified life. By the 1900s, a gradual decline had set in, and by the time India gained independence, many surviving descendants of the sultans had fallen into poverty. Tipu's youngest son, Ghulam Shah, was rather prudent, saving money and investing in properties in Calcutta. The land where the Shaw Wallace building now stands once belonged to him.

In a strange turn of events, a female descendant of Tipu Sultan served as a spy for the British during the Second World War and met a tragic end at the hands of the Nazis in 1944, at the young age of thirty. The poignant story of Noor Inayat Khan, born in Moscow to an American mother and an Indian Muslim father, makes fascinating reading and is brilliantly depicted by Shrabani Basu in the book *The Spy Princess.* Noor became the first woman radio operator to be infiltrated into occupied France in June 1943. Renowned for her bravery and resilience, she was posthumously awarded Britain's highest honour. In 2012, a memorial bust was erected in Gordon Square Gardens, Bloomsbury, London.

## The Sultan Gets a Facelift

Four Anglo-Mysore wars were fought between January 1767 and May 1799. Haider Ali passed away in 1782, during the Second Anglo-Mysore War. Tipu Sultan participated in all four conflicts, winning some battles while losing quite a few.

When Tipu ascended the throne of Mysore, the Marathas demanded the return of territories annexed by his father. However, Tipu was unwilling to give up his inheritance. In response, the Marathas supported a revolt led by the chief of Nargund, who was a tributary of Tipu. In the ensuing battle, Tipu suffered defeat and sought peace. Mohibbul Hasan's contention, 'To win their friendship, he ceded to them Nargund, Kittur and Badami'[3], simply defies logic.

Hasan appears to disregard information that might tarnish Tipu Sultan's reputation. When recounting the events following the surrender of Nargund in 1785, he states:

> The garrison consisting of about 1,650 men marched out of the fort on July 29.... By the end of September all of them had been set free, except Kalopant and Venkat Rao who were sent in chains to the fort of Kabbaldurga along with their families. The reason why the capitulation terms were not observed in the case of these two men was that they had given the Sultan considerable trouble; so he did not want to let them go unpunished.[4]

By reading between the lines, we can discern that Tipu flagrantly disregarded the conventions of war. All individuals who surrendered from the fort were captured and detained for several months. The leaders were sent to the dreaded prison fortress of Kabbaladurga.

Hasan continues:

> But it is incorrect to say that the Desai's 'daughter was reserved for the Sultan's seraglio', for there is no reference to this in the Maratha records. Similarly, the story mentioned in one of the newsletters that Burhan sent for the pretty daughter of Kalopant to see her and to select her for Tipu's harem is nothing but a pure fabrication, for this too is not supported by any reliable evidence. The news-letter report cannot be regarded as authentic, because the information contained in such letters was generally based on hearsay and bazaar gossip.[5]

In this manner, Hasan dismisses several narratives due to the lack of concrete evidence. However, one wonders what exactly qualifies as evidence. Should we expect ravished women to publish memoirs before deeming their stories credible? Hasan's argument that Maratha sources remain silent about the fate of the women captives also lacks merit. When warriors witness their women being captured, raped and carted away, they would likely choose death over publicizing such atrocities. It is an established fact that both Haider Ali and Tipu Sultan maintained sizeable harems. Where did the inhabitants of these harems come from? Did they line up outside the palaces of the sultans, seeking entry to their 'privileged' position?

In the final analysis, Tipu emerges more as a loser than a winner. Gradually, he lost every bit of territory his father had won. Moreover, he exhibited fanaticism rather than practicality, coupled with pathological arrogance. Tipu even ordered that his own name be inserted in the Khutba, the Friday sermon delivered in all mosques within his territory, instead of the name of the Mughal emperor, Shah Alam. As the Mughal influence in India progressively weakened, Tipu Sultan adopted the title of 'Badshah' in 1786 and minted coins bearing his own name. He entrusted the

Qazi of Srirangapatna with composing a treatise on the duties of Muslims, with a special emphasis on jihad.

The historian Kate Brittlebank appears to go to great lengths to whitewash the sins of the father–son team, 'Over the twenty years that Hyder Ali had been in power, he had followed a policy of expanding Mysore's boundaries by reconquering disputed land on the kingdom's borders.'[6]The truth is that every region desired by Haider Ali conveniently became 'disputed land'. While conceding that Haider 'seized parts of Malabar as well as Kodagu', Brittlebank proceeds to justify these unwarranted invasions.[7] Her accounts regarding Malabar are notably inaccurate. Haider Ali's unprovoked attacks on neighbouring territories are justified on specious grounds, such as '[access] to Malabar ports was important for trade, as was the control of Bednur'.[8] The erudite author further rationalizes, 'The incursion into Kodagu was the result of his intervention in a succession dispute.'[9] It seems that Brittlebank heavily relies on the views expressed by Mohibbul Hasan.

Brittlebank's rationalization of the forced conversions and mass deportations is truly spectacular. She remarks, 'This was not a religious policy but one of chastisement. The forced removals occurred both from Kodagu and Malabar, the former as a response to continued resistance against Mysore rule, the latter – Nairs and Christians – as a result of their resistance and perceived treachery in the war.'[10] According to the author, the Kodavas, Nairs and Christians had no right to resist the Mysorean occupation. Since they were unwilling to submit, they needed to be 'chastised'. Conversion and deportation, in her view, were effective methods of chastisement!

Another curious perspective is presented by the learned author, 'By February 1783, Tipu and his army had returned to Mysore; the newly installed ruler had unfinished business to attend to in Malabar, where the East India Company's Bombay army was continuing its aggression.'[11] The statement implies that Tipu had legitimate reasons to be in Malabar, as the company was the aggressor. According to this perspective, the concerns of the locals seemed to be of little significance.

Brittlebank casually states, 'One of the malcontents with whom they (the British) aligned themselves was the Raja of Travancore, Rama Varma.'[12] However, what had the Travancore ruler done to deserve such a disparaging epithet? According to the author, 'Rama Varma had harboured resentments against Mysore since he had fallen out with Haider in the 1760s. The defensive lines he had constructed in 1764 (wrong date!) ran from east to west to protect from invasion an exposed part of Travancore's northern border.'[13] So, the unforgivable offence committed by Rama Varma was protecting his border from an invader. Did Travancore invade Mysore? No questions, please!

Rama Varma is also accused of other crimes. As Brittlebank further observes:

> The Raja was also providing refuge to several Malabar chiefs who did not wish to submit to Mysore. Again, when Tipu asked the Raja to hand over the men, the Raja refused. He then provoked Tipu further by purchasing two coastal islands from the Dutch, islands that Tipu himself had wished to buy.[14]

Rama Varma should not have provided asylum to refugees fleeing the atrocities of the Mysore sultans. When Tipu demanded that he surrender the men under his protection (many of whom were his relatives), Rama Varma should have obliged without hesitation, even knowing they would likely be killed, converted or enslaved. Furthermore, he had no right to purchase any property that Tipu desired. Rama Varma must have been an absolute tyrant and imbecile. Therefore, Tipu was justified in invading his kingdom. After all, even rajas needed to be chastised!

Brittlebank writes, 'Tipu's treatment of his British prisoners of war also implies a man of integrity.... Contrary to the apocryphal reports of extreme suffering, several captives' memoirs confirm that they were treated as well as they could have hoped in any similar situation in Europe.'[15] The Europeans were brutal in their treatment of prisoners, so why should we solely blame Tipu Sultan? Perhaps James Scurry's forced conversion and forced marriage are not considered significant. Maybe we can dismiss his description of Colonel Bailley in leg irons as an isolated incident. Similarly, we might overlook James Bristow's firsthand testimony.

'The cause of Tipu's failure to crush the Nairs lay in the terrain of Malabar which is extremely hilly and thick wooded,' writes Hasan.[16] There were no roads, and the rainy season lasted six months, making warfare impossible. The climate and terrain favoured the 'rebels' and hampered the movement of the Mysoreans. Additionally, the Nairs were supported by the British and the raja of Travancore.[17] The Nairs get no credit, while Tipu gets no blame.

When Tipu visits the Beevi of Cannanore, it is at her invitation. He solemnized the preliminary ceremonies of the marriage between his son Abdul Khaliq and her daughter with the intention of pacifying the Moplahs who were revolting against him.[18] This logic is clearly flawed, and the tone of condescension is absurd, as the Arakkal Beevis of Cannanore had been reigning for many centuries and were truly royal from inception, whereas Tipu was a commoner. In reality, the marriage never took place because Tipu was defeated the following year at Tirurangadi, losing all his Malabar possessions in one stroke.

Some statements by Hasan reveal that not all the Mappilas were aligned with the Mysoreans:

> Owing to misgovernment, the Moplahs of Ernad and Walavanad [Valluvanad] were also discontented.... In 1786 Goorkul [Gurukkal] Moplah of Manjeri rose in rebellion. Owing to the unsettled state of the province, Tipu decided to visit it. He arrived in Calicut early in April 1788 by way of the Tamarassheri pass, without any army or train or artillery.[19]

This is unbelievable! Tipu, the superman, comes without an army, changes the local commanders at Calicut, lays the foundations of a new capital south of Calicut and names it Farukhabad or Farrookhia, orders a new fort to be built. Thankfully, Hasan concedes that all these actions of Tipu ended in failure, 'Many persons from Calicut were compelled to settle there; but during the Third Anglo-Mysore War, after Malabar was occupied by the English, they returned to Calicut, and very soon hardly any trace of the new capital was left.'[20]

Amidst the mayhem, Tipu made land grants to the Sringeri Mutt and a few other temples around Mysore. While he demolished the Varahaswami Temple at Srirangapatna, he spared the Sri Ranganathaswamy Temple. With his enemies closing in on him, Tipu might have also sought the blessings of Hindu gods.

In the concluding chapter of his book, Mohibbul Hasan mentions Tipu's regard for his mother and his caring attitude towards his brother. He states, 'He was also kind towards his half-witted brother, Abdul Karim, although the latter had allowed himself to be used at the time of Haider's death by persons who wanted to exclude him from the succession.'[21] The question arises: Was Abdul Karim really mentally challenged or was he labelled as such by those who preferred Tipu's rule? Conversely, Kirmani refrains from describing Abdul Karim as intellectually impaired. He recounts Tipu's agitation upon learning that the nobles had appointed his brother as dewan following Haider Ali's demise. The relationship between the brothers is glossed over in most historical accounts, with no explanation provided as to why Karim was made the dewan by the nobles without awaiting Tipu's return from Ponnani. To Tipu's credit, he successfully managed a smooth transition of power.

Hasan opines that 'Tipu was the pioneer of road building in Malabar'.[22] Before his time, waterways predominated as the mode of travel and transportation. Assuming Tipu's role as the foremost roadbuilder, questions arise: Who bore the financial cost and the logistical burden, and whom were these roads intended to benefit besides Tipu's army?

C.K. Kareem, greatly influenced by the thoughts of Mohibbul Hasan, adds, 'Kerala under the Mysoreans witnessed great social, political and economic developments that had far-reaching effects.'[23] Were the people of Malabar poverty-stricken and uncivilized before the arrival of the father–son duo? Did they suddenly become rich, civilized and sophisticated? Kareem emphasizes the goal of 'emancipating Kerala from the medieval ways'.[24] What might have been the fate of Malabar if the Mysoreans had not intervened? Would the people have remained in the Stone Age? Kareem bemoans the fact that 'a glorious period of our history remains buried under falsehood'.[25]

To give the devil his due, Tipu did warn the Marathas, the nizam and other rulers about the eventual British domination of India – a prediction that proved accurate. However, had the British not been around, Haider Ali and Tipu Sultan might have extended their dominion over the entirety of South India. It prompts us to contemplate whether we would have preferred British rule over becoming subjects of Tipu Sultan. Personally, I would opt for British governance.

This is not to suggest that the British were benevolent masters. They too perpetrated acts of extreme cruelty. The truth is that the people of the occupied territories had a choice between the frying pan and the fire, and they usually chose the former.

## Tipu in His 'Reformer' Avatar

Tipu Sultan occasionally positioned himself as a social reformer. However, the sincerity of his reformist zeal is questionable, to say the least. While he banned the use of alcohol and all other intoxicants in his territory, he permitted the French to open a liquor shop in the camp to cater to the undeniable needs of the French soldiers. Tipu forbade prostitution and the employment of female slaves in domestic service. He disallowed persons of illegitimate or slave birth from marrying into respectable families. However, he did attempt to arrange royal alliances for his illegitimate son, Fath Haider.

It is also claimed that Tipu abolished the custom of human sacrifice, which was reportedly practised at the temple of Kali Devi in Mysore. However, detailed records from British writers of the time do not mention any instances of human sacrifice. It seems likely that this accomplishment was attributed to Tipu in more recent times. Conversely, there is a descriptive account of a human sacrifice performed at Srirangapatna under Tipu's rule.

Some contemporary historians have consciously scripted and fashioned Tipu Sultan's image as a reformer. They openly seek to discredit past historians who were critical of Tipu's motives and actions, often resorting to a 'shoot-the-messenger' strategy. They offer perverse interpretations and peculiar rationalizations of well-established historical facts. For example, C.K. Kareem writes:

> Blindly following the English historians who twisted and mutilated facts to serve their own ignoble ends, Indian writers of Kerala history were unable to give an objective and genuine history of Kerala. To make matters worse, they allowed their caste and communal prejudices and parochial bias to creep into their writings.[26]

Referring to Tipu's so-called reforms, Kareem informs us:

> Conservative by nature the people were reluctant to abandon their age-old habits and viewed these reforms as an encroachment upon their religious and social rights. They were unaware of the fact that these measures were a part of Tipu Sultan's reforms implemented throughout his domain. The privileged class of the Malabar society felt that they were singled out for ill-treatment. In reality, the majority of the people reaped the benefits of these reforms. But the Nairs and Namboodiris, who together comprised one-fifth of the total population of Malabar, were adversely affected by these administrative innovations.[27]

The only reform Tipu can be credited with is an aggressive policy of tax collection, bordering on extortion. If the act of cutting down pepper vines can be classified as an administrative innovation, then the author certainly has a point. Kareem also states that the Namboothiri landlords sold their lands to the Mappilas and migrated to Travancore.[28] One cannot help but wonder if any group of people would willingly abandon their homes without experiencing any mistreatment or perceiving any serious threat. Throughout history, mass migration has invariably been a tragic story.

Kareem adds:

> When Tipu Sultan decreed to the people in general and Nairs, in particular, to dress up decently so as to cover all parts of their body and to stop the shameful practice of polyandry, the Nair community as a whole felt that this was the preliminary step towards converting them.[29]

Was the sultan justified in dictating what an occupied population should wear and whom they should marry? If polyandry is considered a 'shameful practice', then why is polygyny, often referred to as polygamy, deemed acceptable? The truth is that the sultan himself had multiple partners, and even today, the law permits Muslim men to have up to four wives. Yet, it is the less common practice of polyandry that the author condemns.

Kareem accuses Col Wilks of concocting Tipu's proclamation to the Nairs, purportedly directing them to abandon their 'obnoxious' customs, under threat of conversion to Islam. The 'evidence' supplied in favour of this allegation is the absence of any mention of such a proclamation in the works of Kirmani and other Muslim historians, nor in the diaries of the Tellicherry factors.[30] Kareem also casts doubts on the order found in the Palghat Fort upon its capture by the British. This order, bearing the sultan's sign and seal, supposedly instructed his men to convert everyone in the district to Islam. While Wilks, Logan and various other individuals reference this order, Kareem prefers to view it as a forgery. In fact, Kareem questions the authenticity of every document related to Tipu, including his memoirs, letters and hukumnamahs. He states, 'It is not surprising really that the originators of the above baseless charges should strive to buttress their position by forging any number of such documents.'[31] Kareem also questions whether Kirkpatrick could have possibly fabricated Tipu's letters. Imagine the mathematical probability of a sane individual fabricating 2,000 letters in Persian and then translating a 1,000 of them into English!

Kareem presents a range of innovative rationalizations:

> Even if we accept the proclamation of Tipu to the Nairs of Kerala as genuine there is nothing in it to prove that he was a religious bigot. His mere insistence on the abolition of polyandry and the adoption of civilized mode of dress does not make him a religious bigot. If at all such a proclamation was made, it was only to introduce these reforms which were not even remotely connected with religious propaganda. It is quite legitimate to assume that the original proclamation was tampered with by later historians and deliberately altered to suit their purpose of picturing Tipu as a religious fanatic.[32]

Here, the author indirectly admits that there was indeed a proclamation. Kareem adds, 'If Tipu wanted to use the instrument of military force for conversions, he should have first converted his troops.'[33] Was the learned historian unaware of the Chelas, the Ahmedis and the Usud Ilhyes? What about the Europeans who were forcibly converted, some of whom lived to write their memoirs? Were they all liars? In this context we need to consider what modern psychologists say: We see what we want to see and hear what we want to hear. I would add: We read what we want to read and believe what we want to believe.

Kareem reports that during the negotiations for the Treaty of Seringapatam in 1792, the Maratha vakils suggested including an article 'to prevent Tipoo from continuing the practice of circumcising Hindoos'.[34] If this practice was not ongoing, why would it be proposed as a clause in a major peace treaty?

Kareem liberally accuses the Tellicherry factors of being the primary source of false information regarding the sultan:

> On December 31, 1789, L. Avvon of Tellicherry factory wrote to C.W. Malet that Tipu Sultan was in the suburb of Tellicherry 'to marry his son to the daughter of Bulla Bebby, widow of the

> late Ally Raja, at the celebration of which marriage, 40,000 captives, unhappy families of the Coorg country and other parts of the Malabar coast are to be circumcised.' This was endorsed by Cornwallis in his letter to Malet who was Resident of the Maratta Court. It is clear that this news of the religious atrocity of Tipu Sultan was for the consumption of Marattas and to stir them against the Mysore ruler.[35]

Avvon and Cornwallis both lied. However, James Bristow, who was a prisoner at Srirangapatna at that time, had mentioned Tipu's announcement of his intention to convert 100,000 of his subjects on the occasion of his son's wedding. Thankfully, fate intervened, and the wedding never occurred as Tipu's attack on the Travancore Lines led to the outbreak of the Third Anglo-Mysore War.

Kareem goes on to state, 'When these non-Muslim sources created such falsehood, the Muslim chroniclers also in their attempt to glorify their hero after their heart as the "Champion of Islam" made similar utterances that have become trump cards in the hands of hostile historians.'[36] The author thus divides non-Muslim writers from Muslim writers and segregates historians into 'hostile' and 'friendly' categories. He also summarily dismisses Kirmani's statement that upon the sultan's arrival at Srirangapatna, all the Coorgi prisoners were converted to Islam and termed 'Ahmedis', deeming Kirmani's pronouncements as mere 'hyperbolic utterances' not to be taken literally.[37] The author selectively rejects any viewpoint that does not enhance the sultan's reputation. For example, he attributes the Muslim Gurukkal's revolt to his membership in the landed aristocracy and his dissatisfaction with the sultan's agrarian reforms.[38]

Kareem goes a step further and makes a sweeping generalization, stating, 'Not a specific instance can be pointed out to show that any person was persecuted just because he was not a Muslim. Nor can any particular temple or church be pointed out as having been demolished by the Mysoreans.'[39] This assertion is akin to an ostrich burying its head in the sand.

Kate Brittlebank informs us:

> From 1792 onwards his [Tipu's] reign became more Islamic in character.... He ordered the composition of *khutbas*, sermons on the merits of *jihad*, *'ilm* (religious learning) and prayer, and instructed the Qazi of Srirangapatna to compose a treatise on the duties of Muslims, with an emphasis on jihad.[40]

Tipu's decision to send two emissaries to Mauritius in 1797 is attributed to the purportedly nefarious influence of an unnamed 'Frenchman of dubious origin'.[41] Thus, the blame is shifted from Tipu to the enigmatic foreigner, believed to be Monsieur Ripaud.

In the book *Eternal Kaveri*, edited by George Michell (Marg Publications, 1999), Kate Brittlebank's chapter titled 'Srirangapattana: Tipu's Island Fort' presents some interesting observations. Brittlebank opines that Tipu patronized religious institutions across his kingdom:

> The Sringeri *math*, seat of one of India's four Shankaracharyas (sic), was a well-known recipient of his largesse, and the Nanjundeswara temple at Nanjangud, some 25 kilometres south of the city of Mysore, houses a green jadeite linga donated by him. Not surprisingly, the Sriranganatha temple on the island also received gifts from Tipu. The temple still has in its possession silver vessels with inscriptions that show that they were presented by him.[42]

While this summarizes Tipu's so-called generosity towards Hindu temples, his service to Islam is also elaborated:

> Early in his reign, he ordered the construction of the A'la mosque within the fort. Completed in 1787, the building stands to this day as a focus of local Muslim worship. An impressive structure with two minarets, it is clear that recycled materials were used in its erection: temple pillars, for example, can be seen near the main entrance gate.[43]

Where did the recycled materials come from? Did Tipu destroy a temple located there or did it collapse on its own? These questions remain unanswered. Tipu also erected the Aksa Mosque adjacent to the Gumbaz. In fact, aside from these two mosques in Srirangapatna and the mausoleum of his father and mother (Gumbaz), Tipu Sultan undertook minimal construction. Brittlebank tells us he completed the construction of the Bangalore Palace, initiated by his father. Tipu's Palace within the Srirangapatna Fort was also built by him, however, it has since collapsed.

Brittlebank's description of the Fourth Anglo-Mysore War is indeed intriguing. Tipu's appeals to the Isle de France for military assistance, the Malartic Proclamation, his letters to Napoleon Bonaparte and Zaman Shah of Afghanistan, and the subsequent events are simply brushed under the carpet, and the focus is placed on the perceived malicious intentions of the British. Brittlebank states, 'Seven years later the island (Srirangapatna) was again attacked by the British. Under the aggressive policies of the governor-general, Richard Wellesley, brother of Arthur, the fourth Anglo-Mysore war began when troops led by General George Harris marched into Mysore in March 1799.'[44] The author also opines that it was the treachery of Mir Sadiq that led to Tipu's downfall, 'His Diwan, Mir Sadiq, has come down to us as a notorious traitor; on the Daria Daulat mural his face has been scrubbed out, apparently in consequence of his treachery.'[45] If Mir Sadiq had remained loyal to Tipu, would Mysore have won the war? The truth is that the Mysoreans were facing overwhelming odds – they were surrounded, outnumbered and outclassed. Their defeat was inevitable. If Mir Sadiq had indeed betrayed Tipu, it would only have hastened the imminent end. Interestingly, the local populace of Srirangapatna still maintains that Tipu's downfall was due to the grand betrayal.

Tipu condemned the practice of polyandry in Malabar and Coorg. Since women in Malabar did not traditionally cover themselves above the waist, Tipu decreed that no woman should go outside the house 'naked'. It is said that he offered blouses to women in Malabar who were 'oppressed' in this manner, which is often cited as evidence of his concern and generosity. However, Kirkpatrick remarks that Tipu was quite unsuccessful in enforcing these laws. Many writers have cited innumerable instances of Tipu taking women from conquered territories into his harem after forcibly converting them. However, these accounts are conveniently ignored by the reform brigade.

Tipu instituted changes such as altering the calendar or renaming towns he captured, causing considerable confusion. However, none of these changes persisted beyond his death; the towns quickly reverted to their original names, and his calendar faded into obscurity. Additionally, his pet tigers were shot dead by British soldiers, his family was exiled first to Vellore and then to Kolkata, and his territories were divided among his enemies. In the end, he left no lasting legacy except memories of suffering and animosity. Brittlebank notes, 'Mir Hussein Ali Khan Kirmani, who wrote the most well-known history of Haidar and Tipu, refers to him neither as a *shahid* nor as a *ghazi*, a warrior who fights in defence of Islam.'[46]

Tipu's so-called bravery and reformist agenda do not hold up under scrutiny. He was neither an inventor nor an innovator and left no enduring contributions. Instead, he was known for destruction, burning Calicut to the ground and destroying pepper vines in Malabar. He was a skilled warmonger, winning numerous battles but also suffering significant defeats. Ultimately, he died not on the battlefield but within his own fort.

Tipu possessed the destructive prowess akin to the mythical demon Bhasmasura – he seemed to destroy everything he touched. In Kerala today, only one town retains a part of the name given by Tipu – Feroke. Tipu initially named it Farukkabad, but the locals chose to call it Feroke instead. Similarly, in Wayanad, Ganapathivattom was referred to as Sultan Bathery when Tipu converted it into a military outpost, and it is by this name that the place is known today. However, all other Islamic names reverted to their original vernacular versions after Tipu's death, not only in Malabar but across the entire southern peninsula.

The dynasty of Haider Ali ended with Tipu Sultan, leaving behind no lasting legacy. Their atrocities, however, continued to haunt the memories of their unfortunate victims, with horror stories passed down through generations. This cycle of remembrance is likely to persist into the future, seamlessly blending into the pages of history.

# NOTES

**Chapter 1: The Legacy of the Mysore Sultans**

1 Wilks, Mark (Col). *Historical Sketches,* Vol. III. Originally published in 1817 (Digitized by Internet Archive in 2007), p. 263.
2 Buchanan, Francis. *A Journey from Madras through the Countries of Mysore, Canara and Malabar,* Vol. II. Originally published in 1807. Reprint, Scholar's Choice edition, 2015, p. 455.
3 Moxham, Roy. *The Theft of India: The European Conquests of India, 1498–1765.* HarperCollins, 2016, p. 3.
4 Buchanan, Francis. *A Journey from Madras through the Countries of Mysore, Canara and Malabar,* Vol. II. Originally published in 1807. Reprint, Scholar's Choice edition, 2015, p. 551.
5 Logan, William. *Malabar.* Originally published in 1887. Reprint, Madras Government Press, 1951, p. 450.
6 Wilks, Mark (Col). *Historical Sketches, Vol. III.* 1817 (Digitized by Internet Archive in 2007), p. 40.
7 Kirkpatrick, William. Select Letters of Tippoo Sultaun to Various Public Functionaries. London: Black, Parry and Kingsbury, 1811, p. 3.
8 Buchanan, Francis. *A Journey from Madras through the Countries of Mysore, Canara and Malabar,* Vol. II. Originally published in 1807. Reprint, Scholar's Choice edition, 2015, p. 426.
9 Ibid., p. 328.
10 Bayi, Aswathi Thirunal Gouri Lakshmi. *Sree Padmanabha Swamy Temple,* Bharatiya Vidya Bhavan, 1995, pp. 145–146.
11 Ibid., p. 146.
12 Ibid., p. 146.
13 Bartolomeo, Paolino da San. *A Voyage to the East Indies: Containing an Account of the Manners, Customs, & c. of the Natives, with a Geographical Description of the Country,* edited by John Reinhold Forster, translated by William Johnston. Paris, 1796, p. 104.

14 Ibid., pp. 122–123.
15 Ibid., p. 136.
16 Ibid., pp. 139–140.
17 Ibid., pp. 141–142.
18 Kirkpatrick, William. *Select Letters of Tippoo Sultan to Various Public Functionaries*. London: Black, Parry and Kingsbury, 1811, pp. 255–256.
19 Ibid., pp. 256–257.
20 Ibid., p. 150.
21 Ibid., pp. 151–152.
22 Ibid., p. 3.
23 Bowring, Lewin B. *Hyder Ali and Tipu Sultan and the Struggle with the Musalman Powers of the South*. London: Clarendon Press, 1899, p. 125.
24 Ibid., pp. 126–127, footnote.
25 Ibid., p. 127.
26 Bartolomeo, Paolino da San. *A Voyage to the East Indies*, edited by John Reinhold Forster, translated by William Johnston. Paris, 1796, p. 306.
27 Buchanan, Francis. *A Journey from Madras through the Countries of Mysore, Canara and Malabar, Vol. II.* Originally published in 1807. Scholar's Choice edition, 2015, p. 96.
28 Kirkpatrick, William. *Select Letters of Tippoo Sultan to Various Public Functionaries*. London: Black, Parry and Kingsbury, 1811, p. 114.
29 Bristow, J. *A Narrative of the Sufferings of James Bristow, Belonging to the Bengal Artillery, during Ten Years Captivity with Hyder Ally and Tippoo Saheb*. Calcutta, 1792. Reprint, London, 1793, pp. 108–109.
30 Ibid., p. 39.
31 Ibid., pp. 39–40.
32 Ibid., p. 40.
33 Ibid., pp. 40–41.
34 Ibid., pp. 72–73.
35 Kirkpatrick, William. *Select Letters of Tippoo Sultan to Various Public Functionaries*. London: Black, Parry and Kingsbury, 1811, p. 150.
36 Ibid., pp. 151–152.

37 Hoover, James W. *Men without Hats: Dialogue, Discipline and Discontent in the Madras Army, 1806–1807.* Manohar Publishers and Distributors, 2007, pp. 49–50.
38 Nair, K.K. *By Sweat and Sword: Trade, Diplomacy and War in Kerala through the Ages.* Manohar Publishers and Distributors, 2013, p. 263.
39 Ibid., pp. 263–264.
40 Kirmani, Mir Hussein Ali Khan. *History of Tipu Sultan,* translated from Persian by Col W. Miles, 1864. Reprint, New Delhi: Abhijeet Publications, 2017, pp. 31–32.
41 Ibid., p. 49.
42 MMDLT. *The History of Hyder Shah alias Hyder Ali Khan Bahadur* or *New Memoirs Concerning the East Indies with Historical Notes.* London, 1784, p. 115.
43 Ibid., p. 123.
44 Ibid., p. 124.
45 Ibid., p. 45.
46 Ibid., pp. 41–42.
47 Ibid., p. 43.
48 Peixoto, Eloy Joze Correa. *Memoirs of Hyder Ally from the Year 1758 to 1770,* in *Annual Report of the Mysore Archaeological Department for the Year 1937 (Part IV – Manuscripts).* Bangalore: Government Press, 1938, p. 114.
49 Ibid., pp. 114–115.
50 Ibid., p. 115.
51 Ibid., p. 104.
52 Ibid., p. 119.
53 Ibid., p. 115.
54 Brittlebank, Kate. *Tiger: The Life of Tipu Sultan.* Juggernaut Books, 2016, p. 100.
55 Ibid., p. 101.
56 Ibid., p. 101.
57 Forrest, Denys M. *Tiger of Mysore: Life and Death of Tipu Sultan.* Allied Publishers, 1970, p.133.
58 Ibid., p. 133.

**Chapter 2: Oral Histories and Whispering Walls**

1 Bayi, Aswathi Thirunal Gouri Lakshmi. *Sree Padmanabha Swamy Temple,* Bharatiya Vidya Bhavan, 2014, p. 145.

2 Ibid., pp. 144–145.
3 Ibid., p. 145.
4 Logan, William. *Malabar*. 1887. Reprint, Madras Government Press, 1951, pp. 662–663.
5 Iyer, Chandrika Hariharan. *Hemambika: The Elixir of Life*. 2017, p. 18.
6 Ibid., pp. 20–21.
7 Ibid., p. 21.
8 Ibid., p. 36.
9 Ibid., p. 20.
10 Buchanan, Francis. *A Journey from Madras through the Countries of Mysore, Canara and Malabar, Vol. II*. Originally published in 1807. Scholar's Choice edition, 2015, pp. 350–351.
11 Bartolomeo, Paolino da San. *A Voyage to the East Indies*, edited by John Reinhold Forster, translated by William Johnston. Paris, 1796, p. 142.
12 Jayashanker, S. *Temples of Kannoor District*. Kerala: Directorate of Census Operations, Census of India, 1999, p. 135.
13 Ibid., p. 135.
14 Ibid., p. 137.
15 Ibid., p. 296.
16 Ibid., p. 148.
17 Ibid., p. 148.

**Chapter 3: The Wild Rampage of Haider Naik**

1 Forrest, Denys M. *Tiger of Mysore: Life and Death of Tipu Sultan*. Allied Publishers, 1970, p. 11.
2 Hasan, Mohibbul. *History of Tipu Sultan*. Aakar Books, 1951, pp. 3–4.
3 Sampath, Vikram. *Splendours of Royal Mysore: The Untold Story of the Wodeyars*. Rupa Publications, 2012, p. 1437.
4 Wilks, Mark. *Historical Sketches, Vol. III*. 1817. Digitized by the Internet Archive in 2007, pp. 261–262.
5 Ibid., p. 262.
6 Ibid., p. 262.
7 Ibid., p. 263.
8 Ibid., p. 263.
9 Ibid., p. 267.

10 Ibid., p. 268.
11 Ibid., p. 269.
12 Ibid., p. 270.
13 Ibid., pp. 300–301.
14 Bowring, Lewin B. *Hyder Ali and Tipu Sultan and the Struggle with the Musalman Powers of the South.* London: Clarendon Press, 1899, pp. 28–29.
15 Wilks, Mark. *Historical Sketches, Vol. III.* 1817. Digitized by the Internet Archive in 2007, p. 397.
16 Yazdani, Kaveh. *Mysore at War.* Research Gate, 2019, p. 18.
17 Stewart, Charles. *A Descriptive Catalogue of the Oriental Library of the Late Tippoo Sultan of Mysore: To Which Are Prefixed Memoirs of Hyder Ali Khan and His Son Tippoo Sultan.* Cambridge, 1809, pp. 12–13.
18 Ibid., p. 13.
19 Ibid., p. 13.
20 Wilks, Mark. *Historical Sketches, Vol. I.* 1817. Digitized by the Internet Archive in 2007, p. 411.
21 Stewart, Charles. *A Descriptive Catalogue of the Oriental Library of the Late Tippoo Sultan of Mysore: To Which Are Prefixed Memoirs of Hyder Ali Khan and His Son Tippoo Sultan.* Cambridge, 1809, p. 14.
22 Hasan, Mohibbul. *History of Tipu Sultan.* Aakar Books, 1951, p. 7.
23 Bowring, Lewin B. *Hyder Ali and Tipu Sultan and the Struggle with the Musalman Powers of the South.* London: Clarendon Press, 1899, p. 32.
24 Ibid., p. 33.
25 Ibid., pp. 33–34.
26 Ibid., p. 34.
27 Panikkar K.M. *A History of Kerala, 1498–1801.* Originally published by Annamalai University in 1960. Reprint, Life Span Publishers and Distributors, 2021, pp. 328–329.
28 Rao, C. Hayavadana. *History of Mysore (1399–1799 CE), Vol. II.* Bangalore: Government Press, 1948, pp. 429–430.
29 Ibid., p. 437.
30 Panikkar K.M. *A History of Kerala, 1498–1801.* Originally published by Annamalai University in 1960. Reprint, Life Span Publishers and Distributors, 2021, p. 329.
31 Rao, C. Hayavadana. *History of Mysore (1399–1799 CE), Vol. II.* Bangalore: Government Press, 1948, pp. 439.

32 Ibid., p. 441.
33 Ibid., p. 441.
34 Ibid., p. 442.
35 Ibid., p. 444.
36 Ibid., p. 445.
37 Ibid., p. 447.
38 Ibid., p. 446.
39 Ibid., p. 452.
40 Bowring, Lewin B. *Hyder Ali and Tipu Sultan and the Struggle with the Musalman Powers of the South.* London: Clarendon Press, 1899, p. 41.
41 Rao, C. Hayavadana. *History of Mysore (1399–1799 CE), Vol. II.* Bangalore: Government Press, 1948, p. 466.
42 Ibid., p. 468.
43 Ibid., p. 469.
44 MMDLT. *The History of Hyder Shah alias Hyder Ali Khan Bahadur* or *New Memoirs Concerning the East Indies with Historical Notes.* London, 1784, p. 95.
45 Rao, C. Hayavadana. *History of Mysore (1399–1799 CE), Vol. II.* Bangalore: Government Press, 1948, p. 469.
46 Ibid., p. 470.
47 Ibid., p. 470.
48 Ibid., p. 472.
49 Ibid., p. 472, footnote.
50 Ibid., p. 474.
51 Ibid., p. 498.
52 Ibid., p. 495.
53 Ibid, pp. 497–498.
54 Ibid., pp. 499–500.
55 Ibid., p. 502.
56 Ibid., p. 502.
57 Ibid., p. 503.
58 Ibid., p. 504.
59 Ibid., p. 504.
60 Ibid., p. 505.
61 Ibid., p. 505, footnote.
62 Ibid., p. 513.
63 Ibid., p. 506.
64 Ibid., p. 507.

65 Ibid., pp. 508–509.
66 Ibid., p. 509, footnote.
67 Ibid., p. 512.
68 Ibid., p. 477.
69 Ibid., p. 477.
70 Ibid., p. 477.
71 Rao, C. Hayavadana. *History of Mysore (1399–1799 CE), Vol. III.* Bangalore: Government Press, 1948, pp. 24–25.
72 Ibid., p. 25.
73 Ibid., pp. 26–27.
74 Rao, C. Hayavadana. *History of Mysore (1399–1799 CE), Vol. II.* Bangalore: Government Press, 1948, pp. 515–516.
75 Ibid., p. 516.
76 Bowring, Lewin B. *Hyder Ali and Tipu Sultan and the Struggle with the Musalman Powers of the South.* London: Clarendon Press, 1899, pp. 74–75.
77 Ibid., p. 77.
78 Ibid., p. 77.
79 Ibid., pp. 77–78.
80 Ibid., p. 79.
81 Ibid., p. 80.
82 Ibid., p. 82.
83 Ibid., p. 83.
84 Luther, Narendra. *Legendotes of Hyderabad.* Niyogi Books, 2014, p. 51.
85 Ibid., p. 72.
86 https://www.deccanchronicle.com/nation/current-affairs/051117/rambagh-temple-a-hidden-gem-in-the-hyderabad.html
87 Nair, K.K. *By Sweat and Sword: Trade, Diplomacy and War in Kerala through the Ages.* Manohar Publishers and Distributors, 2013, p. 235.
88 Habib, Irfan (ed.). *State and Diplomacy under Tipu Sultan: Documents and Essays.* Indian History Congress, Tulika Books, 2001, p. 85.
89 Ibid., p. 85.
90 Ibid., p. 85.
91 Ibid., pp. 85–86.
92 Ibid., p. 87.
93 Ibid., p. 87.
94 Ibid., p. 87.

95 Ibid., p. 89.

96 Peixoto, Eloy Joze Correa. 'Memoirs of Hyder Ally from the Year 1758 to 1770', in *Annual Report of the Mysore Archaeological Department for the Year 1937 (Part IV – Manuscripts).* Bangalore: Government Press, 1938, p. 118.

97 Ibid., p. 118.

98 Ibid., p. 118.

99 Ibid., p. 118.

100 Ibid., p. 118.

**Chapter 4: Malabar Invasions and Strange Adoptions**

1 Logan, William. *Malabar.* 1887. Reprint, Madras Government Press, 1951, p. 402.

2 Ibid., p. 402.

3 Wilks, Mark. *Historical Sketches, Vol. I.* 1817. Digitized by the Internet Archive in 2007, p. 358.

4 Ibid., p. 358.

5 Logan, William. *Malabar.* 1887. Reprint, Madras Government Press, 1951, p. 402.

6 Ibid., p. 129.

7 Ibid., p. 400.

8 Peixoto, Eloy Joze Correa. *Memoirs of Hyder Ally from the Year 1758 to 1770,* in *Annual Report of the Mysore Archaeological Department for the Year 1937 (Part IV – Manuscripts).* Bangalore: Government Press, 1938, p. 98.

9 Ibid., p. 99.

10 Ibid., p. 99

11 Ibid., pp. 99–100.

12 Ibid., p. 100.

13 Ibid., p. 100.

14 Ibid., p. 100.

15 Ibid., p. 100.

16 Logan, William. *Malabar.* 1887. Reprint, Madras Government Press, 1951, p. 402.

17 Ibid., p. 403.

18 Ibid., p. 404.

19 Peixoto, Eloy Joze Correa. *Memoirs of Hyder Ally from the Year 1758 to 1770,* in *Annual Report of the Mysore Archaeological Department for*

*the Year 1937 (Part IV – Manuscripts).* Bangalore: Government Press, 1938, p. 103.

20 Ibid., p. 103.

21 Ibid., p. 103.

22 Ibid., p. 104.

23 Panikkar K.M. *A History of Kerala, 1498–1801.* Originally published by Annamalai University in 1960. Reprint, Life Span Publishers and Distributors, 2021, p. 333.

24 Wilks, Mark. *Historical Sketches, Vol. I.* 1817. Digitized by the Internet Archive in 2007, p. 533.

25 Peixoto, Eloy Joze Correa. *Memoirs of Hyder Ally from the Year 1758 to 1770, in Annual Report of the Mysore Archaeological Department for the Year 1937 (Part IV – Manuscripts).* Bangalore: Government Press, 1938, p. 104.

26 Bowring, Lewin B. *Hyder Ali and Tipu Sultan and the Struggle with the Musalman Powers of the South.* London: Clarendon Press, 1899, p. 45.

27 Ibid., p. 46.

28 Kareem, C.K. *Kerala under Haidar Ali and Tipu Sultan.* PhD thesis, Aligarh Muslim University. Cochin: Kerala History Association, 1973, p. 59.

29 Ibid., p. 60.

30 Ibid., p. 62.

31 Ibid., p. 65.

32 Buchanan, Francis. *A Journey from Madras through the Countries of Mysore, Canara and Malabar, Vol. II.* Originally published in 1807. Scholar's Choice edition, 2015, p. 548.

33 Ibid., p. 548.

34 Ibid., p. 549.

35 Panikkar K.M. *A History of Kerala, 1498–1801.* Originally published by Annamalai University in 1960. Reprint, Life Span Publishers and Distributors, 2021, p. 308.

36 https://en.wikipedia.org/wiki/Madayi_Kavu

37 Buchanan, Francis. *A Journey from Madras through the Countries of Mysore, Canara and Malabar, Vol. II.* Originally published in 1807. Scholar's Choice edition, 2015, p. 387.

38 Panikkar K.M. *A History of Kerala, 1498–1801.* Originally published by Annamalai University in 1960. Reprint, Life Span Publishers and Distributors, 2021, p. 22.

39 Buchanan, Francis. *A Journey from Madras through the Countries of Mysore, Canara and Malabar, Vol. II.* Originally published in 1807. Scholar's Choice edition, 2015, p. 555.
40 Hasan, Mohibbul. *History of Tipu Sultan.* Aakar Books, 1951, p. 28, footnote.
41 Wilks, *Historical Sketches, Vol.II,* pp. 453–454.
42 Ibid., p. 454.
43 Ibid., pp. 454–455.
44 Bowring, Lewin B. *Hyder Ali and Tipu Sultan and the Struggle with the Musalman Powers of the South.* London: Clarendon Press, 1899, pp. 121–122.
45 Nair, K.K. *By Sweat and Sword: Trade, Diplomacy and War in Kerala through the Ages.* Manohar Publishers and Distributors, 2013, p. 259.
46 Ibid., p. 260.
47 Kirmani, Mir Hussein Ali Khan. *History of Tipu Sultan,* translated from Persian by Col W. Miles, 1864. Reprint, New Delhi: Abhijeet Publications, 2017, p. 4.
48 Kurup, Pushpa. *Power Women: A Journey into Hindu Mythology, Folklore and History.* Bloomsbury, 2021, pp. 214–215.
49 Ibid., pp. 214–215.
50 Ibid., p. 215.

**Chapter 5: Living by the Sword**

1 Bowring, Lewin B. *Hyder Ali and Tipu Sultan and the Struggle with the Musalman Powers of the South.* London: Clarendon Press, 1899, p. 107.
2 Ibid., p. 109.
3 Ibid., p. 109.
4 Ibid., p. 110.
5 Ibid., p. 110.
6 Ibid., pp. 110–111.
7 Ibid., p. 26.
8 Wilks, Mark. *Historical Sketches, Vol. I.* 1817. Digitized by the Internet Archive in 2007, p. 390.
9 Ibid., p. 390.
10 Ibid., pp. 392–393.
11 Ibid., p. 393.

12 Bowring, Lewin B. *Hyder Ali and Tipu Sultan and the Struggle with the Musalman Powers of the South.* London: Clarendon Press, 1899, p. 112.

13 M.M.D.L.T. *The History of Hyder Shah alias Hyder Ali Khan Bahadur* or *New Memoirs Concerning the East Indies with Historical Notes.* London, 1784, p. 269.

14 Peixoto, Eloy Joze Correa. *Memoirs of Hyder Ally from the Year 1758 to 1770,* in *Annual Report of the Mysore Archaeological Department for the Year 1937 (Part IV – Manuscripts).* Bangalore: Government Press, 1938, p. 113.

15 Ibid., p. 116.

16 Ibid., p. 116.

17 Chetti, P. Stephen Basappa. *A Guide to Seringapatam and Its Vicinity; Historical and Traditional.* Town Press, 1897, p. 8.

18 Beatson, Alexander. *A View of the Origin and Conduct of the War with Tippoo Sultaun; Comprising a Narrative of the Operations of the Army under the Command of Lieutenant-General George Harris, and of the Siege of Seringapatam.* London, 1800, p. 233.

19 Rao, C. Hayavadana. *History of Mysore (1399–1799 CE), Vol. II.* Bangalore: Government Press, 1948, p. 381.

20 Ibid., p. 388.

21 Ibid., p. 393.

22 Ibid., p. 540.

23 Ibid., p. 536, footnote.

24 Ibid., pp. 537–538.

25 Ibid., p. 538, footnote.

26 Ibid., p. 544.

27 Ibid., p. 544, footnote.

28 Ibid., pp. 544–545.

29 Ibid., p. 541.

30 Kirkpatrick, William. *Select Letters of Tippoo Sultan to Various Public Functionaries.* London: Black, Parry and Kingsbury, 1811, p. 217.

31 Ibid., pp. 217–218.

32 Wilks, Mark. *Historical Sketches, Vol. III.* 1817. Digitized by the Internet Archive in 2007, p. 26.

33 Ibid., p. 26.

34 Ibid., pp. 26–27.

35 Ibid., p. 27.

36 Mackenzie, Roderick. *A Sketch of the War with Tippoo Sultaun* or *A Detail of Military Operations, from the Commencement of Hostilities at the Lines of Travancore in December 1789, until the Peace Concluded before Seringapatam in February 1792.* Calcutta, 1799, Appendix 1, p. 1.

37 Ibid., Appendix 3, p. 12.

38 Bowring, Lewin B. *Hyder Ali and Tipu Sultan and the Struggle with the Musalman Powers of the South.* London: Clarendon Press, 1899, pp. 225–226.

39 Ibid., p. 222.

40 Habib, Irfan (ed.). *State and Diplomacy under Tipu Sultan: Documents and Essays.* Indian History Congress, Tulika Books, 2001, p. 98.

41 Ibid., p. 99.

42 Ibid., p. 99.

43 Ibid., p. 99.

44 Ibid., p. 99.

45 Ibid., p. 99.

46 Ibid., pp. 99–100.

47 Ibid., p. 100.

48 Rao, C. Hayavadana. *History of Mysore (1399–1799 CE), Vol. III.* Bangalore: Government Press, 1948, p. 43.

49 Ibid., p. 44.

50 Hasan, Mohibbul. *History of Tipu Sultan.* Aakar Books, 1951, p. 129.

51 Habib, Irfan (ed.). *State and Diplomacy under Tipu Sultan: Documents and Essays.* Indian History Congress, Tulika Books, 2001, p. xii.

52 Ibid., p. xv.

53 Wilks, Mark. *Historical Sketches, Vol. III.* 1817. Digitized by the Internet Archive in 2007, p. 51.

54 Ibid., p. 52.

55 Kirkpatrick, William. *Select Letters of Tippoo Sultan to Various Public Functionaries.* London: Black, Parry and Kingsbury, 1811, p. 446.

56 Ibid., p. 462.

57 Roy, Tirthankar. *The East India Company: The World's Most Powerful Corporation.* Penguin Random House, 2012, p. 162.

58 Habib, Irfan (ed.). *State and Diplomacy under Tipu Sultan: Documents and Essays.* Indian History Congress, Tulika Books, 2001, p. 69.

59 Ibid., p. 76.

60 Ibid., p. 76.

61 Ibid., p. 73.

62 Hoover, James W. *Men without Hats: Dialogue, Discipline and Discontent in the Madras Army, 1806–1807.* Manohar Publishers and Distributors, 2007, p. 80.

63 Habib, Irfan (ed.). *State and Diplomacy under Tipu Sultan: Documents and Essays.* Indian History Congress, Tulika Books, 2001, p. 33.

64 Ibid., pp. 33–34.

65 Ibid., p. 34.

66 Ibid., p. 35.

67 Ibid., p. 33.

68 Ibid., p. 44.

69 Ibid., p. 44.

70 Ibid., p. 45.

71 Ibid., p. 45.

72 Buchanan, Francis. *A Journey from Madras through the Countries of Mysore, Canara and Malabar, Vol. II.* Originally published in 1807. Scholar's Choice edition, 2015, p. 550.

73 Brittlebank, Kate. *Tiger: The Life of Tipu Sultan.* Juggernaut Books, 2016, p.129.

74 https://www.nytimes.com/1927/03/23/archives/jeweler-here-buys-nassak-diamond-worldfamous-stone-held-by-the.html

75 https://www.nytimes.com/1929/01/19/archives/park-av-gem-theft-a-puzzle-to-police-no-clues-unearthed-and-value.html?sq=nassak%2520diamond&scp=11&st=cse

76 https://www.nytimes.com/1970/04/05/archives/nassak-diamond-set-for-auction-parkebernet-to-sell-indian-rarity-on.html

77 Dalrymple, William. *Return of a King: An Indian Army in Afghanistan.* Bloomsbury, 2013, p. 10.

78 Ibid., p. 11.

79 Ibid., p. 2.

80 Ibid., p. 31.

**Chapter 6: Fighting the English**

1 Hasan, Mohibbul. *History of Tipu Sultan.* Aakar Books, 1951, p. 8.

2 Ibid., pp. 8–9.

3 Bowring, Lewin B. *Hyder Ali and Tipu Sultan and the Struggle with the Musalman Powers of the South.* London: Clarendon Press, 1899, p. 50.
4 Ibid., pp. 50–51.
5 Forrest, Denys M. *Tiger of Mysore: Life and Death of Tipu Sultan.* Allied Publishers, 1970, pp. 32–33.
6 Hasan, Mohibbul. *History of Tipu Sultan.* Aakar Books, 1951, p. 9.
7 Forrest, *Tiger of Mysore*, 1970, p. 33.
8 Ibid., p. 33.
9 Bowring, *Hyder Ali and Tipu Sultan*, 1899, pp. 47–48.
10 Ibid., p. 53.
11 Rao, C. Hayavadana. *History of Mysore (1399–1799 ce), Vol. III.* Bangalore: Government Press, 1948, p. 96.
12 Chetti, P. Stephen Basappa. *A Guide to Seringapatam and Its Vicinity; Historical and Traditional.* Town Press, 1897, p. 47.
13 Ibid., pp. 44–45.
14 Hasan, Mohibbul. *History of Tipu Sultan.* Aakar Books, 1951, p. 10.
15 Bowring, *Hyder Ali and Tipu Sultan*, 1899, p. 60.
16 M.M.D.L.T. *The History of Hyder Shah alias Hyder Ali Khan Bahadur* or *New Memoirs Concerning the East Indies with Historical Notes.* London, 1784, p. 408.
17 Ibid., p. 408.
18 Ibid., p. 409.
19 Ibid., p. 410–411.
20 Wilks, Mark. *Historical Sketches, Vol. III.* Originally published in London in 1817. Digitized by the Internet Archive in 2007, pp. 695–696.
21 Hasan, Mohibbul. *History of Tipu Sultan.* Aakar Books, 1951, p. 11.
22 Ibid., p. 12.
23 Bowring, *Hyder Ali and Tipu Sultan*, 1899, p. 67.
24 Ibid., pp. 67–68.
25 Ibid., p. 70, footnote.
26 Ibid., p. 73.
27 Ibid., p. 74.
28 M.M.D.L.T. *The History of Hyder Shah alias Hyder Ali Khan Bahadur* or *New Memoirs Concerning the East Indies with Historical Notes.* London, 1784, p. 413.
29 Ibid., pp. 413–414.

30 Wilks, Mark. *Historical Sketches, Vol. III.* Originally published in London in 1817. Digitized by the Internet Archive in 2007, p. 33.
31 Ibid., p. 33.
32 Ibid., pp. 33–34.
33 Ibid., p. 34.
34 Ibid., p. 34.
35 Hasan, Mohibbul. *History of Tipu Sultan.* Aakar Books, 1951, p. 12.
36 Bowring, *Hyder Ali and Tipu Sultan*, 1899, p. 85.
37 Ibid., p. 90.
38 Ibid., p. 92.
39 Ibid., p. 92.
40 Ibid., p. 92.
41 Hasan, Mohibbul. *History of Tipu Sultan.* Aakar Books, 1951, p. 17, footnote.
42 Bowring, *Hyder Ali and Tipu Sultan*, 1899, pp. 95–96.
43 Ibid., pp. 97–98.
44 Ibid., p. 98.
45 Hasan, Mohibbul. *History of Tipu Sultan.* Aakar Books, 1951, p. 15.
46 Bowring, *Hyder Ali and Tipu Sultan*, 1899, p. 99.
47 Ibid., p. 99.
48 Hasan, Mohibbul. *History of Tipu Sultan.* Aakar Books, 1951, p. 19.
49 Ibid., pp. 19–20.
50 Ibid., p. 20.
51 Bowring, *Hyder Ali and Tipu Sultan*, 1899, p. 101.
52 Ibid., p. 102.
53 Ibid., p. 102.
54 Ibid., p. 103.
55 Ibid., p. 103.
56 Hasan, Mohibbul. *History of Tipu Sultan.* Aakar Books, 1951, pp. 20–21.
57 Bowring, *Hyder Ali and Tipu Sultan*, 1899, pp. 103–104.
58 Hasan, Mohibbul. *History of Tipu Sultan.* Aakar Books, 1951, p. 24.
59 Ibid., p. 24.
60 Bowring, *Hyder Ali and Tipu Sultan*, 1899, pp. 120–121.
61 Bristow, J. *A Narrative of the Sufferings of James Bristow, Belonging to the Bengal Artillery, during Ten Years Captivity with Hyder Ally and Tippoo Saheb.* Calcutta, 1792. Reprint, London, 1793, p. 26.
62 Ibid., p. 28.

63 Bowring, *Hyder Ali and Tipu Sultan*, 1899, pp. 122–123.
64 Bristow, J. *A Narrative of the Sufferings of James Bristow, Belonging to the Bengal Artillery, during Ten Years Captivity with Hyder Ally and Tippoo Saheb*. Calcutta, 1792. Reprint, London, 1793, pp. 70–71.
65 Ibid., pp. 74–75.
66 Ibid., p. 76.
67 Bowring, *Hyder Ali and Tipu Sultan*, 1899, p. 129.
68 Ibid., p. 129.
69 Ibid., p. 130.
70 Wilks, Mark. *Historical Sketches of the South of India, Vol. III*. Originally published in London in 1817. Digitized by the Internet Archive in 2007, p. 33.
71 Ibid., p. 43.
72 Ibid., p. 45.
73 Mackenzie, Roderick. *A Sketch of the War with Tippoo Sultan; Or A Detail of Military Operations, from the Commencement of Hostilities at the Lines of Travancore in December 1789, until the Peace Concluded before Seringapatam in February 1792*. Calcutta, 1799, p. 43, footnote.
74 Ibid., p. 7.
75 Ibid., p. 9, footnote.
76 Ibid., p. 25, footnote.
77 Wilks, Mark. *Historical Sketches, Vol. III*. Originally published in London in 1817. Digitized by the Internet Archive in 2007, p. 48.
78 Bowring, *Hyder Ali and Tipu Sultan*, 1899, p. 141.
79 Ibid., p. 141, footnote.
80 Mackenzie, Roderick. *A Sketch of the War*, 1799, p. 15.
81 Ibid., p. 16.
82 Ibid, p. 17, footnote.
83 Ibid., p. 19.
84 Ibid., p. 19, footnote.
85 Ibid., p. 19, footnote.
86 Hasan, Mohibbul. *History of Tipu Sultan*. Aakar Books, 1951, p. 163.
87 Ibid., p. 163.
88 Chetti, *A Guide to Seringapatam*, 1897, p. 94.
89 Kirmani, Mir Hussein Ali Khan. *History of Tipu Sultan*, translated from Persian by Col W. Miles, 1864. Reprint, New Delhi: Abhijeet Publications, 2017, p. 75.

90 Ibid., p. 75.
91 Ibid., p. 75.
92 Ibid., p. 75.
93 Ibid., p. 75.
94 Ibid., p. 75.
95 Ibid., p. 75.
96 Bristow, J. *A Narrative of the Sufferings of James Bristow, Belonging to the Bengal Artillery, during Ten Years Captivity with Hyder Ally and Tippoo Saheb*. Calcutta, 1792. Reprint, London, 1793, p. 111.
97 Ibid., p. 112.
98 Ibid., p. 113.
99 Ibid., p. 113.
100 Ibid., p. 114.
101 Wilks, Mark. *Historical Sketches of the South of India, Vol. III.* Originally published in London in 1817. Digitized by the Internet Archive in 2007, p. 48.
102 Balakrishna, Sandeep. *Tipu Sultan: The Tyrant of Mysore.* Rare Publications, 2013, p. 153.
103 Bowring, *Hyder Ali and Tipu Sultan*, 1899, p. 142.
104 Ibid., p. 142.
105 Ibid., p. 143.
106 Mackenzie, Roderick. *A Sketch of the War*, 1799, p. 11, footnote.
107 Ibid., p. 12.
108 Ibid., pp. 35–36.
109 Ibid., p. 36.
110 Ibid., p. 37.
111 Ibid., p. 38.
112 Bowring, *Hyder Ali and Tipu Sultan*, 1899, pp. 149–150.
113 Mackenzie, Roderick. *A Sketch of the War*, 1799, p. 74.
114 Ibid., p. 75.
115 Ibid., p. 77–78.
116 Ibid., p. 80.
117 Ibid., p. 80.
118 Ibid., p. 80.
119 Panikkar, K.M. *A History of Kerala, 1498–1801.* Originally published by Annamalai University in 1960. Reprint, Life Span Publishers and Distributors, 2021, p. 394.
120 Ibid., p. 394.

121 Ibid., p. 397.
122 Ibid., p. 403.
123 Bowring, *Hyder Ali and Tipu Sultan*, 1899, pp. 160–161.
124 Ibid., pp. 160–161.
125 Balakrishna, Sandeep. *Tipu Sultan: The Tyrant of Mysore.* Rare Publications, 2013, p. 139.
126 Bowring, *Hyder Ali and Tipu Sultan*, 1899, p. 152.
127 Ibid., p. 153.
128 Ibid., p. 154.
129 Ibid., p. 155.
130 Ibid., p. 156.
131 Ibid., pp. 157–158.
132 Ibid., p. 155.
133 Ibid., p. 155, footnote.
134 Ibid., p. 158.
135 Ibid., p. 163.
136 Ibid., p. 163.
137 Ibid., pp. 166–167.
138 Ibid., p. 168.
139 Ibid., p. 168.
140 Ibid., pp. 170–171.
141 Kirkpatrick, William. *Select Letters of Tippoo Sultan to Various Public Functionaries.* London: Black, Parry and Kingsbury, 1811, pp. 135–136.
142 Mackenzie, Roderick. *A Sketch of the War*, 1799, Appendix 3, p. 17.

**Chapter 7: The Company Devours the Tiger**

1 Dalrymple, William. *The Anarchy.* Bloomsbury, 2019, p. 333.
2 Ibid., p. 332.
3 Chetti, P. Stephen Basappa. *A Guide to Seringapatam and Its Vicinity; Historical and Traditional.* Town Press, 1897, p. 55.
4 Bowring, Lewin B. *Hyder Ali and Tipu Sultan and the Struggle with the Musalman Powers of the South.* London: Clarendon Press, 1899, p. 178.
5 Forrest, Denys M. *Tiger of Mysore: Life and Death of Tipu Sultan.* Allied Publishers, 1970, Appendix II, pp. 341–342.
6 Ibid., Appendix II, p. 342.
7 Chetti, P. Stephen Basappa. *A Guide to Seringapatam and Its Vicinity; Historical and Traditional.* Town Press, 1897, p. 55.

8 Balakrishna, Sandeep. *The Tyrant of Mysore*. Rare Publications, 2013, p. 178.
9 Bowring, Lewin B. *Hyder Ali and Tipu Sultan and the Struggle with the Musalman Powers of the South*. London: Clarendon Press, 1899, pp. 180-181.
10 Ibid., p. 181.
11 Ibid., p. 181.
12 Ibid., p. 181.
13 Ibid., p. 184.
14 Ibid., p. 191.
15 Ibid., p. 191, footnote.
16 Ibid., p. 192.
17 Ibid., p. 192.
18 Ibid., pp. 192–193.
19 Ibid., pp. 195–196.
20 Ibid., p. 196, footnote.
21 Ibid., p. 196.
22 Ibid., p. 196.
23 Ibid., p. 197.
24 Ibid., p. 197, footnote.
25 Ibid., p. 197.
26 Ibid., p. 198.
27 Chetti, P. Stephen Basappa. *A Guide to Seringapatam and Its Vicinity: Historical and Traditional*. Town Press, 1897, p. 65.
28 Ibid. p. 68.
29 Ibid., pp. 70–71.
30 Bowring, Lewin B. *Hyder Ali and Tipu Sultan and the Struggle with the Musalman Powers of the South*. London: Clarendon Press, 1899, p. 199.
31 Ibid., p. 200.
32 Dalrymple, William. *White Mughals*. Delhi: Penguin Books, 2002, p. 193.
33 Bowring, Lewin. B. *Hyder Ali and Tipu Sultan and the Struggle with the Musalman Powers of the South*. London: Clarendon Press, 1899, pp. 200–202.
34 Ibid., p. 204.
35 Ibid., p. 204.
36 Ibid., p. 205.

37 Hoover, James W. *Men without Hats: Dialogue, Discipline and Discontent in the Madras Army, 1806–1807.* Manohar Publishers and Distributors, 2007, pp. 74–75.
38 Bowring, Lewin B. *Hyder Ali and Tipu Sultan and the Struggle with the Musalman Powers of the South.* London: Clarendon Press, 1899, pp. 194–195.
39 Dalrymple, William. *White Mughals.* Penguin Books, 2002, p. 192.
40 Ibid., p. 193.
41 Chetti, P. Stephen Basappa. *A Guide to Seringapatam and Its Vicinity; Historical and Traditional.* Town Press, 1897, p. 86.
42 Bowring, Lewin B. *Hyder Ali and Tipu Sultan and the Struggle with the Musalman Powers of the South.* London: Clarendon Press, 1899, pp. 174–175.
43 Chetti, P. Stephen Basappa. *A Guide to Seringapatam and Its Vicinity: Historical and Traditional.* Town Press, 1897, pp. 111–112.
44 Ibid., p. 112.
45 Ibid., p. 112.
46 Ibid., p. 113.
47 Ibid., pp. 113–115.
48 Ibid., pp. 116–117.
49 Bowring, Lewin B. *Hyder Ali and Tipu Sultan and the Struggle with the Musalman Powers of the South.* London: Clarendon Press, 1899, p. 202.
50 Ibid., p. 202, footnote.
51 Ibid., pp. 223–224.
52 Ibid., p. 224, footnote.
53 Forrest, Denys M. *Tiger of Mysore: Life and Death of Tipu Sultan.* Allied Publishers, 1970, p. 2.
54 Ibid., Appendix V, p. 355.
55 Ibid., p. 354.
56 Ibid., p. 356.
57 https://www.deccanchronicle.com/nation/in-other-news/040616/treasures-lost-and-found.html
58 https://economictimes.indiatimes.com/news/international/world-news/tipu-sultans-sword-fetches-record-rs-143-crore-at-auction/close-connection-to-the-tiger-of-mysore/slideshow/100546956.cms
59 Bowring, p. 204; Beatson, pp. 236–237; Chetti, Panikkar, Balakrishna, et al.

60 https://www.bbc.com/news/world-asia-india-53944723
61 Chetti, P. Stephen Basappa. *A Guide to Seringapatam and Its Vicinity; Historical and Traditional.* Town Press, 1897, pp. 22–23.
62 Ibid., p. 23.
63 Ibid., pp. 23–24.
64 Ibid., p. 16.

**Chapter 8: Firangi Tales**

1 Yazdani, Kaveh. *Mysore at War.* ResearchGate, 2019, p. 20.
2 Scurry, James. *The Captivity, Sufferings and Escape, of James Scurry, Who Was Detained a Prisoner during Ten Years, in the Dominions of Hyder Ali and Tipoo Saib.* Originally published in London in 1824. Reprint, Forgotten Books, 2015, p. 35.
3 Ibid., p. 52.
4 Ibid., p. 62.
5 Ibid., p. 67.
6 Ibid., p. 69.
7 Ibid., p. 69.
8 Ibid., p. 74.
9 Ibid., p. 75.
10 Ibid., p. 141.
11 Ibid., p. 103.
12 Ibid., p. 104.
13 Ibid., p. 108.
14 Ibid., p. 110.
15 Ibid., p. 113.
16 Ibid., p. 129.
17 Ibid., p. 229.
18 Ibid., p. 208.
19 Bristow, J. *A Narrative of the Sufferings of James Bristow, Belonging to the Bengal Artillery, during Ten Years Captivity with Hyder Ally and Tippoo Saheb.* Calcutta, 1792. Reprint, London, 1793, p.21.
20 Ibid., p. 22.
21 Ibid., p. 23.
22 Ibid., pp. 23–24.
23 Ibid., p. 25.
24 Ibid., p. 26.
25 Ibid., pp. 26–27.

26 Ibid., pp. 27–28.
27 Ibid., p. 29.
28 Ibid., p. 30.
29 Ibid., pp. 31–32.
30 Ibid., pp. 34–35.
31 Ibid., p. 45.
32 Ibid., pp. 204–205.
33 Ibid., p. 47.
34 Ibid., p. 48.
35 Ibid., pp. 51–52.
36 Ibid., pp. 52–53.
37 Ibid., p. 54.
38 Ibid., p. 54.
39 Ibid., pp. 54–55.
40 Ibid., p. 55.
41 Ibid., p. 55.
42 Ibid., pp. 55–56.
43 Ibid., p. 56.
44 Ibid., p. 56.
45 Ibid., p. 57.
46 Ibid., p. 57.
47 Ibid., p. 59.
48 Ibid., p. 60.
49 Ibid., p. 61.
50 Ibid., pp. 61–62.
51 Ibid., p. 77.
52 Ibid., pp. 80–81.
53 Ibid., pp. 80–81.
54 Ibid., p. 81.
55 Ibid., p. 81.
56 Ibid., pp. 82–83.
57 Ibid., pp. 85–86.
58 Ibid., p. 87.
59 Ibid., p. 88.
60 Ibid., p. 92.
61 Ibid., p. 92.
62 Ibid., pp. 95–96.
63 Ibid., pp. 96–97.

64 Ibid., p. 91.
65 Ibid., pp. 98–99.
66 Ibid., p. 99.
67 Ibid., p. 100.
68 Ibid., p. 100.
69 Ibid., p. 105.
70 Ibid., pp. 107–108.
71 Ibid., p. 108.
72 Ibid., p. 110.
73 Ibid., pp. 110–111.
74 Ibid., p. 111.
75 Ibid., p. 134.
76 Ibid., p. 134.
77 Ibid., p. 136.
78 Ibid., p. 138.
79 Ibid., p. 138.
80 Ibid., p. 139.
81 Ibid., p. 140.
82 Ibid., p. 141.
83 Ibid., p. 207.
84 Peixoto, Eloy Joze Correa. *Memoirs of Hyder Ally from the Year 1758 to 1770*, in *Annual Report of the Mysore Archaeological Department for the Year 1937 (Part IV – Manuscripts)*. Bangalore: Government Press, 1938, p. 87.
85 Ibid., p. 89.
86 Ibid., p. 89.
87 Ibid., p. 89.
88 Ibid., pp. 89–90.
89 Ibid., pp. 90–91.
90 Ibid., p. 91.
91 Ibid., p. 91.
92 Ibid., pp. 92–93.
93 Ibid., p. 93.
94 Ibid., p. 93.
95 Ibid., p. 94.
96 Ibid., p. 95.
97 Ibid., p. 95.
98 Ibid., p. 97.

99 Ibid., p. 98.
100 Ibid., p. 101
101 Ibid., p. 101.
102 Ibid., p. 101.
103 Ibid., p. 101.
104 Ibid., p. 101.
105 Ibid., p. 102.
106 Ibid., pp. 102–103.
107 Ibid., p. 104.
108 Ibid., p. 105.
109 Ibid., p. 105.
110 Ibid., p. 105.
111 Ibid., p. 107.
112 Ibid., p. 107.
113 Ibid., p. 107.
114 Ibid., p. 107.
115 Ibid., p. 109.
116 Ibid., p. 109.
117 Ibid., p. 109.
118 Ibid., p. 110.
119 Ibid., p. 111.
120 Ibid., p. 111.
121 Ibid., p. 111.
122 Ibid., p. 113.
123 Ibid., p. 113.
124 Ibid., p. 114.
125 Ibid., p. 115.
126 Ibid., p. 115.
127 Ibid., pp. 115–116.
128 Ibid., pp. 116–119.
129 Kirkpatrick, William. *Select Letters of Tippoo Sultan to Various Public Functionaries*. London: Black, Parry and Kingsbury, 1811, p. 488.
130 Ibid., p. 486.
131 Ibid., p. 488.
132 Ibid., p. 488.
133 Ibid., p. 489.
134 Ibid., p. 489.
135 Ibid., p. 490.

136 Wilks, Mark. *Historical Sketches, Vol. I.* Originally published in London in 1817. Digitized by the Internet Archive in 2007, Preface, p. xxxviii.
137 Ibid., Vol. III, p. 24, footnote.
138 Ibid., Vol. III, p. 12.
139 Ibid., Vol. III, pp. 12–13.
140 Ibid., Vol. III, p. 28.
141 Ibid., Vol. III, p. 45.
142 Ibid., Vol. III, pp. 45–46.
143 Stewart, Charles. *A Descriptive Catalogue of the Oriental Library of the late Tippoo Sultan of Mysore, to Which Are Prefixed Memoirs of Hyder Aly and His Son, Tippoo Sultan.* Cambridge, 1809, p. 52.
144 Ibid., p. 55.
145 Ibid., p. 33.
146 Ibid., pp. 33–34.
147 Ibid., p. 42.
148 Ibid., p. 42.
149 Ibid., p. 42.
150 Buchanan, Francis. *A Journey from Madras through the Countries of Mysore, Canara and Malabar, Vol. II.* Originally published in 1807. Scholar's Choice edition, 2015, p. 420.
151 Ibid., p. 420.
152 Ibid., p. 421.
153 Ibid., p. 422.
154 Ibid., p. 432.
155 Ibid., p. 474.
156 Ibid., p. 352.
157 M.M.D.L.T. *The History of Hyder Shah alias Hyder Ali Khan Bahadur* or *New Memoirs Concerning the East Indies with Historical Notes.* London, 1784, p. 25.
158 Ibid., p. 27.
159 Ibid., p. 50.
160 Ibid., p. 50.
161 Ibid., pp. 50–51.
162 Ibid., pp. 52–53.
163 Ibid., p. 64.
164 Ibid., p. 80.
165 Ibid., pp. 92–96.
166 Ibid., pp. 97–98.

167 Ibid., p. 174.
168 Ibid., pp. 188–192.
169 Ibid., pp. 192–193.
170 Ibid., p. 207.
171 Ibid., p. 303.
172 Ibid., p. 311.
173 Ibid., pp. 321-322
174 Ibid., p. 324.
175 Ibid., p. 333.
176 Ibid., p. 416.
177 Ibid., p. 92.
178 Ibid., p. 113.
179 Habib, Irfan (ed.). *State and Diplomacy under Tipu Sultan: Documents and Essays.* Indian History Congress, Tulika Books, 2001, p. 2.
180 Ibid., Notes, p. 100.
181 Ibid., p. 82.
182 Ibid., p. 83.
183 Ibid., p. 84.
184 Ibid., p. 84.
185 Ibid., p. 101.
186 Ibid., p. 101.
187 Ibid., p. 85.
188 Ibid., p. 85.
189 Ibid., p. 86.
190 Ibid., p. 88.
191 Ibid., p. 89.
192 Ibid., p. 86.
193 Ibid., p. 86.
194 Ibid., p. 86.
195 Ibid., p. 86.
196 Ibid., p. 86.
197 Ibid., p. 86.
198 Ibid., p. 87.
199 Ibid., p. 86.
200 Ibid., p. 87.
201 Ibid., p. 90.
202 Ibid., p. 90.
203 Ibid., p. 90.

204 Ibid., p. 90.
205 Ibid., p. 91.
206 Ibid., p. 91.
207 Ibid., p. 92.
208 Ibid., p. 92.
209 Ibid., p. 93.
210 Ibid., p. 94.
211 Ibid., p. 94.
212 Ibid., p. 94.
213 Ibid., p. 93.
214 Ibid., p. 93.
215 Ibid., p. 95.
216 Ibid., p. 95.
217 Ibid., p. 95.
218 Ibid., p. 95.
219 Ibid., p. 93.
220 Ibid., p. 106.
221 Ibid., p. 106.
222 Bartolomeo, Paolino da San. *A Voyage to the East Indies: Containing an Account of the Manners, Customs, &c. of the Natives, with a Geographical Description of the Country,* edited by John Reinhold Forster, translated by William Johnston. Paris, 1796, pp. 68–69.
223 Ibid., p. 50.
224 Ibid., p. 58.
225 Ibid., p. 58.
226 Ibid., pp. 58–59.
227 Ibid., p. 175.
228 Ibid., p. 175.
229 Ibid., p. 65.
230 Ibid., pp. 65–66.
231 Ibid., p. 66.
232 Ibid., p. 76.
233 Ibid., p. 83.
234 Ibid., p. 84.
235 Ibid., p. 23.
236 Ibid., p. 24.
237 Bowring, Lewin B. *Hyder Ali and Tipu Sultan and the Struggle with the Musalman Powers of the South.* London: Clarendon Press, 1899, p. 117.

238 Ibid., p. 119.
239 Ibid., p. 119.
240 Ibid., p. 131.
241 Ibid., p. 132.
242 Ibid., p. 137.
243 Ibid., pp. 206–207.
244 Ibid., p. 227.
245 Beatson, Alexander. *A View of the Origin and Conduct of the War with Tippoo Sultaun; Comprising a Narrative of the Operations of the Army under the Command of Lieutenant-General George Harris, and of the Siege of Seringapatam.* London, 1800, pp. 216–217.
246 Ibid., p. 217.
247 Ibid., p. 220.
248 Ibid., p. 249.
249 Ibid., p. 252.
250 Ibid., p. 261.
251 Ibid., p. 262.
252 Ibid., p. 232.
253 Forrest, Denys M. *Tiger of Mysore: Life and Death of Tipu Sultan.* Allied Publishers, 1970, p. 21.
254 Ibid., p. 21.
255 Ibid., p. 22.
256 Ibid., p. 22.
257 Ibid., p. 22.
258 Ibid., p. 29.
259 Ibid., p. 30.
260 Ibid., p. 30.
261 Ibid., p. 30.
262 Ibid., p. 32.
263 Ibid., Appendix III, p. 343.
264 Logan, William. *Malabar.* 1887. Reprint, Madras Government Press, 1951, p. 139.

**Chapter 9: Chronicles of Non-European Writers**

1 Kirmani, Mir Hussein Ali Khan. *History of Tipu Sultan* translated from Persian by Col W. Miles, 1864. Reprint, New Delhi: Abhijeet Publications, 2017, p. 2.

2 Ibid., pp. 2–3.
3 Ibid., p. 6.
4 Ibid., p. 8.
5 Ibid., p. 9.
6 Ibid., p. 12.
7 Ibid., pp. 12–13.
8 Chetti, P. Stephen Basappa. *A Guide to Seringapatam and Its Vicinity; Historical and Traditional.* Town Press, 1897, p. 1.
9 Ibid., p. 2.
10 Ibid., pp. 4–5.
11 Ibid., p. 2.
12 Ibid., p. 2.
13 Ibid., p. 46.
14 Ibid., pp. 10–11.
15 Ibid., p. 14.
16 Ibid., p. 11.
17 Ibid., pp. 14–15.
18 Ibid., p. 27.
19 Ibid., p. 31.
20 Ibid., p. 43.
21 Ibid., p. 43
22 Ibid., pp. 43–44.
23 Ibid., p. 88.
24 Ibid., p. 88.
25 Rao, C. Hayavadana. *History of Mysore (1399–1799* CE*), Vol. I–III.* Bangalore: Government Press, 1948, p. 19.
26 Ibid., pp. 5–6.
27 Ibid., p. 6.
28 Ibid., pp. 8–9.
29 Ibid., p. 10.
30 Ibid., p. 10.
31 Ibid., p. 43.
32 Ibid., p. 44.
33 Ibid., Vol. II, p. 423.
34 Ibid., pp. 423–424, footnote.
35 Ibid., p. 546.
36 Ibid., p. 546.
37 Ibid., p. 547.

38 Ibid., p. 547.
39 Ibid., pp. 476–477.
40 Hasan, Mohibbul. *History of Tipu Sultan.* Aakar Books, 1951, p. 379.
41 Ibid., p. 395.
42 Ibid., p. 363.
43 Ibid., p. 365.
44 Ibid., p. 366.
45 Ibid., p. 366.
46 Ibid., p. 357.
47 Ibid., p. 363.
48 Ibid., pp. 375–376.
49 Ibid., p. 368.
50 Ibid., p. 413.
51 Ibid., pp. viii–ix.
52 Panikkar, K.M. *A History of Kerala, 1498–1801.* Originally published by Annamalai University in 1960. Reprint, Life Span Publishers and Distributors, 2021, p. 405.
53 Ibid., p. 410.
54 Ibid., p. 418.
55 Ibid., p. 409.
56 Ibid., p. 415.
57 Kareem, C.K. *Kerala under Haidar Ali and Tipu Sultan.* PhD thesis, Aligarh Muslim University. Cochin: Kerala History Association, 1973, Preface, p. iii.
58 Ibid., p. xii.
59 Wilks, Mark. *Historical Sketches, Vol. I.* Originally published in London in 1817. Digitized by the Internet Archive in 2007, p. 301.
60 Kareem, C.K. *Kerala under Haidar Ali and Tipu Sultan.* PhD thesis, Aligarh Muslim University. Cochin: Kerala History Association, 1973, Preface, p. xii.
61 Ibid., Preface, p. x.
62 Ibid., Preface, p. xi.
63 Ibid., p. 19.
64 Ibid., p. 19.
65 Ibid., p. 19.
66 Ibid., p. 20.
67 Ibid., p. 77.
68 Ibid., p. 86.

69 Ibid., p. 99.
70 Ibid., p. 101.
71 Ibid., p. 104.
72 Ibid., p. 104.
73 Ibid., p. 104.
74 Ibid., p. 106.
75 Ibid., pp. 113–114.
76 Ibid., p. 114.
77 Ibid., p. 115.
78 Ibid., p. 278.
79 Ibid., p. 196.
80 Ibid., pp. 196–197.
81 Balakrishna, Sandeep. *Tipu Sultan: The Tyrant of Mysore*. Rare Publications, 2013, p. 30.
82 Ibid., p. 159.
83 Ibid., p.168
84 Ibid., p.127
85 Ibid., p. 61.

**Chapter 10: The Tragedy of Coorg**

1 Rice, Benjamin Lewis. *Mysore and Coorg: A Gazetteer Compiled for the Government of India, (Vol. III: Coorg)*. Mysore Government Press, 1878, p. 175.
2 Belliappa, C.P. *Nuggets from Coorg History*. Rupa Publications, 2008, p. 30.
3 Bowring, Lewin B. *Hyder Ali and Tipu Sultan and the Struggle with the Musalman Powers of the South*. London: Clarendon Press, 1899, p. 65.
4 Belliappa, C.P. *Nuggets from Coorg History*. Rupa Publications, 2008, p. 34.
5 Rao, C. Hayavadana. *History of Mysore (1399–1799 CE), Vol. II*. Bangalore: Government Press, 1948, p. 548, footnote.
6 Ibid., p. 549.
7 Ibid., p. 550.
8 Belliappa, C.P. *Nuggets from Coorg History*. Rupa Publications, 2008, pp. 36–37.
9 Bowring, Lewin B. *Hyder Ali and Tipu Sultan and the Struggle with the Musalman Powers of the South*. London: Clarendon Press, 1899, p. 66.

10 Habib, Irfan (ed.). *State and Diplomacy under Tipu Sultan: Documents and Essays.* Indian History Congress, Tulika Books, 2001, p. 106.
11 Bowring, Lewin B. *Hyder Ali and Tipu Sultan and the Struggle with the Musalman Powers of the South.* London: Clarendon Press, 1899, p. 66.
12 Belliappa, C.P. *Nuggets from Coorg History.* Rupa Publications, 2008, p. 43.
13 Kirmani, Mir Hussein Ali Khan. *History of Tipu Sultan* translated from Persian by Col W. Miles, 1864. Reprint, New Delhi: Abhijeet Publications, 2017, p. 33.
14 Ibid., p. 33.
15 Ibid., p. 33.
16 Ibid., p. 35.
17 Ibid., p. 38.
18 Ibid., p. 39.
19 Ibid., p. 39.
20 Ibid., p. 39.
21 Ibid., p. 40.
22 Ibid., p. 35.
23 Buchanan, Francis. *A Journey from Madras through the Countries of Mysore, Canara and Malabar, Vol. II.* Originally published in 1807. Scholar's Choice edition, 2015, p. 94.
24 Ibid., p. 95.
25 Ibid., p. 96.
26 Ibid., p. 108.
27 Kirkpatrick, William. *Select Letters of Tippoo Sultan to Various Public Functionaries.* London: Black, Parry and Kingsbury, 1811, p. 167.
28 Ibid., p. 167.
29 Ibid., p. 171.
30 Ibid., p. 172.
31 Ibid., p. 174.
32 Buchanan, Francis. *A Journey from Madras through the Countries of Mysore, Canara and Malabar, Vol. II.* Originally published in 1807. Scholar's Choice edition, 2015, p. 95.
33 Kirkpatrick, William. *Select Letters of Tippoo Sultan to Various Public Functionaries.* London: Black, Parry and Kingsbury, 1811, p. 236.
34 Ibid., p. 236, footnote.

35 Ibid., pp. 228–229.
36 Ibid., p. 267.
37 Ibid., p. 269.
38 Bowring, Lewin B. *Hyder Ali and Tipu Sultan and the Struggle with the Musalman Powers of the South.* London: Clarendon Press, 1899, pp. 216–217.
39 Belliappa, C.P. *Nuggets from Coorg History.* Rupa Publications, 2008, p. 47.
40 Hasan, Mohibbul. *History of Tipu Sultan.* Aakar Books, 1951, p. 140.
41 Rice, Benjamin Lewis. *Mysore and Coorg: A Gazetteer Compiled for the Government of India, (Vol. III: Coorg).* Mysore Government Press, 1878, p. 118.
42 Ibid., p. 118.
43 Ibid., p. 119.
44 Ibid., p. 119.
45 Ibid., p. 125.

**Chapter 11: Pazhassi Raja's Uncanny Resistance**

1 Bowring, Lewin B. *Hyder Ali and Tipu Sultan and the Struggle with the Musalman Powers of the South.* London: Clarendon Press, 1899, p. 180.
2 Nair, C. Gopalan. *Wynad: Its Peoples and Traditions.* Originally published in Madras, 1911. Reprint, Gyan Books, 2020, pp. 4–5.
3 Ibid., p. 9.
4 Ibid., pp. 10–11.
5 Ibid., pp. 12–13.
6 Ibid., p. 17.
7 Ibid., p. 25.
8 Ibid., p. 18.
9 Ibid., p. 19.
10 Ibid., p. 26.
11 Ibid., pp. 27–28.
12 Ibid., p. 28.
13 Ibid., p. 28.
14 Ibid., p. 29.
15 Ibid., p. 29.
16 Menon, A. Sreedhara. *Kerala History and Its Makers.* Originally published in 1987. Reprint, D.C. Books, 2020, p. 165.

17 Buchanan, Francis. *A Journey from Madras through the Countries of Mysore, Canara and Malabar, Vol. II.* Originally published in 1807. Scholar's Choice edition, 2015, p. 485.
18 Nair, C. Gopalan. *Wynad: Its Peoples and Traditions.* Originally published in Madras, 1911. Reprint, Gyan Books, 2020, pp. 29–30.
19 Ibid., p. 30.
20 Buchanan, Francis. *A Journey from Madras through the Countries of Mysore, Canara and Malabar, Vol. II.* Originally published in 1807. Scholar's Choice edition, 2015, p. 484.
21 Ibid., pp. 483–484.
22 Ibid., p. 131.
23 Ibid., p. 484.
24 Ibid., p. 131.
25 Menon, A. Sreedhara. *Kerala History and Its Makers.* Originally published in 1987. Reprint, D.C. Books, 2020, p. 166.
26 Ibid., p. 166.
27 Ibid., p. 167.
28 Ibid., p. 167.
29 Ibid., p. 167.
30 Ibid., p. 167.
31 Ibid., p. 167.
32 Ibid., p. 168.
33 Ibid., p. 168.
34 Ibid., p. 168.
35 Ibid., p. 168.
36 Ibid., pp. 168–169.
37 Ibid., p. 169.
38 Ibid., p. 169.
39 Ibid., p. 170.
40 Nair, C. Gopalan. *Wynad: Its Peoples and Traditions.* Originally published in Madras, 1911. Reprint, Gyan Books, 2020, pp. 32–33.
41 Ibid., pp. 34–35.
42 Ibid., pp. 36–37.
43 Ibid., pp. 37–38.
44 Ibid., p. 38.
45 Ibid., p. 39.
46 Ibid., pp. 39–40.

47 Panikkar, K.M. *A History of Kerala, 1498–1801.* Originally published by Annamalai University in 1960. Reprint, Life Span Publishers and Distributors, 2021, p. 421.
48 Buchanan, Francis. *A Journey from Madras through the Countries of Mysore, Canara and Malabar, Vol. II.* Originally published in 1807. Scholar's Choice edition, 2015, p. 499.
49 Ibid., p. 500.
50 Ibid., p. 500.
51 Nair, C. Gopalan. *Wynad: Its Peoples and Traditions.* Originally published in Madras, 1911. Reprint, Gyan Books, 2020, p. 55.
52 Buchanan, Francis. *A Journey from Madras through the Countries of Mysore, Canara and Malabar, Vol. II.* Originally published in 1807. Scholar's Choice edition, 2015, p. 490.
53 Ibid., p. 490.
54 Ibid., p. 518.
55 Ibid., p. 518.
56 Ibid., p. 530.
57 Ibid., p. 532.
58 Ibid., p. 535.
59 Ibid., p. 536.
60 Ibid., p. 536.
61 Ibid., p. 536.
62 Ibid., p. 540.
63 Wilks, Mark. *Historical Sketches, Vol. I.* Originally published in London in 1817. Digitized by the Internet Archive in 2007, pp. 174–175.
64 Forrest, Denys M. *Tiger of Mysore: Life and Death of Tipu Sultan.* Allied Publishers, 1970, p. 269.
65 Ibid., p. 269.

**Chapter 12: Tipu's Temple Run and Jihadist Zeal**

1 Buchanan, Francis. *A Journey from Madras through the Countries of Mysore, Canara and Malabar, Vol. II.* Originally published in 1807. Scholar's Choice edition, 2015, p. 474.
2 Ibid., p. 558.
3 Nair, C. Gopalan. *Wynad: Its Peoples and Traditions.* Originally published in Madras, 1911. Reprint, Gyan Books, 2020, pp.118–119.

4 Ibid., p. 128.
5 Ibid., p. 53.
6 Buchanan, Francis. *A Journey from Madras through the Countries of Mysore, Canara and Malabar, Vol. II.* Originally published in 1807. Scholar's Choice edition, 2015, p. 332.
7 Kirkpatrick, William. *Select Letters of Tippoo Sultan to Various Public Functionaries*. London: Black, Parry and Kingsbury, 1811, p. 406.
8 Ibid., p. 435.
9 Stewart, Charles. *A Descriptive Catalogue of the Oriental Library of the late Tippoo Sultan of Mysore, to Which Are Prefixed Memoirs of Hyder Aly and His Son, Tippoo Sultan.* Cambridge, 1809, p. 52.
10 Wilks, Mark. *Historical Sketches, Vol. III.* Originally published in London in 1817. Digitized by the Internet Archive in 2007, p. 2.
11 Ibid., pp. 14–15.
12 Ibid., p. 4.
13 Ibid., p. 23.
14 Ibid., p. 23.
15 Buchanan, Francis. *A Journey from Madras through the Countries of Mysore, Canara and Malabar, Vol. II.* Originally published in 1807. Scholar's Choice edition, 2015, p. 463.
16 Jayashanker, S. *Temples of Kannoor District.* Kerala: Directorate of Census Operations, Census of India, 1999, p. 61.
17 Ibid., p. 65.
18 Ibid., pp. 70–71.
19 Ibid., p. 75.
20 Ibid., p. 75.
21 Ibid., p. 77.
22 Ibid., p. 77.
23 Ibid., p. 77.
24 Ibid., p. 78.
25 Ibid., p. 83.
26 Ibid., p. 106.
27 Ibid., p. 115.
28 Ibid., p. 140.
29 Ibid., pp. 118–119.
30 Ibid., p. 126.
31 Ibid., p. 130.
32 Ibid., p. 131.

33 Ibid., p. 189.
34 Ibid., pp. 204–205.
35 Ibid., p. 205.
36 Ibid., p. 216.
37 Ibid., p. 217.
38 Ibid., p. 224.
39 Ibid., p. 225.
40 Ibid., p. 225.
41 Ibid., p. 236.
42 Ibid., p. 237.
43 Ibid., p. 237.
44 Ibid., p. 237.
45 Ibid., p. 237.
46 Ibid., p. 237.
47 Ibid., p. 259.
48 Ibid., p. 259.
49 Ibid., p. 267.
50 Ibid., p. 269.
51 Ibid., p. 271.
52 Ibid., p. 283.
53 Ibid., p. 294.
54 Ibid., p. 298.
55 Ibid., p. 299.
56 Ibid., p. 301.
57 Ibid., p. 301.
58 Ibid., p. 321.
59 Ibid., p. 322.
60 Ibid., p. 322.
61 Ibid., p. 322.
62 Ibid., p. 326.
63 Ibid., p. 327.
64 Ibid., p. 327.
65 Ibid., p. 327.
66 Bayi, Aswathi Thirunal Gouri Lakshmi. *Thulasi Garlands*. Bharatiya Vidya Bhavan, 1998, pp. 138–139.
67 Jayashanker, S. *Temples of Kannoor District*. Kerala: Directorate of Census Operations, Census of India, 1999, p. 338.
68 Ibid., p. 338.

69 Ibid., p. 338.
70 Ibid., p. 353.
71 Ibid., p. 353.
72 Ibid., p. 353.
73 Ibid., p. 355.
74 Ibid., p. 355.
75 Jain, Meenakshi. *Flight of Deities and Rebirth of Temples: Episodes from Indian History*. Aryan Books International, 2019. p. 268.
76 Ibid., p. 258.
77 Balakrishna, Sandeep. *Tipu Sultan: The Tyrant of Mysore.* Rare Publications, 2013, p. 193.
78 Bowring, Lewin B. *Hyder Ali and Tipu Sultan and the Struggle with the Musalman Powers of the South.* London: Clarendon Press, 1899, p. 135.
79 Wilks, Mark. *Historical Sketches.* Originally published in London in 1817. Digitized by the Internet Archive in 2007, p. 267.
80 Kirkpatrick, William. *Select Letters of Tippoo Sultan to Various Public Functionaries.* London: Black, Parry and Kingsbury, 1811, pp. 242–243.
81 Ibid., p. 310.
82 Ibid., pp. 315–316.
83 Ibid., pp. 315–316.
84 Bartolomeo, Paolino da San. *A Voyage to the East Indies: Containing an Account of the Manners, Customs, &c. of the Natives, with a Geographical Description of the Country,* edited by John Reinhold Forster, translated by William Johnston. Paris, 1796, p. 137.
85 Ibid., p. 138.
86 Ibid., p. 139.
87 Mackenzie, Roderick. *A Sketch of the War with Tippoo Sultaun* or *A Detail of Military Operations, from the Commencement of Hostilities at the Lines of Travancore in December 1789, until the Peace Concluded Before Seringapatam in February 1792.* Calcutta, 1799, p. 203.
88 Jain, Meenakshi. *Flight of Deities and Rebirth of Temples: Episodes from Indian History*.
Aryan Books International, 2019. pp. 300–301.
89 Ibid., p. 338.
90 Kirkpatrick, William. *Select Letters of Tippoo Sultan to Various Public Functionaries.* London: Black, Parry and Kingsbury, 1811,. Preface, p. xx.

91 Bowring, Lewin B. *Hyder Ali and Tipu Sultan and the Struggle with the Musalman Powers of the South.* London: Clarendon Press, 1899, pp. 217–218.

92 Buchanan, Francis. *A Journey from Madras through the Countries of Mysore, Canara and Malabar, Vol. II.* Originally published in 1807. Scholar's Choice edition, 2015, p. 494.

93 Balakrishna, Sandeep. *Tipu Sultan: The Tyrant of Mysore.* Rare Publications, 2013, p. 307.

94 Buchanan, Francis. *A Journey from Madras through the Countries of Mysore, Canara and Malabar, Vol. II.* Originally published in 1807. Scholar's Choice edition, 2015, p. 328.

95 Bowring, Lewin B. *Hyder Ali and Tipu Sultan and the Struggle with the Musalman Powers of the South.* London: Clarendon Press, 1899, pp. 220–221.

96 Kirkpatrick, William. *Select Letters of Tippoo Sultan to Various Public Functionaries.* London: Black, Parry and Kingsbury, 1811, pp. 11–12.

97 Ibid., pp. 56–57.

98 Ibid., pp. 57–58.

99 Ibid., p. 59.

100 Ibid., p. 59.

101 Ibid., p. 60.

102 Ibid., p. 60.

103 Chetti, P. Stephen Basappa. *A Guide to Seringapatam and Its Vicinity; Historical and Traditional.* Town Press, 1897, pp. 92–93.

104 Ibid., pp. 92–93.

105 Ibid., pp. 94–95.

106 Ibid., p. 87.

107 Chandra, Bipan. *History of Modern India.* Orient BlackSwan, 2009, p. 29.

108 Hasan, Mohibbul. *History of Tipu Sultan.* Aakar Books, 1951, pp. 358–359.

109 Ibid., pp. 358–359.

110 Ibid., p. 359.

111 Ibid., p. 360.

112 Kareem, C.K. *Kerala under Haidar Ali and Tipu Sultan.* PhD thesis, Aligarh Muslim University. Cochin: Kerala History Association, 1973, p. 195.

113 Hasan, Mohibbul. *History of Tipu Sultan*. Aakar Books, 1951, p. 360.
114 Chetti, P. Stephen Basappa. *A Guide to Seringapatam and Its Vicinity; Historical and Traditional*. Town Press, 1897, p. 87.
115 Nair, C. Gopalan. *Wynad: Its Peoples and Traditions*. Originally published in Madras, 1911. Reprint, Gyan Books, 2020, p. 129.

**Chapter 13: Dreams, Letters and Zenana Women**

1 Habib, Irfan (ed.). *State and Diplomacy under Tipu Sultan: Documents and Essays*. Indian History Congress, Tulika Books, 2001, p. 5.
2 Ibid., p. 4.
3 Wilks, Mark. *Historical Sketches, Vol. III*. Originally published in London in 1817. Digitized by the Internet Archive in 2007, p. 25, footnote.
4 Balakrishna, Sandeep. *Tipu Sultan: The Tyrant of Mysore*. Rare Publications, 2013, p. 165.
5 Ibid., p. 160.
6 Kirkpatrick, William. *Select Letters of Tippoo Sultan to Various Public Functionaries*. London: Black, Parry and Kingsbury, 1811, Preface, p. x.
7 Ibid., Preface, p. xiv.
8 Ibid., Preface, p. xvi.
9 Wilks, Mark. *Historical Sketches, Vol. I*. Originally published in London in 1817. Digitized by the Internet Archive in 2007, Preface, p. xxx–xxxi.
10 Ibid., Preface, p. xxxi.
11 Ibid., Preface, p. xxxiii.
12 Kirkpatrick, William. *Select Letters of Tippoo Sultan to Various Public Functionaries*. London: Black, Parry and Kingsbury, 1811, p. 22.
13 Ibid., p. 55.
14 Ibid., p. 87.
15 Ibid., p. 74.
16 Ibid., p. 143.
17 Ibid., p. 191.
18 Ibid., p. 191.
19 Ibid., p. 23.
20 Ibid., pp. 23–24.
21 Ibid., p. 146.
22 Ibid., pp. 163–164.

23 Ibid., p. 123.
24 Ibid., p. 190.
25 Ibid., p. 190.
26 Ibid., p. 191.
27 Ibid., p. 208.
28 Ibid., p. 208, footnote.
29 Ibid., pp. 474–475.
30 Bowring, Lewin B. *Hyder Ali and Tipu Sultan and the Struggle with the Musalman Powers of the South.* London: Clarendon Press, 1899, p. 212.
31 Kirkpatrick, William. *Select Letters of Tippoo Sultan to Various Public Functionaries.* London: Black, Parry and Kingsbury, 1811, p. 222.
32 Ibid., p. 386.
33 Ibid., pp. 387–389.
34 Ibid., pp. 389–390.
35 Ibid., p. 416.
36 Ibid., p. 416, footnote.
37 Ibid., p. 418.
38 Ibid., p. 419.
39 Ibid., p. 420.
40 Ibid., p. 422.
41 Ibid., p. 422.
42 Ibid., pp. 424–425.
43 Ibid., p. 428.
44 Ibid., p. 428.
45 Ibid., p. 433.
46 Ibid., p. 439.
47 Ibid., p. 456.
48 Ibid., pp. 469–470.
49 Ibid., pp. 479–480.
50 Ibid., p. 482.
51 Ibid., p. 483.
52 Ibid., p. 160.
53 Ibid., p. 160.
54 Ibid., pp. 216–217.
55 Ibid., pp. 219–220.
56 Ibid., p. 297.
57 Ibid., p. 314.

58 Ibid., p. 274.
59 Ibid., p. 463.
60 Ibid., p. 464.
61 Ibid., p. 464.
62 Ibid., p. 464.
63 Ibid., p. 471.
64 Ibid., p. 471.
65 Ibid., p. 471, footnote.
66 Ibid., p. 184.
67 Ibid., p. 179.
68 Ibid., p. 193.
69 Ibid., p. 224.
70 Ibid., p. 466.
71 Ibid., p. 472.
72 Ibid., p. 472.
73 Ibid., p. 472, footnote.
74 Ibid., p. 485, footnote.
75 Ibid., p. 486.
76 Ibid., p. 3.
77 Ibid., pp. 3–4.
78 Ibid., p. 3, footnote.
79 Ibid., pp. 4–5.
80 Bowring, Lewin B. *Hyder Ali and Tipu Sultan and the Struggle with the Musalman Powers of the South.* London: Clarendon Press, 1899, pp. 225–226.
81 Kirkpatrick, William. *Select Letters of Tippoo Sultan to Various Public Functionaries.* London: Black, Parry and Kingsbury, 1811, Preface, p. xvii–xviii.
82 Ibid., pp. 431–432.
83 Wilks, Mark. *Historical Sketches, Vol. III.* Originally published in London in 1817. Digitized by the Internet Archive in 2007, p. 25, footnote.
84 Kirkpatrick, William. *Select Letters of Tippoo Sultan to Various Public Functionaries.* London: Black, Parry and Kingsbury, 1811, pp. 18–19.
85 Ibid., p. 19.
86 Ibid., pp. 203–204.
87 Ibid., p. 204, footnote.
88 Ibid., pp. 205–206.

89 Ibid., p. 9.
90 Ibid., p. 9, footnote.
91 Tipu Sultan's dreams in his own handwriting, presented in the name of The Marquis Wellesley to Hugh Inglis Esqr., Chairman of the Court of Directors, by Major Alexander Beatson, late aid de camp to the governor-general (British Library 10 Islamic 3563f.29v).
92 Husain, Mahmud. *The Dreams of Tipu Sultan*. Translated from the original Persian without an introduction and notes. Delhi: Facsimilic Publisher, p. 10.
93 Ibid., pp. 61–62.
94 Ibid., pp. 63–64.
95 Ibid., p. 84.
96 Ibid., pp. 81–82.
97 Ibid., pp. 92–93.
98 Ibid., p. 90.
99 Ibid., pp. 54–56.
100 Ibid., p. 78.
101 Ibid., pp. 78–79.
102 Brittlebank, Kate. *Tiger: The Life of Tipu Sultan*. Juggernaut Books, 2016, p. 81.
103 Mackenzie, Roderick. *A Sketch of the War with Tippoo Sultaun* or *A Detail of Military Operations, from the Commencement of Hostilities at the Lines of Travancore in December 1789, until the Peace Concluded Before Seringapatam in February 1792.* Calcutta, 1799, p. 4, footnote.
104 Chetti, P. Stephen Basappa. *A Guide to Seringapatam and Its Vicinity: Historical and Traditional.* Town Press, 1897, p. 19.
105 Hasan, Mohibbul. *History of Tipu Sultan.* Aakar Books, 1951, p. 372.
106 Wilks, Mark. *Historical Sketches, Vol. III.* Originally published in London in 1817. Digitized by the Internet Archive in 2007, p. 302.

**Chapter 14: Tigers, Rockets and Other Fads**

1 Bowring, Lewin B. *Hyder Ali and Tipu Sultan and the Struggle with the Musalman Powers of the South.* London: Clarendon Press, 1899, p. 211.
2 M.M.D.L.T. *The History of Hyder Shah alias Hyder Ali Khan Bahadur* or *New Memoirs Concerning the East Indies with Historical Notes.* London, 1784, p. 255.

3 Rao, C. Hayavadana. *History of Mysore (1399–1799 CE), Vol. I–III.* Bangalore: Government Press, 1948.
4 Yazdani, Kaveh. *Mysore at War.* ResearchGate, 2019, p. 23.
5 Bowring, Lewin B. *Hyder Ali and Tipu Sultan and the Struggle with the Musalman Powers of the South.* London: Clarendon Press, 1899, p. 223.
6 Kirkpatrick, William. *Select Letters of Tippoo Sultan to Various Public Functionaries.* London: Black, Parry and Kingsbury, 1811, p. 395.
7 Chetti, P. Stephen Basappa. *A Guide to Seringapatam and Its Vicinity; Historical and Traditional.* Town Press, 1897, pp. 99–100.
8 M.M.D.L.T. *The History of Hyder Shah alias Hyder Ali Khan Bahadur* or *New Memoirs Concerning the East Indies with Historical Notes.* London, 1784, p. 28.
9 Wilks, Mark. *Historical Sketches, Vol. III.* Originally published in London in 1817. Digitized by the Internet Archive in 2007, p. 274.
10 Kirkpatrick, William. *Select Letters of Tippoo Sultan to Various Public Functionaries.* London: Black, Parry and Kingsbury, 1811, p. 91.
11 Ibid., p. 92.
12 Ibid., pp. 96–97.
13 Ibid., p. 95.
14 Bowring, Lewin B. *Hyder Ali and Tipu Sultan and the Struggle with the Musalman Powers of the South.* London: Clarendon Press, 1899, p. 212.
15 Kirkpatrick, William. *Select Letters of Tippoo Sultan to Various Public Functionaries.* London: Black, Parry and Kingsbury, 1811, p. 97.
16 Ibid., p. 98.
17 Ibid., p. 98.
18 Ibid., p. 98.
19 Ibid., p. 99.
20 Ibid., pp. 391–392.
21 Kirmani, Mir Hussein Ali Khan. *History of Tipu Sultan* translated from Persian by Col W. Miles, 1864. Reprint, New Delhi: Abhijeet Publications, 2017, pp. 109–110.
22 Kirkpatrick, William. *Select Letters of Tippoo Sultan to Various Public Functionaries.* London: Black, Parry and Kingsbury, 1811, p. 381.
23 Ibid., p. 381, footnote.

24 Ibid., p. 16.
25 Ibid., p. 66.
26 Ibid., p. 214.
27 Ibid., p. 390.
28 Ibid., p. 215.
29 Ibid., p. 216.
30 Ibid., pp. 438–439.
31 Ibid., p. 303.
32 Chetti, P. Stephen Basappa. *A Guide to Seringapatam and Its Vicinity; Historical and Traditional.* Town Press, 1897, p. 25.
33 Ibid., p. 18.
34 Bowring, Lewin B. *Hyder Ali and Tipu Sultan and the Struggle with the Musalman Powers of the South.* London: Clarendon Press, 1899, p. 221.
35 Ibid., pp. 221–222.
36 Habib, Irfan (ed.). *State and Diplomacy under Tipu Sultan: Documents and Essays.* Indian History Congress, Tulika Books, 2001, p. 73.
37 Ibid., p. 78.
38 Kirkpatrick, William. *Select Letters of Tippoo Sultan to Various Public Functionaries.* London: Black, Parry and Kingsbury, 1811, p. 146.
39 Ibid., pp. 310–311.
40 Ibid., p. 231.
41 Ibid., p. 231.
42 Ibid., p. 253.
43 Ibid., p. 253.
44 Wilks, Mark. *Historical Sketches.* Originally published in London in 1817. Digitized by the Internet Archive in 2007, p. 58.
45 Kirkpatrick, William. *Select Letters of Tippoo Sultan to Various Public Functionaries.* London: Black, Parry and Kingsbury, 1811, p. 186.
46 Ibid., p. 186.
47 Ibid., p. 186, footnote.
48 Ibid., p. 187.
49 Ibid., p. 188.
50 Ibid., p. 189.
51 Ibid., p. 209.
52 Ibid., p. 209.
53 Ibid., pp. 239–240.
54 Ibid., pp. 282–283.

55 Ibid., pp. 231–233.
56 Ibid., p. 240.
57 Ibid., p. 187.
58 Ibid., p. 127.
59 Ibid., p. 80.
60 Ibid., p. 212.
61 Ibid., p. 213.
62 Ibid., p. 265.
63 Ibid., pp. 265–266.
64 Bowring, Lewin B. *Hyder Ali and Tipu Sultan and the Struggle with the Musalman Powers of the South.* London: Clarendon Press, 1899, pp. 213–214.
65 Ibid., p. 210.
66 Wilks, Mark. *Historical Sketches, Vol. III.* Originally published in London in 1817. Digitized by the Internet Archive in 2007, p. 308.
67 Ibid., pp. 306–307.
68 Chetti, P. Stephen Basappa. *A Guide to Seringapatam and Its Vicinity: Historical and Traditional.* Town Press, 1897, p. 33.
69 Buchanan, Francis. *A Journey from Madras through the Countries of Mysore, Canara and Malabar, Vol. II.* Originally published in 1807. Scholar's Choice edition, 2015, pp. 165–166.
70 Bowring, Lewin B. *Hyder Ali and Tipu Sultan and the Struggle with the Musalman Powers of the South.* London: Clarendon Press, 1899, p. 209.
71 Wilks, Mark. *Historical Sketches, Vol. III.* Originally published in London in 1817. Digitized by the Internet Archive in 2007, p. 266.
72 Habib, Irfan (ed.). *State and Diplomacy under Tipu Sultan: Documents and Essays.* Indian History Congress, Tulika Books, 2001, p. 22.
73 Wilks, Mark. *Historical Sketches, Vol. III.* Originally published in London in 1817. Digitized by the Internet Archive in 2007, p. 9.
74 Ibid., p. 8.
75 Ibid., p. 9.
76 Ibid., pp. 9–10.
77 M.M.D.L.T. *The History of Hyder Shah alias Hyder Ali Khan Bahadur* or *New Memoirs Concerning the East Indies with Historical Notes.* London, 1784, p. 48.

78 Habib, Irfan (ed.). *State and Diplomacy under Tipu Sultan: Documents and Essays.* Indian History Congress, Tulika Books, 2001, p. xx.

**Chapter 15: Vellore and Other Revolts**

1 Gopalakrishnan, S. (ed.). *The South Indian Rebellions: Before and After 1800.* South Indian History Congress. Palaniappa Brothers, 2007, p. 25.
2 Ibid., pp. 26–27.
3 Ibid., pp. 42–43.
4 Ibid., p. 46.
5 Bayly, C.A. *Empire and Information: Intelligence Gathering and Social Communication in India, 1780–1870.* Cambridge University Press, 1996, p. 209.
6 Hoover, James W. *Men without Hats: Dialogue, Discipline and Discontent in the Madras Army, 1806–1807.* Manohar Publishers and Distributors, 2007, pp. 49–50.
7 Manikumar, K.A. *Vellore Revolt, 1806.* Allied Publishers, 2006, p. 21.
8 Ibid., p. 38.
9 Mount, Ferdinand. *The Tears of the Rajas: Mutiny, Money and Marriage in India 1805–1905.* UK: Simon & Schuster, 2015, p. 72.
10 Manikumar K A. *Foreshadowing the Great Rebellion.* Orient Blackswan, 2021, p. 64
11 Ibid., p. 57.
12 Ibid., p. 58.
13 Ibid., pp. 60–61.
14 Hoover, James W. *Men without Hats: Dialogue, Discipline and Discontent in the Madras Army, 1806–1807.* Manohar Publishers and Distributors, 2007, pp. 242–243.
15 Bayly, C.A. *Empire and Information: Intelligence Gathering and Social Communication in India, 1780–1870.* Cambridge University Press, 1996, p. 90.
16 Ibid., p. 123.
17 Menon, A. Sreedhara. *Kerala History and Its Makers.* Originally published in 1987. Reprint, D.C. Books, 2020, p. 175.
18 Ibid., p. 175.
19 Ibid., p. 176.
20 Ibid., p. 177.
21 Ibid., p. 177.

22 Ibid., p. 177.
23 Ibid., p. 178.
24 Ibid., p. 179.
25 Mount, Ferdinand. *The Tears of the Rajas: Mutiny, Money and Marriage in India 1805–1905*. UK: Simon & Schuster, 2015, p. 76.
26 Ibid., p. 85.
27 Ibid., p. 98.
28 Ibid., pp. 98–99.
29 Chetti, P. Stephen Basappa. *A Guide to Seringapatam and Its Vicinity; Historical and Traditional.* Town Press, 1897, p. 83.
30 Mount, Ferdinand. *The Tears of the Rajas: Mutiny, Money and Marriage in India 1805–1905*. UK: Simon & Schuster, 2015, pp. 101–102.
31 Ibid., p. 103.
32 Ibid., p. 94.

**Chapter 16: Tipu Sultan's Modern Makeover**

1 Hasan, Mohibbul. *History of Tipu Sultan.* Aakar Books, 1951, p. 368.
2 Hoover, James W. *Men without Hats: Dialogue, Discipline and Discontent in the Madras Army, 1806–1807.* Manohar Publishers and Distributors, 2007, p. 74.
3 Hasan, Mohibbul. *History of Tipu Sultan.* Aakar Books, 1951, p. 383.
4 Ibid, p. 91.
5 Ibid, p. 91.
6 Brittlebank, Kate. *Tiger: The Life of Tipu Sultan.* Juggernaut Books, 2016, p. 45.
7 Ibid., p. 45.
8 Ibid., p. 45.
9 Ibid., p. 45.
10 Ibid., p. 46.
11 Ibid., p. 43.
12 Ibid., p. 67.
13 Ibid., p. 67.
14 Ibid., p. 68.
15 Ibid., p. 117.
16 Hasan, Mohibbul. *History of Tipu Sultan.* Aakar Books, 1951, p. 143.
17 Ibid., p. 143.
18 Ibid., pp. 142–143.
19 Ibid., p. 141.

20 Ibid., p. 141.
21 Ibid., p. 373.
22 Ibid., p. 381.
23 Kareem, C.K. *Kerala under Haidar Ali and Tipu Sultan.* PhD thesis, Aligarh Muslim University. Cochin: Kerala History Association, 1973, Preface, p. iii.
24 Ibid., Preface, p. iv.
25 Ibid., Preface, p. iv.
26 Ibid., p. 183.
27 Ibid., p. 182.
28 Ibid., p. 184.
29 Ibid., p. 183.
30 Ibid., p. 186.
31 Ibid., p. 187, footnote.
32 Ibid., p. 187.
33 Ibid., p. 187, footnote.
34 Ibid., p. 189.
35 Ibid., pp. 190–191.
36 Ibid., pp. 191–192.
37 Ibid., p. 192.
38 Ibid., p. 192.
39 Ibid., p. 194.
40 Brittlebank, Kate. *Tiger: The Life of Tipu Sultan.* Juggernaut Books, 2016, p. 74.
41 Ibid., p. 75.
42 Michell, George (ed.). *Eternal Kaveri.* Marg Publications, 1999, p. 52.
43 Ibid., p. 52.
44 Brittlebank, Kate. *Tiger: The Life of Tipu Sultan.* Juggernaut Books, 2016, p. 60.
45 Ibid., p. 60.
46 Ibid., p. 62.

# GLOSSARY

*Ahmedy* – Term used by the Mysore sultans to refer to slave battalions, usually comprising men who were forcibly converted to Islam.

*Acharam* – Rules and protocols passed on from generation to generation and held to be inviolable.

*Acharya* – Spiritual guru or learned person who teaches religious rules and protocols. In modern parlance, it refers to an expert teacher or scholar in any discipline.

*Amrutham/amrit* – The nectar of immortality.

*Angam* – A medieval form of duel.

*Antharjanam* – Namboothiri Brahmin lady, literally meaning 'one who lives indoors'.

*Ariyittu Vazhcha* – An ancient tradition marking the coronation of a ruler. Rice (*ari*) is sprinkled on the prince's head while Vedic chants and rituals accompany the ceremony, followed by the placement of the crown on his head and the sceptre (*chenkol*) in his hand. Today, the tradition continues in various diluted forms as erstwhile royals are feted by common folk bringing gifts of rice, coconuts, etc.

*Asaf/Asoph* – Treasurer, chancellor or custodian of the treasury.

*Balikallu* – Stone altar meant for animal sacrifice found in every temple (*bali* refers to sacrifice and *kallu* means stone).

*Bayadere* – Temple dancer or *devadasi.*

*Bhandaram* – *Hundi* or container for cash found in temples for collecting cash offerings.

*Chaver pada* – Suicide squads of warriors.

*Chekon/chekavan* – A warrior who fights duels; the plural or respectful address is *chekavar.*

*Chela* – Term used by the Mysore sultans to refer to slave battalions, usually comprising men who were forcibly converted to Islam.

*Chembu* – Copper.

*Churika* – A flexible sword, a weapon used by *kalari* practitioners.

*Chuttambalam* – A distinctive feature of Kerala temple architecture, the *chuttambalam* is an outer structure within the temple walls with a stone paved walkway, used by devotees to circumambulate the main shrine. The *dwajasthambam* or sacred flag-post is found here.

*Dalawai/dalawa* – Chief minister who administers the kingdom on behalf of the king.

*Desa/desam* – Country or region.

*Devadasi* - Temple courtesan. The word literally means 'servant of god'. This ancient tradition of dedicating girl children to the gods flourished alongside temples and empires and dates back at least to the 7th century.

*Dwarapalaka* – Doorkeepers or guards, sculptures found in many Hindu temples.

*Ezhava* – A trading caste in the state of Kerala, whose ancestors are said to have originated in Eezham or Eelam (Sri Lanka). Today they form the largest Hindu community, constituting 23 per cent of the state's population.

*Fanam* – Coins issued for use as currency. During the British Raj, the South Indian kingdoms used *panam* or punch-marked coins. Fanam is the anglicized form.

*Faujdar* – Military chief or commander of a battalion, who often had judicial and revenue collection functions.

*Ghar-vapasi* – Literally means 'returning home' and refers to the return of converts to Islam or Christianity to the Hindu fold.

*Gopuram* – The entrance gateway or the top part of a traditional South Indian or Dravidian temple structure, which typically rises in a tapering form and has bulbous finials at the top. Similar to the *shikaras* found in the temples of northern India. Gopurams are usually decorated on the outside with exquisite sculptures and carvings. They grew bigger and more elaborate from the mid-12th century until the imposing gateways came to dominate the temple complex, often surpassing the main sanctum or *vimana* in size and grandeur.

*Gurikkal/gurukkal* – Maestro or teacher, especially one who teaches martial arts, such as *kalariapayattu*.

*Hiranya-garbham* – A ritual performed by Brahmins to elevate people of lower castes to Kshatriya status, especially when the latter have acquired political power but need social sanction.

*Hircarrah/harcarrah/hurcarrah* – Spy or informer.

*Hukumnama* – Ruler's orders in the form of detailed written instructions to officials.

*Hussar* – A member of a class of light cavalry, sporting a colourful military uniform with designer jackets decorated with braids. *Hussars* had a romanticized image of being dashing and adventurous. European armies often had *hussar* regiments, and no doubt they introduced the tradition to India. Several modern armies, including those of Britain and France, retain the designation of *hussars*. The Mysore sultans probably adopted the designation from the French.

*Illam* – Abode of a Namboothiri family.

*Jagir* – Estate or land granted to an official or soldier by an overlord.

*Jambudvipa* – Indian subcontinent as described in ancient Indian texts. *Dvipa* means 'island' or 'continent'. The literal meaning is 'land of jambu trees'. Jambu or jamun is also known as Malabar plum (botanical name 'syzygium cumini'). Emperor Ashoka used the term *Jambudvipa* in the 3rd century to refer to his domain.

*Jetti* – Professional strangler, a man trained to kill people by strangulation, usually at the ruler's command.

*Kalari* – Training ground for martial arts.

*Kalaripayattu* – Indian martial art that originated in North Malabar.

*Karnavar* – Eldest male member of a matrilineal clan.

*Karyasthan* – Trusted aide.

*Kavu* – Sacred grove.

*Kila/qila* – Fort.

*Kiledar/Killedar* – Person in charge of the fort.

*Kshethram* – Temple.

*Kovilakam* – Royal dwelling.

*Kudipaka* – Vendetta.

*Kudumba kshethram* – Family temple.

*Kula-deiyvam* – Clan deity.

*Kula thozhil* – Traditional occupation of a particular community or clan.

*Kunjali Marakkar* – The term refers to four Muslim naval admirals of the Zamorin who fiercely resisted Portuguese incursions into Malabar for nearly a century. The last of the *Kunjalis*, Muhammed Kunjali Marakkar, was martyred in 1600.

*Linga* – Symbol of Lord Shiva, found in all Saivite places of worship.

*Maha-kshethram* – Great temple.

*Makkathayam* – System of patrilineal descent.

*Mappila/Moplah* – Malabar Muslims are known as *Mappilas*. *Moplah* is the anglicized version.

*Marumakkathayam* – System of matrilineal descent and kinship, common in Kerala, especially among the Nairs. It is a system wherein a man's sister's children (*marumakkal*) are his legitimate heirs. Property devolves through the female line.

*Musnud/masnad* – Royal seat equivalent to a throne.

*Mundu/dhoti* – A plain, unstitched garment, usually white, worn by both men and women, tied at the waist in a simple knot.

*Moopan* – Tribal chief.

*Naduvazhi* – Ruler or chief.

*Namboothiri/Nambuthiri/Namboodiri* – This is a generic term for the Brahmins of Kerala.

*Nayak/naik/naiker* – Military rank (e.g., corporal), title conferred on military leaders, also means chief or chieftain. *Nayak* literally means 'hero'.

*Nawab/nabob* – Muslim ruler. *Nabob* is the anglicized spelling.

*Nazar* – Gift to a ruler or overlord (probably a short form of the Hindi word *nazrana*).

*Nercha* – Prayerful offering to a god in anticipation of a special blessing or favour.

*Nivedya/nivedyam/naivedyam* – Food offering to a deity or divinity.

*Ooralar* – Hereditary owners of temples; prominent persons in a village or *taluq* having certain hereditary privileges and well-defined responsibilities, usually relating to temple rituals.

*Paathiri* – Malayalam version of the word 'padre' meaning father. Refers to a Christian priest.

*Pada* – Battalion or group of warriors, usually *Nairs*, hence the term *Nair-pada*. The root is the Tamil word *padai,* which means 'army'.

*Padayottam* – Military march or military run; the term specifically refers to the Mysore sultans' march on Malabar, which spelt terror and ruin.

*Padsha/padasa/pasha/pachcha* – Various ways of spelling *badshah*, a Hindi word meaning king or emperor.

*Padshahlinga* – A greenish jadeite *linga* donated by *Badshah* Tipu Sultan to the Nanjundeswara Temple at Nanjangud in Karnataka.

*Palayakkar/polygar/poligar* – Leader of a military camp. *Poligar* is the anglicized version of the vernacular *palayakkar*. The latter word is derived from *palayam,* which means military camp. In the time of the sultans, the Tamil country was fragmented into several units ruled by *palayakkars* rather than rajas.

*Pallivetta* – A temple ritual wherein the sacred idol is taken out in a procession, with a priest carrying it on his head or in a chariot or astride an elephant.

*Pattam* – Rent paid when a piece of land is leased for cultivation.

*Pattola* – Palm leaf manuscript.

*Peedom* – A sacred pedestal or stool used by *theyyam* performers.

*Ponnakambadi ezhunallathu* – A ceremony involving the transfer of sacred ornaments (*thiruvabharanam*) from the residence of the king to the temple and back again. This is usually accompanied by an armed escort, and elephants or chariots may be used amidst great fanfare.

*Rakshabhogam* – Protection money paid to a military leader to keep him from attacking and looting a region.

*Samuthiri* – See Zamorin.

*Sathya-pareeksha/satya-pariksha* – Trial by ordeal to ascertain truth (similar to *agni pariksha*).

*Shakti-peethas* – Fifty-one locations where the pieces of Goddess Sati's body fell after her horrific self-immolation. These are scattered all over the Indian subcontinent. Kerala's only *Shakti-peetha* is at Kottiyoor in Kannur district.

*Shuddhikalasam* – Purification ritual performed to eliminate the effects of 'pollution' or contamination.

*Sila-vigraham* – Stone sculptured idol.

*Smarthavicharam* – Trial of chastity in accordance with the laws of the *smrithis* or sacred Hindu texts, an odious practice among the Namboothiris of Kerala that prevailed almost until the dawn of independence from Britain. The last trial occurred in Malabar in 1930. The crime was illicit sex, and the punishment was excommunication and banishment. The object of *smarthavicharam* was invariably a woman.

*Srikovil* – Sanctum sanctorum of a temple, the inner chamber where the sacred idol is placed.

*Svaroopam* – Domain or realm of a ruler.

*Tamil Sangam* – The famed assembly of poets that gathered presumably at Madurai between100 BCE and 200 CE, and produced volumes of literature and poetry by hundreds of poets and scholars. The literature is collectively called *Tamil Sangam* literature.

*Thanthri/tantri* – Temple priest.

*Tharavad* – A joint family comprising all the descendants in the female line of one single female ancestor. Clans and ancestral homesteads are also loosely referred to as *tharavad*.

*Thiruvabharanam* – Sacred ornaments that belong to an idol in a temple.

*Theyyam* – An ancient tradition of North Malabar, which forms a captivating blend of folk art and religious ritual. The performers wear elaborate and primitive costumes, dance wildly, play with fire, bless the devotees and utter prophesies.

*Thirumangalyam* – An auspicious object, a symbol of prosperity and good tidings.

*Utsava-thitambu/uthsava thidambu* – Representation of the deity taken out during festivals, usually adorned and carried by the priest on his head during the procession.

*Usud Ilhye* – A term used by the Mysore sultans to refer to slave battalions, usually comprising men who were forcibly converted to Islam.

*Valiya balikallu* – Main sacrificial alter found in Hindu temples.

*Vattezhuthu* – Archaic Malayalam script that was widely used from the 8th to the 15th century.

*Vilakku* – Traditional lamp found in Hindu temples and homes. *Nilavilakku* (or *kuthuvilakku*) is a lamp placed on the ground, while *thookuvilakku* is one hung from a rafter or from the ceiling. *Lakshmivilakku* has an image of Goddess Lakshmi.

*Vadakkanpaatu* – Northern ballads of Malabar.

*Vazhunnavar* – Rulers, landlords, chieftains.

*Vedan/vettakkaran* – Hunter (vetta means 'hunt' in Malayalam)

*Vigraham* – Sacred idol in a temple.

*Wodeyar/Wadiyar* – Ruler of the kingdom of Mysore, name of the dynasty.

*Yakshi* – A bloodthirsty female tree spirit that pounces on humans and drinks their blood. This is the concept of *yakshi* in Kerala. It differs vastly from the benevolent form of tree spirits mentioned in our scriptures where the male is a *yaksha*, *gandharva* or celestial being. Kubera is a famed *yaksha*. Whereas *yakshi* once represented fertility and prosperity, today the word has unpleasant connotations. In Malayalam films, the *yakshi* is portrayed as a fearsome Dracula-like apparition.

*Zamorin* – Anglicized version of Samuthiri, a generic term for the rajas of Kozhikode or Calicut, who came to power around the 12th century and held sway until Haider Ali's invasion of Malabar in 1766 and the subsequent British takeover in 1792. The Portuguese tried but failed to dislodge the Samuthiris.

# REFERENCES

Allen, Charles. *Coromandel: A Personal History of South India*. Little Brown, 2017.

Arora, Namit. *Indians: A Brief History of a Civilization*. Penguin Random House India, 2021.

Ayyar, K.V. Krishna. *The Zamorins of Calicut: From the Earliest Times Down to AD 1806*. Norman Printing Bureau, 1938.

Bayi, Aswathi Thirunal Gouri Lakshmi. *Thulasi Garlands*. Bharatiya Vidya Bhavan, 1998.

———. *Sree Padmanabha Swamy Temple*. Bharatiya Vidya Bhavan, 2014.

Balakrishna, Sandeep. *Tipu Sultan: The Tyrant of Mysore*. Rare Publications, 2013.

Bartolomeo, Paolino da San. *A Voyage to the East Indies: Containing an Account of the Manners, Customs, &c. of the Natives, with a Geographical Description of the Country*, edited by John Reinhold Forster, translated by William Johnston. Paris, 1796.

Basu, Shrabani. *Spy Princess: The Life of Noor Inayat Khan*. Lotus, 2006.

Bayly, C.A. *Empire and Information: Intelligence Gathering and Social Communication in India, 1780–1870*. Cambridge University Press, 1996.

Beatson, Alexander. *A View of the Origin and Conduct of the War with Tippoo Sultaun: Comprising a Narrative of the Operations of the Army under the Command of Lieutenant-General George Harris, and of the Siege of Seringapatam*. London, 1800.

Belliappa, C.P. *Nuggets from Coorg History*. Rupa Publications, 2008.

Bes, Kruijtzer, et al. *Dutch Sources on South Asia, c.1600–1825: Archival Guide to Repositories Outside the Netherlands, Vol. III*, edited by Lennart Bes, Gijs Kruijtzer, Jos Gommans, Alicia Schrikker and Carolien Stolte. Internet Archive, 2001. New Delhi: Manohar Publishers and Distributors, 2015.

Bowring, Lewin B. *Hyder Ali and Tipu Sultan and the Struggle with the Musalman Powers of the South.* London: Clarendon Press, 1899.

Bristow, J. *A Narrative of the Sufferings of James Bristow, Belonging to the Bengal Artillery, during Ten Years Captivity with Hyder Ally and Tippoo Saheb.* Calcutta, 1792 (Reprint, London, 1793).

Brittlebank, Kate. *Tiger: The Life of Tipu Sultan.* Juggernaut Books, 2016.

Buchanan, Francis. *A Journey from Madras through the Countries of Mysore, Canara and Malabar, Vol. II.* Originally published in 1807. Scholar's Choice edition, 2015.

Caldwell, Robert. *Political and General History of the District of Tinnevelly, in the Presidency of Madras, From the Earliest Period to Its Cession to the English Government in 1801 CE.* Madras Government Press, 1881.

Chandra, Bipan. *History of Modern India.* Orient Blackswan, 2009.

Chetti, P. Stephen Basappa. *A Guide to Seringapatam and Its Vicinity: Historical and Traditional.* Town Press, 1897.

Dalrymple, William. *White Mughals.* Penguin Books, 2002.

———. *Return of a King: An Indian Army in Afghanistan.* Bloomsbury, 2013.

———. *The Anarchy.* Bloomsbury, 2019.

Dowson, John. *A Classical Dictionary of Hindu Mythology and Religion, Geography, History and Literature*, Second Edition. London: Trubner & Co., 1888.

Forrest, Denys M. *Tiger of Mysore: Life and Death of Tipu Sultan.* Allied Publishers, 1970.

Grant, James. *Cassell's Illustrated History of India.* London, Paris and Melbourne: Cassell & Co. Ltd, 1890.

Gurukkal, Rajan, and Varier Raghava. *History of Kerala: Prehistoric to the Present.* Orient Blackswan, 2018.

Habib, Irfan (ed.). *State and Diplomacy under Tipu Sultan: Documents and Essays.* Indian History Congress, Tulika Books, 2001.

Hasan, Mohibbul. *History of Tipu Sultan.* Aakar Books, 1951.

Hoover, James W. *Men without Hats: Dialogue, Discipline and Discontent in the Madras Army, 1806–1807.* Manohar Publishers and Distributors, 2007.

Husain, Mahmud. *The Dreams of Tipu Sultan.* Fascimile Publisher, 2015.

Iyer, Chandrika Hariharan. *Hemambika: The Elixir of Life.* 2017.

Jain, Meenakshi. *Flight of Deities and Rebirth of Temples: Episodes from Indian History.* Aryan Books International, 2019.

Jayashanker, S. *Temples of Kannoor District.* Kerala: Directorate of Census Operations, Census of India, 1999.

Kalathil, Roopesh Michael. *Uravidangal Thaedi: Sampaloor Charithrathinte Punarvayana* (Malayalam). Navara Publication, 2016.

Kareem, C.K. *Kerala under Haidar Ali and Tipu Sultan.* PhD thesis, Aligarh Muslim University. Cochin: Kerala History Association, 1973.

Kirkpatrick, William. *Select Letters of Tippoo Sultan to Various Public Functionaries.* London: Black, Parry and Kingsbury, 1811.

Kirmani, Mir Hussein Ali Khan. *History of Tipu Sultan,* translated from Persian by Col W. Miles, 1864. Reprint, New Delhi: Abhijeet Publications, 2017.

Kurup, Pushpa. *Power Women: A Journey into Hindu Mythology, Folklore and History.* Bloomsbury, 2021.

Logan, William. *Malabar.* 1887. Reprint, Madras Government Press, 1951.

Luther, Narendra. *Legendotes of Hyderabad.* Niyogi Books, 2014.

M.M.D.L.T. *The History of Hyder Shah alias Hyder Ali Khan Bahadur* or *New Memoirs Concerning the East Indies with Historical Notes.* London, 1784.

Mackenzie, Roderick. *A Sketch of the War with Tippoo Sultaun* or *A Detail of Military Operations, from the Commencement of Hostilities at the Lines of Travancore in December 1789, until the Peace Concluded before Seringapatam in February 1792.* Calcutta, 1799.

Majumdar, R.C. *Ancient India.* Originally published in 1952. Reprint, Motilal Banarasi Das Publishers, 2018.

Malleson, G.B. *History of Afghanistan from the Earliest Period to the Outbreak of the War of 1878.* London: W.H. Allen & Co., 1878.

Manikumar, K.A. *Vellore Revolt, 1806.* Allied Publishers, 2006.

———. *Vellore.* Orient Blackswan, 2021.

Menon, A. Sreedhara. *Kerala History and Its Makers.* Originally published in 1987. Reprint, D.C. Books, 2020.

Michell, George (ed.). *Eternal Kaveri.* Marg Publications, 1999.

Mount, Ferdinand. *The Tears of the Rajas: Mutiny, Money and Marriage in India 1805–1905.* UK: Simon & Schuster, 2015.

Moxham, Roy. *The Theft of India: The European Conquests of India, 1498–1765.* Harper Collins, 2016.

Mukund, Kanakalatha. *The World of the Tamil Merchant*. Portfolio (Penguin), 2012.

Nainar, S. Muhammad Husayn. *Shaykh Zainuddin Makhdum's Tuhfat al-Mujahidin,* translated from the Arabic. Malaysia: Islamic Book Trust, 2006.

Nair, C. Gopalan. *Wynad: Its Peoples and Traditions.* Originally published in Madras, 1911. Reprint, Gyan Books, 2020.

———. *Malayalathile Mappilamar*. Indian Pouran Press, 1917.

Nair, K.K. *By Sweat and Sword: Trade, Diplomacy and War in Kerala through the Ages*. Manohar Publishers and Distributors, 2013.

Nair, Prof. N. Gopinathan. *Marthanda Varma, Pazhassi Raja, Shaktan Thampuran* (Malayalam). D.C. Books, 2009.

Panikkar, K.M. *A History of Kerala, 1498–1801.* Originally published by Annamalai University in 1960. Reprint, Life Span Publishers and Distributors, 2021.

Peixoto, Eloy Joze Correa. 'Memoirs of Hyder Ally from the year 1758 to 1770', in *Annual Report of the Mysore Archaeological Department for the Year 1937 (Part IV – Manuscripts)*. Bangalore: Government Press, 1938.

Rao, C. Hayavadana. *History of Mysore (1399–1799 CE), Vol. I–III.* Bangalore: Government Press, 1948.

Rice, Benjamin Lewis. *Mysore and Coorg: A Gazetteer Compiled for the Government of India, (Vol. III: Coorg).* Mysore Government Press, 1878.

Roy, Tirthankar. *The East India Company: The World's Most Powerful Corporation*. Penguin Random House, 2012.

Sampath, Vikram. *Splendours of Royal Mysore: The Untold Story of the Wodeyars*. Rupa Publications, 2012.

Scurry, James. *The Captivity, Sufferings and Escape, of James Scurry, Who Was Detained a Prisoner during Ten Years, in the Dominions of Hyder Ali and Tipoo Saib.* Originally published by Henry Fisher in London, 1824. Reprint, Forgotten Books, 2015.

Stewart, Charles. *A Descriptive Catalogue of the Oriental Library of the Late Tippoo Sultan of Mysore, to Which Are Prefixed Memoirs of Hyder Aly and his Son, Tippoo Sultan.* Cambridge, 1809.

Streeter, Edwin W. *The Great Diamonds of the World: Their History and Romance.* London: George Bell & Sons, 1882.

Wilks, Mark. *Historical Sketches of the South of India in an Attempt to Trace the History of Mysoor from the Origin of the Hindoo Government of that State, to the Extinction of the Mahommedan Dynasty in 1799, Vol. I–III.* Originally published in London, 1817. Digitized by the Internet Archive, 2007.

Yazdani, Kaveh. *Mysore at War*. ResearchGate, 2019.

# ABOUT THE AUTHOR

Pushpa Kurup is an IT professional, a history buff, and an independent researcher. She started her career as an officer in the Life Insurance Corporation of India and later moved to Tata Consultancy Services (TCS) as faculty member and Vitalect Technologies as managing director. After a wish-fulfilling corporate career spanning several decades, she decided to hang up her boots and pursue her hobbies.

Pushpa Kurup's recent publications include *Power Women: A Journey into Hindu Mythology, Folklore and History* and *Gods Dancing among Men: The Mystical World of Theyyams of North Malabar*. She wrote *Stars and Saplings: A Biography of Dr. G. Viswanathan*, the authorized biography of the founder-chancellor of VIT (Vellore Institute of Technology) University in 2013. She travels widely, reads plenty of books, and handles consulting assignments involving corporate training and prevention of workplace sexual harassment. She divides her time between Thiruvananthapuram and Kozhikode.